D0215816

Handbook of hospitality operations and IT

Handbook of hospitality operations and IT

Edited by
Peter Jones

Associate Dean (International) and ITCA
Chair of Production and Operations Management
Faculty of Management & Law,
University of Surrey, Guildford, Surrey, UK

AMSTERDAM • BOSTON • HEIDELBERG • LONDON • NEW YORK • OXFORD
PARIS • SAN DIEGO • SAN FRANCISCO • SINGAPORE • SYDNEY • TOKYO
Butterworth-Heinemann is an imprint of Elsevier

Butterworth-Heinemann is an imprint of Elsevier
Linacre House, Jordan Hill, Oxford OX2 8DP, UK
30 Corporate Drive, Suite 400, Burlington, MA 01803, USA

First edition 2008

British Library Cataloguing-in-Publication Data
A catalogue record for this book is available from the British Library

Library of Congress Cataloging-in-Publication Data
A catalog record for this book is available from the Library of Congress

ISBN: 978-0-7506-8753-9

For information on all Butterworth-Heinemann publications
visit our website at elsevierdirect.com

Typeset by Charon Tec Ltd (A Macmillan Company)
www.macmillansolutions.com

Printed and bound in Hungary
08   09   10   10   9   8   7   6   5   4   3   2   1

Contents

Contents

Acknowledgements

This edited text has come into existence through the hard work and dedication of a large number of people. I would therefore like to acknowledge and thank the following for their contribution to this handbook.

First, my thanks to the contributors who authored each of the chapters. Almost without exception, when I asked them if they might contribute, they said 'yes' without any hesitation and submitted their chapters before signing a contract. I thank them for their trust in me to produce something worthy of their efforts. They are truly the most amazing group of colleagues – incredibly knowledgeable, fantastically professional, and so laid back – it has been a joy to work with them.

Second, I would like to thank Novie Johan at the University of Surrey for her help in editing the chapters, especially the citations and references. In a handbook of this kind, it is particularly important that these are as accurate as they can be. Checking this is painstaking and requires hard work. Novie's contribution to this has been invaluable.

Third, my thanks to Professor Abraham Pizam, the series editor, for inviting me to be the editor. Quite simply Abe is a legend in his own lifetime, and I am honoured to be his colleague and friend.

Finally, my thanks to all those at Elsevier who assisted during the final stages of getting the book to print. But most notably thanks to Sally North, who has always supported, encouraged and championed authorship in the hospitality field.

Professor Peter Jones
October 2007

Contributors

Mohamed Fawzy Afify is an assistant lecturer at Faculty of Tourism and Hotels, Menoufia University, Egypt. He has worked in the hotel industry in Egyptian resort properties and is currently doing his Ph.D. at the University of Surrey.

Stephen Ball is head of the Centre for International Hospitality Management Research and a professor of hospitality management at Sheffield Hallam University. He is the chair of the Council for Hospitality Management Education (CHME), the subject body for hospitality management in the UK, and visiting fellow at two other UK universities. He has authored and edited a number of textbooks, and written numerous articles, book chapters, reports and keynote presentations. He co-researched three editions of the British Hospitality Association's annual *British Hospitality: Trends and Statistics* and co-authored *A Review of Hospitality Management Education in the UK* for CHME. His current research interests are varied but relate mainly to hospitality management and entrepreneurship to academic research leadership.

Bonnie Canziani, Ph.D., is the director of the Hospitality and Tourism Management Program at UNCG. Dr. Canziani's expertise is in the area of customer service operations, ecommerce web usability and multicultural issues, such as globalization and immigration, and their impact on the hospitality and tourism industry. She has worked internationally in the design and implementation of management and tourism training for tourism and public service employees. She is a research associate of the Instituto Sul Lavoro in Rome, Italy, for study of stress in service employees and of the Norman Y. Mineta International Institute for Surface Transportation Policy Studies (MTI) at San Jose State University, California. She worked with the

School of Hotel Administration at Cornell University to create academic programmes in various international locations, including Venezuela, Puerto Rico and France.

Robin B. DiPietro, Ph.D., is an assistant professor at the University of Nebraska-Lincoln in the Hospitality, Restaurant and Tourism Management programme. She has 20 years of experience with chain restaurants in the operations, human resources and training areas. She has research interests in multi-unit chain restaurant operations and human resources issues inherent in restaurant operations including motivation, employee retention and staffing issues of organizations.

Thomas Gorin is the manager of Revenue Management at Continental Airlines, and an adjunct professor of Revenue Management at the University of Houston's Conrad N. Hilton School of Hotel and Restaurant Management. Dr. Gorin received his Ph.D. from the Massachusetts Institute of Technology's Center for Transportation and Logistics in September 2004. His doctoral research focused on the impacts of entry in airline markets and the difficulty in assessing predatory practices in the airline industry in light of the competitive effects of airline revenue management and network flows of passengers.

Prof. Peter Jones is ITCA chair of Production and Operations Management in the School of Management at the University of Surrey. He has written, co-authored and edited numerous books and chapters on the subject of hospitality management, as well as presented keynotes and research papers at conferences throughout the world. In 1992 he was the founding president of EuroCHRIE and in 2007–2008 served as International CHRIE President.

Prof. David Kirk is the vice principal of Queen Margaret University in Edinburgh. He wrote the first ever textbook devoted to environmental management in the hospitality industry in 1996, and has continued to research in this field.

Carolyn Lambert, Ph.D., RD, is an associate professor in the School of Hospitality Management at The Pennsylvania State University. Dr. Lambert attained her Ph.D. from the University of Tennessee. Her research interests include the application of operations management techniques to the hospitality industry.

Kate Wonjae Lee, Ph.D., is a revenue manager for the Crowne Plaza Times Square, New York. Before joining InterContinental

Hotels Group, she worked as a revenue analyst for Hilton New York. She also worked as an operations research software engineer for Transport Dynamics Inc. and developed simulation systems for FedEx. She attained a dual-title Ph.D. in hotel management and operations research from The Pennsylvania State University and she has MA from New York University and MS. BS from Yonsei University.

Ingrid Y. Lin is an assistant professor at the School of Travel Industry Management, University of Hawaii at Manoa. Her research areas primarily focus on marketing and consumer behaviour. Her research topics include servicescapes, customer switching/buying behaviours, and cross-cultural studies. She has published in the *Journal of Hospitality and Tourism Research*, the *International Journal of Hospitality Management* and *Journal of Foodservice Business Research*.

Andrew Lockwood is the head of Division of Hospitality and Tourism and Forte Professor of Hospitality Management at the University of Surrey. He worked for international hotel companies both in London and the provinces in a range of managerial positions, before running his own 40-bedroom hotel. He has written and edited 10 books and over 100 articles, chapters and conference papers on the management of hospitality operations. His long-standing research interests lie in the fields of operations and quality management, hospitality education and managerial activity in the hospitality industry.

Robert Christie Mill is a professor at the University of Denver's School of Hotel, Restaurant and Tourism Management in the Daniels College of Business. He has authored or contributed chapters to 12 books, several of which are in multiple editions. Additionally, he has authored numerous articles in both research journals and the trade press.

Dolf A. Mogendorff, Ph.D., FRSA, FIH, is the research director of Eproductive Ltd whose products include industry-leading labour management software for hospitality chains. He is a former professor of hospitality management and has published and lectured internationally, especially on operations management and technological change and innovation.

Karthik Namasivayam is an associate professor at the School of Hospitality Management, The Pennsylvania State University. He researches the connections between organizational practices and consumer satisfaction and has widely published, including in *Psychology & Marketing*, the *International Journal of Service Industries Management* and the *Journal of Hospitality and Tourism Research*.

Peter O'Connor, Ph.D., is a professor of Information Systems at Essec Business School France, where he also serves as Academic Director of Institute de Management Hotelier International (IMHI), Europe's leading MBA program in international hospitality management. His research, teaching and consulting interests focus on distribution, e-commerce and electronic marketing in hospitality and tourism.

Michael Ottenbacher is an associate professor at San Diego State University, California, USA. He received his Ph.D. in marketing from the University of Otago, New Zealand, and he has numerous publications in the areas of innovation, new product development and hospitality management.

Pornpissanu Promsivapallop is a lecturer in the Faculty of Hospitality and Tourism at Prince of Songkla University, Phuket, Thailand. He is currently on sabbatical at the University of Surrey to study for his Ph.D. in the area of factors influencing outsourcing in the hotel industry.

Dennis Reynolds is the associate director and Ivar Haglund Distinguished Professor of Hospitality Management at the Washington State University School of Hospitality Business Management. Dr. Reynolds is a frequent speaker to management groups in Asia, Europe and North America, and has been cited in various media around the globe. Professor Reynolds's research focuses on pathways leading to enhanced managerial efficiency and effectiveness, especially in service organizations, through the application of operations-management tools and techniques. His recent papers have also addressed the related effects of management feedback on subordinate self-efficacy and a new approach to evaluating operational efficiency for multi-unit restaurant organizations.

Stowe Shoemaker teaches at the University of Houston. He is also on the executive education faculty at Cornell University, where he earned his Ph.D. He is the senior author of *Marketing Leadership in Hospitality and Tourism: Strategies and Tactics for a Competitive Advantage* and *Marketing Essentials in Hospitality and Tourism*, both published by Prentice Hall.

Beverley Sparks is a professor with the Department of Tourism, Leisure, Hotel and Sport Management at Griffith University in Australia. Beverley is an active researcher in the area of tourism and hospitality marketing and management, and has published widely. Her current research projects include a three government funded project investigating challenging service encounters from the perspective of both employees and customers. Her past management experience has included Head, School Tourism and Hotel Management (Griffith); Dean International at Griffith University; Director, International Centre of Excellence in Sustainable Tourism Education and Director, Sustainable Tourism CRC Education Program.

Karin Weber is an assistant professor at the School of Hotel and Tourism Management at Hong Kong Polytechnic University. She received her BB (Hons.) degree from Monash University, Australia, her M.Sc. degree in Hotel Administration from the University of Nevada, Las Vegas in the United States, and her Ph.D. in services marketing from Griffith University, Australia. Karin's two major areas of research interest are services marketing and convention tourism/management. Karin is the lead editor and chapter author of a book on convention tourism that has been published by Haworth Press New York in 2002, and has chaired the first Convention and Expo Summit in Asia in 2003.

Paul Whitelaw is a senior lecturer in the School of Hospitality, Tourism and Marketing at Victoria University in Melbourne, Australia, where he lectures in quantitative and computer-based hospitality management systems on undergraduate and postgraduate programmes. Prior to this appointment, Paul was the Foundation Executive Director of The Centre for Hospitality and Tourism Research, Victoria University.

Preface

When writing a text on any subject, the challenge is always how to divide the body of knowledge into separate bits – so that chapters can be written.[1] In some disciplines, there are well-established and commonly used ways of sub-dividing the subject matter. But in hospitality operations and information management, there is not. This is even more challenging when editing a text, since the editor may have a clear view of what should go in each chapter, but each of the contributors may have different views about this. So before explaining how this book is organized, my thanks to all the contributors for their cooperation in allowing me to edit their chapters, so that the book makes sense as a whole (at least to me).

As the title of this book makes clear, this text is concerned with both operations management and information management. These can be thought of, and are often taught, as two separate subjects. So one way to have organized this text would be to have two parts – one focusing on operations and the other on information management. I decided very strongly not to do this because it is my belief that managing information in the hospitality industry without an operations context is meaningless, whilst managing operations without the right information is impossible. The two are inextricably mixed.

In Chapter 1, the underpinning theory of operations management is explained, and one of the emergent ideas from this is that operations (especially in hospitality) involve the processing of materials, customers and information. On this

---

[1] In most chapters you will find footnotes like this one, directing you to relevant content in other chapters – which only serves to illustrate how dividing the body of knowledge into chapters is very artificial.

basis, there are some chapters which focus on just one of these. For instance, Chapter 2 on systems management is largely about materials, Chapter 4 is explicitly about hospitality consumers and Chapter 8 looks at the role of ICT. However, many chapters consider the interaction of processing materials, people and information with regard to those things the operations manager is responsible for – quality, productivity, innovation and so on.

There were three main factors that influenced the choice of topics for each chapter. First, what operations managers do in the hospitality industry itself. Second, the hospitality curriculum – what is taught to students of hospitality. Third, the research that has been conducted into operations and information management in hospitality. One might think that there should be congruence between these three – that the time and effort managers spend on different things are reflected in the topics students are taught and the research that academics do. But this is not the case – for all kinds of reasons that I need not go into here.

So this handbook is designed to be a review of everything we know so far about this subject. In some cases (and hence chapters), this is based on a significant amount of research of all kinds; in other cases it is based more on industry practice, with very limited supporting research evidence. Either way it is hoped that this handbook will be a valuable resource for educators, researchers, students and practitioners of hospitality operations and information management.

Professor Peter Jones
October 2007

Operations management: theoretical underpinnings

Peter Jones

Associate Dean (International) and ITCA Chair of Production and Operations Management Faculty of Management & Law, University of Surrey Guildford, Surrey, UK

Introduction

Operations Management (OM) is the study of how goods get manufactured and service gets delivered. Originally, it was founded on studies of how best to organize factories manufacturing automobiles and other consumer goods. But from the 1970s onwards, a greater emphasis was placed on understanding service operations. A seminal contribution to this was the publication of *The Management of Service Operations* (Sasser et al. 1978) by three distinguished Harvard professors. This book recognized that service firms were playing a greater and greater role in a nation's economic activity and suggested that managing such firms and their operations may be different to practice in manufacturing – an issue we explore later in this chapter.

Johnston (1994) defines OM and its scope and role within an organization. He states: 'operations management … is a body of knowledge, experience and techniques covering such topics as process design, layout, production planning, inventory control, quality management and control, capacity planning and workforce management' (Johnston 1994: 21).

As an academic discipline, OM is highly applied, to the extent that some have argued that it is almost atheoretical (Schmenner and Swink 1998). The applied nature of OM is further illustrated when it is applied to the hospitality industry. Very rarely are managers assigned job titles as 'Operations Managers'. Rather than this generic title, managers with operations responsibility are given specific roles such as Rooms Division Manager, Food and Beverage Manager, Restaurant Manager and so on.

In this introductory chapter, we first consider the general OM theory and identify how this has been applied in the hospitality industry. Key operational trends in the industry are identified, along with the operational strategies firms have adopted. The chapter goes on to discuss the extent to which hospitality is different to other industries, as well as the extent to which it is homogenous or made up of sectors that have features distinctive to each other. Finally, an overview of the OM literature in hospitality is provided in order to identify the scale and scope of research in this field.

Operations management theory

Until the late 1990s, OM was an applied subject, with very little theory. However, based on contributions from Hayes and Wheelwright (1979), Schmenner (1986), Schmenner and Swink

(1998) and Johnston and Jones (2005), five main theories can be identified, for the purposes of this chapter:

1. Theory of Process Choice
2. Theory of Swift and Even Flow
3. Theory of Lean Manufacturing
4. Theory of Performance Frontiers
5. Theory of Service Experience

Each of these theories will now be explained, along with their related propositions or 'laws'.[1] Their relevance and application to the hospitality industry will be explored and hospitality research into these theories will be summarized.

Theory of Process Choice

Hayes and Wheelwright (1979) identified that firms adopted different types of process in order to manufacture products. In their original analysis, they saw this as evolutionary. Firms in an industry would start with hand-making articles, applying craft skills in 'job-shop operation', move on to batch production and then adopt mass production principles. However, it was quickly realized that in some industry sectors, firms did not follow this evolutionary path, but simply adopted the process that best matched their product and their market. Hayes and Wheelwright's analysis was subsequently simplified and process types became distinguished in terms of two main criteria – volume (how many were produced) and variety (the number of different products made). These were generally seen as a trade-off. Firms could produce a wide range of different products, but if they did so, they were likely to have a relatively low volume of output, as in the job-shop operation. Or firms could go for high-volume output, but doing this minimizes the variety of products they produce, as in mass production. A similar analysis has been applied to services (Silvestro et al. 1992).

---

[1] The terms 'proposition' and 'law' have different meanings. Here, 'proposition' is used to denote a generally applicable rule that may have exceptions, whereas a 'law' is used to denote something that always applies. In all instances, 'law' has been used where the authors of the theory have used the term. However, it should be recognized that 'laws' which are applied to social settings, such as operations, may not have the same rigour as the scientific or natural laws found, for instance, in physics or chemistry.

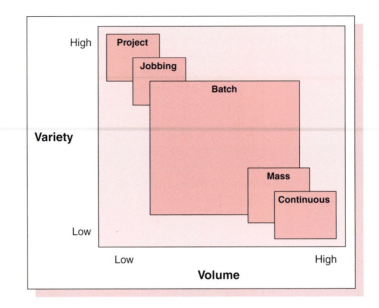

Figure 1.1
Process types in operations (*Source*: Based on Silvestro et al. 1992).

Propositions associated with the Theory of Process Choice

There are two key propositions related to this theory. First, it is proposed that firms have a choice over the type of process they adopt to manufacture their products or deliver their services. The choice they make derives mainly from an assessment of their core capabilities and market demand. Second, it is proposed that there is a trade-off between producing volume *or* variety, as illustrated in Figure 1.1. Across all industries, a major trend has been the so-called *shift along the diagonal* from job shop (low volume, high variety) towards mass production (high volume, low variety). This has been going on throughout the twentieth century and is epitomized by Henry Ford's development of automobile manufacturing.

Process choice in the hospitality industry

In hospitality operations process design, Jones (1988) identified a number of trends, two of which relate to process choice: production lining and decoupling. *Production lining* refers to the concept of breaking down production activities into simple tasks so that they may be organized on a production-line basis, just as Henry Ford production lined the motor manufacturing process in the 1920s. It has long been argued (Levitt 1972) that services, in general, are moving towards more industrialized processes. Indeed, this has actually been termed the McDonaldization of society (Ritzer 2000).

Decoupling refers to the idea of separating, both in place and in time, back-of-house activity from front-of-house activity. Often, the rationale for doing so is that one or the other (usually back-of-house) can be production lined. For instance, a number of health authorities in the UK have created one large central production kitchen for a number of hospitals and introduced cook-chill, so that the kitchen may produce 5,000–6,000 meals for transportation to five or more different hospitals the following day.

Process choice research • • •

There has been no empirical research of process choice in the hospitality industry. However, evidence from industry suggests that the propositions identified above are well understood. A good example of this has been the emergence of budget hotels that greatly reduced the variety and complexity of hotel operations and which have been hugely successful throughout the world.

Theory of Swift and Even Flow

The Theory of Swift and Even Flow 'holds that the more swift and even the flow of materials through the process, the more productive the process is' (Schmenner and Swink 1998). This applies to all types of operation, whether they are job shops, batch production or assembly lines producing goods, or they are professional, batch or mass service operations.

Laws within the Theory of Smooth and Even Flow • • •

There are three laws associated with the Theory of Swift and Even Flow (Schmenner and Swink 1998). These are as follows:

1. Law of variability 1 – the greater the randomness of the process, the lower the productivity.
2. Law of variability 2 – the greater the variability of the requirements of the process, the lower the productivity.
3. Law of bottlenecks – the greater the difference in the rate of flow through stages in a process, the less productive the process.

To these we can add a fourth law:

4. Law of prioritization – in operations of inherent instability, the greater the instability, the greater the prioritization of orders (Westbrook 1994).

Swift and even flow in the hospitality industry • • •

Ensuring 'balance' at all stages of the process is a key feature of designing and operating hospitality operations. When hotels and restaurants are designed, the capacity of each part should match the expected operational needs. For instance, the car park should have sufficient spaces for guests driving to the property; the number of restaurant seats should accommodate the demand for dining; and so on. Likewise, operations seek to reduce randomness and variability. For instance, most hospitality companies adopt standard operating procedures. They also encourage their customers to book ahead, which enables the operation to schedule its labour to meet forecast levels of demand.

Related research • • •

In the hospitality industry, these laws are implicitly understood and applied, but there has been no specific empirical research on them.

Theory of Lean Manufacturing

This theory basically states that productivity is enhanced by applying principles designed to eliminate waste of all kinds. The Japanese guru Taiichi Ohno, former Chief Engineer for Toyota, has identified seven types of waste:

1. doing too much
2. waiting
3. transporting
4. too much inflexible capacity or lack of process flexibility
5. unnecessary stocks
6. unnecessary motions
7. defects

By tackling each of these, Japan has achieved global dominance in a wide number of industry sectors such as motorcycles and electronic goods.

Laws associated with the Theory of Lean Manufacturing • • •

Four laws are associated with the Theory of Lean Manufacturing. These are as follows:

1. Law of scientific methods – labour productivity is improved by applying scientific management principles.
2. Law of quality – productivity improves as quality improves, since waste is eliminated. This is a controversial law that may not hold in all cases, although there is widespread anecdotal evidence that it is generally true.
3. Law of limited tasks – factories that perform a limited number of tasks will be more productive than similar fac-tor-ies with a broad range of tasks.
4. Law of value added – a process will be more productive if non-value-added steps are reduced or eliminated.

Lean manufacturing in hospitality • • •

A major trend that has been in all industries is automation, which is the gradual replacement of a human workforce with machines such as computers and robots. In the hospitality industry, this has been most marked with regard to information processing. Examples of this include front-office operations in hotels, point of sale in fast food restaurants and procurement and inventory management. It can be argued that the McDonalds service delivery system, along with many other delivery systems derived from this, applied many of the ideas developed by Ohno. These ideas were also applied by Taco Bell in the 1980s in redesigning their concept and units and by Ritz Carlton in the 1990s after winning the Malcolm Baldridge Award.[2] But the industry sector that has most recently adopted lean manufacturing is the flight catering sector. Flight kitchens are large-scale producers of inflight meals and engage in a great deal of equipment handling. Operators have significantly improved 'cycle time' (total production time) and reduced waste by the adoption of just-in-time principles.

Hospitality research in lean manufacturing • • •

The Rimmington and Clark (1996) study of hospital catering is an example of research based on this theory, but there has been very little other empirical research.

---

[2] See Chapter 13.

7

Theory of Performance Frontiers

Schmenner and Swink (1998) propose the Theory of Performance Frontiers. The theory is called so because the authors use a production function or performance frontier curve to illustrate this theory. Production function methodology maps 'the maximum output that can be produced from any given set of inputs, given technical considerations'. Schmenner and Swink (1998) expand this economic model by defining inputs to include 'all dimensions of manufacturing performance', as well as defining technical considerations as all choices affecting the design and operation of the manufacturing unit. They suggest, consistent with the OM thinking, that a distinction can be drawn between the 'operating frontier', which represents operational activities within a given set of assets; and the 'asset frontier', which reflects the infrastructural elements or asset utilization of the operations. In effect, the operating frontier models the most effective and efficient use of inputs and the asset frontier models the best design and configuration of transformation inputs.

Laws of the Theory of Performance Frontiers ● ● ●

Within this theory, there are a number of proposed laws:

- Law of cumulative capabilities – an improvement in one manufacturing capability leads to improvements in others. Schmenner and Swink (1998) suggest that such improvements are made over time. Moreover, there may be certain sequences or trajectories of improvement that build one upon the other; for instance quality leads to lower cost, followed by increased speed of delivery.
- Law of diminishing returns – 'as improvement (or betterment) moves a manufacturing plant nearer and nearer to its operating frontier (or asset frontier), more and more resources must be expended in order to achieve each additional incremental benefit'.
- Law of diminishing synergy – the law of cumulative capabilities suggest there is synergy between policies and procedures. This synergy diminishes as a plant approaches its asset frontier.

Application to the hospitality industry ● ● ●

Jones (2002) identified two further process trends in the industry, consistent with this theory – the development of so-called micro-units and the dual- or multi-use of physical infrastructure. Micro-units are food-service outlets of very small size aimed at serving often limited and/or captive markets. They include outlets in petrol-filling stations, cinemas, sports stadia, the workplace and so on. Their growth derives from the fact that more traditional sites are now unavailable and the demand for eating out continues to grow. The final trend of dual- or multi-use of infrastructure is sometimes a consequence of devising micro-units. When a brand is enabled to be delivered inside a small 'footprint', it can be incorporated into an existing outlet.

Performance frontier research in hospitality • • •

De facto, some of the research in the hospitality field that uses data envelopment analysis (DEA) is exploring this theory. DEA is a powerful non-parametric, multivariate, multiple linear programming technique that benchmarks units by comparing their ratios of multiple inputs to produce multiple outputs at the same time. DEA constructs a frontier function in a piecewise linear approach by comparing like units (the decision-making units, DMU) taken from the observed dataset. Since DEA uses the production units that are 'best in its class' as reference material, the method is very much in line with the Theory of Performance Frontiers. DEA has been used for performance and productivity benchmarking in the hotel industry (Johns et al. 1997).[3]

Theory of Service Experience

Hence customers are different to materials in that they sense and respond to their environment. Hence, they interact with the operation and form opinions about their experience.

The following are the laws associated with the Theory of Service Experience (Johnston and Jones 2005) are as follows:

- Law of adaptive experience – a customer process is more productive when customer feedback adapts the process, both immediately (during the transaction) and over the long term.
- Law of matching expectations – a customer process will be more productive if customer expectations are matched with their perceptions.
- Law of cumulative effect – productive customer processes have a cumulative effect on customer expectations.

---

[3] For a detailed discussion of this, see Chapter 12.

Service experience in hospitality • • •

Another trend identified by Jones (1988) is customer participation, otherwise known as self-service. Many hospitality operations now enable their customers to do things for themselves that were previously done for them. It is possible to check into a hotel by using a swipe card system, select salad items for a self-help salad bar and check out of a hotel using the in-room television set.

Hospitality research in service experience • • •

This theory is so new that there is no specific research that has tested the proposed laws. However, research into the servicescape (Chapter 3), self-service (Chapter 5) and service encounter (Chapter 6) has some relationship with this theory.

Distinctive features of the hospitality industry

Within the OM field, there are a number of debates which directly relate to the hospitality industry. These debates focus on the extent to which all operations are the same and whether or not differences between them are significant enough to justify theorizing, researching and managing them differently. The three major areas of debate are as follows:

1. General differences between service and manufacturing.
2. Differences between processing customers and processing materials.
3. Specific differences between cost structures of manufacturing, retail and service.

Differences between services and manufacturing

In 1978, Sasser et al. published their textbook *The Management of Service Operations* and identified four ways in which services differed, to which a fifth (ownership) has since been added:

1. Intangibility – a service is a deed, performance or effort and as such has no physical dimensions that make it objectively measurable,
2. Perishability – services cannot be stored; capacity (such as airline seats, hotel rooms) needs to be filled on each occasion when it is available,

3. Heterogeneity – judgements about service are based on the perception by each individual customer on each individual occasion they purchase the service,
4. Simultaneity – service delivery (by the provider) and consumption (by the customer) happen together, both physically and in real time,
5. Ownership – having purchased the service, customers do not possess any tangible good to show for their expenditure.

However, even when identifying these differences, Sasser et al. (1978) acknowledged that there were very few pure services. Most operations were a bundle of both tangible products and intangible services. Furthermore, many 'manufacturers' provide service and many service firms make things. This has led to a long debate amongst academics, researchers and some practitioners as to the extent to which manufacturing and services are different (see for example Lovelock 1981; Brown et al. 2000; Lowson 2002).

Differences between processing customers and processing materials

Morris and Johnston (1988) suggest there are basically three types of processing:

1. Materials processing operation (MPO) – more commonly referred to as manufacturing.
2. Customer processing operation (CPO) – typically described as a service.
3. Information processing operation (IPO) – mostly considered as services.

Clearly, the Theory of Swift and Even Flow applies to materials processing. However, there is prima facie evidence that it may not apply to customer processing. For instance, Roth and Menor (2003: 146) argue that 'many service management problems are fuzzy and unstructured; are multi-dimensional and complex; and are less conducive to normative, analytical modelling'. They go on to note the ongoing challenges to the management of productivity in services and that further study of the design and delivery of service productivity is warranted. One reason that studying service productivity is challenging is the inherent difficulty in managing such productivity (Johnston and Jones 2004). The Theory of Swift and Even Flow is potentially insightful to the management of operations because it is process focused and built around process issues salient to productivity, for example variability, bottlenecks, quality and so on. The theory undoubtedly proves useful for understanding 'back-room' or 'decoupled' operations, but what about 'front-office' operations, where a critical component of the delivery process is the customer and the customer's direct experience of the service process? Johnston and Jones (2005) argue why the Theory of Service Experience is needed.

Differences between cost structures

It is suggested that service, manufacturing and retail operations have different cost structures and that in hospitality these can be represented by the housekeeping function (rooms), kitchen operation (food) and bar operation (beverage) (Harris and Mongiello 2001). A typical cost structure for each of these functions in a four-star hotel is illustrated in Table 1.1; whilst identifying the relationship between fixed and variable cost is illustrated in Table 1.2.

Table 1.1 Per cent variable costs of four-star hotel revenue

	Rooms	**Food**	**Beverage**
Direct costs	Nil	32%	32%
Miscellaneous costs	4%	8%	2%
Labour costs	16%	35%	16%
Contribution	80%	25%	50%

Table 1.2 Ratio of fixed to variable cost in the hotel industry

	Rooms	**Food**	**Beverage**
Contribution	80%	25%	50%
Fixed costs	High	Low	Low
Variable costs	Low	High	Low
Marginal revenue (i.e. discount)	Yes	No	Maybe

Service operations achieve profitability on the basis of relatively low materials costs and relatively high labour costs, which lead to a high contribution margin. This tends, therefore, to be sensitive to demand fluctuations, making capacity management a key feature of successful OM. According to Heskett, Sasser and Schlesinger (1997), profit in the most successful 'service breakthrough' firms derives from achieving effective market segmentation based on high-volume sales; understanding these segments' needs, values and behaviour; selecting profitable segments; articulating the service concept's benefits; deploying resources efficiently; and creating barriers to entry. A second key factor is having a high level of repeat custom. Apart from this being a form on entry barrier, repeat customers have lower acquisition costs and a closer match between expectation and perception,[4] and make more efficient use of the system.

Manufacturing operations, on the other hand, have relatively high materials cost and high labour costs and hence low margins. In most cases, materials consumption should not be sensitive to demand, as both components and end products have a shelf life. So manufacturing profit derives from the control of materials through all stages of manufacture (storage, production, assembly, etc.) and from the control of labour costs. In the hospitality industry, in the last 10 years, there has been a shift from control towards planning, due to the availability of convenience foods and stable prices, better scheduling and use of peripheral staff and introduction of integrated inventory to POS systems (consistent with the Theory of Lean Manufacturing).

Retail operations cost structure has relatively high materials cost and low labour cost and therefore reasonable margins. These too are insensitive to demand fluctuations due to the shelf life of stock. Hence, retail operations managers make profit through stock control and sales and revenue management (such as direct selling, sales scripts, table-top promotions and merchandizing).

Importance of differences to hospitality industry context

Some argue that hospitality has some distinctive features. For instance, Bowen and Ford (2004) conducted an extensive review of literature to see if there was evidence indicating there are differences in the management of hospitality organizations and manufacturing organizations from the perspective of organizing,

---

[4] For a discussion of this, see Chapter 13.

staffing and commanding. Their results indicated that there are a number of differences between managing a manufacturing firm and a hospitality firm:

- Tasks have to be designed to fit with the degree of inter-action with the customer.
- The 'servicescape' is important.
- Operations must be designed to cope with high degrees of uncertainty.
- Employees must be recruited with the right 'service attitude'.
- Internal marketing may be significant.
- Employees may suffer from boundary-role stress (role conflict, role ambiguity, etc.).
- Customers become 'partial employees'.
- Employee empowerment, especially of front-line staff, may be important.

Bowen and Ford (2004) argue on this case, based on asking hotel executives and managers what they thought. Since most managers think that their industry is unique in some way or the other, often because they have no direct experience of any other industry, this may have biased their conclusions.

Reviews of operations management research in hospitality

Although the hospitality research literature is now quite substantial and growing rapidly, a relatively small proportion of this literature focuses on the area of OM. For instance, in a review of the research, Teare (1996) provides an overview of 'hospitality operations management' articles published in selected journals from 1989 to 1994, but in his summary of the main themes and subthemes (sic), hospitality operations is not referred to at all. Ingram (1996) in a similar review of 820 postgraduate research projects in the hospitality and tourism field comments that in the hospitality area 'most relate to the leisure and hotel sectors while food and catering entries show a marketing or science focus and rarely relate to operational or service issues'. Moreover, as the review of OM theory has demonstrated, there has been very little research designed to test OM laws and propositions.

Jones and Lockwood (1998) specifically explore the nature of hospitality OM research by reviewing 143 articles from 1970 up to 1997. They divide this literature into five areas, gradually shifting from a macro-perspective of hospitality operations down to a micro-perspective of hospitality operations.

They start by considering the industry as a whole, go on to consider research into chain and unit operations, then consider operating systems in accommodation and food and beverage and conclude with a review of the operational interface between providers and customers (the so-called service encounter). They draw three conclusions from this analysis. First, 'there is no lack of terminology, but various definitions, few taxonomies and alternative typologies. This can result in researchers using the same term to describe different phenomena'. Second, a high proportion of the research is 'conceptual in nature'. Third, much of the research is 'phenomenological'. They state: 'it is certainly the case that very little hospitality operations management research is related to the generic discipline of operations management or based on operations research methodologies'.

Drawing on this work, two further analyses of the literature have been published. Lockwood and Ingram (1999) reviewed research in hotel OM, whilst Jones (1999) considered catering OM. Lockwood and Ingram (1999) consider 141 articles by subdividing them into the topics of strategy and environment, property and asset management, human resources, customers and marketing, profitability and yield management, productivity and performance, service and quality and operating systems. Jones (1999) reviews 63 articles by categorizing them into six main areas – classification, systems design and technology, 'operations management', catering managers, menu planning and analysis and chain development and growth.

Since these reviews of the research literature, the situation with regard to OM research in hospitality has worsened rather than improved, with even less output between 2000 and 2005 than in the preceding five years. In a review of hospitality research, Jones (2006) cites only 65 hospitality articles from this millennium, which represented only one-third of the total output he identified in the field. O'Connor and Murphy (2004) reviewed research on information technology in the hospitality industry. Their perspective on its quality mirrors the comments of Jones and Lockwood (1998) made six years earlier. O'Connor and Murphy (2004: 481) state: 'too much of this research (in I.T.) is descriptive … [and] needs more originality in both the topics addressed and the research methods used'.

Summary and conclusion

This chapter has identified and discussed three main issues. First, OM theory has been identified, along with the extent to which this theory has been researched in the hospitality industry.

It is concluded that there has been very little explicit investigation of the propositions and 'laws' that underpin hospitality operations. This might be because the theory itself is relatively new, so there has not been enough time for it to be researched, or because hospitality operations are in some way distinctive or different to other types of operation.

The notion of distinctiveness was therefore the second issues discussed. It was identified that operations have been postulated to vary according to whether they were manufacturing or service; materials or customer processing; or retail, service or manufacturing cost based. It is proposed that in the hospitality industry, it is important to distinguish between MPOs, which are typically back-of-house and CPOs, which are front-of house. The cost structure also has important implications for managing operations.

Finally, there was a discussion of reviews of hospitality research in order to identify the scale and scope of OM research to date. This identified that certain topics, notably quality management and yield (or revenue) management, had received a great deal of attention, but that other topics had rarely been researched.

This book seeks to address these issues by exploring all the topics related to OM. In doing so, each subsequent chapter will discuss both theory and industry practice, explore the nature of the challenges facing management and identify any research contribution that might help managers. Each of the reviews of hospitality OM research discussed above has been unique in terms of their analytical framework. In this book, hospitality operations research is analysed by specifically adopting the generic POM framework, that is the issues of process design and layout, capacity and production planning, materials and inventory control, supply chain management, productivity and workforce management, quality management and innovation. This approach is adopted for two reasons. First, it identifies the scope of hospitality research and therefore helps to identify the future research agenda. Second, it emphasizes the need for future OM research to test the theories and 'laws' stated earlier.

References

Bowen, J. and Ford, R. C. (2004) What experts say about managing hospitality service delivery systems, *International Journal of Contemporary Hospitality Management*, 16, 7, 394–401

Brown, S., Lamming, R., Bessant, J. and Jones, P. (2000) *Strategic Operations Management*, Butterworth Heinemann: Oxford

Harris, P. J. and Mongiello, M. (2001) Key performance indicators in European hotel properties: general managers' choices and company profiles, *International Journal of Contemporary Hospitality Management*, 13, 3, 120–127

Hayes, R. H. and Wheelwright, S. C. (1979) Linking manufacturing process and product life cycle, *Harvard Business Review*, January–February, 133–140

Heskett, J. L., Sasser, W. E. and Schlesinger, L. A. (1997) *The Service Profit Chain*, The Free Press: New York, NY

Ingram, H. (1996) Clusters and gaps in hospitality and tourism academic research, *International Journal of Contemporary Hospitality Management*, 8, 7, 91–95

Johns, N., Howcroft, B. and Drake, L. (1997) The use of data envelopment analysis to monitor hotel productivity, *Progress in Tourism and Hospitality Research*, 3, 2, 119–127

Johnston, R. (1994) Operations: from factory to service management, *International Journal of Service Industry Management*, 5, 1, 20–54

Johnston, R. and Jones, P. (2004) Service productivity: towards understanding the relationship between operational and customer productivity, *International Journal of Productivity and Performance Management*, 53, 3, 201–213

Johnston, R. and Jones, P. (2005) On theory in operations management: a critique from a service perspective, *Unpublished Working Paper*

Jones, P. (1988) The impact of trends in service operations on food service delivery systems, *International Journal of Operations and Production Management*, 8, 7, 23–30

Jones, P. (1999) Operational issues and trends in the hospitality industry, *International Journal of Hospitality Management*, 18, 4, 427–442

Jones, P. (Ed.) (2002) *An Introduction to Hospitality Operations*, 3rd edition, Continuum: London

Jones, P. (2006) From the bottom up: operations management in the hospitality industry. In Brotherton, R. and Wood, R. (Eds.), *Hospitality Management Handbook*, Sage Publications: London

Jones, P. and Lockwood, A. (1998) Hospitality operations management, *International Journal of Hospitality Management*, 17, 2, 183–202

Levitt, T. (1972) Production-line approach to service, *Harvard Business Review*, 50, 5, 20–31

Lockwood, A. and Ingram, H. (1999) Hotel operations management, In Brotherton, B. (Ed.), *Handbook of Contemporary Hospitality Management Research*, 1st edition, Wiley: Chichester, 415–440

Lovelock, C. H. (1981) Why marketing management needs to be different in services, In Donelly, J. H. and George, W. R. (Eds.), *Marketing of Services*, American Marketing Association: Chicago, IL

Lowson, R. H. (2002) *Strategic Operations Management – the new competitive advantage*, Routledge: London

Morris, B. and Johnston, R. (1988) Dealing with inherent variability: the difference between manufacturing and service, *International Journal of Operations and Production Management*, 7, 4, 13–22

O'Connor, P. and Murphy, J. (2004) Research on information technology in the hospitality industry, *International Journal of Hospitality Management*, 23, 5, 473–484

Rimmington, M. and Clark, J. (1996) Productivity measurement in foodservice systems, In Johns, N. (Ed.), *Productivity Management in Hospitality and Tourism*, Cassell: London

Ritzer, G. (2000) *McDonaldisation of Society*, 4th edition, Pine Forge Press: Thousand Islands, CA

Roth, A. V. and Menor, L. J. (2003) Insights into service operations management: a research agenda, *Production and Operations Management*, 12, 2, 145–161

Sasser, W. E., Wyckoff, D. D. and Olsen, M. (1978) *The Management of Service Operations*, Allyn and Bacon: Boston

Schmenner, R. (1986) How can service businesses survive and prosper?, *Sloan Management Review*, Spring, 21–32

Schmenner, R. W. and Swink, M. (1998) On theory in operations management, Journal of Operations Management, 17, 97–113

Silvestro, R., Fitzgerald, L., Johnston, R. and Voss, C. (1992) Towards a classification of service processes, *International Journal of Service Industry Management*, 3, 3, 62–75

Teare, R. (1996) Hospitality operations: patterns in management, service improvement and business performance, *International Journal of Contemporary Hospitality Management*, 8, 7, 63–74

Westbrook, R. (1994) Priority management: new theory for operations management, *International Journal of Operations and Production Management*, 14, 6, 4–24

CHAPTER
• • • • 2

Hospitality systems

Stephen Ball

*Director of the Centre for International
Hospitality Management Research and
Chair of the Council for Hospitality
Management Education (CHME)
Faculty of Organisation and Management
Sheffield Hallam University
UK*

Introduction

One of the earliest contributions to the research literature on hospitality systems was that made by Livingstone and Chang (1978). They collected a series of papers which reported on systems analysis and design applied to foodservice operations at that particular time. Despite being 30 years old, and with much of the specific content now out-of-date, the topics covered in this text remain highly relevant today. They include computer-assisted production planning (Bresnahan 1978), design of centralized production facilities (Livingston 1978), human engineering in foodservice system design (Symington 1978), management information systems for foodservice operations (Gibbons 1978), and the design and operation of a quality assurance program (Schwartz 1978).

When applied to hospitality, 'systems' can have two meanings. First, 'systems' can be explained in terms of how one thinks about and conducts research in hospitality, i.e. through reference to so-called systems theory and analysis. Secondly, 'systems' can be considered as the actual operations themselves – their infrastructure, their layout and organization and their different types. Clearly both of these meanings can be linked – as is done by Ball (1992), when fast food technology and systems of operation are examined. But this linking need not necessarily be done. Systems theory and analysis can be applied to any industry, not just hospitality, and hospitality operations can be classified and analysed without any reference to systems thinking.

In this chapter, systems theory will be briefly explained and research conducted from the above-mentioned perspective will be identified. The chapter will then proceed to discuss the different types of operation and processes found in the hospitality industry. It concludes with a brief review of some of the major systems to be found in hospitality, not discussed elsewhere in this text – focusing on foodservice systems and the physical infrastructure of operations.

Systems theory

As Johns and Jones (1999) explain, in the hospitality industry, the language of systems is ubiquitous – management information systems, property management systems, service delivery systems, central reservation systems, or food production systems are some examples.[1] Mostly these are 'hard' systems, based on technology. But just as important are non-technological systems, sometimes called 'soft' systems, such as employee recruitment policies, selection procedures, customer service training or mystery shopper programmes. The combination of these two is called a socio-technical system, comprising both the physical infrastructure (hard systems) and human activities (soft systems), that enables a hospitality operation to deliver goods and services to customers. Technology can influence individual and group behaviour and the broader social relationships (Kast and Rozenzweig 1970), and foodservice operations can be regarded as socio-technical systems in which technological and social factors are integrated (Collison and Johnson 1980).

There is an important difference between hard and soft systems. Because the former comprise physical artefacts (i.e. equipment, machinery, technology) they behave in predictable ways according to scientific laws. Hence a hard system can be modelled as having precise outcomes which can be quantified precisely and be analysed mathematically. It is what is called 'deterministic'. For instance, it is possible to calculate precisely how long it will take for a deep fat fryer to cook different portion sizes of French fries. Soft systems, on the other hand, involve humans and technology, and human beings do not conform to scientific laws in terms of their behaviour. Hence it is not so easy to calculate precisely how long it will take different workers to prepare a portion of French fries – it will depend on their ability, their skill, their motivation and the context in which they are doing it. This is one reason why many processes have been automated and are computer controlled. They are more reliable as a result.

Although the term 'system' is used widely, it is also misused and hence misunderstood (Kirk 1995). It is often used to 'describe an assembly of parts … [or] package of components which can be purchased "off-the-shelf" with little thought of the way in which they are going to be used'. Kirk goes on to argue that such systems come as ready-made solutions to problems which often fail in practice because of the fact they are not properly designed for the environment in which they are placed. Hence the right way to think of a system is as a set

---

[1] It could be argued that all the remaining chapters in this book are about systems, such as those on the 'servicescape', the 'service encounter' and so on. But it should be noted that few of the authors of these chapters adopt a systems perspective on these topics.

of components and the relations between them, usually configured to produce a desired set of outputs, operating in the context of its environment.

Key aspects of systems

Ball et al. (2004) identify five key aspects of systems theory:

1. the general systems view,
2. systems hierarchy,
3. systems interactions,
4. simultaneous multiple containment (SMC),
5. cohesion and dispersion.

General systems view • • •

The standard systems model shows the relationship between inputs, transformational inputs, processes, outputs and feedback – as illustrated in Figure 2.1. Inputs, or resources, are typically divided into materials, energy and information, whilst outputs are the same, although often described, especially in man-made systems, as product (inputs transformed in the desired way), waste (inputs transformed as a by-product) and residue (unused inputs). The conversion of inputs into outputs is achieved by some kind of transformation process that typically requires 'transformational inputs' such as a physical

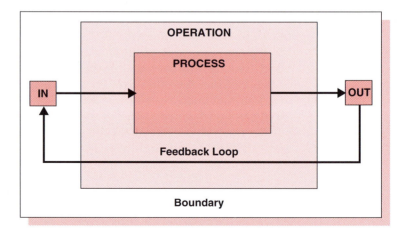

Figure 2.1
The basic systems model.

infrastructure, order, structure and capacity. These largely remain unchanged by the process, although over time machinery wears out, buildings need refurbishment and so on. In order to ensure output conforms to established requirements, it has to be monitored. If there is a deviation from expectation, there is a feedback loop so that the inputs or processes may be adjusted. Finally, this input–process–output activity is situated in a systems environment, i.e. all those things with which the system interacts. This introduces the idea of a systems 'boundary'. The boundary delineates what is 'in' the system and what is 'outside'. Sometimes the boundary is quite clear, but rather fuzzy at other times.

Systems hierarchy • • •

Very few systems operate in isolation from other systems. Many systems are made up of sub-systems and are themselves sub-systems of a larger system. This concept of hierarchy is commonly applied in the hospitality industry to the way in which operations are organized. For example, a restaurant chain (the principal system) is usually made up of a head office and individual restaurants (the first-level sub-system). Each restaurant is organized into departments such as foodservice, bars and food production (second-level sub-system).[2]

Systems interaction • • •

This concept of a hierarchy implicitly means that systems must interact with each other. The outputs of one system may form all, or part, of the inputs of another system. Some processes combine to deliver an accommodation experience to a hotel guest (front office, housekeeping and laundry), whilst others combine to create the foodservice experience for the diner in a restaurant (food preparation, food production, holding/transportation/regeneration, dining and bars). All of these are supported by other systems with which they interact (procurement, stores, maintenance and environmental/waste).

The existence of boundaries, hierarchy and interaction creates a challenge for the operations manager. Boundaries help to clarify where one system ends and another begins, and

---

[2] Another good example is in Chapter 13 where it is explained that quality inspection is part of quality control, and quality control can be part of the quality assurance system.

often where one manager's responsibility starts and ends. But hierarchy and interaction require a great deal of communication and coordination between systems, something that 'boundaries' can hinder or prevent. Sometimes these boundaries are physical, such as the distance between the hotels in a chain or the wall between the kitchen and the restaurant. But sometimes they are organizational and derive solely from the way work and responsibility have been allocated to managers or employees. One of the earliest research studies in hospitality (Whyte 1948) identified the existence of 'boundary conflict' between waiters and chefs in the restaurant industry. Historically, the industry has been quite good at recognizing the problems of physical boundaries and has removed them. One of the unique (at that time) and innovative things about McDonald's was the removal of the traditional barrier between the kitchen and the restaurant. Understanding this helps to explain why there has often been resistance to innovations that cross traditional boundaries, such as business process engineering or total quality management (TQM).

Simultaneous multiple containment

SMC is the idea that systems may exist as sub-systems of more than just one system. Thus, a hotel may be a part of a hotel chain, a member of a trade association, have a team playing in a local sports league and contribute greatly to employment in the city by operating in that labour market. Ball et al. (2004) suggest two implications of SMC. First, the complexity of the system is increased, so that understanding system behaviour and managing its performance becomes more difficult. Secondly, there can be tension between the outputs desired by the different systems. They give the example of a hotel chain in the UK which was interested in why some of its hotels were more able to implement its new 'green' policy[3] than others. The chain found that successful hotels were located in cities (i.e. another 'system') which had already established their own green policies, facilitated separate waste collections and educated the public and hence employees in best practice.

Cohesion and dispersion

The final aspect of systems is concerned with the idea that there must be forces that bind sub-systems together, balanced

---

[3] See also Chapter 17.

by forces that prevent them from merging into one. Ball et al. (2004) suggest franchising is a good example of this, in that operations are 'bound together' by franchising agreements to create chains of independently owned but mutually operated businesses.

Systems principles

Having identified five major elements of systems theory, there are seven principles which govern the behaviour of systems. If systems are to be managed effectively, these seven principles need to be clearly understood (Jones and Johns 1999).

The principle of reactions ● ● ●

In the physical sciences, 'if a set of forces [i.e. a system] is in equilibrium and a new force is introduced then, in so far as they are able, the existing forces will rearrange themselves so as to oppose the new force' (Le Chatelier 1884). This is true of *all* systems – commercial, economic, technological or social – as well as the natural world. Reaction is typically seen in response to the introduction of a new technology or new processes, most often when employees react negatively to the innovation and change. The nature of this reaction might take a variety of forms. It may be slow (such as an increase in employee turn-over after a change has been made) or fast (employees going on strike), and hence it may be chaotic and even catastrophic.

The principle of systems cohesion ● ● ●

Due to multiple systems containment, every system has 'dispersive' forces that seek to break it up, in order to redefine the systems boundaries. At the same time there will be 'cohesive' forces that keep the system together. For any system to continue in its current form, these cohesive and dispersive forces must be balanced. Ball et al. (2004) argue that managers spend a lot of time engaged in activities designed to create cohesion, largely because there are so many dispersive forces. Hence managers draw up plans, budgets and schedules so that colleagues work together towards the same goals; they hold meetings to ensure team members share information; they manage by walking around to observe behaviour and correct any deviance; and they interact with key opinion makers to influence their behaviour in support of the business.

The principle of connected variety ● ● ●

This principle states that the more stable the interaction between systems, the greater the variety and amount of interconnection between them. Recently a number of management ideas have been proposed that build on this principle. For instance, TQM requires a high degree of team work. 'Quality teams are often interdepartmental, and a quality assurance *system* (my emphasis) makes it difficult for divisions to see themselves as independent operators' (Breiter and Bloomquist 1998). Thus, TQM recognizes and values variety, and sets out to deliberately create connections to ensure stability, so as to assure the delivery of established standards.

The principle of adaptation ● ● ●

Since a system exists within an environment, cohesion can only be achieved if the rate of change in both the system and the environment is matched. The hospitality industry is full of examples of this principle in action. Over the years the hospitality industry has adapted to meet changing demographics and changing lifestyles of people. In the hotel industry, there has been development of the motel to match the growth in car ownership, the resort property to reflect the increase in disposable income, and more recently, the all-suite concept to reflect the increases in job mobility and family reunions.

The principle of limited variety ● ● ●

This principle states that the variety of systems is limited by the available space and level of differentiation possible. Hence, whilst new systems will be created to fill any gaps or niches in the systems environment, there is ultimately a limit to how many new systems can do so.

The principle of preferred patterns ● ● ●

This principle highlights the idea that interacting systems will adopt configurations that are locally stable, especially if there is systems variety and a high level of connectivity. This applies especially to managers' attempts to control processes. One of the key elements of TQM is the identification and standardization of processes. Horst Schulze in describing Ritz-Carlton's experience describes how key processes were selected for analysis and how each process was analysed over an 18-month period in order to systematize them. Prior to this study, these processes were all more or less effectively managed, but each hotel did so in slightly different ways influenced by employees' previous experience, working relationships, levels of skill and training and so on. Each hotel had its own preferred pattern based on 'local stability'.

The principle of cyclic progression ● ● ●

This principle suggests that all interconnected systems go through a cyclic progression of five stages:

1. system variety is generated,
2. dominance emerges,
3. variety is suppressed,
4. the dominant mode decays or collapses,
5. survivors emerge to regenerate variety.

Integration of principles

As well as their separate influence on systems, these seven principles may be integrated into a single 'unified systems' model (Hitchins 1992), as illustrated in Figure 2.2. Any manager should keep this model in mind when considering any problem (Johns and Jones 2000). It demonstrates that the world is both extremely complex and dynamic. It may appear to be chaotic. However, the model identifies specific relationships that place structure on this apparent chaos. Thus, the model

● identifies the extent to which the system is stable or unstable,
● helps to forecast likely events in the system environment,
● suggests appropriate plans of action that will counteract negative influences and sustain the system,
● emphasizes that change is inevitable.

To apply and use the model, the notion of hierarchy must be considered. The model should not be applied to more than one level in the hierarchy. A 'one level view' must be adopted, i.e. at an industry, firm, unit or socio-technical system level. Ball et al. (2004) give many examples of the unified systems model at work – the emergence of motels in America, the development of McDonalds, changes in foodservice management contracts and hotel management contracts, the implementation of cook-chill technology and inflight foodservice.

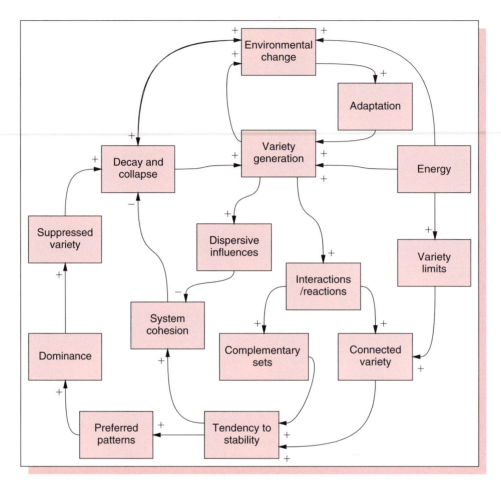

Figure 2.2
The unified systems model (*Source*: Adapted from Hitchins 1992).

Types of hospitality operation and their processes

There are alternative ways of thinking about types of operation. Johnston and Morris (1987) proposed that there are basically three types of operation: materials processing operation (MPO), customer processing operation (CPO) and information processing operation (IPO). Hayes and Wheelwright (1984), however, suggested five types – ranging from continuous through to project – based on two criteria, volume and variety.[4] Jones and Lockwood (2000) combined these two ideas to

---

[4] Discussed in Chapter 1.

develop their classification of operational types in the hospitality industry. They proposed that hospitality operations need to be modelled as either CPOs or MPOs. If an operation is a hybrid, i.e. it processes customers and materials, then it should be divided into its two constituent parts and each categorized accordingly. It should be noted that it is assumed that those operations where food items are mainly prepared from fresh ingredients are typically associated with table service, whereas those using convenience products are linked to cafeteria or counter-style operations. Whilst this is generally true, the industry is considerably diverse in its practice. This classification, by its very nature, simplifies this complexity. Hence the operations identified in Figure 2.3a and b are listed as either predominantly CPO or MPO or hybrid, and then hybrids are divided into their back-of-house and front-of-house systems. Their analysis is shown in Figure 2.3a and b.

Jones and Lockwood (2000) go on to suggest that this analysis of hospitality operations identifies some key aspects of the hospitality industry:

1. Hotels are generally more complex than foodservice operations, simply because other than limited service hotels, they provide both lodging and foodservice.
2. Hybrid operations are more complex to manage than non-hybrid operations.
3. Hospitality MPOs are job shops (e.g. a la carte restaurant), batch production (e.g. cook-chill) or mass production (e.g. fast food).
4. Most hospitality CPOs are service shops (e.g. table-service restaurant) or mass services (e.g. fast food).
5. There is generally a relationship between volume and variety, i.e. the greater the variety the lesser the volume produced (see Table 2.1).
6. It follows therefore that hybrid operations that are batch production MPOs are typically associated with service shop CPOs, whilst mass production matches mass service.

One of the main reasons for classifying operations in this way is to more fully and in more detail understand how each type varies from one another. A highly effective way of doing this is to compare job/service shops with mass production/service. A number of criteria can be used for identifying such differences, as illustrated in Table 2.1. This comparison brings us on to consider process choice in hospitality.

As well as classifying types of operation, some systems analysis has been made of the processes, or sub-systems, within these.

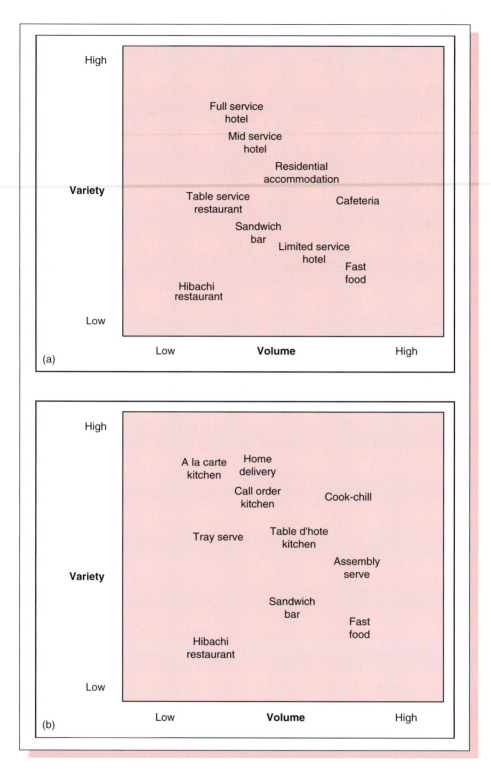

Figure 2.3
Classification of hospitality (a) customer processing operations and (b) materials processing operations (*Source*: Jones and Lockwood 2000).

Table 2.1 Differences between job shops and mass production/service

	Job/service shops	Mass production/service
Volume	Low	High
Mix of services	Diverse	Limited
Demand variation	Lumpy demand accommodated	Preferably stable demand
Pattern of process	Adaptable	Rigid
Process change	Easily accommodated	Costly
Role of equipment	Multi-use	Single use, often automated
Labour skills	Flexible, skilled workers	Generally lower skilled
Job content	Wide in scope	Narrow in scope
Work environment	Individual, craft-based	Visible, paced performance
Economies of scale	Limited	Some
Bottlenecks	Movable and frequent	Identified and predictable
Additions to capacity	May be incremental	Difficult to adjust
Tolerance for excess capacity	Adapt activity of workforce	Adjust staffing levels

Source: Adapted from Sasser et al. (1978) and Schmenner (1986).

Jones (1996) has considered both accommodation and food-service, developing systems models for each of them. He argues that for accommodation there is a *core* system comprising four sub-systems of reservations, reception, overnight stay (housekeeping) and payment (or billing). This is illustrated in Figure 2.4. Besides these, depending on the type of market being served there are ancillary systems that may, or may not, be offered (also shown in Figure 2.4). These sub-systems include laundry, restaurants, bars, business services and leisure services. Jones (1996) identifies that a hotel is largely a CPO, especially for the core system. He then writes about six different types of accommodation operation (business hotel, resort hotel, budget hotel, guest house, hospitality and residential care and hostels).

Foodservice, on the other hand, is an MPO and a CPO. Jones (1993, 1996) and Jones and Huelin (1990) have made a number of attempts to classify foodservice operations based on an analysis of their systems design, technology and configuration.

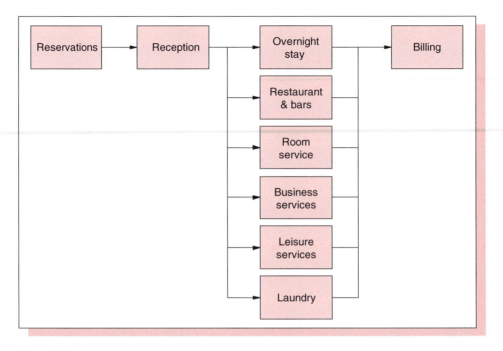

Figure 2.4
A systems model of hotel operations (*Source*: Jones 1996).

They identify 10 sub-systems of foodservice, namely storage, preparation, cooking, holding, transport, regeneration, service, dining, clearing and dishwash. Jones (1996) goes on to suggest that these have been configured in a limited number of ways, within three broad categories – food manufacturing systems, food delivery systems and integrated foodservice systems.

Configuration and layout in hospitality operations

The hospitality industry has tended to regard its processes and related technologies as unique – and in some senses they are. Few, if any, other industries prepare meals, service bedrooms, organize conferences and banquets, serve alcoholic beverages, and provide leisure facilities. Likewise the paint industry only processes paint and the car industry only makes vehicles, but they are seen as sharing some characteristics, along with many other types of manufacturing operation. For it is increasingly being recognized that concepts in relation to process choice, process configuration and process technology can be applied to *all* sectors, including the hospitality industry.

There are four basic layout types found in manufacturing and service settings (Brown et al. 2004). These are

1. fixed position,
2. process layout,
3. product layout,
4. a combination of product and process layout.

Fixed position – refers to a single, fixed position at which the product is assembled or service is processed by workers who move to that position to carry out their work. This layout is applied to products that are heavy, bulky or fragile such as in ship-building, aerospace or dentistry. In hospitality, the provision of accommodation services, i.e. hotel bedrooms, is an example of this kind of layout. Room attendants move from room to room in order to service them. This means that they have to take the technology they need to perform this task with them. The same is true of table-service restaurants – staff go to each table to perform their duties and deliver service.

Process layout – has machines or activities grouped together non-sequentially to allow a range of different products to be made. Products move to a particular location for processing according to need. Workers tend to operate within one area, but may be multi-skilled enough to work across areas. This is the typical layout associated with job shop or batch production. It allows for a wide variety of products to be made in relatively small volumes. Breakdown of one machine does not halt production. Examples of sectors that use this approach are jewellery making, hair-dressing and low-volume furniture manufacturing. Most traditional food production kitchens have a process layout. The kitchen is organized into different sections – larder, sauce, vegetables, pastry and so on – each of which can produce a wide variety of outputs. The technology in each section is carefully selected to support this activity – for instance, a large wooden chopping block in the larder, marble-topped tables in pastry and boiling pans in the vegetable section. The same is true when production is scaled up for cook-chill production, albeit that the equipment is of considerably larger capacity.

Product layout – has machinery dedicated to a particular product, usually laid out in a sequence, with distinct stages in manufacture. Workers are usually required to perform relatively simple tasks at one particular stage in the process. Whenever possible such tasks have been automated. This is the layout associated with mass production. It is used in car manufacture, chocolate production and fast food. One of the reasons that fast food was innovative was that it adopted a product layout in order to achieved high-volume, low-variety mass production style output. The technology of these operations is organized so that raw materials are processed in a highly sequential way by individual crew members. Each worker carries out one or two simple tasks such as cooking the beef pattie, toasting the bun, topping the pattie with dressing, assembling and wrapping the finished product, or serving the customer.

Process/product layout – combines elements of the process layout, such as clusters of machines, with product layout, so that each cluster is organized sequentially. Hence each cluster or cell can produce in high volumes a variety of outputs based around a single product. This, in essence, is mass customization adopted in high-tech manufacturing operations. This layout is probably only found in the flight catering sector. Large-scale food production facilities of this type may be producing up to 50,000 inflight traysets a day. They therefore have product layouts, particularly for the laying up of trays, whilst they have process layouts for the production of different types of meal item, such as starters, main meals and sandwiches.

This analysis of choice and layout identifies some interesting issues with regards to the industry. In manufacturing industry, there is a close fit between operational type and process layout. This derives from the fact that manufacturing is essentially an MPO, and service elements of a product are usually decoupled from the actual manufacture of the product. But in hospitality both customer and materials processing are closely interlinked, leading to a lack of fit between layout and process type. Fortunately (it could be argued) many of the processes in the hospitality industry are relatively simple and do not require sophisticated technology or highly skilled labour. Thus, the lack of fit between the type of process and the process layout has not become an issue. Housekeeping is a good example of this. The processes or activities undertaken to clean a guest room are basically identical and would normally lend themselves to both production-lining and even automation. If it was physically possible, one could envisage a factory in which rooms moved slowly along a production line and as they did so, a worker (or machine) polished the mirror, another vacuumed the floor, and third dusted the lampshades and so on. Of course, this cannot happen due to the size of the room and its fixed position. Hence tasks which could (should?) be dealt with on a mass production basis are actually managed as a job shop.

Systems analysis

The most frequent application of systems analysis and research into systems in hospitality is in the field of foodservice. This is due to the evolution over time of alternative ways of producing, holding and regenerating meals, such as cook-chill, cook-freeze and sous-vide. This has lead to the production of food and its service being separated in time, and often in place, something Jones (1996) refers to as 'decoupling'.[5] The theory behind these systems is essentially that of economies of scale. By decoupling the kitchen from the point of service, production facilities can be centralized, increased in size and operate in isolation from peaks and troughs in short-term demand.

Foodservice systems

A key factor in these systems is ensuring food safety and hence the process by which this is assured. Each system adopts a different 'technological' solution to this. In cook-chill systems the food is cooled to a temperature under 3°C within 90 min of cooking and stored at a maintained temperature of 0–3°C. This has now been further developed into short shelf-life (SSL) systems, where meals may be kept for up to 5 days, and long shelf-life (LSS) systems (Rodgers 2005), where shelf life is extended, usually by pasteurization.

Cook-freeze systems, as the name implies, take the temperature of cooked foods rapidly below freezing to −20°C. The advantage of this approach is that the shelf life is extended to at least 3 months. Disadvantages are that the freezing process expands water molecules in the foodstuff, and when they turn to ice the cell walls break down, potentially making the food mushy. This technology has now introduced some dehydration of meals prior to freezing in order to reduce this effect. But this does require rehydration at the point the meal is being regenerated for use. Another disadvantage is the cost and environmental impact of maintaining freezer equipment.

Sous-vide is a method of cooking that is intended to maintain the integrity of ingredients by heating them for an extended period of time at relatively low temperatures. Food is cooked for a long time, sometimes well over 24 h. But unlike a slow cooker, sous-vide cooking uses airtight plastic bags placed in hot water well below boiling point, around 60°C. The method was developed by Georges Pralus in the mid-1970s for the Restaurant Troisgros (of Pierre and Michel Troigros) in Roanne,

---

[5] See Chapter 1.

France. Sous-vide cooking must be performed under carefully controlled conditions to avoid botulism poisoning. To help with food safety and taste, relatively expensive water-bath machines are used to circulate precisely heated water; differences of even 1°C can affect the finished product. A study by Church and Parsons (1993) reviewed the claims that sous-vide technology improved both shelf life and eating quality, but in doing so presented an increased public health risk. This demonstrated at that time that, although there was some theoretical foundation, in practice the claims were unsubstantiated by their study.

Foodservice systems research

As Rodgers (2004) points out 'Foodservice systems ... development is supported by research in engineering (equipment), food science (safety, quality and nutrition) and operations management (system selection criteria and productivity). As a result, methods vary from microbiological and instrumental to computer modeling and case studies'. In this chapter, it is only the latter type of research that is of relevance. Such research can be done at the macro level, across sectors or at the unit level.

At the sectoral level, Nettles and Gregoire (1996) undertook research into foodservice directors' satisfaction with conventional or cook-chill systems and to determine whether ratings differed based on the type of system. They found that the degree of satisfaction with certain issues differed based on the type of foodservice system the director had selected. Another study by Mibey and Williams (2002) of the foodservice departments in 93 hospitals throughout New South Wales in Australia (covering 51% of hospital beds in the state) compared results with those from similar surveys conducted in 1986 and 1993. Over the previous 8 years there had been a significant increase in the proportion of hospitals using cook-chill foodservice production systems, from 18% in 1993 to 42% in 2001. Hospitals with cook-chill systems had better staff ratios than those with cook-fresh systems (8.3 vs. 6.4 beds/full-time equivalent staff), but there was no significant difference in the ratio of meals served per full-time equivalent (FTE). There was no difference between public and private hospitals in terms of ratios of beds or meals to foodservice staff. Managers using cook-chill systems reported significantly lower levels of satisfaction with the foodservice system compared to those using cook-fresh. A more recent study by Engelund et al. (2007) discusses the change in technology and logistics used in the Danish hospital foodservice during the years 1995–2003.

On the other hand, a number of unit-level studies have also been undertaken. Hartwell and Edwards (2003) investigated a hospital foodservice system that enables patients to see and smell the food on offer and interact with the staff serving the meals. This was done to establish if it resulted in better patient nutritional intake and increased meal satisfaction. Their study showed that nutritional intake was not dependent on the catering systems, but patient satisfaction was improved with the trolley system, where 93% of patients were satisfied compared to 76% with the plate system. This research suggests that nutritionally, the method of meal delivery is immaterial but patients do prefer choice at the point of consumption. Another study by Edwards and Hartwell (2006) investigated the new *Steamplicity* concept, recently introduced into UK hospitals. This system seeks to address some of the current hospital foodservice concerns through the application of a static, extended choice menu, revised patient ordering procedures, new cooking processes and individual patient food heated/cooked at ward level. The aim of their study was to compare a cook-chill foodservice operation against *Steamplicity*. Specifically, the goals were to measure food intake and wastage at ward level, stakeholders' (i.e. patients, staff, etc.) satisfaction with both systems, and patients' acceptability of the food provided. They found that patients preferred the *Steamplicity* system overall and in particular in terms of food choice, ordering, delivery and food quality. Wastage was considerably less with the *Steamplicity* system, although care must be taken to ensure that poor operating procedures do not negate this advantage.

One interesting aspect of both these studies is that their research methodology was experimental. Systems theory lends itself to this methodological approach, which is perhaps used less frequently than it could be in the hospitality operations field. An even smaller scale study also demonstrates this approach. Cocci et al. (2005) adopted a between-groups experimental design to collect data for their study of ergonomically designed worktables, and their contribution to improving the productivity of workers in a foodservice establishment. Their results provided strong support for the statement that ergonomic design contributes to an improvement of about 35% in productivity in a simple, repetitive task environment.

Facilities management in hospitality operations

As well as foodservice systems, another major operational system is the building in which the operation is situated. The management of buildings and their engineering systems is commonly known as 'facilities management'. This has become a discrete and huge body of complex knowledge and the subject of textbooks in its own right.[6] De Bruijn et al. (2001) explore how facilities management should be defined and scoped as an academic discipline by comparing it with hospitality management. But facilities management is relatively rarely mentioned in the operations management field and even more rarely researched. This is because it is a highly technical area, relying less on management expertise and more on engineering knowledge and skills.

Facilities typically have systems designed to

- deliver power and water,
- maintain a comfortable temperature,
- provide adequate lighting,
- remove waste,
- ensure personal safety,
- assist movement within the property,
- ensure the correct functioning of equipment.

Ball et al. (2004) state that the engineering function has four main purposes. The first of these is to ensure these systems operate when they are required. In situations where inputs such as energy and water are from an external provider, operators may need backup systems to ensure they are able to continue operating should external supply be interrupted. The second purpose is to ensure that these systems work properly. A systems failure has the potential to be catastrophic, for instance an electrical fault may cause a fire, a burst pipe result in flooding and so on. Third, the systems must work efficiently. Poorly controlled systems and poorly maintained equipment may result in higher than necessary energy costs. Finally, it is increasingly the case that energy consumption is an environmental issue and systems need to be designed and managed in such a way that their impact is minimized.[7]

In facilities management there are three main 'inputs' which connect the hospitality operation with the environment. These are one or more sources of power, such as electricity, gas or

[6] See, for instance, Stipanuk, D. M. (2002) *Hospitality Facilities Management and Design*, Educational Institute: Lansing, MI or Borsenik, F. D. and Stutts, A. T. (1997) *The Management of Maintenance and Engineering Systems in the Hospitality Industry*, Wiley: New York.

[7] See also Chapter 17.

solar; a water supply; and a drainage system. These external systems are connected to the facility through several technological systems that are often inter-related. These typically include a heating system, ventilation system, lighting and electrical service system, wastewater system, building transportation system and fire safety system.

From an operations' management perspective, other key activities that may need to be managed are the renovation or refurbishment of a property. Hassanien (2007) researched the practice and perception of architects, interior designers and building contractors who make up the external parties involved in the hotel renovation process. In his study, conducted in Egypt, lack of money and limitations by owners were perceived by external companies to be the main obstacles to renovation in all hotel categories.

Summary and conclusions

Discourse about systems in hospitality refers to, and uses, the concept in different ways. Systems theory is a school of thought with its own specific approach to researching the world. But systems thinking is not very theoretical – it is highly applied. In particular, it can be used for analysing hospitality operational activities, i.e. systems analysis, and solving operational problems. Systems thinking can also be used to describe the nature of hospitality operations. Systems exist everywhere in the hospitality industry, can be applied to a vast number of phenomena and can also be considered as the actual operations themselves. What one defines as a system depends on where one defines the system boundaries. This depends in turn on what one wants to study, and why. The notion of systems has a number of valuable implications. Understanding systems and effectively applying them in practice in hospitality can, for instance, facilitate better management. In his book *The Spirit to Serve* (Marriott and Brown 1997), J.W. Marriott Jr., Chief Executive of one of the world's largest and most successful hospitality companies, has written a chapter called 'The devil is in the details, success is in the systems'. In this he writes, 'systems help to bring order to the natural messiness of human enterprise ... Efficient systems and clear rules help everyone to deliver a consistent product and service'. He continues, 'systems have been deeply ingrained for so long in our corporate culture that I'm always a little surprised when I come across companies that aren't as devoted to them as we are'.

References

Ball, S., Jones, P., Kirk, D. and Lockwood, A. (2004) *Hospitality Operating Systems*, Thomson Learning: London, UK

Ball, S. D. (Ed.) (1992) *Fast Food Operations and Their Management*, Stanley Thornes: Cheltenham, UK, 65–82

Breiter, D. and Bloomquist, P. (1998) TQM in American hotels: an analysis of application, *Cornell Hotel and Restaurant Administration Quarterly* 39, 2, 26–33

Bresnahan, R. E. (1978) Optimization of food preparation labor through computer-assisted production planning, In Livingston, G. E. and Chang, C. M. (Eds.), *Food Service Systems*, Academic Press: New York, NY, 189–200

Brown, S., Lamming, R., Bessant, J. and Jones, P. (2004) *Strategic Operations Management*, Butterworth Heinemann: Oxford, UK

Church, I. J. and Parsons, A. L. (1993) Sous-vide cook chill technology, *International Journal of Food Science & Technology*, 28, 6, 563–574

Cocci, S. J., Namasivayam, K. and Bordi, P. (2005) An investigation of ergonomic design and productivity improvements in foodservice production tables, *Foodservice Research International* 16, 3–4, 53–59

Collison, R. and Johnson, K. (1980) A general systems approach to catering, In Glew, G. (Ed.), *Advances in Catering Technology*, Applied Sciences Publishers: Barking, UK

De Bruijn, H., van Wezel, R. and Wood, R. C. (2001) Lessons and issues for defining 'facilities management' from hospitality management, *Facilities*, 19, 13–14, 476–483

Edwards, J. S. A. and Hartwell, H. J. (2006) Hospital food service: a comparative analysis of systems and introducing the 'Steamplicity' concept, *Journal of Human Nutrition and Dietetics*, 19, 6, 421–430

Engelund E., Lassen, A. and Mikkelsen, B. E. (2007) The modernization of hospital food service – findings from a longitudinal study of technology trends in Danish hospitals, *Nutrition & Food Science*, 37, 2, 90–99

Gibbons, H. C. (1978) Management information systems for food service operations, In Livingston, G. E. and Chang, C. M. (Eds.), *Food Service Systems*, Academic Press: New York, NY, 343–358

Hartwell, H. J. and Edwards, J. S. A. (2003) A comparative analysis of plated and bulk trolley hospital foodservice systems, *Food Service Technology*, 3, 3/4, 133–142

Hassanien, A. (2007) An investigation of hotel property renovation: the external parties' view, *Property Management*, 25, 3, 209–224

Hayes, R. H. and Wheelwright, S. C. (1984) *Restoring Our Competitive Edge*, John Wiley: London

Hitchins, D. K. (1992) *Putting Systems to Work*, Wiley: Chichester, UK

Johns, N. and Jones, P. (1999) Systems and management: mind over matter, *Hospitality Review*, 1, 3, 43–48

Johns, N. and Jones, P. (2000) Systems and management: understanding the real world, *Hospitality Review*, 2, 1, 47–52

Johnston, R. and Morris, B. (1987) Dealing with inherent variability: the difference between manufacturing and service, *International Journal of Operations and Production Management*, 7, 4

Jones, P. (1993) A taxonomy of foodservice operations, Presented at 2nd CHME National Research Conference, Manchester Metropolitan University

Jones, P. (1996) *Introduction to Hospitality Operations*, Cassell: London, UK

Jones, P. and Huelin, A. (1990) Thinking about catering systems, *International Journal of Operations and Production Management*, 10, 8, 42–51

Jones, P. and Johns, N. (1999) Systems and management: the principles of performance, *Hospitality Review*, 1, 4, 40–44

Jones, P. and Lockwood, A. (2000) Operating systems and products, In Brotherton, B. (Ed.), *An Introduction to the UK Hospitality Industry*, Butterworth Heinemann: Oxford, UK, 46–70

Kast, F. E. and Rozenzweig, E. (1970) *Organisation and Management*, McGraw-Hill: London, UK

Kirk, D. (1995) Hard and soft systems: a common paradigm for operations management, *International Journal of Contemporary Hospitality Management*, 7, 5, 13–16

Le Chatelier, H. L. (1884) A general statement of the laws of chemical equilibrium, *Comptes rendus*, 99, 786–789

Livingston, G. E. (1978) Designing centralised food production facilities, In Livingston, G. E. and Chang, C. M. (Eds.), *Food Service Systems*, Academic Press: New York, NY, 261–274

Marriott, J. W. and Brown, K. A. (1997) *The Spirit to Serve*, Harper Business Press: New York, NY

Mibey, R. and Williams, P. (2002) Food services trends in New South Wales hospitals 1993–2001, *Food Service Technology*, 2, 2, 95–103

Nettles, M. F. and Gregoire, M. B. (1996) Satisfaction of foodservice directors after implementation of a conventional or cook-chill foodservice system, *Foodservice Research International*, 9, 2, 107–115

Rodgers, S. (2004) The review of foodservice systems and associated research, *Foodservice Research International*, 14, 4, 273–290

Rodgers, S. (2005) Selecting a food service system: a review, *International Journal of Contemporary Hospitality Management*, 17, 2, 157–169

Sasser, W. E., Olsen, R. P. and Wyckoff, D. D. (1978) *Management of Service Operations*, Allyn & Bacon: Newton, Mass

Schmenner, R. (1986) How can service businesses survive and prosper?, *Sloan Management Review*, Spring, 21–32

Schwartz, R. N. (1978) Design and operation of a quality assurance program in a multiunit food service operation, In Livingston, G. E. and Chang, C. M. (Eds.), *Food Service Systems*, Academic Press: New York, NY, 405–412

Symington, L. E. (1978) The role of human engineering in food service systems design, In Livingston, G. E. and Chang, C. M. (Eds.), *Food Service Systems*, Academic Press: New York, NY, 343–356

Whyte, W. F. (1948) *Human Relations in the Restaurant Industry*, McGraw-Hill: New York, NY

CHAPTER 3

The servicescape

Karthik Namasivayam

Associate Professor
School of Hospitality Management
The Pennsylvania State University
USA

Ingrid Y. Lin

Associate Professor
School of Travel Industry Management
University of Hawaii at Manoa
Honolulu, U.S.A.

Introduction

No matter who you are, where or how you live; what your physical, mental and spiritual requirements [are] – your environment is essential to your mental balance. Leatrice Eiseman

Recent advances in the services literature suggest that what service consumers seek is an 'experience' (Gilmore and Pine 2002). Service organizations are exhorted to provide memorable experiences to their consumers. A service 'product' is a combination of intangible and tangible components. Organizations that provide the most appropriate combination of the two are most likely to achieve competitive success. While it is important to recognize that the actual service provided is intangible, the setting in which any service is provided is constituted of both tangible and intangible elements. The environment in which a service is provided, therefore, plays a very important role in the creation and facilitation of a consumer's service experience. The service environment is termed the 'servicescape' and represents the artificial and psychological, landscape in which a service experience is organized and delivered by service providers and experienced by consumers.

Servicescapes have a particularly important role to play in a service establishment. Consumers seek evidence of the eventual 'quality' of the intangible service from observing the tangible elements – that is, the servicescape (Berry and Parasuraman 1991). Therefore, the more intangible a service is, the more managerial attention is required towards servicescape elements (Shostack 1977).

A servicescape is described as the physical environment of an organization encompassing several different elements such as overall layout, design and decor. The servicescape also includes atmospherics such as lighting, colours and music. Servicescapes are important since they influence consumers' cognitive, emotional and physiological states, as well as their behaviours. Service organizations therefore employ elements of the servicescape and atmospherics to motivate consumer satisfaction and repeat purchase behaviour. Organizations also use servicescape elements to direct and manage consumer interactions with the organization (e.g. in fast food restaurants) and thereby increase operational efficiencies.

The effect of environments on individuals has been investigated extensively adopting various fundamental theoretical domains. Among the more important theories explaining individuals' reactions to environments are those proposed by Lewin (1951), who proposed that human behaviour is a function of the environment and individual differences (expressed as $B = f(P, E)$) and models developed by others using Gestalt psychology. These and other theoretical frames have been applied to model individual behaviour in service settings. Such an understanding permits managers to better design and manage the 'moments of truth' that are so vital to the success of a service business (Carlzon 1987). Research in this area has also shown that the physical environment in which a service is provided has an important effect on consumer satisfaction (Turley and Milliman 2000).

The objective of this chapter is to provide a fuller understanding of the effects of servicescapes on consumers in a service setting. To achieve this goal, the chapter begins with definitions of the servicescape. Next, the effects of the servicescape on consumer behaviour are described using theoretical perspectives, mainly from environmental psychology. The chapter goes on to review research in the effects of various elements of the servicescape such as music, scents and colour on consumers. Finally, the key issues are summarized and implications for managers discussed.

Defining the servicescape

Initial research in servicescapes was largely in the context of retail operations, but later research recognized the importance of the role of servicescapes in other services, including hospitality. For example, Kotler (1973) analysed the role of store interiors and exteriors in motivating sales of manufactured products. He noted that store interiors and exteriors (i.e. the servicescape) had a strong effect on store sales volumes. Later, Bitner (1992) extended the concept more specifically in the context of services, including both employees and customers in her analysis.

A servicescape consists of all elements that can be employed to influence both employee and customer behaviour in the service setting. This is especially important in the service industry due to the element of co-production in which the service is produced by both the employee and consumer together.[1] Moreover, the service is generally produced and consumed simultaneously (Bitner 1992; Zeithaml et al. 1985). Elements such as lighting, signage, textures, colour, music, fragrances and temperature of the environment all contribute to creating a servicescape. Bitner summarizes the different elements into three composite dimensions, namely ambient conditions;

---

[1] See also Chapter 4.

spatial layout and functionality; and signs, symbols and arte-facts. It must be noted that different industries will use different combinations of the elements to influence particular forms and sets of behaviour. For example, a fast food operation depends on a different set of environmental cues than a fine-dining restaurant. Thus, the choice of servicescape in an organization is dependent on its strategic market orientation.

Environmental psychologists note that in studying the effects of environments on human behaviour, it must be recognized that the environment is often in the background. The individual is often unaware, directly, of the effects of any single element in the environment; it is the cumulative effect that is powerful and complex (Russell and Snodgrass 1987). It is therefore important for service managers to recognize that their design of the servicescape has a subtle yet powerful effect on consumer and employee behaviour. Opposed to a strictly operations design view in which managers concentrate on achieving higher efficiencies, it is suggested that the effects of particular choices in signage, layout or other elements of the servicescape on employee and consumer emotions, attitudes and behaviours have to be attended to by managers.

Venolia (1988) adopting a counselling psychology perspective notes that the servicescape consists of the actual physical dimensions and also a mental dimension (i.e. messages imparted to consumers by the physical environment) and an emotional dimension (i.e. the emotional responses an environment evokes). These dimensions reflect the fact that environments affect individuals physically, psychologically, emotionally and spiritually.

Definitions of the servicescape in the consumer literature have expanded from a strict attention to the physical environment in which a service is provided. Tombs and McColl-Kennedy (2003) propose a 'social-servicescape model' and suggest that not only the physical aspect but also the social aspect (other customers and service providers in the environment) affect consumer behaviour. More recently, Rosenbaum (2005) speaks of 'symbolic servicescapes'. He suggests that certain elements in a servicescape may evoke the same meaning for people of a given ethnicity and that such elements may function in a symbolic manner. Rosenbaum (2005: 258) notes that 'ethnic consumers may respond both to a *physical* servicescape and to a *symbolic* servicescape' when considering whether or not to patronize an establishment.

In summary, the servicescape has been described as having both physical and non-physical dimensions. The progression of definitions suggest that researchers are moving away from a strict and narrow definition of servicescapes comprising phys-ical and tangible elements to one that is comprehensive and includes social, psychological and contextual elements. The next section reviews theoretical frames that have been used to analyse the effects of the servicescape on human behaviour. While most of the literature has discussed the impact of the servicescape on consumer behaviour, there is some research in employee reactions to servicescapes. In this chapter, however, servicescape effects on individuals are discussed without pref-erence for one or the other group of individuals. Managers and researchers should note that different elements have different effects, given particular situations. For example, the length and design of a queuing system will have an effect on con-sumers who are in a hurry.[2] Or the type and texture of floor-ing becomes of paramount interest to an employee who has to stand on her feet for long hours.

Theoretical and methodological frames adopted in servicescape research

A number of different theoretical frames have been adopted in describing the effects of servicescapes on humans. The area of environmental psychology has a rich tradition of research exploring the connections between human behaviour and the environment in which such behaviour occurs, with a view to enhancing positive outcomes from such interactions.

Researchers in environmental psychology propose the 'person-in-environment system' as the unit of analysis in research projects. This perspective requires researchers to account for not only the characteristics of the individual but also 'the complexity of the real-life situation (Wapner et al. 2000: 296). This perspective calls for a transactional and contextual approach to understanding the person–environment relation-ships. As the authors note, 'the person and the environment are considered parts of the whole' and 'the relations are viewed as part of an integrated process rather than as unidirectional chains of cause–effect relationships' (Wapner et al. 2000: 291). However, as Aubert-Gamet (1997) argues, most studies in servicescapes have adopted a positivist research orientation. Adopting this perspective implies that researchers assume a correspond-ence between the elements of the servicescape and individuals' behavioural, emotional or cognitive outcomes in the given space.

---

[2] See also Chapter 5.

Research in this frame seeks to understand and predict consumers' behaviours, given a set of servicescape elements. Thus, research has adopted either a natural science or a human science method to analysing the human–environment relationship. In natural science approaches, researchers focus on observable behaviour and seek explanations rooted in the environment for such behaviour. Contrastingly, a human science perspective 'specifies as its goal the understanding of experience, or the explication of structural relationships, patterns, or organization that specifies meaning' (Walsh et al. 2000: 303). In this context, the work of Lefebvre (cited in Aubert-Gamet 1997) is relevant. His conceptualization of space draws on postmodern constructivist paradigm that argues for a space co-constructed by both architect and consumer (Aubert-Gamet 1997). Consumers are seen as appropriating the space and both constructing and attributing meaning to it.

The main theoretical streams in environmental psychology may be usefully divided as cognitive theories and affective theories. Thus, theoretical frames emphasizing the role of perceptual processes (e.g. Lee 2003; Baroni 2003; Bonaiuto et al. 2003) fall in the cognitive theory camp, while those that describe the nature of individuals' attachment to an environment (Guiliani 2003) are affective. Besides this, theories have also been developed that seek to explain the social setting, individuals' attitudes towards a setting and its effect on individual behaviour in particular environments (Staats 2003). Membership in particular groups may also influence individuals' behaviours in settings or their attitudes towards certain environments. Hence, identity theories have been applied to explain person–environment interactions (Twigger-Ross et al. 2003).

While the broader discipline of environmental psychology is developing new theoretical frames, among the more common perspectives researchers in servicescapes have adopted is the S-O-R (stimulus-organism-response) model (Donovan and Rossiter 1982). This research stream developed from Lewin's (1951) formula relating to human behaviour and the environment: $B = f(P, E)$, where behaviour (B) is modelled as a function (f) of the interaction between the person (P) and the environment (E). According to this model, various environmental stimuli (such as music, crowding, lighting, colour and temperature) have an effect on individuals' emotions, cognitions and feelings. As a consequence, individuals respond to these stimuli by adopting behaviours that enhance their well-being. This framework has dominated much of the research in servicescapes.

The S-O-R model, adopting a more emotional frame, explores the interactions between the environment and the person, whereas environmental researchers following the principles of Gestalt psychology attempt to provide a more cognitive explanation of the interactions. According to Gestalt psychologists, perception is a function of multiple sources of input from the environment and from one's own predispositions, expectations, motives and knowledge gleaned from past learning experiences (Goldstein 1999; Schiffman and Kanuk 1978). All of these elements together produce an individual's picture of the world. People generally receive a variety of stimuli from a servicescape and then organize them cognitively into groups and form images from the stimuli as a whole. The Gestalt approach explains how individuals organize mental figure-like images and how such images are both organized and perceived through various sensory aids, such as visual, audio and olfactory sensations.

Unlike research that seeks to outline the connections between the environment and individuals' affective responses, Gestalt researchers attempt to understand and describe how environments influence individuals' mental models, schema and perceptual frames. Researchers following the principles of Gestalt psychology 'believed that a perception cannot be meaningfully deconstructed into its elementary components ... the attempt to break down and reduce a perception to its presumed elementary sensory units would be to lose sight of the perception itself' (Lin 2004: 165). According to Lin (2004), individuals first organize their perceptions, which then influence their affective reactions and subsequent secondary cognitive processing and behaviours. Opposite to the S-O-R model described earlier, Gestalt principles assume proactive individuals who consciously and, oftentimes, proactively organize their interactions with the environment (Namasivayam and Lin 2004). Tombs and McColl-Kennedy (2003: 453) note that '[individuals'] behaviors may not necessarily be directly affect driven but may require some cognitive appraisals'.

Cue utilization theory describes products or services as consisting of a number of cues that 'serve as surrogate indicators of the product's quality' (Reimer and Kuehn 2005: 786). The theory treats cues as either intrinsic or extrinsic to the product or service. In the case of manufactured products, physical attributes of a product such as size or shape serve as intrinsic cues, while extrinsic cues include brand names and price. However, it is suggested that in the case of services, because of simultaneous production and consumption, the only intrinsic cues available are in the servicescape itself. The theory is used to model individuals' information search processes and consequent behaviour, in a consumption setting. The role of servicescapes as an influence on the information search processes is thus modelled using the perspective of cue utilization theory.

Recognizing that not just physical characteristics of the environment but also social characteristics (such as other consumers in the setting) have an effect on consumer behaviour, researchers conceptualize a social-servicescape (Tombs and McColl-Kennedy 2003). The authors integrate three socially oriented theories – Social Facilitation (Zajonc 1965), Behaviour Settings (Barker 1968) and Affective Events Theory (Weiss and Cropanzano 1996) – to develop their concept of social-servicescapes. Drawing on existing research, the concept includes five key elements (Tombs and McColl-Kennedy 2003: 458):

1. purchase occasion (context);
2. social density (physical elements);
3. displayed emotion of others (social elements);
4. customer's affective responses (internal responses); and
5. customer's cognitive responses (either as intention of behaviour or as actual behaviours).

This perspective moves research away from a narrow delineation of the servicescape as a set of physical and intangible elements to include other consumers in the setting as an important component of the servicescape. Similarly, the occasion of purchase is also taken into account to explain consumer behaviour in servicescapes.

As noted earlier, researchers also speak of a symbolic servicescape. This line of reasoning is informed by sociological research that suggests 'ethnic groups maintain distinct symbolic universes, which evoke common meanings among members' (Rosenbaum 2005: 260). The author extends Bitner's (1992) argument that consumers pay attention to signs, symbols and artefacts in a servicescape to receive meaning and to recognize their similarity (or difference) from other individuals in the setting. Thus, servicescape elements serve to construct symbolic spaces which have meaning for individuals. Such meaning will then subsequently drive their behaviour. This line of research implicitly draws on theorizing that suggests that identity formation and appropriation are part of the person–environment interaction.

Servicescape research is developing rapidly by incorporating existing theoretical frames, including fresh perspectives and refining our understanding of the effects of servicescapes on consumer behaviour. However, a number of methodological challenges present themselves in the research of environment–person behaviour. As Bechtel et al. (1987: 5) note, the interface of physical environment and human functioning needs special attention to research methods because 'there is the question as to who or what is the basic unit of analysis. In most social science research, it is the person, group, or societal aggregate. In environmental research, it is as much, if not more the space or place that the person or agglomeration [is using]'. More recently, authors suggest meta-analysis (Stamps III 2002), experience sampling (Hektner and Csikszentmihalyi 2002), geographic information systems (Golledge 2002) and structural equation modelling (Corral-Verdugo 2002) to research environmental issues. Wapner et al. (2000) suggest that researchers should be aware that their assumptions about natural science or human science will drive their research methods. They do not, however, suggest that one has predominance over the other – when the number of variables being examined are reasonable, natural science methods such as experimentation may be usefully adopted. However, should the researcher be more interested in understanding or describing processes underlying the person–environment interaction and changes in these processes, they suggest adopting 'more descriptive, phenomenological methods' (Wapner et al. 2000: 11). Walsh et al. (2000) note that research in this discipline has included narrative sketches and videotapes, self-report survey instruments and idiotape analysis. Aubert-Gamet (1997) notes that servicescape researchers have borrowed analytic tools from many disciplines including anthropology, sociology and semiotics. However, it is preferable to use multiple methods and to adopt triangulation wherever possible (Lin 2004).

Environmental stimuli

The various elements of the servicescape that constitute stimuli may be broadly classified as visual, auditory and olfactory. Visual stimuli include, among others, colour, lighting, space and function and layout and design (Lin 2004). Colour can be considered as one of the most powerful aspects of an environment. The right colours and colour combinations will stimulate or relax an individual in any given environment. Much research has been conducted on the effect of colour on individual reactions (Eiseman 1998). Colour can be decomposed into three interrelated dimensions: hue (red, blue, green, etc.), value (or the degree of lightness or darkness) and intensity (or the degree of saturation of a colour – for example, bright red). Colours have been shown to enhance introversion or extroversion, incite anger or relaxation and influence physiological responses (Elliot et al. 2007). In a retail setting, Bellizzi et al. (1983) found that colours affect consumers' purchase behaviours and their perceptions of store image. Individuals have been found to attribute different emotions to different colours, with light colours representing positive emotions while darker ones representing negative emotions (Boyatzis and Varghese 1994). Researchers also noted a gender effect (Hemphill 1996) and an age effect (Silver and Ferrante 1995) in terms of preference for colours. More importantly, certain colours evoked strong physiological reactions (Kwallek and Lewis 1990): men's depression, confusion and anger was associated with working in offices with a high-saturated colour (green, blue, purple, red, yellow or orange); some colours such as blue and violet decreased individuals' blood pressure, pulse and respiration rate (Ward 1995). These findings together have demonstrated the strong influence of environmental colours on individuals' reactions.

Similarly, the type of lighting in an environment directly influences an individual's perceptions of the definition and quality of the space. Lighting influences an individual's perceptions of form, colour, texture and enclosure (Ching 1996). The physical, emotional, psychological and spiritual aspects of space are highlighted and revealed by lighting (Kurtich and Eakin 1993). Natural and artificial lighting have each shown to have different effects on individuals' physiological functioning (Hastings et al. 1980). Areni and Kim (1994) showed that brighter stores cause customers to handle goods more but does not result in increased time spent at store or sales. Flynn (1992) described several psychological dimensions of artificial lighting that caused similar reactions across individuals. These dimensions include people's impressions of visual clarity, spaciousness, relaxation, privacy and pleasantness. For example, environments in which lighting is designed to harmonize with furniture and accessories is perceived as more pleasant than environments in which lighting does not harmonize with other elements of the room (Steffy 1990).

Auditory cues include music and noise in an environment. Many studies have shown that music can be used as an effective tool to minimize the negative consequences of waiting in a service operation (Hui et al. 1997). More recently, Sweeney and Wyber (2002) found that consumers rated a retail environment as more pleasurable and the merchandize on offer as of higher quality if they liked the music being played. In their 1993 study, Yalch and Spangenberg found that younger consumers spent more time shopping when background music was played. Another study by Areni and Kim (1993) demonstrated the differing effects of classical and top-forty music on wine shoppers. Playing classical music resulted in significantly higher sales because it led consumers to buy more expensive items. Classical music was found to make bank consumers feel more positively towards the environment (Yalch and Spangenberg 1993). Dube et al. (1995) found that music appears to influence the quality of buyer–seller interactions. Thus, music has been shown in a number of settings and environments to have an important effect on individuals' psychological state and consequently their behaviours. Indeed, on 27 September 2007, Intercontinental Hotels & Resorts issued a press release announcing a 'global acoustic programme'. They reported that in addition to ethnographic research, they had interviewed 1100 guests throughout the world and found that 'two out of three were passionate about music and very clear about the styles of music they prefer'. Hence, this company believes 'music is an integral part of the guest experience' (Intercontinental Hotels & Resorts 2007).

Olfactory cues as influences on consumer behaviour have also been extensively investigated. Exposure to specific odours determines various psychological processes such as mood, cognition, person perception, sexual behaviour and ingestive functions (Martin 1994). Baron (1997) found that mall shoppers who smelled baking cookies or roasting coffee were significantly likely to spontaneously help a same-sex stranger than people not exposed to such smells. Research has shown that when the odour is congruent with the product class being examined, consumers spend more time on processing product information, are more holistic in their processing and are more variety seeking compared to when the odour is incongruent (Mitchell et al. 1995; Spangenberg et al. 1996).

Intervening moderators or mediators

From the sample of research described above, it is clear that individual elements in the environment have an important effect on consumer behaviour. While research aimed at exploring and making clear the effects of individual or sets of environmental elements on behaviour is important, it is also important to account for 'consumers' psychological processing and evaluation' (Lin 2004: 174). Research has also focused on moderators and mediators that may alter the relationship between such servicescape elements and outcomes. Lin (2004) provides a useful summary of the relationships: she distinguishes between micro- and macro-level factors that intervene between the servicescape attribute and individuals' cognitive or affective processing of the information. Some micro-level factors that may moderate the relationship include personality, cognitive style, level of involvement and other demographic variables such as gender and age. Macro-level factors that may impact the relationship include cultural factors (e.g. individualism versus collectivism) and the socio-cultural setting (e.g. church or theme park). Timko et al. (2000) suggest that there should be a match between individuals' personal traits and the nature of environmental demands in order to obtain positive affective and behavioural outcomes. Researchers also suggest that personality predispositions influence individuals' evaluative responses to an environment (Lin 2004; Nasar 2000). Russell and Snodgrass (1987) noted that a number of individual differences such as arousal seeking tendencies, prior mood and prior expectations influence the relationship between individual and environment. While much research in environmental psychology has investigated these and other variables, less work has been conducted in this area in the context of consumer behaviour.

At the macro-level, a number of interesting perspectives have been developed. Timko et al. (2000) note that social environments have unique 'personalities' and the management of environmental personality to be accessible to individuals who have a range of personality types is very important. In another perspective, environments are considered as personal contexts – spaces constructed and construed by individuals in a manner suiting their particular needs (Little 2000). Thus, individuals may 'construct' restorative niche spaces within larger environmental boundaries. Such spaces are very personal and idiosyncratic; one person's restorative niche may be another's discordant space! Barker (1968) on the other hand conceives of spaces as 'behaviour-settings', that is, spaces are said to bound a definite set of behaviours within a time–space dimension. Individuals who are in church or at a discotheque adopt the norms of the behaviour setting they find themselves in.

Mention must also be made about the issue of levels of analysis: it is possible to study servicescapes at the level of the individual, the group or the organization. It is perhaps important to account for the different processes that impact consumer behaviour at these various levels of conceptualization. The type and nature of moderators or mediators that has to be accounted for will change depending on the level of analysis. For example, it is possible that personality factors will have a greater role to play at the individual level of analysis compared to groups. In groups, it is possible that group socio-cultural factors moderate the relationship between environments and individuals in the group. Moreover, it is also important to account for the temporal element: Namasivayam and Lin (2004) describe servicescape impacts before and after a consumer transacts with a service provider. Consumers are said to process environmental information differently based on their temporal location with reference to the service interaction. It is important, therefore, for servicescape researchers to account for these and other potential moderators and mediators.

Implications of the servicescape's effect on consumers

Research in environmental psychology concerns itself with accounting for the effects of environments on human behaviour. Thus, the main focus of research is to explore how different elements in the environment can be managed to produce positive effects on humans in the environment. In the domain of consumer behaviour, servicescape research has documented the effect of the environment on consumers' behaviours including time spent in the store (Grossbart et al. 1990), retention of customers (Babin and Attaway 2000), purchasing behaviour (De Mozota 1990), product choice (Buckley 1991), quality (Reimer and Kuehn 2005), satisfaction (Bitner 1990) and dissatisfaction (Morrin and Ratneshwar 2000).

Environmental psychologists have been concerned with similar outcomes, but they have also been concerned with the degree to which an environment facilitates or blocks an individual's plans (Russell and Snodgrass 1987). According to this view, individuals select certain environments in order to carry out a 'plan'. To the extent an environment supports the attainment of such planned goals, the environment will be seen in positive light. Researchers note that the outcomes of such frustration of plans can be emotional. Individuals may react to frustrated motives with anger, sadness or even depression. Bitner (1992) categorizes individuals' responses as internal and behaviour. Individuals' internal responses include cognitive (beliefs, categorization and symbolic meaning), emotional (mood and attitude) and physiological (pain, comfort, movement and physical fit). Individuals' behaviours include approach and avoidance behaviours. Approach behaviours include attraction, stay and explore, spend money and carry out plan, while avoidance behaviours include all the opposites of approach. Donovan and Rossiter (1982) showed that the environment influenced individuals' shopping enjoyment, financial expenditures, time spent browsing and store exploration. More recent perspectives suggest that individuals' appropriate space for their own purposes and the extent to which the environment permits such appropriation will affect their behaviour (Aubert-Gamet 1997).

Future research

The notion of 'experience' has been suggested as an alternative to 'commoditization'. Hospitality managers are exhorted to provide 'a memorable experience – one that creates a lasting memory for each guest' (Gilmore and Pine 2002: 87). The authors suggest that the way to do this is to use 'services as the stage and goods as props to engage individual customers in an inherently personal way' (Gilmore and Pine 2002: 88). As has been discussed here, hospitality environments are considered key factors in managing customers' experiences. Hospitality researchers may want to explore the idea of the Gestalt and the customer experience. To what extent do consumers include the environment while 'experiencing' a service?

More research is required exploring the interaction of factors at the individual level and the environment. The notion of person–environment fit should be more fully explored to outline the connections between particular personalities and their preferred environments. Such knowledge can motivate more targeted design of servicescape elements. While there are broad generalities such as pink environment for girls and blue for boys, a more thorough investigation of the connections between personality and environment will aid in the design of appropriate spaces. Hogan and Roberts (2000: 12) note that 'the interaction in a person–situation interaction is between a person's identity, the role he or she must play in an interaction, the agenda for the interaction and the implications of the interaction for a person's reputation'. Individuals in a social setting may be conscious of their identity and may actually use the social setting in constructing their identities (Twigger-Ross et al. 2003). Applying the precepts of identity theory (Tajfel 1978, 1981; Breakwell 1986) may clarify how individuals use servicescapes to realize or construct identity and thus help hospitality managers better manage the interaction. Also as noted earlier, theorists conceptualize a social-servicescape in which the social environment is presented as an important factor determining consumers' affective and cognitive outcomes (Tombs and McColl-Kennedy 2003). Thus, more research is needed accounting for the influence of the social environment on individuals.

A number of research questions can be generated based on the extant gaps in the literature. For example, what are the effects of different environmental attributes in different hospitality settings? What are the effects of different colours in different hospitality settings? What kind of music is the most appropriate in a bar? How do individuals react to ceiling heights and which reaction is the most appropriate in a given space and for a specific function? Which element/s has/have the greatest role to play in individuals' reactions and sense making? Do individuals evaluate each element, or do they take into account a set of specific markers to make sense of hospitality environments? That is, do all individuals engage in Gestaltic evaluations? How does the idea of categorization influence how individuals process environmental information? Do individuals associate particular environmental markers with particular brands? More research is warranted in understanding consumers' evaluative processes.

For managers, there exists a rich stream of research that provides information about how to design spaces that maximize various target behaviours (e.g. time spent in the restaurant – managers may want to minimize the length of time customers occupy the seat!). However, more research in social-servicescapes, symbolic servicescapes and servicescapes as important influences on individuals' identity may provide managers with a more sophisticated toolbox.

Summary and conclusions

This chapter summarized the main areas of research in servicescapes. A number of novel theoretical frames were briefly reviewed. In sum, it can be noted that while the research in environmental psychology has advanced, there is little progress in theoretical underpinnings in servicescape research (important exceptions have been noted in this chapter). Researchers and managers will benefit greatly with more theorizing and empirical research in this area.

References

Areni, C. and Kim, D. (1993) The influence of background music on shopping behavior: Classical versus top-forty in a wine store, *Advances in Consumer Research*, 20, 336–340
Areni, C. and Kim, D. (1994) The influence of in-store lighting on consumers' examination of merchandise in a wine store, *International Journal of Research in Marketing*, 11, 2, 117–125

Aubert-Gamet, V. (1997) Twisting servicescapes: diversion of the physical environment in a re-appropriation process, *International Journal of Service Industry Management*, 8, 1, 26–41

Babin, B. J. and Attaway, J. S. (2000) Atmospheric effect as a tool for creating value and gaining a share of customer, *Journal of Business Research*, 49, 2, 91–99

Barker, R. G. (1968) *Ecological Psychology*, Stanford University Press: Stanford, CA

Baron, R. A. (1997) The sweet smell of … helping: effects of pleasant ambient fragrance on prosocial behavior in shopping malls, *Personality and Social Psychology Bulletin*, 23, 5, 498–503

Baroni, M. R. (2003) Cognitive processes theories and environmental issues, In Bonnes M., Lee T. and Bonaiuto, M. (Eds.), *Psychological Theories for Environmental Issues*, Ashgate Publishing: Hants, UK, 63–94

Bechtel, R. B., Marans, R. W. and Michelson, W. (1987) *Methods in Environmental and Behavioral Research*, Van Nostrand Reinhold Company: New York

Bellizzi, J. A., Crowley, A. E. and Hasty, R. W. (1983) The effects of color in store design, *Journal of Retailing*, 59, 1, 21–45

Berry, L. L. and Parasuraman, A. (1991) *Marketing Services: Competing through Quality*, Free Press: New York

Bitner, M. J. (1990) Evaluating service encounters: the effects of physical surroundings and employee responses, *Journal of Marketing*, 54, 2, 69–82

Bitner, M. J. (1992) Servicescapes: the impact of physical surroundings on customers and employees, *Journal of Marketing*, 56, 2, 57–71

Bonaiuto, P., Giannini, A. M. and Biasi, V. (2003) Perception theories and the environmental experience, In Bonnes, M., Lee, T. and Bonaiuto, M. (Eds.), *Psychological Theories for Environmental Issues*, Ashgate Publishing: Hants, UK, 95–136

Boyatzis, C. J. and Varghese, R. (1994) Children's emotional associations with colors, *Journal of Genetic Psychology*, 155, 1, 77–85

Breakwell, G. M. (1986) *Coping with Threatened Identities*, Methuen: London

Buckley, P. G. (1991) An S-O-R model of the purchase of an item in a store, *Advances in Consumer Research*, 18, 1, 491–499

Carlzon, J. (1987) *Moments of Truth*, Ballinger Publishing Company: Cambridge, MA

Ching, F. (1996) *Architecture: Form, Space and Order*, Van Nostrand: New York

Corral-Verdugo, V. (2002) Structural equation modeling, In Bechtel, R. B. and Churchman, A. (Eds.), *Handbook of Environmental Psychology*, Wiley: New York, 256–270

De Mozota, B. B. (1990) Design as a strategic marketing tool, In Oakley, M. (Ed.), *Design Management*, Blackwell Reference: Cambridge, MA, 73–84

Donovan, R. J. and Rossiter, J. R. (1982) Store atmosphere: an experimental psychology approach, *Journal of Retailing, 58*, 1, 34–57

Dube, L., Chebat, J. C. and Morin, S. (1995) The effects of background music on consumers' desire to affiliate in buyer–seller interactions, *Psychology and Marketing, 12*, 4, 305–319

Eiseman, L. (1998) *Colors for Your Every Mood*, Capital Books, Inc.: Sterling, VA

Elliot, A. J., Maier, M. A., Moller, A. C., Friedman, R. and Meinhardt, J. (2007) Color and psychological functioning: the effect of red on performance attainment, *Journal of Experimental Psychology: General*, 136, 1, 154–168

Flynn, J. E. (1992) *Architectural Interior Systems: Lighting, Acoustics and Air Conditioning*, 3rd edition, Van Nostrand Reinhold: New York

Gilmore, J. H. and Pine, II, B. J. (2002) Differentiating hospitality operations via experiences: why selling services is not enough, *Cornell Hotel and Restaurant Administration Quarterly*, 43, 3, 87–96

Giuliani, M. V. (2003) Theory of attachment and place attachment, In Bonnes, M., Lee, T. and Bonaiuto, M. (Eds.), *Psychological Theories for Environmental Issues*, Ashgate Publishing: Burlington, VT, 137–170

Goldstein, B. (1999) *Sensation and Perception*, Pacific Grove, CA: Brooks/Cole

Golledge, R. G. (2002) The open door of GIS, In Bechtel, R. B. and Churchman, A. (Eds.), *Handbook of Environmental Psychology*, Wiley: New York, 244–255

Grossbart, S., Hampton, R., Rammohan, B. and Lapidus, R. S. (1990) Environmental dispositions and customer response to store atmospherics, *Journal of Business Research*, 21, 225–242

Hastings, A. C., Fadiman, J. and Gordon, J. S. (1980) *Health for the Whole Person*, Westview Press: Boulder, CO

Hektner, J. M. and Csikszentmihalyi, M. (2002) The experience sampling method: measuring the context and content of lives, In Bechtel, R. B. and Churchman, A. (Eds.), *Handbook of Environmental Psychology*, Wiley: New York, 233–243

Hemphill, M. (1996) A note on adults' color–emotion associations, *Journal of Genetic Psychology*, 157, 275–281

Hogan, R. and Roberts, B. W. (2000) A socioanalytic perspective on person–environment interaction, In Walsh, W. B., Craik, K. H. and Price, R. H. (Eds.), *Person-Environment Psychology: New*

Directions and Perspectives, Lawrence Erlbaum Associates: Mahwah, NJ, 1–23

Hui, M. K., Dube, L. and Chebat, J. (1997) The impact of music on consumers' reactions to waiting for services, *Journal of Retailing,* 73, 1, 87–104

Ingrid, I. Y. and Lin, I. Y. (2004) Evaluating a servicescape: the effect of cognition and emotion, *International Journal of Hospitality Management,* 23, 2, 163–178

Intercontinental Hotels & Resorts (27 September 2007) *Global Acoustic Programme,* London Press release

Kotler, P. (1973) Atmospherics as a marketing tool, *Journal of Retailing,* 49, 4, 48–64

Kurtich, J. and Eakin, G. (1993) *Interior Architecture,* Van Nostrand Reinhold: New York

Kwallek, N. and Lewis, C. M. (1990) Effects of environmental colour on males and females: a red or white or green office, *Applied Ergonomics,* 21, 4, 275–278

Lee, T. (2003) Schema theory and the role of socio-spatial schemata in environmental psychology, In Bonnes, M., Lee, T. and Bonaiuto, M. (Eds.), *Psychological Theories for Environmental Issues,* Ashgate Publishing: Hants, UK, 27–62

Lewin, K. (1951) *Field Theory in Social Science,* Harper: New York

Lin, Y. I. (2004) Evaluating a servicescape: The effect of cognition and emotion, *International Journal of Hospitality Management,* 23, 163–178

Little, B. R. (2000) Free traits and personal contexts: expanding a social ecological model of well-being, In Walsh, W. B., Craik, K. H. and Price, R. H. (Eds.), *Person-Environment Psychology: New Directions and Perspectives,* Lawrence Erlbaum Associates: Mahwah, NJ, 87–116

Martin, G. (1994) *Pre- and Post-Prandial Human Scalp EEG Response to Food odour Using the Brain Electrical Activity Mapping Technique,* Doctoral Dissertation, University of Warwick, UK

Mitchell, D. J., Kahn, B. E. and Knasko, S. C. (1995) There's something in the air: effects of congruent or incongruent ambient odor on consumer decision making, *Journal of Consumer Research,* 22, 2, 229–238

Morrin, M. and Ratneshwar, S. (2000) The impact of ambient scent on evaluation, attention and memory for familiar and unfamiliar brands, *Journal of Business Research,* 49, 2, 157–165

Namasivayam, K. and Lin, I. Y. (2004) Accounting for temporality in servicescape effects on consumers' service evaluations, *Journal of Foodservice Business Research,* 7, 1, 5–22

Nasar, J. L. (2000) The evaluative image of places, In Walsh, W. B., Craik, K. H. and Price, R. H. (Eds.), *Person-Environment Psychology: New Directions and perspectives*, Lawrence Erlbaum Associates: Mahwah, NJ, 117–168

Reimer, A. and Kuehn, R. (2005) The impact of servicescape on quality perception, *European Journal of Marketing*, 39, 7/8, 785–808

Rosenbaum, M. S. (2005) The symbolic servicescape: your kind is welcomed here, *Journal of Consumer Behavior*, 4, 4, 257–267

Russell, J. A. and Snodgrass, J. (1987) Emotion and the environment, In Stokols, D. and Altman, I. (Eds.), *Handbook of Environmental Psychology*, Vol. 1, Wiley: New York, 245–280

Schiffman, L. G. and Kanuk, L. L. (1978) *Consumer Behavior*, Prentice-Hall: Engelwood Cliffs, NJ

Shostack, G. L. (1977) Breaking free from product marketing, *Journal of Marketing*, 41, 2, 73–80

Silver, N. C. and Ferrante, R. (1995) Sex differences in color preferences among an elderly sample, *Perceptual and Motor Skills*, 80, 920–922

Spangenberg, E. R., Crowley, A. E. and Henderson, P. W. (1996) Improving the store environment: do olfactory cues affect evaluations and behaviors? *Journal of Marketing*, 60, 2, 67–80

Staats, H. (2003) Understanding proenvironmental attitudes and behavior: an analysis and review of research based on the theory of planned behavior, In Bonnes, M., Lee, T. and Bonaiuto, M. (Eds.), *Psychological Theories for Environmental Issues*, Ashgate Publishing: Burlington, VT, 171–202

Stamps III, A. E. (2002) *Meta-Analysis*, In Bechtel, R. B. and Churchman, A. (Eds.), *Handbook of Environmental Psychology*, Wiley: New York, 222–232

Steffy, G. (1990) *Architectural Lighting Design*, Van Nostrand Reinhold: New York

Sweeney, J. C. and Wyber, F. (2002) The role of cognitions and emotions in the music–approach–avoidance behavior relationship, *The Journal of Services Marketing*, 16, 1, 51–69

Tajfel, H. (1978) *Differentiation Between Social Groups: Studies in the Social Psychology of Intergroup Relations*, Academic Press: London

Tajfel, H. (1981) *Human Groups and Social Categories*, Cambridge University Press: Cambridge, UK

Timko, C., Moos, R. H. and Finney, J. W. (2000) Models of matching patients and treatment programs, In Walsh, W. B., Craik, K. H. and Price, R. H. (Eds.), *Person-Environment Psychology: New Directions and Perspectives*, Lawrence Erlbaum Associates: Hillsdale, NJ, 169–196

Tombs, A. and McColl-Kennedy, J. R. (2003) Social-services-cape conceptual model, *Marketing Theory*, 3, 4, 447–475

Turley, L. W. and Milliman, R. E. (2000) Atmospheric effects on shopping behavior: a review of the experimental evidence, *Journal of Business Research*, 49, 193–211

Twigger-Ross, C., Bonaiuto, M. and Breakwell, G. (2003) Identity theories and environmental psychology, In Bonnes, M., Lee, T. and Bonaiuto, M. (Eds.), *Psychological Theories for Environmental Issues*, Ashgate Publishing: Burlington, VT, 27–62

Venolia, C. (1988) *Healing Environments*, Celestial Arts: Berkeley, CA

Walsh, W. B., Craik, K. H. and Price, R. H. (2000) Person-environment psychology: a summary and commentary, In Walsh, W. B., Craik, K. H. and Price, R. H. (Eds.), *Person-Environment Psychology: New Directions and Perspectives*, Lawrence Erlbaum Associates: Hillsdale, NJ, 297–326

Wapner, S., Demick, J., Yamamoto, T. and Minami, H. (2000) Epilogue: similarities and differences across theories of environment–behavior relations, In Wapner, S., Demick, J., Yamamoto T. and Minami, H. (Eds.), *Theoretical Perspectives in Environment-Behavior Research*, Kluwer Academic/Plenum Publishers: New York, pp. 11, 289–306

Ward, G. (1995) Colors and employee stress reduction, *Supervision*, 56, 2, 3–5

Weiss, H. M. and Cropanzano, R. (1996) Affective events theory: a theoretical discussion of the structure, causes and consequences of affective experiences at work, *Research in Organizational Behavior*, 18, 1–74

Yalch, R. F. and Spangenberg, E. (1993) Using store music for retail zoning: a field experiment, In McAlister, L. and Rothschild, M. L. (Eds.), *Advances in Consumer Research*, Vol. 20, Association for Consumer Research: Provo, UT, 632–636

Zajonc, R. B. (1965) Social facilitation: a solution is suggested for an old unresolved social psychological problem, *Science*, 149, 269–274

Zeithaml, V., Parasuraman, A. and Berry, L. L. (1985) Problems and strategies in services marketing, *Journal of Marketing*, 49, 2, 33–46

CHAPTER 4

Hospitality customers: their roles in service blueprints

Bonnie Farber Canziani

Director, Hospitality and Tourism Management
Department of Recreation, Tourism, and
Hospitality Management
University of North Carolina Greensboro

Introduction

A number of business disciplines have built theory that describes the relationship of an organization with its customers. From a marketing perspective, the customer is a source of earnings, market intelligence or word-of-mouth promotion; hospitality managers can benefit by understanding the manipulable dimensions of consumer behaviour that suggest directions for firm strategy. From the viewpoint of organizational theorists, the customer is an environmental partner who impacts structure, division of labour, human resources and other policies. Traditional operations management views the customer as the source of demand triggering desired levels of production, as a trading partner in the supply chain impacting the throughput rate, and as a source of operational uncertainty.

More recently, research has examined how customer participation in an operation impacts firm productivity and profitability and how uncertainty may be reduced by appropriate task assignment and supervision of customer roles in business organizations. The insertion of the customer into the hospitality service delivery system is of particular interest and to this end we explore the progress which has been made toward understanding how exactly the customer and the hospitality firm commingle to achieve their goals. Drawing upon an integrated literature base, a framework for managing customer participation in the hospitality firm is presented. This may assist future research on the significant roles performed by customers and provides insight into related tactical issues that require managerial attention in hospitality operations. The chapter begins by examining how customers engage in relations with hospitality firms – to set the stage for understanding how what customers do (their participation in the organizational system) impacts the hospitality operation and ultimately the customer's own perception of service.

The customer–hospitality firm relationship

Customers have relationships with hospitality firms at multiple levels of analysis, such as

(a) with the general industry or field of interest, e.g. *a customer seeking hotel rooms who includes Marriott in the potential choice list*;
(b) with a firm, e.g. *a member of Marriott's hotel reward program*;
(c) with a firm's sub-units, e.g. *a Marriott at Greensboro Airport hotel guest*; or

(d) with employees or agents of the firm, e.g. *Marriott customer in the process of interacting with a Marriott employee.*

In this chapter, the focus is on customers' relations with the organizational and operational systems in a hospitality firm rather than on their relationships with the more generalized hospitality industry or with any firm's individual employees.[1] There are several driving forces in the hospitality industry that create an environment where customers and hospitality firms are likely to increase their interaction with each other; these include the organizational technology inherent in hospitality business, the push for continuous quality initiatives and investment in customer relationship management (CRM) technology.

Table 4.1 summarizes the many ways used to describe various types of customer–firm relations in business research. Customer relations with hospitality firms generally are construed as requiring some type of contact or transaction to occur between an organization and its customers. However, the term *contact* has multiple meanings. *Contact* can relate to employee sales calls directed to clients (Kestnbaum et al. 1998), to dyadic service encounters between *contact* employees and their customers (Solomon et al. 1985) or to Chase and Tansik's (1983) notion that firms can be contrasted as high contact or low contact on the delivery mode and frequency of interaction required by their core technologies. This latter concept of contact is significant to understanding customer relations because it suggests that the primary organizational technology found in an industry can impact how customers are expected to (or expect themselves to) interact with firms in that industry.

Long-linked technology historically drives firms to buffer the technical core from the environment by decoupling low-contact and high-contact organizational units and developing certain employees as *contact* specialists who serve as boundary coordinators. *Mediating technologies* are those where service firms e.g. real estate agents connect external clients or agents to each other. *Intensive service* technologies (most common in the hospitality field) require face-to-face communication or frequent feedback from clients and result in operational personnel increasing their boundary spanner roles (Aldrich and Herker 1977). In the hospitality sector, customers are often inseparable from the core technology of the firm. In hospitality services, organizational work is affected by the presence of customers, since many hospitality firms deal with unique client

---

[1] See also Chapter 6.

Table 4.1 Common descriptors of the customer–firm relationship

Term	Definition
Attachment	Customer dedication, commitment, productivity, and affective response to a company (Ulrich et al. 1991; Ball and Tasaki 1992)
Contact	Ranges from high (face-to-face communication or required presence of the customer during the service production) to low (customer kept away from core personnel and operations) (Chase and Tansik 1983)
Encounter	Dyadic interaction between a service employee and a customer (Solomon et al. 1985) or single customer–server interaction where neither expects future interaction (Gutek et al. 1999)
Interaction	A communication process leading to exchange (Booms and Nyquist 1981)
Loyalty	Retention or brand loyalty measured as spending or usage behaviour (Guest 1964). Affective loyalty equivalent to attachment as defined above (Fournier 1998)
Participation	Absorbing the customer into the service firm to reduce input uncertainty and maximize efficiency (Bowen and Jones 1986; Eiglier and Langeard 1977). Self-service is an extreme form of participation (Bateson 1985; Dabholkar 1996; Walker and Craig-Lees 1999)
Transaction	Game or exchange between persons to minimize costs and maximize gains (Bowen and Jones 1986; Dsouza and Jaykumar 1995)

requirements as well as mandatory client presence at the time of service production. It is in the hospitality firm that there is most evidence of line personnel and clients physically in contact with each other, coordinating tasks and exchanging information in the processing of client needs (Mills et al. 1983).

Moving from customer contact to customer participation

Understanding the idea of customer contact is not enough to fully grasp the impact of customers on a hospitality organization. We need to investigate more deeply the role of customers in the hospitality service blueprint. Customers represent human capital (Lepak and Snell 1999) for a hospitality firm. Customer intelligence must be tapped to achieve relevant organizational learning (Huber 1991; Crossan et al. 1999) and customer skill may be viewed as core rather than peripheral assets (Barney 1991). Successful strategies procuring customer feedback have traditionally been used to leverage customer preference and purchase behaviour in sales and design of hospitality products. In addition, quality management initiatives in the hospitality industry[2] have increasingly sought to increase contact of technical core employees with both suppliers and customers in order to increase organizational responsiveness to customer needs.

Two major trends in strategic business management and marketing reinforce our belief that customers are already viewed as a resource for the service firm: first, the proliferation of CRM technologies and second, the emergence of a field known as knowledge management. Investment in CRM technology largely assists firms to personalize product offerings and services to customers in response to data collected on customer preferences and habits (Sullivan 2001). In the hotel sector, for many years guest loyalty cards have been a way to achieve this. But even in high-volume, short-transaction operations, such as coffee shops, this is now possible. In the UK, Costa Coffee encourages customers to use pre-paid swipe cards to speed up their transaction time. These cards then record customer preferences and behaviour enabling the company to target promotions at customers by email – since the cards can only be purchased via the internet in the first place.

Due to current technological capacity for retaining vast data stores of customer information, firms are now promoting customer retention for the long term, looking to personalize and extend the relationship with the customer as much as possible, when the customer is assessed to be a profitable transaction partner (Grossman 1998). Since the costs of managing the relationship vary according to customer profiles and competencies, knowing the level of profitability from customers must be part of the decision to retain customers (Gronroos 1994; Kaplan and Narayanan 2001). Expanding this notion of 'profitable', the hospitality firm has a vested interest not only in promoting customer actions that increase revenues, but also in promoting customer actions that result in greater efficiency and reduced transaction costs.

However, one of the more challenging problems is that many CRM systems are not balanced in capturing information about the full spectrum of activities customers carry out in their transactions with the firm. They are generally focused on activities

---

[2] See Chapter 13.

within the marketing department rather than offering insights into customer actions on the operations side of hospitality businesses.

It is in the service firm that we see the most evidence of service blueprints merging line personnel and clients in impromptu teams that coordinate tasks and exchange information in the improvisation of solutions to client needs. In their seminal work of the costs of handling customers, Lefton and Rosengren (1966) present two dimensions of the relations between organizations and clients: longitudinal (duration) and lateral (depth) aspects of the firm's relationship with the client. Costs of managing the relationship were seen to vary according to the firm's need for extended transactions or post-transaction follow-up and/or deeper knowledge of a client's 'biography'. Every service firm incurs a variety of transaction costs that relate to the efficiency of the interaction between customers and service employees. Reducing these transaction costs can be as important to the profit picture as increasing sales of existing products and services or expanding into new service arenas before the competition. The idea of a relationship between firm and customer that minimizes the costs for each party is central to Gronroos' *customer lifecycle model* (1994). Knowing the level of profitability from customers is part of the decision to retain customers (Kaplan and Narayanan 2001).

More recently, researchers (Hsieh et al. 2004; Xue and Harker 2002) have examined how customer participation in organizational work impacts firm productivity and profitability and how uncertainty and operational costs may be reduced by appropriate task assignment and supervision of customer roles in the organization. The abilities of employees and customers to work as a team to negotiate win-win outcomes and perform expected tasks (Mills et al. 1983) have taken precedence as factors in the success of the service delivery system.

In recent decades, service company strategies in human resources, e.g. corporate downsizing and outsourcing of personnel, and augmentation of self-service options, e.g. Internet websites, have contributed to the pressing need to view customers as a complement and, at times, an alternative to employee labour (Eiglier and Langeard 1977; Fitzsimmons 1985; Kelley et al. 1990; Lovelock and Young 1979). A prime example of this is the self-service system. Managers as well are increasingly called upon to decide which resources and tools should be transferred to the customers for self-service (Bateson 1985), raising the need for firms to examine the potential wear and tear on these resources accessed by customers, and the need for customer training.[3] It can be argued that the consideration of customers as alternatives to traditional employee-based human capital (Lepak and Snell 1999) is a rational extension of the organizational and human resources trends over the past half-century treating organizational labour as increasingly impermanent and external, as exemplified by proliferating outsourced labour contracts. Ford and Heaton (2001) discuss guests as 'quasi-employees' and ways in which their performance might be managed. With this in mind, we turn now to the various roles via which customer participation in operations may manifest itself.

Defining customer roles and customer participation

Based on a review of pertinent literatures, Table 4.2 identifies a set of core customer roles that define customer participation in the work of a hospitality firm: termed generally as The Investor, The Engineer, The Broker, and The Auditor. A description of how each role manifests itself in the various literatures follows. The enactment and mastery of these roles by customers are postulated to produce customer capital in the same way that employee labour translates into human capital for the firm.

Manifestations of the investor

The *buyer* is the heart of the study of consumer behaviour. A buyer examines, purchases and uses products and services – buyers invest time and money in the acquisition of a firm's

Table 4.2 Classification of customer roles in firm–customer relationships

Primary role name	Consumer behaviour and marketing manifestation	Organizational and management theory manifestation	Operations management manifestation
Investor	Buyer	Exchange partner	End user
Engineer	Co-designer	Influencer	Co-producer
Broker	Promoter	Coordinator	Co-consumer
Auditor	Evaluator	Validator	Inspector

---

[3] See also Chapter 5.

offerings. In the management literature, we find the manifestation of the customer as the *exchange partner* who invests resources and personal trust in relationships with the firm. Customers and firms may be motivated to form higher-order coalitions with each other that can provide them with the requisite resources for sustainability (Oliver 1990; Pfeffer and Salancik 1978). For example, as investment partners, customers invest capital in companies through the purchase of their stock or equivalent financial vehicles. Lastly, operations management offers us the *end user* who contributes time, attention, energy and skill in the deployment of company products and services for his/her personal problem solving. This role is significant across all types of products and services, and very important to the post-purchase or post-delivery stages of product and service support, e.g. as indicated by customer willingness to use buyer guides, information manuals or Internet support links.

Manifestations of the engineer

The *co-designer* is another widely accepted role for customers (Kaulio 1998) who are often asked by market researchers to estimate their personal utility for new product/service attributes. Customers may express desire for services that are not yet offered, or are presently offered by a competitor, or may practice design engineering when they let firms know when transfer of products into a new cultural setting may not work. For instance, when Holiday Inn first opened in the UK, its brand standard was to offer hot beverages to guests by room service delivery. But British guests, predominantly tea rather than coffee drinkers, were used to having beverage making facilities in their hotel room, so that they could brew their own tea. Holiday Inn had to re-think its approach in this new setting. This issue of whether 'end user' customers are equal or better than 'expert designers' is potentially worth investigating further in the service context. Organizational theory suggests the additional manifestation of the *influencer*; this customer is involved in social engineering and impacts organizational design at various levels, e.g. lobbying for codes and regulations and exhibiting pressure through various interest groups. Organizational structures can be indirectly engineered by customers, seen in the many boundary spanner sub-units (Aldrich and Herker 1977), such as sales and marketing, customer relations and legal counsel, which have been institutionalized over time in many business firms to handle customer concerns speedily and accurately (Albrecht and Zemke 1985; Peters and Waterman 1982). Finally, the customer as construction engineer is apparent in the *Co-producer*, seen when, during the service process, customers explain to employees the special needs aspects of their requests and fulfil their own tasks to customize service offerings, since many times the service outcomes hinge on the customers' doing their own parts well.

Manifestations of the broker

In marketing, the *Promoter* is a word-of-mouth communicator, who, according to Arndt (1967), is a key tool in the growth of a customer base. Customers' experience and familiarity with a product permit them to share this prior knowledge with other potential consumers (Alba and Hutchinson 1987). Company websites are posting testimonials and quotes from their customers, and customers are offering encouragement on their own homepages. In creative broker fashion, consumers even purchase goods and services on behalf of others, seeking to bring them into the fold of avid users of a product or service. Next, organizational theory notes that customers can act as the *Coordinator* in two significant ways. First, they may require as part of their contractual stipulations that the service firm form an alliance with selected external organizations. For example, a buyer may require that a real estate agent cooperate with the buyer's preferred attorney or lender. Secondly, customers may also serve as message brokers to facilitate the transfer of information (or materials) from one service unit or worker to another in the service firm. Hotel guests checking out may identify to the front desk personnel any late charges that may be pending from room service, breakfast or phone services. Lastly, customers co-exist with other customers, enacting the role of the *Co-consumer*. This has proven to be a boon in situations where multiple customer goals and perceived outcomes are well matched, e.g. a comedy club where one customer's response can bring forth positive vibes in others. However, there are many occasions where customer behaviour has an unwanted impact on other customers. Mixing smokers and non-smokers or families with children and no-kids couples are traditional trouble spots for restaurant visits. How customers are socialized to conduct themselves around other customers is a complex issue for which study is overdue (Jones 1995). Social presence of others can even constrain or embarrass a buyer, e.g. when engaged in a purchase or situation that is viewed as having negative social overtones (Dahl et al. 2001).

Manifestations of the auditor

Many customers play a critical role in the valuation of firms by providing feedback and ratings of quality that drive share value. As part of the client–firm feedback loop, customers acting as the *Evaluator* have been continuously involved in the rating and evaluation of services and products they have experienced. When Marriott developed the Fairfield Inn concept they incorporated into the checkout process an online system for recording guest feedback on their stay. The *Validator* endorses a firm's strategic business investments by agreeing to use new service methods or technologies and upholds practices related to the firm's broader social agenda by joining in a firm's environmental or safety programs, e.g. conserving water or energy during hotel stays. As the *Inspector*, customers play a role in assuring the integrity and consistency of their own service experience by performing formative spot checks at will. An example of formal inclusion of this role in the service blueprint is when a restaurant guest may be asked to sample the wine during service but prior to its being shared with other guests.

Managing customer roles in the service blueprint

The first step for a hospitality firm is to identify which of the customer roles enumerated in this chapter have utility for the firm's organizational mission and service blueprint. The firm needs to decide whether or not increasing customer task fulfilment or competency in these roles is a potential factor in decreasing operational costs or increasing customer satisfaction and perceived market value of the service or of the firm. It is understood that customers cannot be socialized or trained in the same manner as traditional employees, but identifying opportunities to ask customers to engage in necessary task activities is a logical progression from the creation of this role inventory. Division of labour is a decision normally made by firm managers. However, as illustrated above, the nature of service processes often dictates the involvement of customers in the rendering of the service – such involvement may occur without adequate organizational forethought. We hope to change this through conscious application of knowledge about customer roles. In order to leverage the inherent potential in the deployment of customer activity in service processes, firms must identify which of the described customer roles are significant to their service delivery systems, and, when feasible, determine the optimal assignment of work to the customer.

Coordinating work among firm representatives and customers then becomes a strategic managerial activity.

Seminal work (Thompson 1967) portrays three forms of coordinated organizational workflow: pooled, serial or reciprocal. *Pooled interdependence* reflects organizational actors in independent task roles with no or very minimal need for transfer of information or resources, e.g. a customer interacting with a vending machine has little say or relationship with the stocker or vending company. *Serial interdependence* exists among units or actors when the outputs of one unit are required as inputs for another, e.g. plating food on a banquet line across multiple stations. *Reciprocal interdependence* indicates a movement of resources or information back and forth among units in the creation of products or services, e.g. caterer planning a banquet needing to constantly exchange information with the client about menus, guest lists and set-ups. A complementary approach to defining work interdependence adds a fourth level: *team interdependence,* and suggests that the types of task interdependence in the team arrangement are at least fourfold: interdependence based solely on the aggregation of results of members of a group working individually on similar tasks; interdependence based on sharing of tasks; full interdependence with constant collaboration and mutual support; and interchangeability (Drexler and Forrester 1998). Levels of interdependence are impacted by measurable elements such as the number of resources exchanged, the frequency of interaction, permitted slack in the system and the direction of the resource flow, as well as the costs of coordination strategies (Lawrence and Lorsch 1967; Thompson 1967; McCann and Ferry 1979; Victor and Blackburn 1987).

Van de Ven et al. (1976: 332) found that as levels of workflow interdependence increased within organizational work units, there resulted 'a slight *decrease* in the use of hierarchy and a large *decrease* in the use of bureaucratic plans for coordinating activities'. Interpersonal mutual adjustment in goals and activities at the micro-level was in greater evidence. This is significant in that hospitality companies almost already represent higher levels of workflow interdependence among servers as well as expecting clients and servers to work together. This means that scripted approaches to service delivery will be continuously in conflict with the human tendencies to negotiate mutually satisfying procedures among members of the interdependent work team, and particularly among clients and servers. The abilities of employees and customers to work *as a team* to negotiate win-win outcomes and perform expected tasks (Mills et al. 1983) thus take precedence as

73

factors in the success of the hospitality delivery system. Basic to the understanding of teamwork is the dimension of *trust* (Ganesan and Hess 1997; Mayer et al. 1995; Morgan and Hunt 1994; Schurr and Ozanne 1985) which facilitates the recognition of shared purpose and interdependent team member roles in generating successful service outcomes.

Add to this mix the question of status: how customers are perceived and how they perceive themselves. Are they subordinate, superior or partner to the firm? In many businesses, customer service traditions require deference to the client. Leveraging customer competency in these operations requires the blending of deferential etiquette with influence tactics to socialize clients to increasingly complex roles asked of them in the service production system. Additionally, the degree of social distance (Hage et al. 1971) perceived between customers and servers will impact the communication styles adopted by each during service transactions and in certain service scenarios, e.g. in cultures where server–client relationships are strongly hierarchical, will increase the firm's capacity to monitor and possibly direct customer role performance. Doctor–patient relationships will take on a demeanour significantly distinct from that of a hotel guest requesting information from the concierge.

As an addendum to the discussion on customer–server interdependencies in the hospitality service blueprint, it should be emphasized that managers should decide which resources and tools should be transferred to the customers for self-service (Bateson 1985). Managers need thus to predict the potential wear and tear on self-service equipment, materials, and the need for customer training so that customers can serve themselves adequately. If parallel options are available, e.g. offering both self-service and employee-assisted checkout lanes in supermarkets, then the costs of using these different options simultaneously must be evaluated. Most likely servers will need to be trained to 'train' the customers in the work tasks the customers are being asked to perform, e.g. the myriad airline clerks running out to the kiosks to assist untrained customers trying to check in. Added problems arise if the hospitality firm has obtained the technology to be used by the clients from an outside vendor who has minimal interest or ability to provide adequate support during the client orientation phase of technology adoption.

Although customers may be targeted for training (Noel et al. 1990), they are not normally subject to the performance appraisals of service firm supervisors (Larsson and Bowen 1989; Kelley et al. 1992). Sanctions will be more difficult to apply since few data are presently collected by firms on customers' activities in the various roles described above. Thus, managers must decide which critical customer tasks must be monitored or evaluated and which left unobserved – will one sample customer activity in a manner similar to the appraisal of employee performance? In essence, the appropriate level of supervision over customer work must be determined from a cost/return perspective. However, there is a large body of anecdotal evidence that owner-operators of small hospitality businesses routinely refuse to serve 'underperforming' customers – notably customers in the co-consumer role who detract significantly from the ambience of the bar or restaurant.

Furthermore, difficulties in monitoring customer performance as a discrete measure from employee performance may arise that are comparable to the problems of assessing team member performance in group work. Team measurement difficulties are compounded by the use of customers as evaluators of service quality through customer feedback systems. It is likely that, as obligatory customer participation increases in the service blueprint, customers will attribute negative outcomes to the employee, while attributing positive outcomes either equally to server and customer or solely to their own efforts (Weiner 2000). In any case, once customer roles have been identified as useful for the service firm, the question of developing customer competency must be visited. The effective design of the servicescape can help in this regard.[4]

Leveraging customer competencies in their defined roles

If and when customers are to be included in the skill set of an organization, critical steps must be taken to assess and enhance customer competencies in relation to the tasks they are expected to perform (Canziani 1997). It is intriguing to note that the various business disciplines have recognized roles that bear resemblance to each other in terms of the skills required for the embedded tasks. What often varies across each row of Table 4.2, however, is the structural level or unit with which customers interact as they fulfil the role. If we examine the first general role of *The Investor*, in the deployment of each of its manifestations (*buyer/exchange partner/end user*) we find a need for customer attention skills in the identification, comparison and deployment of technical features of products and services in

---

[4] See Chapter 3.

order for customers to comprehend the inherent utility of their coalition with the service firm or with its products and services. Speed and ease of learning about new products or systems, ability to visualize and obtain benefits from products or services, and desire to repeat process or product usage again are all factors. The development of text-based materials and content-heavy support information may be a critical success factor in preparing customers to be effective in these roles. Media delivery modes for multiple learning styles may comprise face-to-face encounters, telephone, websites or written documents.

The next row related to *The Engineer* (*co-designer/influencer/co-producer*) calls for customer competency in negotiating win-win outcomes and willingness to accept trade-offs. Skills such as communicating detailed instructions, personal information and self-interest in a socially appropriate manner are also critical. Group, such as forums and focus groups, and personal interaction will be emphasized as modes for conducting these types of customer activity. Following this thread of competency needs analysis, we note that the competencies useful to the three activities of *promoter/coordinator/co-consumer* related to the role of *The Broker* are those of educating and coordinating others as well as translating interests as middleman or matchmaker in social networks. Lastly, the various manifestations of *The Auditor* role (*evaluator/validator/inspector*) essentially require similar cognitive observation, retention and judgment skills but expect customers to offer feedback at different stages of the relationship: during use, post-use and even previous or subsequent to the relationship life span.

At this point, we turn to specific customer–service firm relationship variables that may influence the customer's levels of participation in the roles that have been identified in the previous section.

Variables impacting the customer's participation behaviour

As a construct, motivation to participate is relatively unwieldy; it can in turn refer to a customer's internal or psychological frame of mind or to an external reward or sanction system. We do not in this section attempt more than a look at three understudied factors that relate to aspects of the service firm-client relationship and may influence the level of or the success of customer participation. These comprise the expected duration of a transaction, types of interaction patterns, and the degree of perceived customer obligation. Understandably, these factors are viewed primarily as moderating control variables, rather than specific tactics of a motivational strategy that the service firm might apply to encourage customer participation.

Expected duration of a hospitality transaction

That a relationship covers an extended period of time is implicit in the literature (Bendapudi and Berry 1997; Czepiel 1990; Gronroos 1994; Grossman 1998; Gutek et al. 1999). Referring back to Table 4.1, it is apparent that the descriptors in the table vary on a temporal dimension in that *attachment* and *loyalty* are measures related to a longer time horizon than would be applicable with *interaction* or *encounter* profiles. In contrast to the fuzzier time span of a relationship, the endpoint of a hospitality transaction is normally predictable and largely dictated by the nature of the industry itself. Transactions may be conceived of as a set of interactions between client and firm, where the ultimate goal is the purchase and consumption of a hospitality product or service. There is not a binding customer–firm relationship inherent in the transaction itself; although if the service or product experienced by the customer is satisfactory, the customer might choose to transact with the firm again at a future time, ultimately committing to a long-term relationship. Indeed, the marketing literature has strived to build a theoretical connection between service transaction quality, customer satisfaction and the retention or economic value of customers over time (Bejou et al. 1996; Bhagat and Williams 2002; Goodman et al. 1995). Nonetheless, transactions between customers and hospitality companies are an interesting source of data and should be inspected for their inherent influences on the nature of customer participation.

Weick (1976: 5) states 'given the context of most organizations, elements both appear and disappear over time ... The question of what is available for coupling and decoupling ... is an eminently practical question for anyone wishing to have some leverage on a system'. Brass (1981: 332) posits that work teams take the form of 'an arrangement of differentiated task positions into an integrated workflow ... that may cross formal group boundaries or even organizational boundaries'. In the context of Weick's definition, we can define transactions as situationally constrained tight couplings of persons, technologies, resources and tasks that need not artificially separate or permanently bond organizational employees from/to organizational clients. These couplings or interactions between clients and service employees may take many different shapes; they may be finite, repeated or continuous; serial or phasal;

episodic or periodic; long or short in duration; they may occur among the same individuals or groups or among changing partners. One characteristic of transactions in particular can impact the degree to which customer participation takes place in a hospitality service blueprints: transaction duration.

The premise that different categories of products and services have distinct expected or natural durations for the average length of transaction is reflected in Hume's (2000) three types of transactions: episodic, extended and continuous, furthering earlier definitions of discrete versus continuous transactions (Lovelock 1983). It is appropriate to distinguish among three service delivery durations, since some purchases have clear beginnings and endings, and others are longer if not indefinite in nature. Table 4.3 offers examples of service industries that might fall into each of three ordinal categories which we have rephrased from Hume's work as finite, renewable and continuous.

Continuous services are essentially delivery systems that extend over time without noticeable cessation of service, e.g. signing up for a bank account or club membership that promises rendering of service over an extended period of time and is billed to the customer on a periodic basis. Industries selling continuous services often have an easier time retaining customers due to the psychological and time costs customers encounter when trying to switch banks, doctors and so on. Hospitality firms, such as hotels and restaurants, whose services are generally conducted as finite encounters have to work harder to retain customers, since there is a clearly identifiable ending to each transaction at which point the clients may reconsider their affiliation with that particular hospitality firm and seek alternative sources of service. Given that the natural duration of hospitality transactions is shorter than in some industries, hospitality companies have a harder time developing the competencies of their customers who participate

Table 4.3   Transaction durations exemplified

Duration of transactions	Service examples
Finite	Making a purchase at a fast food outlet
Renewable	Enrolling in a college
Continuous	Signing up for utilities

in their service blueprints because they may not stick around long enough to learn the ins and outs of any locale's particular operational blueprint. Moving customers from finite to renewable transaction status is a goal when increasing the presence of knowledgeable or 'trained' customers will help the firm reduce costs of service and the need to continuously orient new customers.

Interestingly, anomalies in actual transaction durations can be positive or negative for either the customer or the firm. For example, sport club customers that renew contracts year after year may be positive influences on the organization, incurring lower costs and exhibiting higher satisfaction with services due to increased familiarity with club operations and facilities. Conversely, students who take longer to graduate from a high school or college due to system or personal constraints may exhibit dissatisfaction or disruptive behaviours. Retention strategies are most appropriately applied when the actual transaction duration is shorter than the expected duration, and extending it would bring increased marginal utility to both transaction partners. Another consideration with respect to profiling transactions is that of significant interaction patterns that may be observed in any industry or firm.

Types of client–firm interaction patterns

Transactions can be further categorized in terms of the density, predictability and clustering of the couplings or interactions between the client and the service firm. The interaction patterns compared across transactions (comparing across firms or across industries) may vary due either to variation in service firm blueprints or policies or to the fact that situational and interpersonal elements drive the pattern and behaviours of interactions as well.

Much like measuring cell density in a tissue sample, transaction density or the total number of client–server couplings during a selected observation period can be measured. Both the hospitality firm and the client can affect the number of couplings, the former through service design (Shostack 1987) and the latter by service usage. Low-density service designs are those where the number of couplings between the service firm and the client are expected to be few. For instance, a carwash transaction involves an average of six discrete encounters with people or equipment: queuing up, requesting service level, paying for the service, interacting with vending machines in the waiting room, tipping the attendant and exiting safely from the parking lot. High-density transactions can comprise a vast number of possible client–firm interactions, for instance, transacting a hotel stay with reservations, valets, front desk, housekeeping, guest shop, health spa and room service or enrolling in college which requires orientation, course selection, class attendance, library visits and so on. Since density reflects the number of 'moments of truth' (Carlzon 1987) embedded in the service blueprint, hospitality companies should be aware of the potential for service failure points in transactions involving extended service blueprints. It will also require more effort on the part of customers to sail through the many interactions embedded in a high-density hotel visit than it would during a lower-density fast-food transaction.

Often the client–firm interactions in a transaction correlate with serial occurrence or phasal interdependence (Johnston 1995) among service tasks in a service blueprint, for example calling for a reservation occurs prior to the actual restaurant visit or hotel stay. Many times, defects in the transfer of persons, their possessions or their data across service firm employees or units compromise later encounters and reduce overall perceptions of service quality. Requiring the customer to be the one transferring the data – such as relying on them to give a drink ticket to a banquet server, to keep their parking or coat check stub with them or to give a confirmation code to the front desk – is always rife with potential for service failure. So hospitality companies that build customer participation into these serial tasks should be aware of the potential consequences.

Knowing when the client–service firm encounter will take place is another issue. A predictable service firm–client encounter is one where both the service firm and the client have a mutual expectation for its eventuality – whether the precise time and place are known or not. For instance, a dentist will expect to see patients every 6 months for a routine examination. Predictability is enhanced when the firm has power to apply sanctions in the case of no-shows or cancellations, as when there are credit card charges for hotel no-shows. Periodicity of encounters may also reflect the cyclical demand for services, such as annual visits to the tax accountants, summer rentals of the same beach house year after year or hair sessions at the beauty salon every 3 weeks. Different customers will have different levels of episodic usage of a facility or service firm as well – for example restaurant guests stopping on the highway for a quick bite en route to their destination. Random events can generate the need for unanticipated service firm–client interaction, as in terrorist acts prompting increases in the purchase of travel insurance or a dead battery sparking a call to AAA. Such interactions are often associated with increased customer stress levels. Planning for customer participation is obviously harder in the face of uncertainty regarding when and if customers will make contact with the firm. Developing self-service options may be one way to sustain perceptions of responsiveness when customer visits are hard to predict (Walker and Craig-Lees 1999).

Clusters of interactions may be built into the service process, such as when the service firm requires numerous encounters during new patient or student registration or facility, equipment or software orientation. Subsequent transaction phases may exhibit fewer interactions that are firm-driven – e.g. an occasional mailing to a dental patient or optional nutrition seminar offered to a health spa member. Moreover, clustering of unanticipated interactions can occur around client problems with the product or process in the service delivery system resulting in repeated contacts with service representatives to seek remedy or recovery. The administrative expense of managing interaction clusters is expected to be higher, due to increased costs of customer education and socialization or the need to process information and preserve customer goodwill in complaint handling. Clustered interactions may also augment time, communication and travel costs for clients, diminishing customer perceptions of value.

Transaction duration and interaction patterns infer moments of truth in a quality sense, but also infer vital opportunities for creating relationship bonds between firm and clients through the process of social obligation. Revisiting the concepts in Table 4.1, we see they range from the behavioural (*interaction*) to the affective (*attachment* or *emotional loyalty*). Customers can demonstrate a wide range of affective responses to an individual employee in the firm, to the firm and its values or practices (such as Starbucks versus Enron) or to the industry (such as the entertainment or tobacco industry). Pleasant or successful interactions with employees have been seen to increase customer liking of or loyalty to the firm (Schneider et al. 1980), particularly in the case where attitudes of positive employee attachment to the firm are exhibited to the customer (Ulrich et al. 1991).

Degree of perceived obligation

Customers may transact with a service firm on the basis of transience (no commitment), implicit or social obligation or explicit contractual obligation (see Table 4.4). The feeling of social obligation or bonding is enhanced during interactions between the employees of the firm and customers (Wilson 1995). Customers perceive linkages with individual boundary spanners to be stronger and more critical than an abstract relationship with a faceless company (Albrecht and Zemke 1985; Zeithaml et al. 1990; Berry 1995). This is particularly true when customers believe these employees possess knowledge and skills that are unique in the firm and well matched to their needs, especially if the client's tie to that employee is viewed as more exclusive than ties experienced by other customers (Burt 1997).

Research on the quality of service (Bitner et al. 1990; Parasuraman et al. 1985; Scheuing and Edvardsson 1994) has underscored the importance of moving beyond the merely tangible or material aspects of customer purchases to incorporate such measures as assurance and empathy experienced in service encounters. Estimating consumer-side utilities for new products or service elements by deciphering customer ratings is a die-hard decision activity in most businesses. Utility functions or measures must include client responses to interpersonal and environmental features as well as the technical elements of a product (Easton and Pullman 2001) to fully grasp the motivations for transaction initiation and closure and customer perceptions of value. As seen in the case of obligation, customer rationalization for staying in relationships with firms can derive from non-economic benefits such as genuine liking of personnel, facilities or even other customers (Bendapudi and Berry 1997).

Firms may also use marketing tactics to promote a pseudo or actual membership (Lovelock 1983) with the firm. Such tactics can include bonus cards or points for increased purchases, perquisites or corporate-labelled giveaways for good customers, or regular mailings or other communications implying that the customer is one of the 'family'. De Wulf et al. (2001)

Table 4.4 Types of obligation exemplified

Obligation	Service examples
None/transient	Having a drink in a bar whilst on holiday
Implicit/social	Using the same restaurant regularly
Explicit/contractual	Joining a health club

have determined that investment in activities that promote the perception of consumer–firm relationships can add to customers' perceptions of value and increase their demonstration of loyalty behaviours. However, as with strategies for extending transaction duration, firms need to be cautious in their deployment of tactics to increase the perception of obligation to the firm. Obligation in the face of boredom or unsatisfactory service encounters can lead to organizational costs in terms of the customer's decreased attachment, negative appraisal and word-of-mouth.

Additionally, Feld (1997) found that contact with multiple persons in a network is associated with persistence of social ties over time. Lovett et al. (1997) suggest that client trust in the organization has a positive correlation with the number of connections to the firm. Determining the benefits versus costs of a client interacting with more than one service agent in an organization is a key managerial activity. This is supported by evidence that 'employee quit rates partially mediate the relationship between [high-involvement] human resources practices and sales growth' (Batt 2002: 587). Methods to offset the customer satisfaction consequences of a key contact employee leaving the firm include staff rotation, employee service teams, informal networking with multiple employees and one-stop shopping (Bendapudi and Leone 2001).

Summary and conclusion

In summary, the literature calling for an examination of customer relationships and participation in service blueprints of hospitality firms has been reviewed. A framework of customer roles has been proposed with the expectation that hospitality firms need to have a broad understanding of the roles customers take on and how customers interact with all parts of the organization. The enactment and mastery of these roles by the customer conceivably impacts the productivity and profitability of the firm. The framework forces managers to think of customer participation as cost in almost every strategic decision, not only those related to marketing or purchase decisions. Other strategic uses of the framework include helping the service firm acknowledge its own role in the development of customer competency and avoid single-minded focus on employee-based human resource strategies. Customer task motivation is likely to vary across the different customer roles due to variations in customer skill levels and preference for different types of work. The types and costs of communication modes employed are also influenced by the work tasks embedded in each customer role. The ability to discriminate among customer roles and associated competencies may stimulate managerial action to develop customers as significant human capital for the service firm.

This was followed by insights on managing customer participation which has both operational and strategic implication for the design and implementation of service blueprints including customer work. The discussion on the transaction duration, interaction patterns and social obligation is particularly fruitful in that it captures the need to discriminate among diverse profiles of customer transactions with the firm and provides insight into additional factors that impact the degree to which customers may participate in the service blueprint.

Future research endeavours may seek to answer the following questions:

- What are the core customer roles and required competencies that define customer participation in specific industries?
- What types of customer–firm task interdependence are found in each of the various roles?
- In *what contexts* and *how* do organizations orient and develop customers to perform each of their determined roles?
- How do competing strategies for customer role assignments, and planned shifts in role responsibilities from the service firm to the customer impact productivity of the firm or satisfaction of the customer?

References

Alba, J. W. and Hutchinson, J. W. (1987) Dimensions of consumer expertise, *Journal of Consumer Research*, 13, 4, 411–454

Albrecht, K. and Zemke, R. (1985) *Service America: Doing Business in the New Economy*, Dow-Jones-Irwin: Homewood, IL

Aldrich, H. and Herker, D. (1977) Boundary spanning roles and organizational structure, *Academy of Management Review*, 2, 2, 217–230

Arndt, J. (1967) Word of mouth advertising and informal communication, In Cox, D. F. (Ed.), *Risk Taking and Information Handling in Consumer Behavior*, Harvard University Press: Cambridge, MA, 188–239

Ball, A. D. and Tasaki, L. H. (1992) The role and measurement of attachment in consumer behavior, *Journal of Consumer Psychology*, 1, 2, 155–172

Barney, J. (1991) Firm resources and sustained competitive advantage, *Journal of Management*, 17, 1, 99–120

Bateson, J. E. G. (1985) Self-service consumer: an exploratory study, *Journal of Retailing*, 61, 3, 49–76

Batt, R. (2002) Managing customer services: human resource practices, quit rates and sales growth, *Academy of Management Journal*, 45, 3, 587–597

Bejou, D., Edvardsson, B. and Rakowski, J. P. (1996) A critical-incident approach to examining the effects of service failures on customer relationships: the case of Swedish and U.S. airlines, *Journal of Travel Research*, 35, 1, 35–40

Bendapudi, N. and Berry, L. L. (1997) Customers' motivations for maintaining relationships with service providers, *Journal of Retailing*, 73, 1, 15–37

Bendapudi, N. and Leone, R. (2001) How to lose your star performer without losing your customers, too, *Harvard Business Review*, 79, 10, 104–112

Berry, L. L. (1995) *On Great Service: A Framework for Action*, Free Press: New York, NY

Bhagat, P. S. and Williams, J. D. (2002) Leveraging relationships in marketing: a motivational perspective, *Journal of Relationship Marketing*, 1, 3/4, 39–67

Bitner, M. J., Booms, B. H. and Tetreault, M. S. (1990) The service encounter: diagnosing favorable and unfavorable incidents, *Journal of Marketing*, 54, 1, 71–84

Booms, B. H. and Nyquist, J. (1981) Analyzing the customer/firm communication component of the services marketing mix. In Donnelly, J. H. and George, W. R. (Eds.), *Marketing of Service*, American Marketing Association: Chicago, IL, 172–177

Bowen, D. E. and Jones, G. R. (1986) Transaction cost analysis of service organization–customer exchange, *Academy of Management Review*, 11, 2, 428–441

Brass, D. J. (1981) Structural relationships, job characteristics, and worker satisfaction and performance, *Administrative Science Quarterly*, 26, 331–348

Burt, R. S. (1997) A note on social capital and network content, *Social Networks*, 19, 4, 355–373

Canziani, B. F. (1997) Leveraging customer competency in service firms, *International Journal of Service Industry Management*, 8, 1, 5–25

Carlzon, J. (1987) *Moments of Truth*, Ballinger Publishing: Cambridge, MA

Chase, R. B. and Tansik, D. A. (1983) The customer contact model for organizational design, *Management Science*, 29, 9, 1037–1050

Crossan, M. M., Lane, H. W. and White, R. E. (1999) An organizational learning framework: from intuition to institution, *Academy of Management Review*, 24, 3, 522–537

Czepiel, J. A. (1990) Service encounters and service relationships: implications for research, *Journal of Business Research*, 20, 1, 13–21

Dabholkar, P. A. (1996) Consumer evaluations of new technology-based self-service options: an investigation of alternative models of service quality, *International Journal of Research in Marketing*, 13, 1, 29–51

Dahl, D. W., Manchanda, R. V. and Argo, J. J. (2001) Embarrassment in consumer purchase: the roles of social presence and purchase familiarity, *Journal of Consumer Research*, 28, 3, 473–481

De Wulf, K., Odekerken-Schröder, G. and Iacobucci, D. (2001) Investments in consumer relationships: a cross-country and cross-industry exploration, *Journal of Marketing*, 65, 4, 33–50

Drexler, A. B. and Forrester, R. (1998) Interdependence: the crux of teamwork, *HR Magazine*, 43, 10, 52–62

Dsouza, D. E. and Jaykumar, M. (1995) A game theoretic approach to modeling service encounters, *International Journal of Management*, 12, 3, 276–288

Easton, F. F. and Pullman, M. E. (2001) Optimizing service attributes: the seller's utility problem. *Decision Sciences*, 32, 2, 251–275

Eiglier, P. and Langeard, E. (1977) A new approach to service marketing. In *Marketing Consumer Services: New Insights Report*, Marketing Science Institute: Cambridge, MA, 77–115

Feld, S. L. (1997) Structural embeddedness and stability of interpersonal relations, *Social Networks*, 19, 1, 91–95

Fitzsimmons, J. A. (1985) Consumer participation and productivity in service operations, *Interfaces*, 15, 3, 60–67

Ford, R. C. and Heaton, C. P. (2001) Managing your guest as a quasi-employee, *Cornell Hotel and Restaurant Administration Quarterly*, 42, 2, 46–55

Fournier, S. (1998) Consumers and their brands: developing relationship theory in consumer research, *Journal of Consumer Research*, 24, 4, 343–371

Ganesan, S. and Hess, R. (1997) Dimensions and levels of trust: implications for commitment to a relationship. *Marketing Letters*, 8, 4, 439–448

Goodman, P. S., Fichman, M., Lerch, F. J. and Snyder, P. R. (1995) Customer–firm relationships, involvement, and customer satisfaction, *Academy of Management Journal*, 38, 5, 1310–1324

Gronroos, C. (1994) From marketing mix to relationship marketing: towards a paradigm shift in marketing, *Management Decision*, 32, 2, 4–20

Grossman, R. P. (1998) Developing and managing effective consumer relationships, *The Journal of Product and Brand Management*, 7, 1, 27–40

Guest, L. P. (1964) Brand loyalty revisited: a twenty-year report, *Journal of Applied Psychology*, 48, 2, 93–97

Gutek, B., Bhappu, A. D., Liao-Troth, M. A. and Cherry, B. (1999) Distinguishing between service relationships and encounters, *Journal of Applied Psychology*, 84, 2, 218–233

Hage, J., Aiken, M. and Marrett, C. B. (1971) Organization structure and communications, *American Sociological Review*, 36, 5, 860–871

Hsieh, A., Yen, C. and Chin, K. (2004) Participative customers as partial employees and service provider workload, *International Journal of Service Industry Management*, 15, 2, 187–199

Huber, G. P. (1991) Organizational learning: the contributing processes and the literature, *Organization Science*, 2, 1, 88–115

Hume, M. (2000) The influence of duration and complexity on the customer satisfaction equation: building a case for the complex episodic service encounter, *Proceedings of the Australian and New Zealand Marketing Academic Conference (ANZMAC) 2000 Visionary Marketing for the 21st Century: Facing the Challenge*

Johnston, R. (1995) The zone of tolerance: exploring the relationship between service transactions and satisfaction with the overall service, *International Journal of Service Industry Management*, 6, 2, 46–61

Jones, P. (1995) Managing customer-customer interactions within the service experience, *Management Research News*, 18, 12, 54–60

Kaplan, R. S. and Narayanan, V. G. (2001) Measuring and managing customer profitability, *Journal of Cost Management* 15, 5, 5–15

Kaulio, M. A. (1998) Customer, consumer and user involvement in product development: a framework and a review of selected methods, *Total Quality Management*, 9, 1, 141–149

Kelley, S. W. Donnelly, J. H. Jr. and Skinner, S. J. (1990) Customer participation in service production and delivery, *Journal of Retailing*, 66, 3, 315–335

Kelley, S. W., Skinner, S. J. and Donnelly, J. H. Jr. (1992) Organizational socialization of service customers, *Journal of Business Research*, 25, 3, 197–214

Kestnbaum, R. D., Kestnbaum, K. T. and Ames, P. W. (1998) Building a longitudinal contact strategy, *Journal of Interactive Marketing*, 12, 1, 56–62

Larsson, R. and Bowen, D. E. (1989) Organization and customer: managing design and coordination of services, *Academy of Management Review*, 14, 2, 213–233

Lawrence, P. and Lorsch, J. (1967) *Organization and Environment*, Harvard University Press: Cambridge, MA

Lefton, M. and Rosengren, W. R. (1966) Organizations and clients: lateral and longitudinal dimensions, *American Sociological Review*, 31, 6, 802–810

Lepak, D. P. and Snell, S. A. (1999) The human resource architecture: toward a theory of human capital allocation and development, *Academy of Management Review*, 24, 1, 31–48

Lovelock, C. H. (1983) Classifying services to gain strategic marketing insights, *Journal of Marketing*, 47, 3, 9–20

Lovelock, C. H. and Young, R. F. (1979) Look to consumers to increase productivity, *Harvard Business Review*, 57, 3, 168–178

Lovett, S., Harrison, D. A. and Virick, M. (1997) Managing boundary spanner–customer turnover connection, *Human Resources Management Review*, 7, 4, 405–424

Mayer, R. C., Davis, J. H. and Schoorman, F. D. (1995) An integration model of organizational trust. *Academy of Management Review*, 20, 3, 709–734

McCann, J. E. and Ferry, D. L. (1979) An approach for assessing and managing inter-unit interdependence, *Academy of Management Review*, 4, 1, 113–119

Mills, P. K., Chase, R. B. and Margulies, N. (1983) Motivating the client/employee system as a service production strategy, *Academy of Management Review*, 8, 2, 301–310

Morgan, R. M. and Hunt, S. D. (1994) The commitment–trust theory of relationship marketing, *Journal of Marketing*, 58, 3, 20–38

Noel, J. L., Ulrich, D. and Mercer, S. R. (1990) Customer education: a new frontier for human resource development, *Human Resource Management*, 29, 4, 411–434

Oliver, C. (1990) Determinants of interorganizational relationships: integration and future directions, *Academy of Management Review*, 15, 2, 241–265

Parasuraman, A., Zeithaml, V. A. and Berry, L. L. (1985) A conceptual model of service quality and its implications for future research, *Journal of Marketing*, 49, 4, 41–50

Peters, T. J. and Waterman, R. H. (1982) *In Search of Excellence: Lessons from America's Best Run Companies*, Harper and Row: New York, NY

Pfeffer, J. and Salancik, G. (1978) *The External Control of Organizations: A Resource Dependence Perspective*, Harper and Row: New York, NY

Scheuing, E. E. and Edvardsson, B. (1994) Service integrity, *Managing Service Quality*, 4, 4, 24–31

Schneider, B., Parkington, J. J., and Buxton, V. M. (1980) Employee and customer perceptions of service in banks, *Administrative Science Quarterly*, 25, 2, 252–267

Schurr, P. H. and Ozanne, J. L. (1985) Influence on exchange processes: buyers' preconceptions of a seller's trustworthiness and bargaining toughness, *Journal of Consumer Research*, 11, 4, 939–953

Shostack, G. L. (1987) Service positioning through structural change, *Journal of Marketing*, 51, 1, 34–43

Solomon, M. R., Surprenant, C., Czepiel, J. A. and Gutman, E. G. (1985) A role theory perspective on dyadic interactions: the service encounter, *Journal of Marketing*, 49, 1, 99–111

Sullivan, J. L. (2001) The challenges and rewards of personalizing customer interactions, *Customer Interaction Solutions*, 19, 10, 50–51

Thompson, J. (1967) *Organizations in Action,* McGraw-Hill: Chicago, IL

Ulrich, D., Halbrook, R., Meder, D., Stuchlik, M. and Thorpe, S. (1991) Employee and customer attachment: synergies for competitive advantage, *Human Resource Planning*, 14, 2, 89–103

Van de Ven, A. H., Delbecq, A. L. and Koenig, R. (1976) Determinants of coordination modes within organizations, *American Sociological Review*, 41, 2, 322–338

Victor, B. and Blackburn, R. S. (1987) Interdependence: an alternative conceptualization, *Academy of Management Review*, 12, 3, 486–498

Walker, R. H. and Craig-Lees, M. (1999) Integrating technology and customer service: reconciling managerial and customer needs to mutual satisfaction, *Proceedings of the International Services Marketing Conference*, Brisbane, pp. 31–33

Weick, K. E. (1976) Educational organizations as loosely coupled systems, *Administrative Science Quarterly*, 21, 1, 1–19

Weiner, B. (2000) Attributional thoughts about consumer behavior, *Journal of Consumer Research*, 27, 3, 382–387

Wilson, D. T. (1995) An integrated model of buyer–seller relationships, *Journal of the Academy of Marketing Science*, 23, 4, 335–345

Xue, M. and Harker, P. T. (2002) Customer efficiency: concept and its impact on e-business management, *Journal of Service Research*, 4, 4, 253–267

Zeithaml, V. A., Parasuraman, A. and Berry, L. L. (1990) *Delivering Quality Service – Balancing Customer Perceptions and Expectations*, Free Press: New York, NY

CHAPTER 5

Waiting lines and self-service

Carolyn U. Lambert

Associate Professor
The Pennsylvania State University
School of Hospitality Management
University Park, PA

Kate Wonjae Lee

Revenue Manager
InterContinental Hotels Group
(Crowne Plaza Times Square Manhattan)
New York, NY

Introduction

Most customers dislike waiting in service lines (Katz et al. 1991; Jones and Dent 1994; Kumar et al. 1997). Customers generally view time as a valued resource, so they may decide that the wait is too long and leave the line or not return (Friedman and Friedman 1997; Pruyn and Smidts 1998). Traditionally, operations management techniques have been used to adjust the number of service points or improve the efficiency of the service process. These techniques are successful over time; however, since demand is not known with certainty in many service situations, it may exceed capacity in the short term. When these situations occur, the customers' psychological experience needs to be managed by influencing the perceived waiting time. The customers' perceived waiting time might influence their view of the service quality (Katz et al. 1991). While hospitality managers are continually striving to decrease actual waiting time or manage perceived waiting time, costs must be evaluated. In response to these operating costs, self-service technologies have been incorporated into many service firms. Research on these theoretical concepts of waiting and self-service technologies is based on tenets in marketing, psychology and operations management.

This chapter is divided into four major sections. The first section investigates perceived waiting time research related to psychology and consumer behaviours. The second section examines the possible relationship between waiting time, service quality, and customer satisfaction. The third section explores the ways of managing waiting time management by using psychology, operations research, and management science. Finally, the fourth section discusses the introduction of technology in self-service and customer reactions.

Perceived waiting time experience and social-psychological theory

Perceived waiting time refers to the customer's perception of the duration of waiting time (Taylor and Fullerton 2000). Individuals perceive waiting time subjectively, based on personal experience and their reaction towards waiting time (Maister 1985). Clemmer and Schneider (1993), Dubé-Rioux et al. (1989) and Pruyn and Smidts (1998) explored the background of these interactions and models in their attempts to suggest the mechanisms of how individuals make decisions, analyse the outcomes of decisions, feel about events, cooperate with difficult situations, and judge other people (Dubé et al. 1991). These models can be applied to individual reactions towards waiting time in similar ways, such as how an individual feels about waiting time, how one cooperates with the waiting situation and how one judges service providers during waiting time (Hui and Tse 1996). These social-psychological theories and models include dissonance theory, attribution theory, negative affection, field theory, a resource allocation model, an uncertainty reduction model and a sense of control model.

Dissonance theory states that waiting time information prior to the wait reduces a person's dissatisfaction while he is waiting (Clemmer and Schneider 1993). The basic premise of dissonance theory is that a person feels discomfort when he experiences two discordant cognitions (Festinger 1957). To reduce this feeling of discomfort, the person tries to justify his decision by convincing himself that the outcome is worth the effort. Therefore, customers who have prior knowledge of the specific length of waiting have a tendency to accept waiting, and their dissatisfaction is reduced. Clemmer and Schneider's (1993) research investigated how a prior notice of waiting time affected customers' satisfaction of waiting lines in banks. Their research results showed that giving prior information on the duration of waiting time significantly influenced customer satisfaction. Customers who were informed about the duration of waiting time had significantly higher satisfaction levels than those who did not receive any information.

While dissonance theory explains how individuals try to justify their own decisions, attribution theory explains how individuals understand events, define causes and assign blame for different outcomes (Jones and Davis 1965). Attribution theory states that when an individual judges another person's behaviours, he also has a tendency to evaluate the person's intention. For example, if customers recognize that a service provider is making an effort to reduce waiting time, customers will place less blame on the service provider (Bitner 1990; Clemmer and Schneider 1993). Baker and Cameron (1996) stated that if a service provider were busy doing clerical activities instead of serving, customers would be dissatisfied because they perceive the service provider is making them wait longer. This may increase customers' negative affections towards waiting time. Taylor (1994) focused on how delay might cause customers' negative affective reactions such as uncertainty and anger, and how these negative affective reactions influence the overall evaluation of service. Taylor also pointed out that negative affective reactions influenced the overall evaluation of service, and ultimately customers' intention to return. She surveyed airline passengers who were waiting for flights to explore the relationships between delay, negative affective reactions, and evaluation of service. Results showed that these negative affective reactions were stronger if the customer thought that the service provider controlled waiting time and if the customer was less occupied during waiting time. Taylor concluded that delay indirectly influences the overall evaluation of service and this influence is mediated by negative reactions. Houston et al.'s (1998) study of bank customers confirmed higher levels of negative affect when customers perceived that the bank controlled the wait.

While Taylor (1994, 1995) focused on control of delay and degree of filled time, Dubé et al. (1991) focused on the stage of service when the delay occurred. In a field experiment with high-school students, an 8-min delay was artificially created during three different stages of the service process: The delay occurred either before the service started (preprocess), in the middle of the service procedure (in-process) or after the service had finished (post-process). Dubé-Rioux et al. concluded that the delays that occurred preprocess and post-process caused stronger negative affective reactions than when the delay occurred in-process of the service procedure.

This conclusion is consistent with Lewin's (1943) field theory, which states that an individual is goal directed. If there are barriers to make the goal hard to reach, the individual feels a negative affect. Therefore, these barriers are the source of negative affective reactions in a person's psychological field. For example, in a restaurant, the customer's main goal is to consume a meal. When waiting time becomes too long, the customer feels upset because the delay keeps the customer from accomplishing the goal of dining. For this service situation, the delay is a source of negative affective reaction. When delays occur during preprocess or post-process, customers feel like they are outside of the process scope, and the impact of delay on customers' feelings is stronger. On the contrary, when delays happen during in-process, customers feel like they are inside the process scope, which makes them 'inside of the goal region', and delays at this point do not cause intensive negative feelings. Hui et al. (1998) used this basic experimental model, but added three categories of delays: procedural, correctional and unknown. Procedural delays occurred when customers had to wait due to an existing queue and correctional delays were atypical due to service breakdowns, such as computers being out of service. Unknown delays were procedural delays that weren't explained. Hui et al. (1998) found that procedural and unknown delays yielded more negative impacts on customer responses during the preprocess stage than the in-process stage, while correctional delays yielded the opposite affect. While Hui et al. (1998) and Dubé-Rioux et al. (1989) and Dubé et al. (1991) claimed that the timing of delay at different stages of the service process can magnify negative affective reactions, Zakay (1989) asserted that a person's cognitive time estimate is a key factor for the length of perceived waiting time.

The resource-allocation model (Zakay 1989) states that providing waiting information will diminish customers' awareness of the passage of time. When a person is more conscious about the time spent waiting, he may reduce their service evaluation. However, distractions and information would make a person less conscious about the length of time. For example, if a person watches TV during the waiting period, he will pay less attention to the passage of time, and the perceived waiting time will be reduced. Hui and Tse (1996) found that providing information about the waiting time significantly improved customers' evaluations of service. When customers were told the waiting duration and queuing information, customers' attention towards the passage of time was reduced. Katz et al. (1991) investigated bank customers' perceived waiting time and found that if management gave waiting duration information to customers, it reduced customers' perceived waiting time, but did not increase service satisfaction.

Another possible reason for better service evaluations when waiting time information is provided is based on the uncertainty reduction model. The uncertainty reduction model states that people tend to have stress when uncertainty exists. Applying this premise to waiting situations, the uncertainty of duration and cause of waiting could make customers more stressed (Osuna 1985). Information such as expected waiting time, cause of waiting and the number of people ahead of the customer reduces the uncertainty of the waiting situation. Since the customer knows how long the waiting time will be, what causes the wait and how many people are waiting, the customer understands the whole waiting situation, which reduces uncertainty. Consequently, this information reduces stress and enhances service evaluation (Taylor 1994). Absence of control also can cause stress for the waiting customers, because a sense of control significantly influences people's psychological reactions towards stressful situations (Langer and Saegert 1977). Hui and Tse (1996) tested the value of information on the waiting duration and queuing length on customers' evaluation of service. Results showed that for short waits (5 min), no information was needed; for intermediate waits (10 min), waiting duration information was evaluated higher than queuing information; and for long waits (15 min), queuing information was more effective than waiting duration information.

To determine the effects of offering wait duration information and explanations for delays, Groth and Gilliland (2006) developed a laboratory test using students. Results indicated that providing no explanation led to more positive attitudes than when the service provider caused the delay. These results are not consistent with Hui and Tse (1996); however, the delay in the Groth and Gilliand study was 15 min. A conceptual framework that combines attribution theory and assimilation-contrast theory, based on perceptions and expectations, cultural models of time perception, and social injustice was proposed by Nie (2002). Nie encouraged further research on the relationships between the factors within the framework.

Another potential factor is 'social regard'. Butcher and Heffernan (2006) define this as 'making the customer feel valued in the social interaction'. They conducted an experimental in a café setting, adjusting actual wait times and friendliness of the service employee and offering an employee apology for the wait. The level of social regard perceived by the customers influenced their positive word of mouth and repeat visitation intention.

In summary, social and psychological theories help to explain the mechanism of how individuals react or feel towards waiting time. However, these social and psychological theories must be integrated with the marketing aspects of service quality and customer satisfaction for a more complete view of waiting behaviour.

Waiting time, service quality and customer satisfaction

Service quality and customer satisfaction are directly related to operational success; however, they are difficult to manage because they are intangible and hard to quantify.[1] For several decades, many research studies were conducted to investigate service quality and customer satisfaction. Research on customer satisfaction started in the 1970s, and service quality research started in the 1980s (Oh and Parks 1997). In this section, research studies that relate waiting time to customer satisfaction and service quality will be reviewed to explore how perceived or actual waiting times might influence customer satisfaction or evaluation of service quality.

---

[1] See also Chapter 13.

Customer satisfaction is considered to be a response rather than an attitude, and service quality is considered to be an attitude or global judgement (Oh and Parks 1997), which also influences customer satisfaction (Cronin and Taylor 1992). Generally, extended waiting time is considered to be a negative factor for evaluation of service quality and customers' satisfaction (Chebat and Filiatrault 1993). Davis and Vollman (1990) found a direct relationship between actual waiting time and satisfaction in a fast food setting. A later study by Davis and Heineke (1998) explored the same issue.

Parasuraman et al. (1985) suggested that delay would negatively influence several attributes, and consequently the overall evaluation of service. Berry and Parasuraman (1991) also stated that promptness or punctuality is an important element of service reliability, which is a strong attribute of overall evaluation of service quality for customers. Using these premises in a study with airline passengers, Taylor (1994) concluded that waiting time influences overall evaluation of service quality negatively. An extended waiting time lowered customers' evaluation for the tangible and reliability attributes of service quality Taylor (1995).

Roslow et al. (1992) suggested that waiting time and service quality are two main keys to determine customer satisfaction. From their research with bank customers, they concluded that waiting time is a more important determinant of customer satisfaction than service quality. Tom and Lucey (1995) agreed that there are negative relationships between waiting time and customer satisfaction, and customers are satisfied when they wait for shorter time periods than they expected. Pruyn and Smidts (1998) also suggested that the disconfirmation of personal acceptable waiting time and perceived waiting time influences appraisal of the wait, and the appraisal of the wait influences satisfaction. They stated that perceived waiting time is a stronger determinant of customer satisfaction than actual waiting time.

Lee and Lambert (2005) surveyed customers in a scramble cafeteria to determine if service quality was influenced by the discrepancy between the expected waiting time and the perceived waiting time. Their results supported results by Parasuraman et al. (1985) in that the discrepancy influences the reliability aspect of service quality, but not tangibility, responsiveness or assurance aspects. Customers whose perceived waiting time was longer than either their expected or reasonable time reported lower satisfaction scores.

Hwang and Lambert (2005) utilized the scenario method to determine satisfactory, unsatisfactory and very unsatisfactory waiting times for customers in a multi-stage restaurant.

Customers' waiting times for being greeted, being seated, ordering, being served, receiving the check and paying varied, depending on what level of service they were willing to accept; however, they ranked the greeting and ordering stages as the most important stages.

Customers' assessment of service quality and their overall satisfaction is clearly related to their waiting time. These concepts need to be further explored to determine the interrelationships between the various waits and the customers' expectations.

Waiting time management

Reducing waiting time has been an important issue for the service industry since waiting time influences customer satisfaction and their evaluation of service quality. Perception management and operations management are two major approaches to managing waiting time (Tom and Lucey 1995). Perception management focuses on reducing perceived waiting time and is based on cognitive psychology and marketing theories. On the other hand, operations management focuses on reducing actual waiting time and is based on management science and operations research theories.

Perception management: managing perceived waiting time

Maister (1985) proposed that unoccupied time, preprocess waits, uncertain waits, unexplained waits, unfair waits and solo waits are perceived to be longer than occupied time, in-process waits, known waits, explained waits and group waits. Therefore, by manipulating these waiting conditions, managers might be able to influence perceived waiting time.

Another well-known principle is giving more control to customers choosing waiting lines (Haynes 1990). For example, different telephone numbers may be available depending on customers' needs such as orders, customer services and bill inquiry. In this way, customers have more control over their selection of queues, and they tolerate longer waiting times. However, contrary to this, a study by Groth and Gilliland (2006) surveyed 135 customers of two fast food stores – one with a single wait line and the other with multiple lines. They found no difference in actual wait times, but those in the single line system perceived their wait time to be shorter.

In their study on placement of delays, Dubé et al. (1991) found that customers preferred to wait in an integrated format rather than a segregated one. For example, customers preferred to wait 8 min at once rather than to wait 5 min in one line and 3 min in a second line. Therefore, they suggested that service providers should minimize waiting time before and after service, and should integrate a series of short waiting steps into a longer waiting period.

Management also can add electronic news boards and clocks that show estimated waiting time to reduce perceived waiting time and boredom (Katz et al. 1991). Jones and Peppiatt (1996) found that customers who were idle estimated waiting times longer than people who were occupied, either by watching TV or because they were in a group. Chebat et al. (1993) investigated the effects of musical and visual cues on perceived waiting time. The tempo of music had no effect on perceived waiting time, but the high amounts of visual information reduced perceived waiting time. Chebat et al. (1995) investigated the effects of mood on time perception and acceptance of waiting. They concluded that a customer's happy mood improved the acceptance of waiting but had no impact on time estimations.

Baker and Cameron (1996) emphasized the importance of service environment attributes, such as lighting, temperature, music, colour, furnishings and spatial layout for managing perceived waiting time. They insisted that the higher the level of lighting, the greater the temperature beyond the range of comfort, the warmer the colour, and the higher the level of discomfort of furnishings, the more the negative effects and the longer the perceived waiting times. In a subsequent study, Cameron et al. (2003) examined the effects of music, wait-length evaluation, and mood on customers' overall experience. Although music preference influenced wait-length evaluation and mood, only mood influenced customers' attitude towards the experience.

Improving the aesthetic appearance of the waiting environment can reduce negative affects of waiting time on satisfaction (Pruyn and Smidts 1998). Video displays, wall magazines, mirrors and product samples also distract attention from waiting time.

This section explored how managers can influence perceived waiting time by enhancing waiting environment. While this approach uses cognitive and psychological disciplines to improve customer satisfaction related to perceived waiting time, a second approach uses management science and operations management theories to reduce objective waiting time.

Operations management: management of actual waiting time

Management science and operations management disciplines frequently apply scheduling, simulation, forecasting and process design methodologies to reduce actual waiting time. Queuing theory is one of the most important theories used to study actual waiting time. In the following section, queuing theory will be reviewed.

Hornik (1984) stated that individuals have a tendency to overestimate waiting time, after he investigated the relationship between actual waiting time and perceived waiting time. Actual waiting time, which is the objective or clocked waiting time, has been studied using queuing theory from the operations and management science discipline. Queuing theory was developed in the early 1900s by A. K. Erlang to study fluctuating demands in telephone traffic. After World War II, Erlang's work was extended to general business applications, and today it is used extensively in both manufacturing and service industries.

Since waiting time is considered to be a key factor for customer satisfaction, fast food restaurants aggressively use these methods to reduce waiting time. In 1978, Burger King introduced specialty sandwiches. By using a simulation model, they found that a new sandwich would cause a service delay of 8 sec, which would cause a $39 million loss in sales capacity for Burger King. Additionally, Burger King applied simulation modelling to determine the optimal distance between the order station and the drive-through window to minimize waiting time, to project the number of workers needed and to decide their placement in the restaurant (Swart and Donno 1981).

Similarly, Hueter and Swart (1998) used an integrated set of operations research models in Taco Bell, by applying a forecasting model for predicting customer arrivals, a simulation model for determining optimal labour requirements and an integer programming model for scheduling and allocating employees to minimize labour cost. Hueter and Swart observed when customers would likely leave a waiting line because they perceived the waiting time to be excessive and found that after actual waiting time exceeded 5 min, customers' perceived waiting time increased exponentially. They decided that a 3-min average time in a queue was an optimal level of waiting since only 2.5% of customers who wait 3 min will leave the line. Lee and Lambert (2007) used customer survey results to determine the acceptable waiting time for customers in a scramble cafeteria. Simulation was utilized to determine the number of employees needed per station to reach the desired waiting time goal. While the desired waiting time, that is 3 min, was reached in most stations, the grill station required renovation or menu changes to reach the goal.

Service process design affects the wait that customers experience, so several researchers (Sheu and Babbar 1996; Kolesar and Green 1998) have explored alternate service process designs. Sheu et al. (2003) compared four queuing service designs to determine the best process design. They recommended that system designs be flexible so managers could switch process systems based on parameter values, such as ordering time, preparation time and demand. Using system information based on approximations, Whitt (1999) developed algorithms to predict the waiting time of new customers or customers in line.

Another approach to reduce the objective waiting time is based on using time as a form of price. Ittig (1994, 2002) modelled aggregate customer demand as a function of the average waiting time to determine the number of servers needed to maximize profit. Waiting line segmentation gives options to customers who are willing to pay a premium for faster service (Friedman and Friedman 1997). Using segmentation reduced the average number of customers in a queue and the average time in a queue, and they suggested that segmentation is useful for a very congested system.

However, there may be circumstances where consumers are deterred from leaving the queue, so-called reneging behaviour, by the length of the queue. Zhou and Soman (2003) found that as the number of people behind in the queue increases, the consumer is less likely to renege, largely because their affective state improves. This derives from making social comparisons with others (in the queue) and regarding those behind them as less fortunate.

In summary, several researchers have focused on how to reduce either perceived waiting time or actual waiting time. These research studies provide good suggestions that management can implement. The interdisciplinary approach of both psychology and operations research gives a better understanding of the relationship among perceived and actual waiting time, customer satisfaction, and service quality. Although research on customer–service provider interactions has been extensive, research on interactions between customers and technological interfaces is less advanced. As self-service technologies continue to expand in the hospitality industry, this area is becoming more critical for research.

Self-service technologies

As labour costs increased in the 1990s, firms began to look at technology for answers. The solutions found included self-service methods of ordering and paying. Self-service refers to situations when the customer performs all aspects of a service encounter without help from employees, such as ATMs and automated hotel checkout (Bitner 2001). While customers were becoming more comfortable with technology, research was not available to support customer acceptance (Meuter and Bitner 1998). Meuter et al. (2000) explored service interactions using self-service technologies to determine the sources of satisfaction and dissatisfaction. Using the critical incident method through a web survey, the researchers collected 823 responses of which 56% were positive reactions and 44% were negative ones. Major reasons cited for positive experiences included that the technology was better than the alternative, that it worked successfully and that it helped solve a problem. Negative experiences were due to technology failure, poor design, and process failure. Meuter et al. (2000) recommended that firms identify how customers evaluate self-service technologies in order to design satisfactory technologies. Based on customer decision-making research, Dabholkar (1996) proposed and tested two models of service quality for technology-based self-service systems. Using a scenario approach, Dabholkar surveyed college students about using self-service technology at fast food restaurants. Waiting time showed a highly significant negative effect on intention and a significantly negative effect on expected service quality. These results should warn managers to install enough self-service stations to minimize waiting lines. Recommendations for future studies included the identification of additional situational influences and exploration of various combinations of situational influences. Also, different population groups need to be studied to reflect differences according to gender, age and cultural group.

Consumers rate a service negatively when waiting times are long (Pruyn and Smidts 1998) or there are delays (Taylor 1994, 1995). Dabholkar and Bagozzi (2002) questioned if the same were true for technology-based self-service models. They examined situational influences of perceptions of waiting and crowding in a quick-service scenario-based survey. They hypothesized that if customers perceive a long waiting time, the relationship between perceived ease of use and attitude towards technology-based self-service would be strengthened. Results supported the hypothesis. Dabholkar and Bagozzi (2002) recommended that managers emphasize the ease of use and enjoyment of using technology-based self-service to counteract long waiting lines. However, as waiting time increases, customers will use alternate options, so the authors reiterated their recommendation that managers need to have sufficient self-service stations to minimize waiting times.

In 2005, Meuter et al. recognized that research on self-service technologies had focused on individual differences (Parasuraman and Colby 2001), and on attitudinal models to determine intentions (Dabholkar and Bagozzi 2002). To further the literature base, they explored the fundamental factors that influence customers to try new self-service technologies and developed a model to predict self-service technology trial behaviour. Using an Internet-based ordering system, results showed that role clarity, the consumer's understanding of the process, and extrinsic motivation, including price discounts and time savings, were the dominant variables that predicted the use of the self-service ordering system. Thus, increased experience with the Internet increases the probability of a customer's use of self-service technologies, and this experience also improves role clarity, motivation and ability, which increases the probability of use.

These results suggest that future research should determine the predictors of role clarity and the strength of these relationships. Also, the influences on commitment to self-service technologies and the differential influences of role clarity, motivation and ability during the adoption process need to be explored. The impact of using self-service technologies on customer loyalty and profitability is another important research thread. Managers need to understand the implications of the shift away from interpersonal interactions and how they can maintain trust and loyalty within customer relations.

Summary and conclusions

Time is a very valuable asset for every person, and waiting time may cause unpleasant feelings of customers, and this would ultimately influence the future success of business. Researchers generally agree that waiting influences service quality evaluations and customer satisfaction ratings. Additionally, many variables have been shown to affect the waiting evaluation, including the perceived wait time, the placement of the wait, the environment of the waiting area and the availability of distractions. However, the interactions of these variables should be addressed to determine the strength of each. Many of these studies were completed in laboratories or using scenario-based surveys. To verify the results, they need to be replicated in various real service settings.

The relationships among satisfaction, service quality, affective reaction, perceived waiting time and objective time could be explored using structural equation modelling to obtain a more complete model. Additionally, simulation models could be developed to conduct cost analysis for customers' waiting time, intention to return, and labour to help managers determine waiting time strategies. Coupled with operations management techniques, research on social psychological aspects of waiting should suggest appropriate solutions for hospitality managers.

The substitution of technology for face-to-face interactions in service encounters has increased opportunities for research. Since customers will continue to expect quality service, researchers need to explore how waiting time and service delays affect customer satisfaction in a variety of self-service environments. Variables such as age, gender, customer readiness, enjoyment, physical environment and safety aspects will need to be evaluated for their relative importance and their impact on the adoption process. As self-service technologies advance, such as pay at table, and food ordering at the gas pump, the pivotal attributes of these technologies need to be addressed to determine how they can be improved. While Meuter et al. (2000) found that role clarity, motivation and customer ability are significant, the main drivers of role clarity should be explored further. The strength of each of the antecedent predictors of consumer readiness, such as perceived risk, previous experience and need for interaction should be determined. Hospitality firms wanting to use self-ordering would benefit by knowing how to attract customers. Then the relative importance of role clarity, motivation and ability on each stage of the adoption process should be explored. These research studies should be designed to validate the existence of the moderating variables and then determine the direction and impact in various settings.

References

Baker, J. and Cameron, M. (1996) The effects of the service environment on affect and consumer perception of waiting time: an integrative review and research propositions, *Journal of the Academy of Marketing Science*, 24, 4, 338–349

Berry, L. L. and Parasuraman, A. (1991) *Marketing Services: Comparing Through Quality*, Free Press: New York

Bitner, M. J. (1990) Evaluating service encounters: the effects of physical surroundings and employee responses, *Journal of Marketing*, 54, 2, 69–82

Bitner, M. J. (2001) Service and technology: opportunities and paradoxes, *Management Service Quality*, 11, 6, 375–379

Butcher, K. and Heffernan, T. (2006) Social regard: a link between waiting for service and service outcomes, *International Journal of Hospitality Management*, 25, 34–53

Cameron, M. A., Baker, J., Peterson, M. and Braunsberger, K. (2003) The effects of music, wait-length evaluation, and mood on a low-cost wait experience, *Journal of Business Research*, 56, 6, 421–430

Chebat, J., Gelinas-Chebat, C. and Filiatrault, P. (1993) Interactive effects of musical and visual cues on time perception: an application to waiting lines in banks, *Perceptual Motor Skills*, 77, 995–1020

Chebat, J. C. and Filiatrault, P. (1993) The impact of waiting in line on consumers, *International Journal of Bank Marketing*, 11, 2, 35–40

Chebat, J. C., Gelinas-Chebat, C., Vaninski, A. and Filiatrault, P. (1995) The impact of mood on time perception, memorization, and acceptance of waiting, *Genetic, Social, & General Psychology Monographs*, 121, 4, 411–424

Clemmer, E. C. and Schneider, B. (1993) Managing customer dissatisfaction with waiting: applying social-psychological theory in a service setting, *Advances in Services Marketing and Management*, 2, 213–229

Cronin, J. J. and Taylor, S. A. (1992) Measuring service quality: a reexamination and extension, *Journal of Marketing*, 56, 3, 55–68

Dabholkar, P. A. (1996) Consumer evaluations of new technology-based self-service options: an investigation of alternative models of service quality, *International Journal of Research in Marketing*, 13, 29–51

Dabholkar, P. A. and Bagozzi, R. P. (2002) An attitudinal model of technology-based self-service: moderating effects of consumer traits and situational factors, *Journal of the Academy of Marketing Science*, 30, 3, 184–201

Davis, M. M. and Heineke, J. (1998) How disconfirmation, perception and actual waiting times impact customer satisfaction, *International Journal of Service Industry Management*, 9, 1, 64–73

Davis, M. M. and Vollmann, T. E. (1990) A framework for relating waiting time and customer satisfaction in a service operation, *Journal of Services Marketing*, 4, 1, 61–69

Dubé, L., Schmitt, B. H. and Leclerc, F. (1991) Consumers' affective response to delays at different phases of a service delivery, *Journal of Applied Social Psychology*, 21, 10, 810–820

Dubé-Rioux, L., Schmitt, B. H. and Leclerc, F. (1989) Consumers' reactions to waiting: when delays affect the perception of service quality, In Srull, T. K. (Ed.), *Advances in Consumer Research*, 16, Ann Harbor, MI: Association for Consumer Research, 112–125

Festinger, L. A. (1957) *A Theory of Cognitive Dissonance*, Stanford University Press: Stanford, CA

Friedman, H. H. and Friedman, L. W. (1997) Reducing the "wait" in waiting-line systems: waiting line segmentation, *Business Horizons*, 40, 4, 54–58

Groth, M. and Gilliland, S. W. (2006) Having to wait for service: customer reactions to delays in service delivery, *Applied Psychology: An International Review*, 55, 1, 107–129

Haynes, P. J. (1990) Hating to wait: managing the final service encounter, *Journal of Service Marketing*, 4, 4, 20–26

Hornik, J. (1984) Subjective vs. objective time measures: a note on the perception of time in consumer behavior, *Journal of Consumer Research*, 11, 1, 615–618

Houston, M. B., Bettencourt, L. A. and Wenger, S. (1998) The relationship between waiting in a service queue and evaluations of service quality: a field theory perspective, *Psychology and Marketing*, 15, 8, 735–753

Hueter, J. and Swart, W. (1998) An integrated labor-management system for Taco Bell, *Interfaces*, 28, 1, 75–91

Hui, M. K., Thakor, M. V. and Gill, R. (1998) The effect of delay type and service stage on consumers' reactions to waiting, *Journal of Consumer Research*, 24, 4, 469–479

Hui, M. K. and Tse, D. K. (1996) What to tell consumers in waits of different lengths: an integrative model of service evaluation, *Journal of Marketing*, 60, 2, 81–90

Hwang, J. and Lambert, C. U. (2005) Customers' identification of acceptable waiting times in a multi-stage restaurant system, *Journal of Foodservice Business Research*, 8, 1, 3–16

Ittig, P. T. (1994) Planning service capacity when demand is sensitive to delay, *Decision Sciences*, 25, 4, 541–559

Ittig, P. T. (2002) The real cost of making customers wait, *International Journal of Service Industry Management*, 13, 3, 231–241

Jones, E. E. and Davis, K. E. (1965) From acts to dispositions: the attribution process in person perception, In Berkowiz, L. (Ed.), *Advances in Experimental Social Psychology*, Vol. 2, Academic Press: New York, 219–266

Jones, P. and Dent, M. (1994) Improving service: managing response time in hospitality operations, *International Journal of Operations and Production Management*, 14, 5, 52–58

Jones, P. and Peppiatt, E. (1996) Managing perceptions of waiting times in service queues, *International Journal of Service Industry Management*, 7, 5, 47–61

Katz, K. L., Larson, B. M. and Larson, R. C. (1991) Prescription for the waiting-in-line blues: entertain, enlighten, and engage, *Sloan Management Review*, 32, 2, 44–53

Kolesar, P. and Green, L. (1998) Insights on service system design via a normal approximation to Erlang's delay formula, *Production and Operations Management*, 7, 282–293

Kumar, P., Kalwani, M. U. and Dada, M. (1997) The impact of waiting time guarantees on customers' waiting experiences, *Marketing Science*, 16, 4, 295–314

Langer, E. J. and Saegert, S. (1977) Crowding and cognitive control, *Journal of Personality and Social Psychology*, 35, 3, 175–182

Lee, W. and Lambert, C. (2005) The effect of waiting time and affective reactions on customers' evaluation of service quality in a cafeteria, *Journal of Foodservice Business Research*, 8, 2, 19–37

Lee, K. W. and Lambert, C. U. (2007) Using simulation to manage waiting time in a cafeteria, *Information Technology in Hospitality*, 15, 4, 127–141

Lewin, K. (1943) Defining the 'field at a given time', *Psychological Review*, 50, 292–310

Maister, D. (1985). The psychology of waiting lines, In Czepiel, J. A., Solomon, M. and Suprenant, C. (Eds.), *The Service Encounter*, Lexington Books: Lexington, MA, 113–123

Meuter, M. and Bitner, M. (1998) Self-service technologies: extending service frameworks and identifying issues for research, In Grewal, D. and Pechmann, C. (Eds.), *AMA Winter Educator's Conference Proceedings: Marketing Theory and Applications*, Vol. 9, American Marketing Association: Chicago, 12–19

Meuter, M. L., Bitner, M. J., Ostrom, A. and Brown, S. (2005) Choosing among alternative service delivery modes: an investigation of customer trial of self-service technologies, *Journal of Marketing*, 69, 2, 61–83

Meuter, M. L., Ostrom, A. L., Roundtree, R. I. and Bitner, M. (2000) Self-service technologies: understanding customer satisfaction with technology-based service encounters, *Journal of Marketing*, 64, 3, 50–64

Nie, W. (2000) Waiting: integrating social and psychological perspectives in operations management, *Omega*, 28, 6, 611–629

Oh, H. and Parks, S. C. (1997) Customer satisfaction and service quality: a critical review of the literature and research implications for the hospitality industry, *The Council on Hotel, Restaurant, and Institutional Education*, 20, 3, 35–64

Osuna, E. E. (1985) The psychological cost of waiting, *Journal of Mathematical Psychology*, 29, 1, 82–105

Parasuraman, A. and Colby, C. (2001) *Techno-Ready Marketing: How and Why Your Customers Adopt Technology,* Free Press: New York

Parasuraman, A., Zeithmal, V. and Berry, L. (1985) A conceptual model of service quality and its implications for future research, *Journal of Marketing,* 49, 4, 41–50

Pruyn, A. and Smidts, A. (1998) Effects of waiting on the satisfaction with the service: beyond objective time measures, *International Journal of Research in Marketing,* 15, 4, 321–334

Roslow, S., Nicholls, J. A. F. and Tsalikis, J. (1992) Time and quality: twin keys to customer service satisfaction, *Journal of Applied Business Research,* 8, 2, 80–86

Sheu, C. and Babbar, D. (1996) A managerial assessment of the waiting-time performance for alternative service process designs, *International Journal of Management Science,* 24, 6, 689–703

Sheu, C., McHaney, R. and Babbar, S. (2003) Service process design flexibility and customer waiting time, *International Journal of Operations and Production Management,* 23, 8, 901–917

Swart, W. and Donno, L. (1981) Simulation modeling improves operations, planning, and productivity of fast food restaurants, *Interfaces,* 11, 6, 35–47

Taylor, S. (1994) Waiting for service: the relationship between delays and evaluations of service, *Journal of Marketing,* 58, 2, 56–69

Taylor, S. (1995) The effects of filled waiting time and service provider control over the delay on evaluations of service, *Journal of the Academy of Marketing Science,* 23, 1, 38–48

Taylor, S. and Fullerton, G. (2000) Waiting for service: perceptions management of the wait experience, In Swartz, T. A. and Iacobucci, D. (Eds.), *Handbook of Services Marketing and Management,* Sage: Thousand Oaks, CA, 171–190

Tom, G. and Lucey, S. (1995) Waiting time delays and customer satisfaction in supermarkets, *The Journal of Service Marketing,* 9, 5, 20–29

Whitt, W. (1999) Predicting queuing delays, *Management Science,* 45, 6, 870–888

Zakay, D. (1989) Subjective time and attentional resource allocation: an integrated model of time estimation, In Levin, I. and Zakay, D. (Eds.), *Time and Human Cognition: A Life Span Perspective,* North Holland: Amsterdam, 365–397

Zhou, R. and Soman, D. (2003) Looking back: exploring the psychology of queuing and the effect of the number of people behind, *Journal of Consumer Research,* 29, 4, 517–530

The service encounter

Beverley Sparks

Professor, Griffith Business School
Tourism, Sport and Services
Innovation Research Centre
Gold Coast Campus
Griffith University
Australia

Karin Weber

Assistant Professor
School of Hotel and Tourism Management
Hong Kong Polytechnic University
Hung Hom, Kowloon
Hong Kong, SAR, China

Introduction

Hospitality businesses rely, to a large degree, on creating positive customer experiences. A core component of achieving this goal is to gain an understanding of the importance of the times when a customer comes into contact with the business and especially the service personnel. These contact points are frequently called 'moments of truth' (Grönroos 1988) and serve as events where customers evaluate whether the business meets their expectations. A key component of these 'moments of truth' is made up of what is commonly called a service encounter, and represents the time(s) when customers and staff interact.

While various aspects of service encounters have been investigated in a number of service industries, the focus of this chapter is primarily on the hospitality industry. What makes the hospitality industry different from other service sectors? Perhaps the most important difference is that it is primarily about creating key, positive experiences. The hospitality sector is very much an experience-driven industry. This chapter discusses a service encounter, the factors that affect a service encounter, the outcomes of a service encounter, the issue of service failure and recovery and finally the best way to manage this important phenomenon.

Defining a service encounter: single, sequence and chains

A service encounter is that period of time during which the customer and the service firm interact in person over telephone or through other media (Shostack 1985). Essentially, a service encounter has been defined as a social interaction involving one human being interacting with another (Czepiel et al. 1985). Given the high degree of person-to-person interaction and, quite frequently the absence of an exchange of tangible goods, the service encounter becomes a critical component of service quality. There are three key players involved in a service encounter that shape the outcome of any encounter: the *service firm*, which sets policies and guidelines; the *employees*, who enact the policies of the firm; and the *customer*, who seeks to satisfy a range of needs and wants. Chandon et al. (1997) propose several service encounter dimensions on the basis of which a service encounter can be assessed. These dimensions and their subcategories differ depending on whether it is the customer or the firm doing the assessment. From the customer's view, the service provider's perceived competence (expertise), listening skills and dedication are likely to be key in assessing the service received. From the employee's view, customer courtesy, efficiency in terms of getting the transaction completed and personal (employee) satisfaction are likely to be key in the assessment process.

Original work by Czepiel et al. (1985) identified seven key characteristics of a service encounter that can be considered the distinguishing factors when analysing service encounters. Briefly, service encounters usually

- are goal oriented
- are undertaken as part of work activities
- are primarily a stranger relationship
- are narrow in scope: only surface topics of conversation
- are mostly task oriented
- mostly follow a pre-defined set of rules to facilitate the interaction
- involve the roles of service provider and client (customer)

It is probably true to say that service encounters are alike in that they have certain common distinguishing characteristics; however, due to the dynamic nature of human interactions, every encounter differs to some degree. Many service encounters have been considered in isolation in that they have been considered outside a broader context. Often when researchers consider service encounters, they merely think about individual events rather than connections between them.

While much research has focused on discrete service encounters, more recent studies have examined multiple service encounters, or sequences of events. For example, Verhoef et al. (2004) approached the service encounter as a sequence of events. In particular, they tested a model on how events contribute to an overall evaluation of a sequence of events and found that while the average performance during the encounter is important, peak performances are critical for satisfaction formation. Thus, from a managerial point of view, it is important not only to manage the overall performance of the service encounter but also to generate a number of positive peak performances. Apart from peak performances, the performance trend – that is whether positive or negative performances are first or last in the sequence as well as the quality of the final performance in a service sequence – also significantly impacts customer evaluations (Hansen and Danaher 1999). In a hotel context, management has not only to be mindful of the average quality of the encounters a hotel guest has with various staff for the check-in process (e.g. porter, check-in clerk and bell boy) but also ensure that unexpected extras, for example, can lead to perceived peak performances from the customer's point of view.

Svensson (2004) goes one step further, referring to service encounter chains where one service encounter by one service provider affects the quality of another service encounter by a different service provider. Thus, the quality of a service encounter in a hotel restaurant may impact a subsequent service encounter with staff at the same hotel's spa. Time, context and performance potentially affect the overall evaluation by a customer of these service encounter chains. The notion of service encounter chains is relevant not only intra-organizationally but also equally, if not more, for inter-organizational service encounters, in service networks or alliances. These situations will be discussed in more detail later in this chapter. So, to summarize at this point, service encounters are critical moments of truths, which can be evaluated from the firm's or the customer's point of view. The service encounter can be a single discrete encounter or part of a larger sequence or chain of events. Indeed, many discrete encounters may accumulate over time to form a longer lasting service relationship. Next, we turn to the issue of how enduring a service encounter might be.

Service encounters and service relationships

The literature makes a clear differentiation between a service encounter and a service relationship (Czepiel 1990; Gutek 1995), whereby a series of service encounters with a particular provider may or may not evolve into a service relationship. Gutek (1995) developed a taxonomy that differentiates among three types of service interactions: the encounter, the relationship and the pseudo-relationship. Service relationships are characterized by customers and providers that have *personal knowledge* of one another a history of *prior interaction* and an *anticipated future*. In a service relationship, a customer is inclined to attribute a successful encounter to the individual service provider's internal characteristics ('he is a good receptionist') but failure to external factors ('he must be having a bad day'). Conversely, in a service encounter, there is typically a lack of intimacy and familiarity between the provider and customer; thus success is often dismissed as resulting from external factors ('it was an easy job'), while failure is related to internal factors ('the receptionist was useless').

Service relationships are expensive to develop, as more staff time must be dedicated to looking after individual customers. As a result, service relationships are rare compared to service encounters. Yet, given the benefits of increased customer loyalty that can result from relationships, Gutek et al. (1999)

argue that a hybrid – a pseudo-relationship – has developed that combines the practicalities and economy of the service encounter with the loyalty-inducing features of the relationship. Instead of developing a personal relationship with the customer, service firms develop customer knowledge by building customer databases. To induce loyalty, service firms offer rewards and incentives. In addition, Gutek et al. (1999) found evidence of a link between the type of relationship a customer has with a service provider and the frequency of interaction. Specifically, they noted that customers having a service relationship with a service provider have more service interactions than customers who have not.

Relative to the service relationship, the service encounter has an advantage in terms of time and cost efficiency and offers easy access to customers to engage in the service encounter at their convenience. These advantages, however, are somewhat outweighed by its disadvantages, namely the service encounters' impersonal nature, limited choice options, potential opportunistic behaviour by a provider due to its one-time nature and a provider's lack of flexibility and autonomy to tailor service to a customer's needs. In contrast, the advantages of the service relationship include a continuing pattern of interaction, with the compilation of customer history and the anticipation of future patronage. Service relationships are more likely to satisfy instrumental and expressive needs and provide greater customization. Disadvantages of service relationships include high switching costs for the customer, uncertainty of getting better service with another provider and possible guilt and hurt feelings of dissolving relationship. For both the provider and the customer, it will take time and effort to develop a good relationship. The customer is limited to see the provider when available, with potentially long wait times.

At this point it may be useful to pause and reflect on the service encounter – relationship distinction. What examples exist within the tourism or hospitality domains? Take airlines as an example. For most economy class passengers (non-business frequent fliers), travel will involve a series of encounters with various entities. First, on arrival at the airport, the traveller will most likely check in some luggage and seek a seat allocation; next, boarding the plane, the traveller will be welcomed on board and directed to a seat by the cabin crew; third, in transit the traveller will probably have service encounters while receiving a meal or requiring some attention from the cabin crew; finally, the traveller will depart the aircraft bidding staff farewell and collect the luggage. Each of these interactions is indicative of standard service encounters, probably characterized by a lack of familiarity or intimacy. Rather each of these encounters is most typically one of negotiated politeness, which is accepted as part of the service delivery process. These service encounters are mainly about efficient, polite and safe service. Now, consider a restaurant patron who has been going to the same restaurant for the past 10 years. In such a situation, the interaction might more closely resemble a relationship rather than an encounter. The restaurant owner may personally greet the loyal patron, which may be followed by a lengthy exchange about recent family events. Given the frequent patronage, a special dish may be prepared or a complimentary bottle of wine be offered. The guest may also get a more personal farewell from either the owner or the wait staff. Thus, in contrast to the service encounter, there is a more personal element involved in a relationship where individual exchanges may also last longer.

Internal versus external service encounters

As previously mentioned, the customer and the employee are two of the key players of a service encounter. Traditionally, the focus of research has been on the external service encounter, that is, the encounter between an employee of a service provider and a customer as the service recipient. However, literature also points to internal service encounters whereby the employees of a company are the customers. The notion of an internal customer follows from the services marketing triangle proposed by Kotler and Armstrong (1991) that illustrates the relationships between a company, its employees and its customers. External marketing refers to the interactions between a service firm and its customers, while interactive marketing relates to the interactions between employees and customers. The latter interactions are termed the service encounter and have been the focus of most research (Bitner et al. 1990). Internal marketing, the third type of marketing in the services marketing triangle, is concerned with the relationship between the service firm and its employees. This leads to the notion of the internal service encounter whereby the needs of the employees, that is, the internal customers, have to be met. The concept of an 'internal service encounter' is rather different from the one of 'internal marketing' in that the former is about how employees of one department serve employees of another department, while the latter is about how the organization (mainly through its human resources department) serves its employees. An internal service encounter may, therefore, be defined as the dyadic interaction between employees in different departments of the organization in which the providers have the responsibility to respond to the needs of their internal customers.

To illustrate the concept of an internal customer in a hotel context, a waiter may be considered the internal customer of the chef who prepared a specific dish, the chef being the internal customer of the storekeeper who, in turn, is the internal customer of the purchasing agent. All of them are internal customers of the payroll department. The internal customer/service encounter concept, while not without its critics (Harari 1991; Stewart 1997), has been widely adopted in the hospitality industry. For example, Bill Marriott, Jr, chairman of Marriott Hotels, argues that employees must be satisfied before external customers will be satisfied. Only if these internal customers are satisfied, he reasons, will they love their jobs and feel a sense of pride in the hotel. This, in turn, will lead to external customers being well served (Kotler and Armstrong 1991). Similarly, Hal Rosenbluth, president of Rosenbluth Travel, contends that the employees in his company 'have to come first, even ahead of customers' (Rosenbluth 1991: 33) as the external customer will never be uppermost in employees' minds if they are not happy with their jobs.

Several studies have examined the concept of the 'internal service encounter.' Paraskevas (2001), for example, explored an internal service chain in three international city hotels and identified the events and behaviours (service dimensions) that distinguish a successful internal service encounter from a non-successful one. He found that interpersonal relations affect to a great extent all internal service encounters in a hotel. Professionalism, dependability and conscientiousness of the internal suppliers, their communication skills and the consideration they show to their internal customers were other critical factors influencing internal service encounters.

Yoon et al. (2001) established that the service climate contributes directly to employee job satisfaction and work effort and indirectly impacts consumers' perceptions of employee service quality. Both job satisfaction and work effort affect consumer perceptions of employee service quality. Surveying 149 hotels, González and Garazo (2006) found that select dimensions of organizational service orientation – enhancing freedom to make decisions during service encounters, increasing service training and rewarding service – will increase employee job satisfaction, which in turn positively affects organizational citizenship behaviour, in particular, employee loyalty. Finally, service communication leadership was also found to have a significant direct relationship with employee organizational citizenship behaviour, pointing to the need for management to clearly communicate with employees service expectations while at the same time soliciting employee ideas, opinions and suggestions.

Given their unique role, customer contact employees are often referred to as boundary spanners, serving both internal and external customers. Yet, this dual role can lead to potential role conflict. Chung and Schneider (2002) tested a framework to understand antecedents and consequences of such role conflicts and saw it emerge as a discrepancy between what employees think customers want and what management rewards employees for doing. Attitudinal (satisfaction) and behavioural (absenteeism) outcomes are the result of role conflict. Thus, while it is important to understand the service encounter from a customer perspective, the internal service encounters are also vital to the operation of a successful hospitality firm.

Influence of technology

Previously, service encounters have been characterized as 'low tech, high touch', with research focusing primarily on the interpersonal dynamics of encounters. In particular, the service encounter has been conceived of as being a primarily human interaction. However, while human interactions in the service encounter are still paramount, advances in technology have been altering various facets of encounters. Research on the changing nature of service delivery and the subsequent impact on customers is lagging behind the technology adoption in practice (Bitner et al. 2000). Acknowledging the influence of technology on the service encounter, Parasuraman (1996) modified the traditional services marketing triangle to incorporate technology as the forth dimension, apart from the company, employees and customers. Bitner et al. (2000) developed a technology infusion matrix that provides insights into how technology can improve the service encounter. On the one hand, technology can be used by contact employees to customize the encounter and facilitate an effective service recovery following a service failure or as a means of delighting customers. On the other hand, customers can also use technology to independently facilitate customization and for service recovery and customer delight. For example, Ritz Carlton, known for its service excellence standards, created an extensive database of preferences of its frequent guests that can be utilized to provide unexpected services to the guest, such as arranging the guest's favourite flowers in the room or serving a preferred tea.

Apart from the development of frameworks to incorporate technology into the traditional service encounter, several distinct research streams have emerged. For example, several authors have examined the adoption of self-service technology (Curran et al. 2003; Curran and Meuter 2005). Study findings indicate that different factors influence attitudes towards the adoption of different self-service technologies such as ATMs, phone and online banking. Another stream of research centres on the investigation of differences of traditional service encounters and technology-facilitated service encounters. For example, Colgate et al. (2005) noted differences in perceived relational benefits between traditional and Internet customers. Snellman and Vihtkari (2003) compared complaining behaviour in traditional and technology-based service encounters, with a particular focus on negative critical incidents in a retail banking setting. Contrary to predictions, the authors did not detect significant differences in the rates of complaints between the two service encounter types, suggesting the high incidence of traditional complaining behaviour as a possible explanation. However, customers who complained about technology-based service encounters experienced a greater response rate to their complaint from the provider than those who complained about traditional service encounters.

Finally, Hogg et al. (2003), in a study on professional health care service encounters, direct attention to the emergence of parallel service encounters whereby a consumer interacts with both technology and the health care professional. In particular, the Internet allows customers to obtain information about their condition, which, in turn, changes the nature of the face-to-face encounter with the health care professional and presents challenges to professionals in terms of relationships and their professional judgement. Similarly, in a hotel context, potential guests use the Internet to obtain information about facilities and services of a hotel property in addition to comparing its price on the hotel's website with that offered by various Internet vendors. In such instances, technology allows for more informed decision making with potential follow-on effects on guest expectations and the quality of the service encounter. Airlines are relying more and more on technology for the delivery of many services that were once done by staff on a personal face-to-face basis. For instance, customers book airline tickets online, sometimes arranging their own seat allocation prior to arriving at the airport, or they check themselves in on arrival and arrange a seat allocation, just leaving the task of depositing their luggage. These 'service encounters' are influenced by interaction with technology rather than a person.

Influences on the service encounter performance

Consumers' evaluation of a service encounter and any future decision-making process are affected by several factors. Broadly, these factors can be divided into environmental factors and individual and staff factors. To discuss the former, literature on atmospherics is assessed. The latter reviews literature pertaining to the effect of staff service pre-disposition and attitudes, communication skills, emotional labour and control or efficiency.

Atmospherics

Kotler (1973) introduced the term 'atmospherics' to refer to the intentional control and manipulation of environmental cues. Atmospherics bears close resemblance to Bitner's (1992) 'servicescape',[1] a reference to the built environment as opposed to the natural or social one that has the potential not only to create a firm's image but also to influence the behaviour and feelings of customers and employees.

Culture

A considerable growth in tourism has originated from non-Western countries. As greater mobility of tourists arises from countries, such as China, it calls into question the subject of how to deal with customers who might be used to a completely different set of norms in a service encounter. As we have already noted, service encounter interactions between customers and frontline staff consist of a mix of social, work and consumer behaviour. Thus, it is reasonable to expect that customers' cultural orientations can influence how they experience and evaluate service (Becker 2000). Lee and Sparks (2007) found that Chinese customers were especially concerned about 'protecting face' or avoiding embarrassing situations. As a consequence, care needs to be taken to maintain a harmonious service interaction when dealing with people from this culture. More work needs to be undertaken in this area to better understand how customers from different cultures evaluate service encounter experiences.

---

[1] This is discussed in detail in Chapter 3.

Staff attitude/service pre-disposition

Several studies have examined the requisite characteristics and skills of employees that will have an impact on consumer evaluations of service encounters. Basing his research on Bitner et al.'s work (Bitner et al. 1990; Gremler and Bitner 1992; Bitner et al. 1994), Varca (2004) proposed requisite skills for service providers along three dimensions: skills, personality and attitudes. Oral communication skills, stress tolerance, empathy, social sensitivity and behavioural flexibility rated highest. Jackson et al. (2002), in their analysis of job advertisements, found that the skills stated as necessary by employers in sales and personal services settings are social skills and personal characteristics. Likewise, a recent examination of nearly 100 human resource professionals in the United States responsible for hiring entry-level hospitality industry employees revealed that the top two criteria were pride in appearance and good attitude (Martin and Grove 2002). Literature abounds with reference to the need for 'soft skills' such as social and interpersonal skills as a critical requirement for hospitality staff (Burns 1997). Employees are expected to be responsive, courteous and understanding. More recently, Nickson et al. (2005) proposed the term 'aesthetic labour', referring to people who are employed on the basis of 'looking good' or 'sounding right'. While the initial selection of appropriate staff is critical for any hospitality business, continued training is equally important to ensure that service encounters are not only meeting but also exceeding customer expectations. The customization of the service experience by frontline employees is central in this context (Bettencourt and Gwinner 1996). Staff training as a means to managing the service encounter will be discussed later in this chapter.

Communication

Perhaps key to any service encounter, but especially a face-to-face interaction, is the communication aspect of the service. As many researchers (Czepiel 1990; Sparks and Callan 1992) acknowledge, the service encounter is very much about a social interaction. As a result, much of the research has at its core issues of communication. Indeed, Nikolich and Sparks (1995) argued that communication facilitates the task dimension of the service interaction while also having the potential to make the customer feel valued and important. Communication effectiveness is vital to the service encounter as it aids in optimizing the service delivery process. Moreover, communication, especially the interpersonal interactions between providers and customers, forms the basis of many service quality evaluations. Early work by Parasuraman et al. (1985) highlighted the importance of responsiveness, courtesy, empathy and communicative aspects of the service provider's behaviour in the evaluations consumers make about service purchases. Employers seem to recognize the importance of what might be called 'softer' service skills – those that are interpersonal in orientation. Nickson et al. (2005) found that employers rated social and interpersonal skills as highly important (99% agreement), much higher than they rated the importance of technical skills (48% agreement). They also found that employers believed applicants for service provider roles tended to lack the social and interpersonal skill required for the position (indeed this was as high as 88% believing this to be the case). Why is it that interpersonal skills are so important in the hospitality industry? One reason is that customers are easily able to determine whether they have received good service when they use interpersonal treatment as an indicator. Most of us know if we have been treated with respect, dignity and appropriate social standing (Bies 2001). As Gabbott and Hogg (2000) point out, within a service interaction there is a complex language of communication that takes place, which involves not only the spoken word but also a range of non-verbal behaviours. Non-verbal communication can actually make a significant difference as to how a customer might perceive an otherwise identical event. Using video stimulus material, Gabbott and Hogg (2000) were able to demonstrate that the same service event was evaluated quite differently when non-verbal communication varied.

Emotional labour

Implicitly, the service encounter demands the delivery of pleasant service. This is because to a large extent, there is an understanding that service providers' positive emotional displays are associated with matching consumer's positive affect. As a result, it is commonplace to hear the management mantra of 'service with a smile', as advocated by Pugh (2002). A rising interest in the concept of emotional labour is evident from the research literature (see for example, Grandey and Brauburger 2002). Emotional labour is the concept that service providers will manage their own emotional state, often suppressing actual felt emotions and engaging in acting out of other (sometimes not felt) emotions. In an effort to meet the demands of the job, such as those of a restaurant waiter, the employee might regulate his or her own emotions, modifying what is displayed in order to meet the role. Early research by Rafaeli and Sutton (1989) demonstrated that many service personnel are required to act in ways that may not be congruent with what is actually being felt emotionally. Related to emotional labour is the concept of emotional contagion, which conceptualizes the idea that the observation of another's emotional expression will invoke the same emotional reactions in the observer (Pugh 2002). For instance, a happy and smiling receptionist should engender similar feelings in the guest who is checking in. Thus, it is understandable that in hospitality jobs it is desirable for the service personnel to act in a welcoming and warm manner. However, as suggested, this may not be without challenges for the frontline staff member.

Control and efficiency

An issue for many hospitality firms is how to balance the control and efficiency of the operations. As Bateson (2000) has pointed out, the service encounter may sometimes be characterized by a 'three cornered' struggle for control. That is, the customer, the frontline service staff member, and the firm's management are all vying to control the encounter. Quite frequently the needs of each party might differ, which may result in some sense of struggle. Take for example the process of a guest checking into a hotel. The guest has a need for a speedy check in, getting a nice room (perhaps with an ocean view), the right configuration (a king-size bed) and friendly treatment. Meanwhile, the frontline service provider wants to get the correct paperwork completed and quick allocation of a room, all in an efficient manner. Once again, communication is central to the effective conduct of a service encounter. A considerable component of communication between the frontline staff member and the guest will revolve around getting specific tasks done, whether it be checking out of a hotel or arranging for a reservation to be made. Furthermore, management has views on how the service encounter might be conducted. This might lead to the service provider (frontline staff) having to meet efficiency targets rather than dedicating time to the customer. Such tensions can lead to feelings of a struggle between the parties to control the service encounter.

In summary, the very nature of most customer service work brings with it incredible demands, especially for pleasantness, smiles and a generally polite demeanour. Research has coined the term 'display rules' to describe what service staff are required to do as part of their everyday job. That is, within the service encounter, the staff are expected to suppress any negative emotions or feelings and display customer friendly, polite behaviour. At a broader level, this type of work is often called 'emotional labour'. The service encounter is the characteristic of the point in time that is very demanding emotionally, presenting management with many challenges to keep service staff motivated and happy. A considerable amount of communication work is about controlling the service encounter and making certain work-related actions in an efficient and speedy manner.

Evaluation of service encounters

Customer perceptions of service encounters are important elements of perceptions of quality, customer satisfaction, and service loyalty (e.g., Solomon et al. 1985; Bitner et al. 1990). Evaluation of a service encounter depends on several factors, including the attitudes of frontline staff and the behaviour of customers. Service encounters in which the expectations of customers are not met have received considerable attention in the literature. As noted by Hart et al. (1990), due to the number of uncontrollable factors and the nature of a service with its inherent characteristics, it is impossible to assure a 100% error-free service, that is, service failures are inevitable. Yet, Zemke and Bell (1990) noted that while in manufacturing industries allowances are typically made for breakage, spoilage or items that do not meet required standards, the same does not necessarily hold true for service systems that are often managed as though service failures are impossible.

Service failures

The probability of a service failure depends on a number of factors. For example, new employees, technology and first-time customers may increase service failure rates (Michel 2001). If a service failure occurs and customers experience dissatisfaction, they may either directly complain to the organization or alternatively simply engage in negative word-of-mouth communication that is detrimental to the organization (Blodgett et al. 1997). If the former is the case, the organization has an opportunity to rectify the situation by means of an effective service recovery. Therefore, while service failure is inevitable, dissatisfied customers are not, provided that the service recovery is effective (Hart et al. 1990). Service recovery has been defined as the actions a service provider takes in response to a service failure (Grönroos 1988), aimed at returning the customer to a state of satisfaction. However, service recovery has to go beyond putting things back to normal; it is critical to consider the kind of processes and outcomes that will enhance customer perceptions (Johnston 1995).

Service recovery

Several studies found that the ability to recover from a service failure favourably affects customers' evaluation of the service and the organization (Smith and Bolton 1998; Tax et al. 1998). Yet, according to a study by Hart et al. (1990), more than 50% of customers felt more negative about the organization after they had complained about a service failure. Therefore, not only an understanding of the importance of service recovery but also that of appropriate measures and procedures is critical. In this context, Sparks and McColl-Kennedy (2001) argued that while previous research has established the importance of effective service recovery, the exact measures and procedures appear to be much less established.

Recovering a failed service delivery can take several forms. Rectifying the original service breakdown is considered the most desirable option, though it may not always be feasible; for example, if a flight has been delayed (Sparks 2001). Explanations for the service failure, an apology, compensation in the form of a refund or discount and providing customer input into the service recovery process are additional measures service providers can draw upon in the service recovery process (Goodwin and Ross 1990; Hoffman et al. 1995; Blodgett et al. 1997). However, equally, and in many instances more important than the provision of these individual measures are the timeliness and the manner in which these service recovery measures are offered to the customer (Blodgett et al. 1993, 1997).

Sundaram et al. (1997) suggested that the more critical the consumption of a service is to a customer, the greater is that customer's desire for the service to be performed without major shortcomings; if shortcomings do arise, a greater effort will be expected from the provider's service recovery. Studies by Webster and Sundaram (1998), Tax et al. (1998) and Blodgett et al. (1997) confirmed the importance of service criticality. Hoffman and Kelley (2000) proposed a number of additional factors that impact the evaluation of service recovery effectiveness, namely the depth of the customer–service provider relationship, the duration and degree of customization of the service encounter and customers' switching costs. Consequently, the relative effectiveness of service recovery strategies is situation specific (Levesque and McDougall 2000).

Several studies suggested that a service provider's inability or unwillingness to recover effectively from a service failure and the consequent repeated disconfirmation of service expectations are likely to result in dissatisfied customers (Parasuraman et al. 1985; Johnston and Fern 1999). After all, customers experience what Bitner et al. (1990) referred to as a 'double deviation' from expectations in that the firm failed to deliver the initial service and then the service recovery. Conversely, effective service recovery may lead to customer satisfaction (Fornell and Wernerfelt 1987; Hart et al. 1990; Bitner et al. 1994; Johnston 1995). Service recovery effort has also been linked to satisfaction in that the greater the effort by a service provider to recover in an excellent manner, the greater the customer satisfaction (Goodwin and Ross 1992; Kelley and Davis 1994; Smith et al. 1999; Tax et al. 1998). Recognizing that staff may be unable to respond in a timely manner to a service failure, Colenutt and McCarville (1994) established that in some instances, the involvement of the customer in the service recovery following an explanation, apology and discount offer could lead to satisfaction.

Word-of-mouth communication refers to an exchange of thoughts, ideas, or comments between two or more consumers, none of whom is a marketing source (Mowen and Minor 1998). That is, they tell others, external to the transaction, of their (dis)pleasure with the service and service provider. The importance of effective service recovery is highlighted when considering that customers who experience a service failure tell 9–10 people about their poor service experience, while satisfied customers only tell four to five individuals about their positive experience (Collier 1995). Several studies confirmed that ineffective service recovery leads to negative word-of-mouth communication (Richins 1983; Bitner et al. 1994; Blodgett et al. 1995). Conversely, service recovery that is marked by courteous and respectful treatment is likely to result in positive word-of-mouth communication (Blodgett et al. 1997). Maxham (2001) noted that a high level of effort in service recovery resulted in greater positive word-of-mouth communication than only moderate service recovery effort.

In examining the effect of word-of-mouth communication, one has to take into consideration not only the impact on friends, relatives and colleagues but also the one resulting from submissions to a third party like a consumer claims tribunal following a service failure, whereby the ineffective service recovery becomes a matter of public record. If covered widely in the press, the impact on the service provider may be much more damaging and widespread than if confined to individual cases (Fisher et al. 1999).

Repeat purchase intentions are closely linked to customer satisfaction (Yi 1990). As is the case with customer satisfaction, a successful service recovery may also positively contribute to future repeat purchase intentions (Goodwin and Ross 1992; Blodgett et al. 1997; Sparks and Bradley 1997). Kelley et al. (1993) suggested that retention exceeded 70% for customers who experienced a satisfactory service recovery. Conversely, switching behaviour as a result of ineffective service recovery has also been reported, especially after a failure in a core service (Keaveney 1995; Dube and Maute 1996). Yet, even if a service failure is not resolved to the satisfaction of the customer, they may remain with the service provider. Switching costs; the lack of perceived alternatives; constraints in terms of time, money and choice; habit and inertia represent possible reasons (Bitner 1990). Alternatively, customers may switch to another firm even if satisfied with a service recovery: In these instances, constraining factors may be of a low magnitude (Colgate and Norris 2001). Therefore, it is important to differentiate between positive attitudes about a service provider and repeat purchase when discussing loyalty (Dick and Basu 1994).

Loyalty is of importance to a firm for a number of reasons. Loyal customers are the most profitable customers since they tend to spend more over a long time period. The 'lifetime' value of loyal customers can be enormous (Reichheld and Sasser 1990). At the same time, costs can be substantially decreased. Furthermore, loyal customers represent a source of positive word-of-mouth communication, often resulting in referral business. The customer retention model developed by Bain & Company illustrates how the creation and maintenance of a relationship generates profit (Jacob 1994). Repeat sales, reduced selling costs, increased customer value and increased new business from referrals are all factors contributing to increased profitability.

Multiple service encounters

Researchers have devoted considerable attention to the study of service failure and recovery in recent years (Tax et al. 1998; Smith et al. 1999; DeWitt and Brady 2003). Yet, the vast majority of previous research has concentrated on the impact of a single service failure event, in part facilitated by the critical incident technique. However, the evaluation of multiple service encounters results in overall service evaluations (Bolton and Drew 1991). Numerous studies confirmed that there is a high correlation between the evaluation of service encounters and more global service evaluation measures (Bitner and Hubbert 1994; Surprenant and Solomon 1987).

More recently, several researchers have begun to investigate how multiple service failure events over an extended time period influence consumer evaluations (Mittal et al. 1999, 2001), consistent with the notion of a distinction between encounter and cumulative satisfaction (Bitner and Hubbert 1994). However, research to date has neglected the investigation of the effects of service encounters in situations in which two or more service organizations are involved in the service provision, as is the case in strategic alliance settings.

Weber (2006) investigated the link between service failure events and more global evaluations of organizations and their partners. She based her research program on work by Cropanzano et al. (2001), who have recently suggested that the investigation of justice has tended to pay attention to one of two paradigms: the event paradigm or the social entity paradigm. In the event paradigm, researchers have investigated a range of microelements that lead to the formation of event fairness judgements. Thus, a customer may evaluate a service event on the basis of distributive, procedural or interactional justice elements. In contrast, other researchers have focused on the evaluation of the social entity (either a service provider as a person or the organization as a whole). Thus, from this perspective, customers make more global judgements about the fairness of the service provider or organization overall. Weber's work is situated within the airline industry and investigates micro service failure events as well as the implications for airline and alliances brands. Her research found that consumers form both justice perceptions of an entity for a particular event and justice perceptions at a more global, general level. These justice perceptions are related to all four dimensions of justice: distributive, procedural, interactional and informational justice. Event and global fairness were identified as additional consumer evaluations whereby the event fairness refers to a summary judgement of an entity in a particular situation, based on an evaluation and weighing of individual event justice perceptions. In contrast, global fairness relates to a summary judgement of an entity in general, based on an evaluation of event fairness and global justice perceptions over time and across events.

So what do service encounters across organizations that are affiliated, either loosely in a network or more closely in a strategic alliance, mean for the hospitality industry? Research on the positivity effect and brand alliances (Rao et al. 1999; Folkes and Patrick 2003) points to the potential transfer of consumer perceptions of the actions of a single employer in a firm to that of the entire firm and from one brand to another, respectively. However, in a service failure context that involves various alliance partners, Weber's (2006) findings showed that the effect of interactional justice is confined to the organization dealing with the service failure, that is, there appears to be no transfer in consumer perceptions and subsequent responses from the actions of one alliance partner to other alliance entities. In other words, if an employee of a hospitality business is courteous and respectful and displays empathy, or alternatively is rude and does not expend effort when addressing a service failure, their actions will not automatically affect a customer's perceptions of the alliance partner.

Managing the service encounter

This chapter has covered quite a bit of ground in terms of reviewing the extant literature on service encounters and related topics. It now turns to addressing some key aspects a manager might want to consider to optimize the service encounter. From the perspective of operations management, there are a number of issues to consider.

Selection and recruitment of suitable employees

Identifying the right employees is not an easy task but the one that managers should be focused on. Perhaps all too often in the hospitality industry, there is a tendency to place a low priority on recruitment and selection, especially when it comes to small or medium-sized businesses. On the basis of the review presented in this chapter, it would be advisable for managers to focus on appointing staff who have a customer-oriented attitude, which is depicted by the ability to communicate effectively, work as part of a team, are resilient to customer and emotional demands and understand the importance of the service encounter within the broader context of service quality.

Appropriate induction and training of employees

Once employees have been appointed, managers must provide appropriate induction programs to set the standard of what is expected from an employee. It is essential to remember that people (staff) are the face of most service organizations. It is the frontline staff member who welcomes the customer and facilitates a smooth transaction. Training programs to assist in both the delivery of task related activities and communication skills relevant to the service encounter are required. Supervisors or managers can ensure that service personnel operate with some sort of script to deliver friendly and polite service. Often, in many part of the hospitality industry, personnel are recruited without any basic skills in customer service. As a result, managers must identify quality training programs that will ensure that the customer experience is enhanced whenever there is a 'moment of truth'.

Providing appropriate levels of empowerment in the job role

Some researchers have investigated the topic of empowerment (Lashley 1995) and provide a compelling argument for ensuring that the frontline staff has the latitude in decision making to provide satisfying service to the customer. McColl-Kennedy and Sparks (2003) showed that the ability of the frontline personnel to think more laterally about feasible options was a key factor in determining customers' satisfaction with the organization. In a series of focus groups, respondents recounted incidents where negative perceptions and feelings were increased because employees could not or did not offer any possible options or solutions for customers who had experienced a service failure. If managers can work toward empowering the frontline staff to use their own initiative to deal with customer problems, it is likely that a more customer-focused work environment will result.

Systems for optimizing the service encounter

Managers need to ensure that there are good systems in place to facilitate the offering of service to customers. This requires undertaking various analyses of the service delivery processes. Some researchers have suggested using service blueprints (Shostack 1992) to gain insight to the overall service process and to identify any points in the process that may be subject to error. A blueprint provides a visual representation of the activities and the subsequent sequence of events required for providing a customer with a service. Blueprints cover the activities that are both front and back of house. Service encounter contacts can be depicted in a blueprint diagram, and a manager can attempt to identify any vulnerable points. By plotting the components of service in this manner, a manager can also provide a training tool to staff so that additional care can be taken to optimize customer satisfaction points. Managers in hospitality firms should also monitor the delivery of service via feedback mechanisms such as customer satisfaction questionnaires.

Mechanisms to monitor the performance of staff in the service encounter role

Managers can monitor performance through various mechanisms including mystery shoppers, observation by supervisors and the development of rating criteria to be used in assessment.[2] Much of this material can be used to provide ongoing feedback to service staff. As Hinkin and Schriesheim (2004) note, it is not uncommon for hospitality service personnel to be uninformed about the day-to-day quality of their job performance. A conclusion to be drawn (Hinkin and Schriesheim 2004) is that feedback is vital and it should focus on behaviour. By focusing on behaviour, it provides an opportunity for the frontline staff to learn and mould behaviour to that most effective service. Testa and Sipe (2006) provide an overview of a systems-based approach to improving service delivery and suggestions on how to improve service:

- define and communicate issues;
- train and educate employees;
- improve processes;
- evaluate results and provide feedback;
- celebrate successes.

Within each of these five areas Testa and Sipe (2006) suggest using a range of tools to facilitate the objective under consideration. Thus, under 'train and educate', a tool might include a service standards workshop aimed at improving communication between the frontline staff and customers.

---

[2] These are discussed in Chapter 13.

Summary and conclusion

The service encounter is an important point in the delivery of hospitality services. It is the time when customers come into contact with the firm and ultimately make a range of evaluations about the firm and their own desire to patronize or recommend the firm to others. The service encounter is dynamic and varies from one episode to another. However, there are a number of scripted or ritualized aspects of the service encounter that assist in its efficiency. Service encounters can be considered discrete one-off events, accumulated events or a chain of events. Similarly, service encounters can occur in multiple but linked organizations (such as an alliance) and result in evaluations that might affect affiliated organizations. A key aspect of the service encounter is the communication that occurs and encompasses both verbal and non-verbal aspects. The service encounter is also subject to failure, and negative experiences are likely to result in negative outcomes such as customer dissatisfaction, the loss of customers and negative word-of-mouth communication. Managers need to be proactive to optimize the service encounter. Actions can include selecting appropriate service-oriented staff, providing regular training on the service encounter, ensuring that staff are empowered to deal with issues arising in the service encounter and monitoring the effectiveness of service delivery at the frontline.

References

Bateson, J. E. G. (2000) Perceived control and the service experience, In Swartz, T. A. and Iacobucci, D. (Eds.), *Handbook of Services Marketing and Management*, Sage Publication: Thousand Oaks, CA

Becker, C. (2000) Service recovery strategies: the impact of cultural differences, *Journal of Hospitality and Tourism Research*, 24, 4, 526–538

Bettencourt, L. A. and Gwinner, K. (1996) Customization of the service experience: the role of the frontline employee, *International Journal of Service Industry Management*, 7, 2, 3–20

Bies, R. J. (2001) Interactional (in)justice: the sacred and the profane, In Greeberg, J. and Cropanzano, R. (Eds.), *Advances in Organizational Justice*, Stanford University Press: Stanford, CA, 89–118

Bitner, M. (1990) Evaluating service encounters: the effects of physical surroundings and employee responses, *Journal of Marketing*, 54, 2, 69–82

Bitner, M. J. (1992) Servicescapes: the impact of physical surroundings on customers and employees, *Journal of Marketing*, 56, 2, 57–71

Bitner, M. J., Booms, B. H. and Mohr, L. A. (1994) Critical service encounters: the employee's viewpoint, *Journal of Marketing*, 58, 4, 95–106

Bitner, M. J., Booms, B. H. and Tetreault, M. S. (1990) The service encounter: diagnosing favorable and unfavourable incidents, *Journal of Marketing*, 54, 1, 71–84

Bitner, M. J., Brown, S. W. and Meuter, M. L. (2000) Technology infusion in service encounters, *Journal of the Academy of Marketing Science*, 28, 1, 138–149

Bitner, M. J. and Hubbert, A. R. (1994) Encounter satisfaction versus overall satisfaction versus quality: the customer's voice, In Rust, R. T. and Oliver, R. L. (Eds.), *Service Quality: New Directions in Theory and Practice*, Sage Publication: Thousand Oaks, CA, 72–94

Blodgett, J. G., Granbois, D. H. and Walters, R. G. (1993) The effects of perceived justice on complainants' negative word-of -mouth behavior and repatronage intentions, *Journal of Retailing*, 69, 4, 399–428

Blodgett, J. G., Hill, D. J. and Tax, S. S. (1997) The effects of distributive, procedural and interactional justice on postcomplaint behaviour, *Journal of Retailing*, 73, 2, 185–210

Blodgett, J. G., Wakefield, K. L. and Barnes, J. H. (1995) The effects of customer service on consumer postcomplaining behaviour, *Journal of Services Marketing*, 9, 4, 31–42

Bolton, R. N. and Drew, J. H. (1991) A multistage model of customers' assessment of service quality and value, *Journal of Consumer Research*, 17, 4, 375–84

Burns, P. M. (1997) Hard-skills, soft-skills: undervaluing hospitality's 'service with a smile', *Progress in Tourism and Hospitality Research*, 3, 3, 239–248

Chandon, J. L., Leo, P. Y. and Philippe, J. (1997) Service encounter dimensions – a dyadic perspective: measuring the dimensions of service encounters as perceived by customers and personnel, *International Journal of Service Industry Management*, 8, 1, 65–86

Chung, B. G. and Schneider, B. (2002) Serving multiple masters: role conflict experienced by service employees, *Journal of Services Marketing*, 16, 1, 70–87

Colenutt, C. E. and McCarville, R. E. (1994) The client as problem solver: a new look at service recovery, *Journal of Hospitality and Leisure Marketing*, 2, 3, 23–35

Colgate, M., Buchanan-Oliver, M. and Elmsly, R. (2005) Relationship benefits in an Internet environment, *Managing Service Quality*, 15, 5, 426–436

Colgate, M. and Norris, M. (2001) Developing a comprehensive picture of service failure, *International Journal of Service Industry Management*, 12, 3, 215–233

Collier, D. A. (1995) Modeling the relationships between process quality errors and overall service process performance, *Journal of Service Industry Management*, 64, 4, 4–19

Cropanzano, R., Byrne, Z. S., Bobocel, D. R. and Rupp, D. E. (2001) Moral virtues, fairness heuristics, social entities, and other denizens of organizational justice, *Journal of Vocational Behaviour*, 58, 2, 164–209

Curran, J. M. and Meuter, M. L. (2005) Self-service technology adoption: comparing three technologies, *Journal of Services Marketing*, 19, 2, 103–113

Curran, J. M., Meuter, M. L. and Surprenant, C. F. (2003) Intentions to use self-service technologies: a confluence of multiple attitudes, *Journal of Service Research*, 5, 3, 209–224

Czepiel, J. A. (1990) Service encounters and service relationships: implications for research, *Journal of Business Research*, 20, 1, 13–21

Czepiel, J. A., Solomon, M. R., Surprenant, C. F. and Gutman, E. G. (1985) Service encounters: an overview, In Czepiel, J. A., Solomon, M. R. and Surprenant, C. F. (Eds.), *The Service Encounter: Managing Employee/Customer Interaction in Service Businesses*, Lexington Books: Lexington, MA, 3–15

DeWitt, T. and Brady, M. K. (2003) Rethinking service recovery strategies: the effect of rapport on consumer responses to service failure, *Journal of Service Research*, 6, 2, 193–207

Dick, A. S. and Basu, K. (1994) Customer loyalty: toward an integrated conceptual framework, *Journal of the Academy of Marketing Science*, 22, 2, 99–113

Dube, L. and Maute, M. (1996) The antecedents of brand switching, brand loyalty and verbal responses to service failure, In Swartz, T. A., Bowen, D. E. and Brown, S. W. (Eds.), *Advances in Services Marketing and Management*, Vol. 5, JAI Press: Greenwich, CT, 127–151

Fisher, J. E., Garrett, D. E., Arnold, M. J. and Ferris, M. E. (1999) Dissatisfied consumers who complain to the better business bureau, *Journal of Consumer Marketing*, 16, 6, 576–589

Folkes, V. S. and Patrick, V. M. (2003) The positivity effect in perceptions of services: seen one, seen them all? *Journal of Consumer Research*, 30, 1, 125–137

Fornell, T. C. and Wernerfelt, B. (1987) Defensive marketing strategy by customer complaint management: a theoretical analysis, *Journal of Marketing Research*, 24, 4, 337–46

Gabbott, M. and Hogg, G. (2000) An empirical investigation of the impact of non-verbal communication on service evaluation, *European Journal of Marketing,* 34, 3/4, 384–398

González, J. V. and Garazo, T. G. (2006) Structural relationships between organizational service orientation, contact employee job satisfaction and citizenship behaviour, *International Journal of Service Industry Management,* 17, 1, 23–50

Goodwin, C. and Ross, I. (1990) Consumer evaluations of responses to complaints: what's fair and why, *Journal of Consumer Marketing,* 7, 2, 39–47

Goodwin, C. and Ross, I. (1992) Consumer responses to service failures: influence of procedural and interactional fairness perceptions, *Journal of Business Research,* 25, 2, 149–163

Grandey, A. and Brauburger, A. (2002) The emotional regulation behind the customer service smile, In Lord, R., Klimoski, R. and Kanfer, R. (Eds.), *Emotions in the Workplace,* Jossey-Bass: San Francisco, CA, 260–294

Gremler, D. and Bitner, M. J. (1992) *Classifying service encounter satisfaction across industries.* Proceedings of the American Marketing Association Summer Educators. Chicago, IL, 346–352

Grönroos, C. (1988) Service quality: the six criteria of good perceived service quality, *Review of Business,* 9, 3, 10–13

Gutek, B. A. (1995) *The Dynamics of Service: Reflections on the Changing Nature of Customer/Provider Interactions*, Jossey-Bass: San Francisco, CA

Gutek, B. A., Bhappu, A. D., Liao-Troth, M. A. and Cherry, B. (1999) Distinguishing between service relationships and encounters, *Journal of Applied Psychology,* 84, 2, 218–233

Hansen, D. E. and Danaher, P. J. (1999) Inconsistent performance during the service encounter: what's a good start worth? *Journal of Service Research*, 1, 3, 227–235

Harari, O. (1991) Should internal customers exist? *Management Review,* 80, 7, 41–43

Hart, C. W. L., Heskett, J. L. and Sasser, W. E. (1990) The profitable art of service recovery, *Harvard Business Review,* 68, 4, 148–156

Hinkin, T. R. and Schriesheim, C. A. (2004) "If you don't hear from me you know you are doing fine": the effects of management nonresponse to employee performance, *Cornell Hotel and Restaurant Administration Quarterly*, 45, 4, 362–372

Hoffman, K. D. and Kelley, S. W. (2000) Perceived justice needs and recovery evaluation: a contingency approach, *European Journal of Marketing,* 34, 3/4, 418–432

Hoffman, K. D., Kelley, S. W. and Rotalsky, H. M. (1995) Tracking service failures and employee recovery efforts, *Journal of Services Marketing,* 9, 2, 49–61

Hogg, G., Laing, A. and Winkelman, D. (2003) The professional service encounter in the age of the Internet: an exploratory study, *Journal of Services Marketing*, 17, 5, 476–494

Jackson, M., Goldthorpe, J. and Mills, C. (2002) *Education, employers, and class mobility.* Paper presented at the International Sociological Association Research Committee 28 Meeting, University of Oxford, Oxford

Jacob, R. (1994) Why some customers are more equal than others, *Fortune*, 149–154

Johnston, R. (1995) Service failure and recovery: impact, attributes and process, In Swartz, T. A., Bowen, D. E. and Brown, S. W. (Eds.), *Advances in Services Marketing and Management*, Vol. 4, JAI Press Inc.: London, 211–228

Johnston, R. and Fern, A. (1999) Service recovery strategies for single and double deviation scenarios, *The Service Industries Journal*, 19, 2, 69–82

Keaveney, S. M. (1995) Customer switching behaviour in service industries: an exploratory study, *Journal of Marketing*, 59, 2, 71–82

Kelley, S. W. and Davis, M. A. (1994) Antecedents to customer expectations for service recovery, *Journal of the Academy of Marketing Science*, 22, 1, 52–61

Kelley, S. W., Hoffman, K. D. and Davis, M. A. (1993) A typology of retail failures and recoveries, *Journal of Retailing*, 69, 4, 429–452

Kotler, P. (1973) Atmospherics as a marketing tool, *Journal of Retailing*, 49, 4, 48–64

Kotler, P. and Armstrong, G. (1991) *Principles of Marketing*, Prentice Hall: Englewood Cliff, NJ

Lashley, C. (1995) Towards an understanding of employee empowerment in hospitality services, *International Journal of Contemporary Hospitality management*, 7, 1, 27–32

Lee, Y. L. and Sparks, B. A. (2007) Gaining a better understanding of Chinese perceptions of service failure and service recovery within the hospitality industry, *Journal of Hospitality and Tourism Research*, 31, 4, 504–529

Levesque, T. J. and McDougall, G. H. G. (2000) Service problems and recovery: an experiment, *Canadian Journal of Administrative Science*, 17, 1, 20–37

Martin, L. and Grove, J. (2002) Interview as a selection tool for entry-level hospitality employees, *Journal of Human Resources in Hospitality and Tourism*, 1, 1, 41–47

Maxham, J. G. (2001) Service recovery's influence on consumer satisfaction, positive word-of-mouth, and purchase intentions, *Journal of Business Research*, 54, 1, 11–24

McColl-Kennedy, J. R. and Sparks, B. A. (2003) Application of fairness theory to service failures and service recovery, *Journal of Service Research*, 5, 3, 251–266

Michel, S. (2001) Analyzing service failures and recoveries: a process approach, *International Journal of Service Industry Management*, 12, 1, 20–33

Mittal, V., Katrichis, J. M. and Kumar, P. (2001) Attribute performance and customer satisfaction over time: evidence from two field studies, *Journal of Services Marketing*, 15, 5, 343–356

Mittal, V., Kumar, P. and Tsiros, M. (1999) Attribute-level performance, satisfaction, and behavioral intentions over time: a consumption-system approach, *Journal of Marketing*, 63, 2, 88–101

Mowen, J. C. and Minor, M. (1998) *Consumer Behaviour*, Prentice-Hall: Upper Saddle River, NJ

Nickson, D., Warhurst, C. and Dutton, E. (2005) The importance of attitude and appearance in the service encounter in retail and hospitality, *Managing Service Quality*, 15, 2, 195–208

Nikolich, M. A. and Sparks, B. A. (1995) The hospitality service encounter: the role of communication, *Hospitality Research Journal*, 19, 2, 43–56

Paraskevas, A. (2001) Internal service encounters in hotels: an empirical study, *International Journal of Contemporary Hospitality Management*, 13, 6, 285–292

Parasuraman, A. (1996, 5 October). *Understanding and leveraging the role of customer service in external, interactive, and internal marketing.* Paper presented at the Frontiers in Services, Nashville, TN

Parasuraman, A., Zeithaml, V. and Berry, L. L. (1985) A conceptual model of service quality and its implications for future research, *Journal of Marketing*, 49, 4, 41–50

Pugh, S. D. (2002) Emotional regulation in individuals and dyads: causes, costs and consequences, In Lord, R. G., Klimoski, R. J. and Kanfer, R. (Eds.), *Emotions in the Workplace*, Jossey-Bass: San Francisco, CA, 147–182

Rafaeli, A. and Sutton R. (1989) The expression of emotion in organisational life, In Straw, L. C. B. (Ed.), *Research in Organisational Behavior*, Vol. 11, JAI Press: Greenwich, CT

Rao, A. R., Qu, L. and Ruekert, R. W. (1999) Signalling unobservable quality through a brand ally, *Journal of Marketing Research*, 36, 2, 258–268

Reichheld, F. F. and Sasser, W. E. (1990) Zero defections: quality comes to services. *Harvard Business Review*, 68, 5, 105–111

Richins, M. L. (1983) Negative word-of-mouth by dissatisfied consumers: a pilot study, *Journal of Marketing*, 47, 1, 68–78

Rosenbluth, H. (1991) Tales from a nonconformist company, *Harvard Business Review*, 69, 4, 26–36

Shostack, G. L. (1985) Planning the service encounter, In Czepiel, J. A., Solomon, M. R. and Suprenant, C. F. (Eds.), *The Service Encounter: Managing Employee/Customer Interaction in Service Businesses*, Lexington Books: Lexington, MA, 243–254

Shostack, G. L. (1992) Understanding services through blueprinting. In Swartz, T. A., Bowen, D. E. and Brown, S. W. (Eds.), *Advances in Services Marketing and Management: Research and Practice*, Vol. 1, JAI Press: Greenwich, CT, 75–90

Smith, A. K. and Bolton, R. N. (1998) An experimental investigation of customer reactions to service failure and recovery encounters: paradox of peril? *Journal of Services Research*, 1, 65–81

Smith, A. K., Bolton, R. N. and Wagner, J. (1999) A model of customer satisfaction with service encounters involving failure and recovery, *Journal of Marketing Research*, 36, 3, 356–372

Snellman, K. and Vihtkari, T. (2003) Customer complaining behaviour in technology-based service encounters, *International Journal of Service Industry Management*, 14, 2, 217–231

Solomon, M. R., Surprenant, C., Czepiel, J. A. and Gutman, E. G. (1985) A role theory perspective on dyadic interactions: the service encounter, *Journal of Marketing*, 49, 1, 99–111

Sparks, B. (2001) Managing service failure through recovery, In Kandampully, J., Mok, C. and Sparks, B. (Eds.), *Service Quality Management in Hospitality, Tourism, and Leisure*, Haworth Press: New York, 193–221

Sparks, B. and Bradley, G. (1997) Antecedents and consequences of perceived service provider effort in the hospitality industry, *Hospitality Research Journal*, 20, 3, 17–34

Sparks B. and Callan V. J. (1992) Communication and the service encounter: the value of convergence, *International Journal of Hospitality Management*, 11, 3, 213–224

Sparks, B. and McColl-Kennedy, J. R. (2001) Justice strategy options for increased customer satisfaction in a services recovery setting, *Journal of Business Research*, 54, 3, 209–218

Stewart, T. A. (1997, 3 February). Another fad worth killing, *Fortune*, 135, 2, 119–120

Sundaram, D. S., Jurowski, C. and Webster, C. (1997) Service failure recovery efforts in restaurant dining: the role of criticality of service consumption, *Hospitality Research Journal*, 20, 3, 137–149

Surprenant, C. F. and Solomon, M. R. (1987) Predictability and personalization in the service encounter, *Journal of Marketing*, 51, 2, 86–96

Svensson, G. (2004) A customized construct of sequential service quality in service encounter chains: time, context, and performance threshold, *Managing Service Quality*, 14, 6, 468–475

Tax, S. S., Brown, S. W. and Chandrashekaran, M. (1998) Customer evaluations of service complaint experiences: implications for relationship marketing, *Journal of Marketing*, 62, 2, 60–76

Testa, M. R. and Sipe, L. J. (2006) A systems approach to service quality: tools for hospitality leaders, *Cornell Hotel and Restaurant Administration Quarterly*, 47, 1, 36–48

Varca, P. E. (2004) Service skills for service workers: emotional intelligence and beyond, *Managing Service Quality*, 14, 6, 457–467

Verhoef, P. C., Antonides, G. and Hoog, A. N. d. (2004) Service encounters as a sequence of events: the importance of peak experiences, *Journal of Service Research*, 7, 1, 53–64

Weber, K. (2006) Consumer responses to service failure events in strategic alliances: a justice theory perspective, PhD thesis, Griffith University, Queensland, Australia

Webster, C. and Sundaram, D. S. (1998) Service consumption criticality in failure recovery, *Journal of Business Research*, 41, 2, 153–159

Yi, Y. (1990) *A critical review of consumer satisfaction.* Paper presented at the American Marketing Association, Chicago

Yoon, M. H., Beatty, S. E. and Suh, J. (2001) The effect of work climate on critical employee and customer outcomes: an employee-level analysis, *International Journal of Service Industry Management*, 12, 5, 500–521

Zemke, R. and Bell, C. (1990) Service recovery: doing it right the second time, *Training*, 27, 6, 42–48

Electronic distribution

Peter O'Connor

Professor, Information Systems
Essec Business School, France

Introduction

Technology fulfils a number of roles in hospitality and tourism, acting as 'a creator, protector, enhancer, focal point and/ or destroyer of the tourism experience' (Stipanuk 1993: 267). However, many believe that technology's greatest impact on this industry is on how the product is being sold. Electronic channels of distribution, particularly those enabled by the Internet, have forever changed the way in which tourism suppliers interact with the customer. This is clearly an operations management issue, as well as a marketing one.

The network of distribution channels (electronic and traditional) continues to rapidly evolve, and has been identified as one of the five most volatile factors affecting the hotel industry (Olsen et al. 1995). To gain an understanding of the importance and complexity of this arena, this chapter explores the development of hotel electronic channels of distribution. Research into how such channels should be managed is explored, and gaps in our current knowledge highlighted. The chapter is divided into three main sections. The first examines distribution, in general, to identify developments in the electronic arena. This is followed by an analysis of the growth of electronic channels, particularly those based on the Web, and the effect they have had on how tourism is being distributed. Lastly, current issues in the management of electronic distribution are explored, and the lack of quality and empirical research in the area highlighted.

Channels of distribution

The manner in which companies bring their products to the marketplace is a cornerstone of any competitive strategy. In their landmark paper, Porter and Millar (1985) specifically cite distribution as one of the primary – as opposed to support – activities of a firm, highlighting its importance for long-term success. Effective distribution is particularly important for hotels, where the product it is highly perishable (Vialle 1995). A hotel room left unsold cannot be stored and subsequently offered for sale at a later date. Revenue is effectively lost forever, making the sale of each room each night at an optimum price extremely important for profitability.[1]

Channels of distribution form a key element in meeting this challenge. A channel of distribution has been defined as any organized and serviced system, created or utilized to provide

---

[1]This is discussed further in Chapter 11.

convenient points of sale and/or access to consumers, away from the location of production and consumption, and paid for out-of-marketing budgets (Middleton 1994). In general, companies need help in distributing their products. With physical goods (e.g. a soft drink), arrangements must be made to get the product to where the customer can buy it. The distribution channel helps move the good from the producer to the consumer, overcoming the major time, place and possession gaps that separate it from those who would use it. Intermediaries, be they wholesalers or brokers, typically play a critical role in this process. Through their contacts, experience, specialization and scale of operation, intermediaries allow firms to gain better access to markets that they could working on their own (Kotler et al. 1996).

With physical products, the intermediary often takes possession of the product to be distributed, making concepts such as product flow, ownership flow and title transfer important. However, with less tangible products such as a hotel stay, it is information – about availability, prices, qualities and convenience – that is transferred (Poon 1993). While some might argue that the concept of a distribution channel, thus, does not apply, others feel that it is even more applicable (Duke and Persia 1993). Middleton (1994) points out that the inability to create physical stocks of products adds to, rather than reduces, the importance of distribution process. Creating and facilitating access for consumers is one of the principal ways to manage demand for highly perishable products.

One of the key functions of a distribution channel is to get the product from its producer to where the customer can buy it. However, with hotel rooms, the hotelier is usually both the producer and seller simultaneously (Lewis et al. 1995). The challenge, therefore, is not how to get the product to the retailer, but how to get the customer to the hotel. The literature suggests that this is best achieved by making it as convenient as possible for customers to find and book the hotel. In fact, Go and Pine (1995: 307) define a channel of distribution as one that provides 'sufficient information to the right people at the right time and in the right place to allow a purchase decision to be made, and to provide a mechanism where the consumer can make a reservation and pay for the required product'.

Information has been described as the 'lifeblood' of tourism, as without it, a potential customer's ability to book is severely limited (Wagner 1991). The intangibility, heterogeneity and diversity of the tourism product mean that consumers depend on accurate, timely, high-quality information to help them differentiate among competing properties (Poon 1994). Recent changes in society have heightened this need. Time is a scarce commodity for most consumers, making leisure travel an important emotional investment that cannot be easily replaced if something goes wrong (Pollock 1995). This makes the annual holiday or even the weekend break risky, which has prompted consumers to seek out as much information as possible to both reduce risk and bridge the gap between expectations and experience (Zsamboky 1998). This heightened information search makes the fast, efficient exchange of data – between the hotel and the customer; the hotel and intermediaries; and intermediaries and the customer – increasingly important in the distribution process (O'Brien 1999).

Travellers have traditionally acquired information from a wide variety of sources, including directly from the hotel itself or through various travel intermediaries. *Travel agents* act as advisors to the customer, relieving them of much of the burden of searching for suitable products and using their prior know-ledge and experience to help match customers with travel experiences. In many cases, they also act as a reservation serv-ice, completing the booking on behalf of the end consumer (Palmer and McCole 2000). *Tour operators*, on the other hand, act as consolidators, packaging various travel components (such as air, hotel, car hire, transfers and other destination serv-ices) together and marketing them as a single seamless product, which may subsequently be sold directly or through the travel agent network. Some national and regional *tourism organiza-tions* also act as intermediaries, distributing information and processing bookings for suppliers in their region (Laws 1997). In each case, the intermediary's prime objectives are to facilitate the search and purchase processes. Information flow is critical, to the extent that Poon (1994) maintains that there is in effect a dual production system in tourism. While suppliers naturally have to produce products (in this case, hotel room nights), to survive, they must also distribute information about the price, availability, quality, convenience and conditions of purchase of their product. Poon claims that, in the case of travel products, this provision of appropriate information is as important for success as the quality of the actual products themselves.

Information has traditionally been provided to both end con-sumer and intermediary as printed media (such as brochures, guidebooks or flyers). However, developing such material is costly, time consuming and labour intensive. More importantly, its content is static by definition, while much of the data needed to make a reservation (e.g. availability and rates) is dynamic and changes frequently. Applying information technology to this function is a natural development of Porter's theory of com-petitive advantage. Porter and Millar (1985) point out that value chain activities that represent a large proportion of overall costs need to be carefully scrutinized as it is here that opportunities exist for competitive advantage. This is particularly true where such activities 'have a significant information processing component or are critical to differentiation' (Porter and Millar 1985: 152). As we have seen, hotel distribution is both information intensive and critical for placement with both consumers and intermediaries. Within tourism, distribution also typically represents a significant proportion of overall costs, making the application of information technology to distribution very logical (O'Connor and Frew 1998). For this reason, information-technology-based systems, or electronic distribution systems, have become an almost universal feature of tourism (Bennett 1993).

In addition to disseminating information, distribution channels have a second but equally important function – providing a mechanism for customers to make a booking (Castleberry et al. 1998). The convenience with which consumers can purchase is critical, particularly when the sale is being facilitated through an intermediary, who by definition has an interest in handling the most easily sold products and could direct clients to competing suppliers if their product is more easily accessible (Bennett 1993). In the past, the booking process involved the customer (or their agent) contacting the hotel during the limited opening hours of the reservations department to confirm availability and rate; comparing them with proposals from other suppliers; and then re-contacting the hotel to make a reservation (Bennett 1996). Distribution took at least three steps – searching, contacting and finally booking – which were ineffective and inefficient for all concerned. Electronic systems allow travellers to make reservations in a fraction of the time, cost and inconvenience characteristic of manual methods by directly interacting with the hotel's reservation system (Connell and Reynolds 1999). Given such benefits, the use of electronic distribution within tourism would appear to be a foregone conclusion. However, diffusion has not affected all sections of the industry equally. The growth of electronic distribution channels in the hotel sector is examined next.

The development of hotel electronic distribution

In *Being Digital*, Negroponte described the convergence of IT, telecommunications and content as the single most important event shaping the business environment (Negroponte 1995). This digital convergence is part of a trend driving computers to ubiquity in everyday life – so much so that they are deemed essential for survival in today's world – and giving rise to a digital economy where speed, agility, connectivity and the ability to amass and subsequently employ knowledge are key competitive ingredients (Tapscott 1996). In the hospitality industry, electronic distribution channels represent the quintessential example of the convergence of technology, communications and content.

According to Karcher (1995), electronic distribution systems in tourism began as inventory systems implemented by the airlines in early 1960s. Originally developed as internal control systems, their scope was expanded in the early 1970s by installing terminals in travel agencies and the travel departments of large firms, giving customers direct access to flight availability and pricing information, as well as the ability to make reservations directly on the system. Making such facilities available in this way greatly reduced administrative and labour costs, while at the same time greatly increasing the efficiency of the booking process (O'Connor 1999).

Deregulation of the U.S. airline industry in the 1970s accelerated system adoption. New airlines, coupled with more competition on each route, resulted in an exponential increase in the number of fare options available, making the use of a computerized system to a large extent essential to help untangle the complex range of options available (Hitchins 1991). Developing and operating such systems was expensive. As the investment could not be recouped based solely on the transaction fees generated from airline segments, most of these developing Global Distribution Systems (GDS) incorporated complementary travel products alongside their airline flights (Knowles and Garland 1994). As a result, today's GDS distribute a broad range of travel products, including scheduled and charter airline flights, hotels and other forms of accommodation, car rental, package holidays, ferry, rail and bus tickets, cruise packages, yachting, excursions, theatre tickets and even flowers and champagne. In effect, they provide a one-stop-shop for all the information and reservation needs of a travel agent (Emmer et al. 1993).

One of the first complementary products distributed through GDS was hotel accommodation. Although traditionally reluctant to embrace technology (Siguaw et al. 2000), with electronic distribution systems, hotels were able to benefit from the experience gained by the airline companies (Schulz 1994). At first, many tried to incorporate room inventory directly onto the airline systems. However, as the GDS were designed specifically to distribute airline seats, incorporating the data requirements of the more diverse hotel product was difficult (Emmer et al. 1993). Both the type and the amount of data that could be stored was limited, leading to simplified, abbreviated or truncated descriptions, and only a limited number of room rates could be incorporated onto the system. Travel agents quickly found that they could obtain more favourable rates by contacting hotel properties directly and, as a result, quickly lost confidence in this initial solution (McGuffie 1994). Hotel chains subsequently began to develop their own computerized systems, with database architectures and methods of operation more adapted to the hotel product, linking them with the GDS through interfaces to give access to the travel agent market (Burns 1994). As each GDS served different geographical markets and hotels needed to be connected to multiple systems in order to effectively cover the marketplace, this still required the development of several complex and expensive interfaces. To overcome this, the major international hotel companies cooperated to develop a 'universal switch' – a bi-directional translator connecting each hotel Central Reservation System (CRS) to the numerous GDS platforms (Werthner and Klein 1999).

However, the capital cost and expertise required to develop and operate a CRS was still substantial, putting it to all intensive purposes outside the reach of smaller companies. Instead of operating their own systems, many chose to outsource electronic distribution to specialist third parties. Costs are typically on a per-reservation basis, allowing the hotel to profit from electronic distribution with little or no capital outlay. Such an approach is particularly attractive to smaller groups and independents, who in many cases also join marketing consortia primarily as a way of gaining cost-effective access to electronic distribution. Participation in Destination Management Systems (DMS) – which typically distribute a comprehensive range of tourism products from a given geographical region – could also be regarded as following a similar strategy (Frew and O'Connor 1999).

The arrival of Internet commerce

Until the mid 1990s, hotel electronic channels of distribution were essentially as described above – a linear status quo where systems cooperated with each other in a mutually beneficial relationship to facilitate distribution (see Figure 7.1). The system was in effect a closed user group, operating over proprietary networks and not available to non-members (Wade 1998). Use of such distribution channels was lucrative, but expensive and lacking in flexibility. This (together with a variety of developments in the external environment) convinced many hotels of

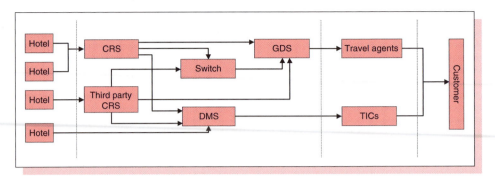

Figure 7.1
The proprietary electronic distribution channels.

the need to find an alternative way to distribute their product (Dombey 1998).

In 1994, the introduction of the Web as a mainstream communications medium provided such an opportunity (Smith and Jenner 1998). In addition to allowing suppliers to distribute directly to consumers, the Web provided a potentially more effective selling medium than the older text-based GDS, allowing images, multimedia and even video to be delivered on demand to supplement highly detailed – yet at the same time highly focused – description data (Murphy et al. 1996). Distribution cost could be greatly reduced by selling over the Web, as the transaction cost of processing voice calls was eliminated and selling directly to the consumer implied the reduction or even elimination of commissions (Helsel and Cullen 2005). The Web also facilitated access to customers with a high propensity to travel, presented little or no barriers to entry, and provided companies with enhanced opportunities to communicate directly with customers (Jeong and Lambert 1999). As a result, electronic commerce was quickly exploited by tourism suppliers and has had a profound effect on the way in which travel products are marketed, distributed, sold and delivered (Williams and Palmer 1999).

Dis-intermediation and re-intermediation

Perhaps the most significant effect of the Internet on tourism has been the way in which it shattered the pre-existing network of distribution channels. As electronic commerce grew, most actors in the tourism value chain started to compete with each other by creating their own consumer-focused websites, while at the same time continuing to cooperate with each other as they had done in the past (Coyne 1995). The situation was well summarized by Dombey (1998) who described it as 'little short of a technological stampede. Up and down the traditional distribution chain, … providers are working feverishly to re-engineer their travel systems … to bypass both the GDS and the travel agent to create a direct link with the customer'. Paradoxically, in addition to there being more competition, there was also more cooperation. A key attraction of many online travel intermediaries is that they are 'full-service', providing consumers with the ability to research and purchase their entire trip on a single site (Ader et al. 1999). To achieve this, they need both detailed content and access to reservation facilities from multiple vendors, which they can only get by cooperating with other distribution providers (Wade and Raffour 2000). Thus multiple non-exclusive virtual alliances have been formed, with companies cooperating with each other to develop new synergistic relationships. The coexistence of competition and cooperation has given rise to a phenomenon which Werthner and Klein (1999) have dubbed 'coopetition'!

As was discussed above, one of the key promises of Internet distribution was that the restrictive and expensive network of intermediaries that previously characterized tourism would be bypassed. For hotel companies, the advantages of setting up their own website are clear – few up-front capital costs, no periodic fees, lower transaction costs, a supplemental source of reservations and increased customer loyalty. This has made Web-based distribution very attractive, particularly for the many smaller establishments that could not afford to be included in the GDS channels (Wade 1998). Although initially slow to respond, by 1999, over 90% of hotel chains had a website, with nearly 80% of these providing some kind of reservation facilities (O'Connor and Horan 1999). In 2006, over one in four bookings in the United States originate online, up from one in twelve in 2002 (PhoCusWright 2006). While online booking levels currently lag in Europe, given the growth in e-commerce and the suitability of travel for sale on the Web, online travel sales in Europe should quickly follow U.S. trends and increase from their 2004 level of Euro 19 billion to approximately Euro 42 billion in 2006 (Carroll and O'Connor 2005).

However, the Internet has created just as many intermediaries as it has displaced (Connolly 1999). As early as 1995, companies from outside the industry identified the potential of travel as a product for sale online, and have attacked and positioned themselves strongly in the emerging distribution network (Nealon 1998). In general, such companies have positioned themselves as general-purpose travel retailers, providing a comprehensive range of information and booking services, usually in cooperation with existing intermediaries and suppliers as was discussed above. Coming from outside the sector, they have no pre-existing relationships or historical emotional baggage, which permits them to question existing methods of operation and gain competitive advantage by doing things differently (Castleberry 1998).

In short, the Web prompted major change in the travel distribution arena. While prior electronic distribution channels were linear, closed and dedicated, the emerging model (see Figure 7. 2) is better described as multi-dimensional, with most participants able to distribute information to, and complete a transaction with, a customer using a variety of different routes (Anderson Consulting 1998). Channels continue to evolve and have become increasingly interconnected as intermediaries form strategic alliances and attempt to develop multiple routes to the customer. Both the number of channels and the complexity of their inter-network are increasing, and the distinction between channels has also become less distinct as systems become connected at multiple levels, as illustrated in Figure 7.2. While most would like to route bookings to direct channels, the domination of the marketplace by online travel intermediaries means that third-party distribution is likely to remain an integral part of the way in which travel gets sold for the foreseeable future (Ader et al. 1999). And since no single system has enough capability or reach to place a product in front of all potential buyers, hotels need to utilize multiple parallel channels (both online and offline) to effectively address the marketplace. Managing this portfolio of channels has become increasingly difficult, but at the same time essential to both profitability and long-terms survival. Key questions include which channels to use; how to set prices across multiple channels, all communicating simultaneously with the marketplace; and how to encourage customers to use direct channels, both to minimize costs and to gather data for management of the customer relationship?

Managing hotel channels of distribution

As discussed above, the growth in the number and complexity of the hotel electronic distribution channels has resulted in a variety of interrelated challenges in terms of how to effectively manage this growing network. Channel choice has become increasingly complex as the number of options increases and as new and innovative business models are introduced. The relative cost of using each alternative may be a key factor, and one

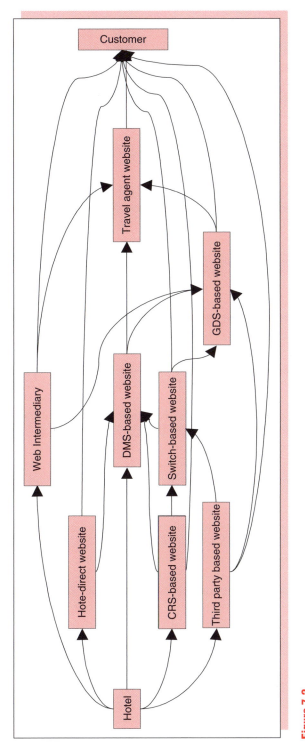

Figure 7.2
A new model of hotel electronic distribution channels.

which varies greatly as a result of the development of alternative forms of remuneration to the commission system traditionally associated with offline travel agents. However, as will be discussed, adopting purely a cost perspective towards channel assessment may be a mistake. Pricing over simultaneous channels is also problematic, while more strategic issues, such as ownership of customer data, also need to be actively managed.

The channel choice decision

Selecting 'an appropriate distribution channel is paramount to success and important if hotel firms are to grow top line revenues and control overhead, yet the number of choices facing hospitality executives is overwhelming' (Connolly et al. 2000: 12). Lewis et al. (1995) claim that such channel management is the backbone of distribution and that every organization must take the time to evaluate current systems and organize a cohesive plan for improvements. Kotler et al. (1996) argue that a well-managed distribution system makes the difference between being a market leader and struggling for survival. Perhaps the situation is best summarized by Andersen Consulting, who maintain that hotel companies urgently need to get better at managing their electronic channels, understanding the profitability of each and developing tactics to drive traffic through their preferred channels (Anderson Consulting 1998). Hence the question arises as to how to decide between alternative channels?

According to Avison and Horton (1988), the most common technique used to evaluate information systems projects is cost-benefit analysis – 'an analysis to determine whether the favourable results of an investment are sufficient to justify the cost of pursuing that alternative' (Shim and Siegel 1995: 97). However, performing such analysis with IT-related projects, particularly those related to electronic distribution, is problematic as costs and benefits are difficult to predict (Applegate et al. 1996). In particular, the benefits arising from adopting a distribution channel can be hard to quantify. Basing evaluations on bookings volume generated is problematic as it may not be possible to establish with certainty which bookings are influenced by which channel. For example, direct websites play an important role in convincing customers to make reservations, even if the actual booking itself is processed through another channel (Connolly et al. 1998). Using bookings volume as a metric would overlook such customers and thus underestimate the importance of the channel. Industry experts claim that online travel sales are undervalued by as much as 25% because of this trend. Furthermore, bookings volume ignores the value of each booking. However, this in itself is also not a valid metric, as, in addition to suffering from the limitations discussed above (i.e. the difficulty in attributing revenue to a particular channel), it ignores cost of distribution. Each channel has different costs – both direct such as commissions and fees, and indirect costs associated with managing the channel (Lugli 1999). Given the interconnectivity of channels discussed earlier, it has become impossible to precisely quantify the cost of accepting a particular booking (Dev and Olsen 2000). Thus, given the number of unknowns, uncertainties and assumptions, cost-benefit analysis has clear limitations (Weill 1991).

Similar challenges exist with capital budgeting techniques. Coming from manufacturing, these evaluate investments based on 'realized effectiveness and productivity gains, in terms of labour savings, increased output and lower unit costs' (Connolly 1999: 69). As such, they tend to focus on cost displacement, to omit strategic implications, to be biased towards short-term returns and to set unjustly high hurdle rates in situations involving high perceived risk, such as with technology investments (Clemons and Weber 1990). While theoretically well grounded, such techniques place too little emphasis on drivers of value such as customer satisfaction, strategic positioning and access to markets. As a result, their utility for evaluating distribution-related projects is limited by the large variety of non-financial factors that need to be taken into account (Ballantine and Stray 1999).

The marketing literature proposes that distribution channels should be evaluated in terms of reach. However, simply choosing channels with the largest potential audience is not always the best solution, as a more focused approach may be more effective (Anderson Consulting 1998). Connolly et al. (1998: 44) cite 'speed, reliability, accuracy, flexibility and functionality' as important in channel evaluation in addition to the cost factors discussed above. Similarly, Kotler et al. (1996) acknowledge flexibility – how easy it is to change the terms and condition of sale – to be of key importance. Kotler also focuses on control – how much influence suppliers have over the manner in which the product is distributed. Can they dictate price, or are distributors free to discount or increase prices if they so wish? Both control and flexibility are often related to the length of the distribution chain (Lewis et al. 1995). Shorter distribution chains (with fewer intermediaries) mean less commission and less need for coordination. The fewer the middlemen, the more the profit and the less the potential for errors. Palmer and McCole

(2000) support this view by pointing out that shorter distribution channels are needed for perishable and complex products – both prime characteristics of a hotel room. Future potential is also a factor that needs to be taken into consideration (Horwath and Horwath 1992). Both technology and markets are rapidly evolving, and when evaluating distribution channels, their future as well as their current potential needs to be examined (Siguaw and Enz 1999).

Traditional models of competitive advantage are based on Porter's five forces model, with firms gaining an advantage by exploiting its strengths relative to those of its competitors (Ohmae 1992). Competitive advantage from technology results when the firm achieves economies of scale, reduce costs, create barriers to entry, build switching costs, change the basis of competition, add customer value, alter the balance of power with suppliers, provide first mover effects, or generates new products as a result of the use of that technology (Applegate et al. 1996). Thus, evaluating projects from a strategic perspective requires going beyond operations to assess their role and importance for company success (Olsen 1993). Taking a more strategic viewpoint balances short- and long-term benefits against capital expenditure, ongoing costs and other factors. However, with strategic issues, measurement difficulties are enhanced as it becomes even more difficult to quantify the tangible benefits.

Thus, choosing between alternative channels of distribution is not a simple process. Deficiencies exist in existing appraisal techniques, yet researchers have to date failed to provide a valid alternative. Collective wisdom now recommends a multi-dimensional approach taking a broad range of factors – not just the technical costs and monetary benefits – into account (O'Connor and Frew 2004). However, hotels have traditionally been poor at using formal methodologies for project evaluation. Whitaker (1987: 231) found that less than half of hotel computer system installations had been preceded by a formal systems analysis. In most cases, the decision process 'consisted of a series of ad hoc and uncoordinated decisions based on vague intentions'. Similarly, Murphy et al. (1996: 71) found that 'few businesses based their Internet investment on anything more than a back-of-the-envelope calculation – 18% had done no analysis at all, while only 12% had justified their investment under the scrutiny typically required within their organization'. Jung and Butler (1999) found that 40% of respondents did not measure the success of their website in any way.

Everyone seems to be using every channel, and no one is prepared to follow the airlines to take control of distribution (Stoltz 1998). Like hotels, airlines rank distribution costs as one of their largest expenses (following fuel and payroll), but in contrast consider them highly controllable. Many have capped travel agent commissions to drive bookings towards more low-cost channels, a strategy which has been highly successful. However, to date, no hotel company has tested or implemented any similar strategy. Most treat distribution channels as analogous to shelf space in a grocery store. Under this type of thinking, more is better as it increases the chances of customer selection. However, additional channels cannot be added infinitum. In many cases, the cost of entering and maintaining these channels outweighs the benefits. Complex technology is needed to support the distribution of room inventory over multiple channels, and the costs of operating this infrastructure increase almost exponentially as additional channels are added. Complexity and the rapid pace of change make it difficult to choose the right mix of channels, yet increased competition, shortages of capital and rising costs make such management essential (Olsen 1997).

Costs and remuneration

Before the growth of the Web as a distribution medium, compensation of intermediaries was relatively straightforward. Travel agents received a standardized commission of 10% in return for selling rooms, while tour operators received highly discounted room rates on the understanding that they would only be sold as part of all-inclusive packages, thus disguising the fact that they had been discounted. Where the sale was facilitated by a technology-based system, such as the GDS or a Switch, a transaction fee for servicing the reservation was also paid by the hotel (O'Connor 1999).

At the beginning of the Internet boom, this model more or less remained the same, as online intermediaries initially positioned themselves as consumer travel agents operating in the online environment (O'Connor and Frew 1998). In most cases, they drew their hotel inventory from the GDS, and collected a normal commission just like an offline agent. However, this arrangement was less than ideal for two reasons. First, hotel inventory on the GDS was primarily business focused, being composed of properties from major hotel chains located in major cities and thus not a good match with the needs of the online intermediary's more leisure-orientated clients. Secondly, the compensation they earned selling such rooms was minimal. After investing in their technological infrastructure, investing heavily in building online brands and merchandizing to make the sale, their remuneration was still only the 10% commission traditional paid to offline travel agents. As was discussed earlier, many of these intermediaries had their origins outside the travel sector and thus were more willing to challenge traditional ways of doing business. Under pressure from the stock market to continue their rapid growth and to become profitability, online intermediaries needed a more attractive and more profitable source of hotel rooms.

Their solution lay in what became known as the *merchant model* – an adaptation of how hotels had traditionally worked with tour operators. Hotels would contract a specified number of rooms each night (known as an allocation) to an online intermediary at a net rate (i.e. free of commission). Intermediaries could then offer these rooms for sale online at whatever price they wished. When they sold a room, they passed the reservation back to the hotel, paying the agreed net rate and pocketing the difference as their margin. If their allocation went unsold, they could release the rooms back to the hotel before their cut-off time without penalty. In an economic climate where hotels were scrambling to fill rooms at any cost, such an arrangement seemed like a win-win situation. Hotels got access to a powerful new channel of distribution to help fill rooms that would otherwise have remained empty, while online intermediaries got access to more hotel rooms and could potentially make higher margins as they, not the supplier, determined the retail price.

However, merchant contracts tended to be biased heavily in favour of intermediaries. Control over inventory and retail price quickly became problematic (O'Connor and Frew 2004). Online intermediaries had fixed allocations of rooms, substantial discounts and total control over retail price and could undercut hotels' direct prices by accepting lower margins, or earn supernormal profits by selling their allocation at a premium when the hotel itself was sold out. Many saw the relationship as unbalanced as the intermediary took no risk (Carroll and Siguaw 2003). If they sold their allocation, they collected their margin, but if they failed, they could return rooms at no penalty, leaving the latter with unsold inventory at the last minute. Hotel companies slowly began to realize that the merchant model meant that they no longer controlled how, and at what price, their product was being sold (O'Connor and Piccoli 2003). At the 2004 Berlin Hotel Industry Investment Conference, speakers cited this threat to profitability as the biggest single challenge facing the industry. Furthermore, as occupancy levels rose, hotels found themselves tied into restrictive contracts for allocations at highly discounted rates. The merchant model then had a negative effect as they were committed to selling rooms at rates lower what could be achieve by selling directly or through other channels. Although intermediaries subsequently reduced their margins (particularly for larger hotel groups with superior negotiating power), industry estimates still place the typical cost of selling a room over the merchant model at over double that of commission-based sales (Carroll and O'Connor 2005).

Given the resistance that has developed to the merchant model, newer forms of intermediary have instead opted for a pay-per-performance compensation model. Meta-search sites in particular seek compensation based on the volume of business that they deliver to the hotel. This can be based on a cost-per-click model, with the intermediary receiving payment for each visitor they despatch to a website, or cost-per-purchase, with the intermediary only receiving payment if that customer subsequently buys. Unlike the merchant model, there are no allocations or discounts to be managed, just payment if and when a sale is made. Although still relatively uncommon, this model has the potential to become popular as it balances the cost minimization needs of the hotel against the revenue requirements of the intermediary, rewarding those who successfully deliver business to the hotel.

Pricing over multiple simultaneous channels

Pricing is a key element of distribution and one that has been made more difficult by the growth of the Web (Enz 2003). As was discussed above, most hotels now use multiple simultaneous channels of distribution to address the marketplace (Buhalis and Laws 2001). While giving hotels more reach, this is problematic as the resulting transparency means that consumers can easily comparing the product offered on each one in terms of price and features (Stone et al. 2002). Yesawich et al. (2000) claim that almost six out of ten leisure travellers now actively seek out the lowest possible price when booking travel services by shopping alternative distribution channels. Dedicated software tools and websites (known as Metasearch) that automate this comparison process (e.g. TravelAxe, Sidestep, cheapaccommodation.com and Kayak.com) are also available. These facilitate price comparison across dozens or potentially hundreds of online retailers, reporting back with the most appropriate or cheapest match (Varini et al. 2003).

Thus, by reducing search costs, the Internet has intensified price competition (Jiang 2002). Any variations or inconsistencies in price are potentially immediately apparent to the consumer, thus necessitating a logical, consistently implemented, pricing strategy. However, many researchers (see for example

O'Connor and Piccoli 2003; Varini et al. 2003) claim that hotels are haphazardly setting prices on electronic distribution channels without really understanding how their actions affect revenue and profitability. For example, a study by Thompson and Failmezger (2005) showed that cheaper rates can frequently be obtained through intermediary sites rather than on hotel brand direct sites. Not only finding the same product at different prices on different sites is confusing for the customer (Biswas 2004), but also having a cheaper price on a third-party site may result in the cannibalization. Existing customers, who might have booked direct, may now book through the intermediary as a result of the lower price. Such third-party bookings also result in a lower net contribution, as commissions, processing fees and other transaction costs usually have to be paid on intermediary bookings. Furthermore, inconsistent or illogical pricing lowers customer satisfaction levels (Murphy and Schegg 2004), can potentially alienate the customer (Kimes 2002) and ultimately result in lost sales (Sinha 2000).

To prevent this, many companies have developed more logical approaches to pricing across multiple channels. Some, for example Marriott International or Hyatt International, use a price consistency strategy – offering the same rate to customers irrespective of the channel – online or offline – being used to make the booking. Thus, customers booking on third-party websites, through travel agents, through the call centre, on the direct website or through the hotel property get offered the same rate irrespective of the point-of-sale. However, this approach ignores the cost of using a channel, and as a result the company will end up with a lower net contribution when the booking is processed through a third party. For this reason, some companies promise cheaper rates to customers booking directly through their brand website, in effect sharing the saving in cost in order to motivate direct bookings. An estimated 43% of hotel companies now promise such best rate guarantees to customers booking through their brand website (KPMG 2005).

Whatever strategy is used, it must be implemented consistently and communicated effectively (Hanks et al. 2002). Unfortunately 'pricing in the hotel industry appears to be unscientific, self-defeating, myopic and not customer-based' (Danziger et al. 2004: 6). O'Connor's (2003) study of international hotel chains found that 'no single channel consistently offered the lowest prices' and that the 'lowest prices were often offered on the channels with the highest transaction costs' (O'Connor 2003: 94). This lack of a comprehensive pricing strategy means that hotels have, to a large extent, lost control over the sale of their product in the online environment

(Murphy and Schegg 2004). While disengaging from merchant contracts can be difficult and painful, leadership has come from international hotel chains, such as Intercontinental Hotel Group (IHG). Taking a strategic decision as to how the company wanted to work with intermediaries, IHG withdrew its inventory from Expedia and Hotels.com, two of the most prominent online travel intermediaries, as the latter were not willing to cooperate with IHG's new business terms (Carroll and O'Connor 2005). Such decisive action is not typical. The KPMG (2005) worldwide industry survey indicates that the majority of hotels have not, to date, implemented a coherent pricing/distribution strategy.

The availability of multiple potential channels of distribution has also made yield management[2] more difficult (Choi and Kimes 2002). However, little empirical research has been published on how the process should be adapted to cope with this changing environment. Choi and Kimes (2002) use a simulation to demonstrate the applicability of yield management techniques to multi-channel problems. More practical advice comes from Noone and Griffin (1999) who propose combining Activity-Based Costing with yield management principles in what they call Customer Profitability Analysis. Noting that the cost of using channels can vary greatly, sophisticated yield management needs to focus not just on rate achieved but also on distribution cost to maximize net revenue (Choi and Kimes 2002). To achieve this, higher prices should be incorporated on channels with higher transaction costs (O'Connor and Piccoli 2003). Other things being equal, the higher rate would either compensate for the higher distribution cost or alternatively drive customers towards cheaper direct channels, thus delivering other branding and marketing benefits associated with having direct contact with customers (Helsel and Cullen 2005).

Having higher prices on intermediary channels may be difficult as hotels may not be able to set the actual retail price. With the merchant model, the hotel provides a net rate free of commission, which the intermediary then marks up by varying amounts (Carroll and O'Connor 2005). Thus, it is the intermediary, not the hotel, who sets the retail price and can undercut direct channels simply by accepting a low markup. Furthermore, the aforementioned transparency of the Internet makes it easy for customers to compare prices across multiple channels. If prices vary illogically, perceived unfairness can lead customers to defect, spread negative information and initiate other actions that damage the seller (Xia et al. 2004). Consistent

---

[2]See also Chapter 11.

pricing across all channels would address this issue, but suffers similar challenges to successful implementation.

Ownership of the customer

Hotels face an increasingly competitive market where the basis of competition is changing. While 'location, location, location' remains a key issue, a hotel's location is a given, at least in the short run. Attracting and retaining customers based on service, facilities or amenities is similarly problematic; as such attributes have, to a large extent, become relatively standardized. Competition based on price is unattractive as it can lead to a downward spiral resulting in uneconomical rates for all suppliers, driven in part by consumers' aforementioned ability to easily compare prices over the Internet (O'Connor 2002). And consumers are displaying less brand loyalty than in the past, eroding another one of the competitive methods on which hotels have traditionally relied (Gamble et al. 1999). For these reasons, many companies are turning towards attempting to build long-term relationships with the customer as a way of adding value and differentiating themselves from their competitors (Francese and Renaghan 1990).

One of the great promises of Internet commerce is the ability to interact directly with customers – past and potential – to build meaningful long-term relationships. Developing such relationships is thought to increase customer loyalty, which is important because such customers stay longer, buy more and buy more often (Dowling 2002). Acquiring new customers is thought to be between five and seven times more expensive than keeping existing ones (Kotler 1997), while another oft-quoted statistic is that companies can improve profitability by between 25% and 85% by reducing customer defections by only 5% (Reichheld and Sasser 1990). Over time, a company can leverage its relationships to learn about individual customers' needs, wants and expectations and use this information to market more effectively and to provide more tailored customer service (Peppers and Rodgers 1994). This should result in higher profitability, from increased sales as a result of higher responsiveness to marketing efforts, from reduced customer acquisition costs, and from customers willing to pay a premium for 'better' service (Dowling 2002).

Success in building such relationships is thought to revolve around effectively capturing data about customers so that they can be profiled accurately to identify their individual needs and idiosyncratic expectations, and to generate actionable customer knowledge for both marketing and operations uses (Gamble et al. 1999). Relationship building is also about consistency – specifically the ability to consistently treat different customers differently (Newell 2000). However, achieving this, particularly in large multi-unit, geographically dispersed hotel chains, can be problematic. Customer recognition is a key enabler of both success factors. However, this is severely threatened by the explosion in number and complexity of electronic distribution channels discussed earlier.

Online travel intermediaries operating under the merchant model in particular tend to pass minimal information about each reservation back to the hotel – typically just the guest name, date of arrival and length of stay – which severely limits the latter's ability to provide customers with appropriate levels of recognition. Similarly, the absence of complete data makes marketing efforts difficult, and may lead to data duplication and data redundancy (Piccoli et al. 2003). From a strategic perspective, such customers are in any case being encouraged to develop relationships with the online intermediaries rather than with the hotel. In each case, the intermediary in question has provided them with a solution to their travel problem. Next time they have a need, their instinct will be to return to the intermediary, who not only provided them with a solution in the past but also offers a one-stop-shopping experience. As this relationship develops, they build up thrust with the intermediary, which potentially allows them to be diverted to competing products. Online intermediary's adoption of marketing and merchandising techniques borrowed from the retailing sector accelerates this trend. While much criticism of the merchant model has focused on profit margins and control over price, strategically this loss of ownership of the customer is much more worrying, and should be a prime motivator for driving customers directly. While no hotel company has as yet followed the airlines in actively discouraging indirect bookings by not awarding loyalty points or forbidding upgrades on seats booked through online intermediaries, such steps may be necessary in order to ensure that customers interact with the hotel directly during the distribution process.

Summary and conclusions

This chapter has given an overview of the origins and development of electronic distribution as it affects the hotel sector. The importance of information distribution for hotel product has been explored, and the role that technologies can play in making accurate, relevant and timely information available to consumers at the appropriate stage of their purchase decision-making process has been explained. The importance of providing reservations facilities – to allow a consumer or an intermediary to book a room with minimum inconvenience – has also been highlighted, and the range of channels traditionally available to help in this process described. It has been shown how the arrival of the Web has acted as a catalyst in hotel distribution – breaking the pre-existing 'status quo' and encouraging both new developments and competition. This has in turn led to an explosion in the type, complexity and number of electronic distribution channels available.

Hoteliers now have a vast range of potential channels through which they can distribute their product. Channels vary greatly, from both operational and strategic perspectives, making management of the distribution space increasingly difficult. The arena is in a continual state of flux as a result of technological advancements, new and emerging distribution players and periodic shifts in the balance of power among suppliers, buyers and intermediaries (O'Connor 1999). An in-depth understanding of this highly complex and dynamic arena is essential for today's hospitality managers. Guidance from published research is sadly lacking (O'Connor and Murphy 2004). Most existing studies lack both rigour and relevance, and offer few concrete suggestions as to how to manage this increasingly complex subject area. The research potential is outstanding for those motivated to dig into this fascinating area.

References

Ader, J., LaFleur, R. and Falcone, M. (1999) *Internet Travel: Point, Click, Trip: An Introduction to the On-Line Travel Industry*, Bear Stearns: New York, NY

Anderson Consulting. (1998) *The Future of Travel Distribution: Securing Loyalty in an Efficient Travel Market*, Anderson Consulting: New York, NY

Applegate, L., McFarlan, F. and McKenney, J. (1996) *Corporate Information Systems Management: The Issues Facing Senior Executives*, 4th edition, Irwin: Chicago, IL

Avison, D. and Horton, J. (1988) Evaluation and information system development, In Avison, D., Fitzgerald, G., Bjorn Andersen, N., Gresser, J., De Marco, M., Dedene, G. and Cavallari, M. (Eds.), *Investimenti in Information Technology nel settore bancario*, FrancoAngeli: Florence

Ballantine, J. and Stray, S. (1999) Information systems and other capital investments: evaluation practices compared, *Logistics Information Management*, 12, 1/2, 78–93

Bennett, M. (1993) Information technology and travel agency: a customer service perspective, *Tourism Management*, 14, 4, 259–266

Bennett, M. (1996) Information technology and database for tourism, In Seaton, A. and Bennett, M. (Eds.), *Marketing of Tourism Products: Concepts Issues and Cases,* International Thomson Business Press: London, UK, 423–450

Biswas, D. (2004) Economics of information in the web economy: towards a new theory? *Journal of Business Research,* 57, 7, 724–733

Buhalis, D. and Laws, E. (2001) *Tourism Distribution Channels: Practices, Issues and Transformations,* Continuum: London, UK

Burns, J. (1994) Seamless – the new GDS connectivity standard, *H & A Report,* 3, 5, 5–9

Carroll, B. and O'Connor, P. (2005) *European Hotels: Managing Hospitality Distribution (Preview),* PhoCusWright: Sherman, CT

Carroll, B. and Siguaw, J. (2003) The evolution of electronic distribution: effects on hotels and intermediaries, *Cornell Hotel and Restaurant Administration Quarterly,* 44, 4, 38–50

Castleberry, W. (1998, February) *The Booking Process: The Developers' Perspective,* Paper presented at the EuroHotec, Nice, International Hotel and Restaurant Association: Paris

Castleberry, J., Hempell, C. and Kaufinan, G. (1998) Electronic shelf space on the global distribution network, *Hospitality and Leisure Executive Report,* 5(Spring), Andersen Consulting, New York, NY, 19–24

Choi, S. and Kimes, S. (2002) Electronic distribution channels' effect on hotel revenue management, *Cornell Hotel and Restaurant Administration Quarterly,* 43, 3, 23–31

Clemons, E. and Weber, B. (1990) *Making the Information Technology Investment Decision: A Principal Approach,* In Sprague, R. (Ed.), Proceedings of the 23rd Annual Hawaii International Conference on System Sciences: Emerging Technologies and Applications: Track IV, IEEE Computer Society Press: Los Almos, CA, 147–156

Connell, J. and Reynolds, P. (1999) The implications of technological developments on tourism information centres, *Tourism Management,* 20, 4, 501–509

Connolly, D. (1999) *Understanding Information Technology Investment Decision Making in the Context of Hotel Global Distribution Systems: A Multiple-Case Study,* Unpublished PhD thesis, Virginia, Blacksburg

Connolly, D., Olsen, M. and Allegro, S. (2000) *The Hospitality Industry and the Digital Economy: An Executive Summary of Key Technology Trends Surfaced at the Lausanne Think Tank,* International Hotel and Restaurant Association: Paris

Connolly, D., Olsen, M. and Moore, R. (1998) The internet as a distribution channel, *Cornell Hotel and Restaurant Administration Quarterly*, 39, 4, 42–54

Coyne, R. (1995) The reservations revolution, *Hotel and Motel Management*, 210, 13, 54–57

Danziger, S., Israeli, A. and Bekerman, M. (2004) Investigating pricing decisions in the hospitality industry using the behavioral process method, *Journal of Hospitality and Leisure Marketing*, 11, 2/3, 5–17

Dev, C. and Olsen, M. (2000) Marketing challenges for the next decade, *Cornell Hotel and Restaurant Administration Quarterly*, 41, 1, 41–47

Dombey, A. (1998, January) *Separating the Emotion from the Fact – The Effects of New Intermediaries on Electronic Travel Distribution*, Presented at ENTER Information and Communications Technology in Tourism, Istanbul, Turkey, International Federation for Information Technology in Tourism

Dowling, G. (2002) Customer relationship management: in b2c markets, often less is more, *California Management Review*, 44, 3, 87–104

Duke, C. and Persia, M. (1993) Effects of distribution channel level on tour purchasing attributes ad information sources, *Journal of Travel and Tourism Marketing*, 2, 2/3, 37–55

Emmer, R., Tauck, C. and Moore, R. (1993) Marketing hotels using global distribution systems, *Cornell Hotel and Restaurant Administration Quarterly*, 34, 6, 80–89

Enz, C. (2003) Hotel pricing in a networked world, *Cornell Hotel and Restaurant Administration Quarterly*, 44, 1, 4–5

Francese, P. and Renaghan, L. (1990) Data-base marketing: building customer profiles, *Cornell Hotel and Restaurant Administration Quarterly*, 31, 1, 60–63

Frew, A. and O'Connor, P. (1999) Destination marketing system strategies: refining and extending an assessment framework, *Information Technology and Tourism – Applications, Methodologies, Techniques*, 2, 1, 3–13

Gamble, P., Stone, M. and Woodcock, N. (1999) *Up, Close and Personal: Customer Relationship Marketing @ Work*, Kogan Page: London, UK

Go, F. and Pine, R. (1995) *Globalization Strategy in the Hotel Industry*, Routledge: New York, NY

Hanks, R., Cross, R. and Noland, R. (2002) Discounting in the hotel industry: a new approach, *Cornell Hotel and Restaurant Administration Quarterly*, 43, 94–103

Helsel, C. and Cullen, K. (2005) *Hotel Distribution Nirvana: A Multi-Channel Approach*, HEDNA: Falls Church, VA

Hitchins, F. (1991) The influence of technology on UK travel agents, *Travel and Tourism Analyst*, 3, 88–105

Horwath and Horwath. (1992) *Hotels of the Future – Strategies and Action Plan*, International Hotel Association: London, UK

Jeong, M. and Lambert, C. (1999) Measuring the information quality of lodging web sites, *International Journal of Hospitality Information Technology*, 1, 1, 63–75

Jiang, P. (2002) A model of price search behavior in electronic marketplace, *Internet Research: Electronic Network Applications and Policy*, 12, 2, 181–190

Jung, H.-S. and Butler, R. (1999, June) *The Perceptions of the Internet as a Marketing Tool by Representative of the Hotel Industry*, Paper presented at the Hospitality Information Technology Association Annual Worldwide Conference, Edinburgh, Scotland, Hospitality Information Technology Association: Edinburgh

Karcher, K. (1995) The emergence of electronic market systems in the European tour operator business, *EM – Electronic Markets*, 5, 1, 10–11

Kimes, S. (2002) Perceived fairness of yield management, *Cornell Hotel and Restaurant Administration Quarterly*, February, 21–30

Knowles, T. and Garland, M. (1994) The strategic importance of CRSs in the airline industry, *EIU Travel and Tourism Analyst*, 4, 4–16

Kotler, P. (1997) *Marketing Management: Analysis, Planning and Control*, 9th edition, Prentice Hall: Englewood Cliffs, NJ

Kotler, P., Bowen, J. and Makens, J. (1996) *Marketing for Hospitality and Tourism*, Prentice Hall: Upper Saddle River, NJ

KPMG (2005) *Global Hotel Distribution Survey 2005 – Managing Pricing Across Distribution Channels*, KPMG: London, UK

Laws, E. (1997) *Managing Package Tourism*, International Thomson Business Press: London, UK

Lewis, R., Chambers, R. and Chacko, H. (1995) *Marketing Leadership in Hospitality: Foundations and Practices*, 2nd edition, Van Nostrand Reinhold: New York, NY

Lugli, F. (1999, January) *CRS, GDS and the Internet*, Paper presented at the EurHotec, Vienna, International Hotel and Restaurant Association

McGuffie, J. (1994) CRS development in the hotel sector, *Travel and Tourism Analyst*, 2, 53–68

Middleton, V. (1994) *Marketing in Travel and Tourism*, 2nd edition, Butterworth-Heinemann: Oxford, UK

Murphy, J., Forrest, E., Wotring, C. and Brymer, R. (1996) Hotel management and marketing on the internet, *Cornell Hotel and Restaurant Administration Quarterly*, 37, 3, 70–82

Murphy, J. and Schegg, R. (2004, June) *The Best Room Rate Depends, but Better Not Call*, Proceedings of the Hospitality Information Technology Conference, Dallas, Texas, Hospitality Information Technology Association: Paris, 201–215

Nealon, T. (1998) New age travellers, *Revolution*, Accessed 8 October 2007 online http://www.brandrepublic.com/login/News/122446/

Negroponte, N. (1995) *Being Digital*, Vintage Books: Knopf, NY

Newell, F. (2000) *Loyalty.com*, McGraw-Hill: New York, UK

Noone, B. and Griffin, P. (1999) Managing the long-term profit yield from market segments in a hotel environment: a case study on the implementation of customer profitability analysis, *International Journal of Hospitality Management*, 18, 2, 111–128

O'Brien, P. (1999) Intelligent assistants for retail travel agents, *Information Technology and Tourism*, 2, 3/4, 213–228

O'Connor, P. (1999) *Electronic Information Distribution in Tourism and Hospitality*, CAB International: Oxford, UK

O'Connor, P. (2002) An analysis of the online pricing strategies of the international hotel chains, In Woeber, K., Frew, A. J. and Hitz, M. (Eds.), *Information and Communications Technologies in Tourism 2002*, Springer-Verlag Wien: New York, pp. 285–293

O'Connor, P. (2003) On-line pricing: an analysis of hotel company practices, *Cornell Hotel and Restaurant Administration Quarterly*, 44, 1, 88–96

O'Connor, P. and Frew, A. (1998, March) *The Evolution of Hotel Electronic Distribution.* Paper presented at the Joint HSMAI/EuroCHRIE conference, Oslo, Norway

O'Connor, P. and Frew, A. (2004) An evaluation methodology for hotel electronic channels of distribution, *International Journal of Hospitality Management*, 23, 2, 179–199

O'Connor, P. and Horan, P. (1999, June) *Failing to Make the Connection? – An Analysis of Web Reservation Facilities in the Top 50 International Hotel Chains*, Paper presented at the Hospitality Information Technology Association Worldwide Conference, Edinburgh, Hospitality Information Technology Association

O'Connor, P. and Murphy, J. (2004) Research on information technology in the hospitality industry, *International Journal of Hospitality Management*, 23, 5, 473–484

O'Connor, P. and Piccoli, G. (2003) Marketing hotels using global distribution systems: revisited, *Cornell Hotel and Restaurant Administration Quarterly*, 44, 5/6, 105–114

Ohmae, K. (1992) *The Mind of the Strategist: Business Planning for Competitive Advantage*, Penguin Books: New York, NY

Olsen, M. (1993) International growth strategies of major US hotel companies, *EIU Travel and Tourism Analyst*, 3, 51–64

Olsen, M. (1997) *Events Shaping the Future and Their Impact on the Multinational Hotel Industry,* International Hotel Association: Paris

Olsen, M., Murthy, B. and Inagaki, T. (1995) *Scanning the Business Environment of the Multinational Hotel Industry,* International Hotel Association: Paris

Palmer, A. and McCole, P. (2000) The virtual re-introduction of travel services: a conceptual framework and empirical investigation, *Journal of Vacation Marketing,* 6, 1, 33–47

Peppers, D. and Rodgers, M. (1994) The only business to be in is the business of keeping customers, *Marketing News,* 28, 3, 6

PhoCusWright (2006) *U.S. Online Travel Overview,* PhoCusWright: Sherman, CT

Piccoli, G., O'Connor, P., Capaccioli, C. and Alvarez, R. (2003) Customer relationship management – a driver for change in the structure of the U.S. lodging industry, *Cornell Hotel and Restaurant Administration Quarterly,* 44, 4, 61–73

Pollock, A. (1995) The impact of information technology on destination marketing, *EIU Travel and Tourism Analyst,* 3, 66–83

Poon, A. (1993) *Technology and Competitive Strategies,* CAB International: Wallingford

Poon, A. (1994) The new tourism revolution, *Tourism Management,* 15, 2, 91–92

Porter, M. and Millar, V. (1985) How information gives you competitive advantage, *Harvard Business Review,* 63, 4, 149–160

Reichheld, F. and Sasser, E. (1990) Zero defections quality comes to services, *Harvard Business Review,* 68, 5, 301–307

Schulz, C. (1994) Hotels and travel agents: the new partnership, *Cornell Hotel and Restaurant Administration Quarterly,* 35, 2, 45–50

Shim, A. and Siegel, T. (1995) *Dictionary of Accounting Terms,* Hauppauge: New York, NY

Siguaw, J. and Enz, C. (1999) Best practices in information technology, *Cornell Hotel and Restaurant Administration Quarterly,* 40, 5, 58–71

Siguaw, J., Enz, C. and Namasivayam, K. (2000) Adoption of information technology in U.S. hotels: strategically driven objectives, *Journal of Travel Research,* 39, 2, 192–201

Sinha, I. (2000) Cost transparency: the net's real threat to prices and brands, *Harvard Business Review,* 78, 2, 43–50

Smith, C. and Jenner, P. (1998) Tourism and the internet, *Travel and Tourism Analyst,* 1, 62–81

Stipanuk, D. (1993) Tourism and technology: interactions and implications, *Tourism Management, 14, 4,* 267–278

Stoltz, C. (1998, 15 November) The e-travel revolution is over, *Washington Post*, p. E01

Stone, M., Hobbs, M. and Khaleeli, M. (2002) Multichannel customer management: the benefits and challenges, *Journal of Database Marketing*, 10, 1, 39–52

Tapscott, D. (1996) *The Digital Economy: Promise and Peril in the Age of Networked Intelligence*, McGraw-Hill: New York, NY

Thompson, G. and Failmezger, A. (2005) *Why Customers Shop Around: A Comparison of Hotel Room Rates and Availability across Booking Channels*, Cornell University School of Hotel Administration, The Center for Hospitality Research: Ithaca, NY

Varini, K., Engelmann, R., Claessen, B. and Schleusener, M. (2003) Evaluation of the price-value perception of customers in Swiss hotels, *Journal of Revenue and Pricing Management*, 2, 1, 47–60

Vialle, O. (1995) *Les GDS dans L'Industrie Touristique*, Organisation Mondiale de Tourisme (World Tourism Organisation): Madrid

Wade, P. (1998) *L'Impact des Nouvelles Technologies sur les Systems d'Information et de Reservation*, Conseil Nationale de Tourisme: Paris

Wade, P. and Raffour, G. (2000) L'internet, un nouveau canal de distribution, *ESPACES*, April, 170, 19–21

Wagner, G. (1991) Lodging's lifeblood, *Lodging Hospitality*, 15 December, 105

Weill, P. (1991) The information technology pay off: implication for investment appraisal, *Australian Accounting Review*, 2, 11, 36–42

Werthner, H. and Klein, S. (1999) *Information Technology and Tourism – A Challenging Relationship*, Springer-Verlag: New York/ Vienna

Whitaker, M. (1987) Overcoming the barriers to successful implementation of information technology in the UK hotel industry, *International Journal of Hospitality Management*, 6, 4, 229–35

Williams, A. and Palmer, A. (1999) Tourism destination brands and electronic commerce: towards synergy? *Journal of Vacation Marketing*, 5, 3, 263–275

Xia, L., Monroe, K. and Cox, J. (2004) The price is unfair! A conceptual framework of price fairness perceptions, *Journal of Marketing Research*, 68, 4, 1–15

Yesawich, Pepperdine and Brown (2000) *National Leisure Travel Monitor*, Yesawich, Pepperdine and Brown: Orlando

Zsamboky, G. (1998) How will the internet change your business? *Tourism Trendspotter*, 1, 1, 11–14

CHAPTER 8

ICT and hospitality operations

Paul A. Whitelaw

*Senior Lecturer, School of Hospitality,
Tourism and Marketing
Senior Associate of the Centre for
Tourism and Services Research at Victoria
University, Melbourne, Australia*

Introduction

As reviews of information and communications technology (ICT) research demonstrate (Frew 2000; O'Connor and Murphy 2004), this subject has been researched from a variety of perspectives. However, because the technology often transcends traditional ways of managing operations and organizing activities, it is not easy to select specific research studies in the operations field or to categorize them. In particular, the Internet and web-based systems are enabling new business models and ways of doing things that blur the distinction between operations and marketing (as the previous chapter on electronic distribution demonstrates). Nonetheless, this chapter explores the types of technology now in use in the industry and how ICT has changed operations in particular. In doing this, three themes emerge: the first is how ICT has put more power in the hands of the guest; second, how ICT has improved the operational efficiency of service staff; and finally, how ICT has improved information flows to senior management thus providing more capacity for understanding, forecasting and strategic planning. Further, the exploration of these issues will also consider ways in which these emerging technologies can provide fresh insight into long-established service management theory.

These perspectives assume that there is a current benchmark of automation – such as hotels having a computerized reservation and rooms management system and bars with food and beverage management systems. Thus, the focus of this chapter will be on how new and emerging ICT will improve the efficacy and efficiency of these systems. For many years, up to around 2000, the hotel industry tended to operate 'bespoke' or custom-designed systems designed exclusively for use in their operations. Often these systems did not integrate with each other, as they were purchased from different vendors or used different platforms. Cline and Warner (1999) found that 82% of the 327 executives in their global survey believed that this had a negative financial impact on the industry. So important was this issue that the American Hotel and Lodging Association set up a working group to investigate the integration of different IT systems commonly used in the industry. More recently web-enabled platforms have been developed that address this issue.

The evolution of this technology needs to be seen in light of the ongoing development of the industry. Several authors (Connolly and Olsen 2001) have argued that the industry is abandoning some elements of its craft traditions and pursuing a more ruthless, commercial agenda. Efficiency of resources, revenue growth and cost cutting are seen as essential management practices needed to drive shareholder value. At the same time, harnessing internal and external resources to meet guests' needs, wants and objectives while still earning profit is seen as paramount. High-speed, high-quality information flow between the guest and the hotel is seen as the key to driving revenue (by meetings guests' needs) and maximizing profit (by improving efficiency and cutting costs). However, at the same time, despite the proliferation of loyalty programs, the market has seen a decline in traditional notions of customer loyalty, further exacerbating the need to quickly and clearly understand the guests' needs and then marshall resources to meet them.

More power to the guest

ICT has resulted in a blurring of work and leisure (Davis and Meyer 1998). People often combine business trips with pleasure and vice versa. Travellers today sport all of the high-technology appendages seen throughout the society: beepers, mobile phones and laptops. They bring these devices with them whether they are travelling for business or pleasure, and when they arrive at their destinations, they expect to have a place where they can readily use these devices without hassle or frustration. This requires hotels to provide a workspace, as well as access to the outside world via modems and the Internet, without the guest needing to search for appropriate access ports, re-wire the room, or re-arrange the furniture and lighting. A digital infrastructure is essential for competing in the future.

Guests therefore remain connected to their worlds no matter where they are physically and no matter why they are travelling. So the industry can no longer label travellers by the traditional, distinctive categories of business, leisure or group. Hence the behaviour of guests will increasingly reflect their individual lifestyle far more than their purpose of travel. Connolly and Olsen (2001) call such guest 'tribal travellers'. This will be the case throughout the so-called 'guest cycle'.

The first part of the guest cycle, which typically involves some form of information search, has been extensively expanded by the Internet[1]. Some of these information channels are formal and official, such as hotel websites, travel agent websites and even destination promotion websites.

---

[1] This is discussed fully in Chapter 7.

However, there has also been explosive growth in external or informal information sources such as blogs and online travel forums that are maintained by individuals who do not have a vested interest in the commercial well-being of the hospitality industry. In some instances, these blogs have emerged as key, authoritative sources of 'inside information' for visitors. For example, it is possible to go online and read the personal reviews of people who have stayed at the hotel you are contemplating staying in when you next travel.

The second phase of the guest cycle, involving the purchase decision, has also been significantly changed by the emergence of ICTs. Whether directly with the hotel, through an airline or travel agent or through a major online consolidator such as Amadeus or Galileo, the ICT-literate guest can compare prices between properties and book, secure and pay for their room online all during the one computer session, irrespective of the prospective guest's location or time of day.

In the next stage of the guest cycle, check-in and residence, it is now possible for guests to pre-allocate their room via the Internet, and in some instances, via their personal digital assistant (PDA) or mobile phone as they approach the hotel. In this environment, it is possible for a guest to book and allocate their room online, alert the hotel of their impending arrival in advance and thus collect their pre-coded room key from the concierge or porter on arrival without ever having to speak to any other hotel staff or stop and queue at the front desk. Just as credit cards can now be used to access, pay and exit boom gates at car parks, hotel room locks and other outlets in the hotel can be programmed to read a credit card. The emerging PDA technology could see PDAs emit a signal to unlock the hotel door by pressing a pin number electronically issued by the hotel without needing a hotel-issued security card or the guest's credit card.

Finally, in the last part of the guest cycle, check out, the guest can simply depart the hotel without having to check out at the front desk. Some hotel companies are now developing policies wherein if the guest has stayed previously, not argued the bill and paid by credit card, then in subsequent visits the guest only needs to indicate that they will pay by the same credit card and the hotel will not require any formal check-in procedure, signature or check-out procedure – the guest is free to come and go. The account is settled when the hotel staff confirm that the room is vacated – all charging information is on electronic file – and so there is no need to disturb the guest whatsoever.

As can be seen, the advent of these technologies places greater control in the hand of the guests. They can more critically shop around, compare prices and choose exactly what room they want (within the price category they pay), and movement and expenditure in and around and out of the hotel is greatly expedited. While there is no evidence of this trend in foodservice yet, it is also entirely feasible for guests to book and allocate their own tables in a restaurant in the same fashion as they can for hotel rooms and airline seats.

Power to the staff

It is now appropriate to look at how these emerging technologies can improve the operating performance of hospitality operations. Consistent with Michael Porter's various theories relating to competitive advantage (Porter 1985), a hospitality operation can use the technology to pursue either a least cost producer strategy or a high value-added strategy. In the first instance, the technology can be used to improve the operating efficiency of staff, thus creating the potential for the business to pass on savings. However, in the second instance, it can be used to improve the richness of the customer experience and thus justify maintaining high prices.

For example, it is feasible for hotels to fully automate their reservations systems – in the same fashion as airlines have. By having guests book and allocate their own rooms, the hotel can generate considerable savings by reducing its reservation staff. These costs savings can then be passed onto the consumer in the form of lower prices.

The technology also presents many opportunities in full-service restaurants. Each waiter can be issued with a PDA which enables her to take orders at the table which are then directly transmitted to the kitchen. When the food is ready, the PDA can immediately alert the waiter. As a result of these arrangements, the waiter does not have to leave the dining room to place the order and will spend a minimum of time out of the room collecting food for serving. How the restaurant elects to utlize this technology will be a function of the competitive advantage it seeks to pursue. If the restaurant sees itself as a 'low cost' producer, it will use this technology to employ less wait staff with a view to passing some of the cost savings onto the guests. In contrast, if the restaurant is a 'value added' producer, the time saved by the waiter can be spent in the dining room enhancing the level of service and, by implication, the guest experience.

Somewhat ironically, until fairly recently hospitality firms were not using ICT as the means to train employees in the use of ICT! Cline and Warner (1999) found that training in technology was predominantly on-the-job, with CD-Rom (32%), interactive television (20%) and the Internet (5%) relatively little used. This has now changed significantly. For instance, Hilton University is one of the world's most sophisticated web-based, online training and development systems (www. hilton-university.com).

Power to the managers

These systems can be used by management to better control operations and understand the business and thus better forecast and plan for the future (Gates 1999).

Understanding the customer

Each interaction with a customer or potential customer is a chance to learn and collect more information about these individuals and update their profiles. Creating repositories to store and share this information and these profiles throughout the entire enterprise becomes a fundamental operating principle of the knowledge economy. Connolly and Olsen (2001) argue that 'knowledge, knowledge, knowledge' will replace 'location, location, location' as the three most important sources of competitive advantage. They suggest that companies must focus on developing guest intelligence systems with the same diligence that military organizations pursue intelligence gathering. This implies seeking, collecting and storing the right data, validating the data, sharing the data throughout the entire organization and using this data throughout all levels of the organization to create personalized, unique customer experiences. New tools for data warehousing and data mining and Internet tools such as Firefly, BroadVision, Jango and others are emerging to help collect this raw data, analyze it and decipher intelligent meaning from it.

While hotel companies today have rich customer databases, they are often ineffectively utilized. Moreover, the data are incomplete or inaccurate and stored across multiple, incompatible databases. It is important to recognize that data, like knowledge, are perishable. To that end, hotel companies should continually update their guest databases and use every customer interaction point as a knowledge-building opportunity. Each customer interaction is a learning experience, and each contact is a chance to collect new information about that guest. These data can then be used to determine what needs guests have and what they are seeking to have fulfilled so that these needs can be pre-empted. If used appropriately, these data become the critical link in creating the 'magic experience' that guests seek. Because these interactions represent important relationship-building opportunities, hotel companies must be cautious of relinquishing control of these processes in favor of third parties and intermediaries. The value of guest data is too important and too valuable to be placed in the hands of others. Who knows how these data may be used in the future to steer one's loyal customer base to a competitor or alternative product or service offering? Technology has placed greater control in the hands of the guest within the guest cycle. While the traditional structure of the guest cycle remains relatively unchanged, the level of engagement and activity undertaken by the guest has increased significantly.

Controlling the business

Given that the hospitality industry operates on strict adherence to operating standards, the technology can be employed to ensure that operating standards, particularly with regards to timeliness, are met. For example, when the waitress places an order on her PDA, the time of placing the order and the time of collecting the order, including the name of the sous chef, can be recorded for subsequent analysis such as comparing this time to the kitchen operating standards. Similarly, in the dining room, the time taken by the waitress to respond to her PDA to collect the food from the kitchen can be recorded so that efficiency in the dining room can also be monitored.

The technology can also be used to improve operational control in bars. Rather than have staff use swipe cards to activate the cash register, bar staff can wear a unique identifying, magnetized wrist band, not unlike a wrist watch. The beverage pourers (spirit, soft drink and beer) and the cash register can then be activated by sensing the unique wrist band. By tracking the pouring actions, the cash register can automatically compile and cost the order thus saving the bar person having to key any sales information. While this can expedite service, it also provides a means of securing high-value beverages; they cannot be poured without sensing an authorized wrist band and once beverages are poured the system expects the staff to account for the pour by way of charging a guest.

These cash registers can be integrated into the property's security system. Any unauthorized access of either the pourers or the cash register, or too long delay between the pouring of a drink and the processing of the sale on the cash can trigger an alarm. For example, if the cash register is tampered with, the duty manager's PDA could emit an alarm. The PDAs can even be programmed to immediately report abnormally high levels of activity. In highly sophisticated systems, this alarm can trigger an appropriately positioned closed-circuit television camera, which in turn can broadcast an image of the cash register and surrounds on the duty manager's PDA screen. Therefore, irrespective of where the duty manager is, she can quickly view the screen, ascertain the situation, make a decision and then communicate her decision to staff.

Understanding the business

These advanced cash registers and pouring systems can be integrated into a more comprehensive, contemporaneous stock control and payroll system. Detailed reports on beverage popularity and profitability can be promptly produced at the end of each trading period. Similarly, staff activity, showing what beverages are sold, average check and other staff performance measures can be produced at the end of each shift. This system can also act as the basis of detailed activity-based accounting systems, which can provide management with highly detailed accounting information about the operational and financial performance of the bars, selling points, staff and beverages as well as trading periods, and even types of guests. For example, the system can calculate typical order and average spend by different type of settlement method.

In a similar fashion, in residential hotels, detailed accounting reports can analyse the revenue and profitability of different room types and rate brackets, market segments, days of the week and even wings or floors of the hotel. The ability to analyse and re-analyse from various perspectives gives the hospitality manager a high level of insight into the way the business operates. This information can greatly help improve operating performance.

While customer satisfaction research has a long and chequered history, in-room technology can greatly enhance a hotel's appreciation of the needs and wants of its guests. Online surveys through television or Internet service, obviously with an appropriate incentive, can be employed to get a better understanding of the guest's needs. Because these surveys are online, no delays, errors or other problems associated with data re-keying can occur, thus improving the quality of the data. Clever, innovative and interesting survey design can also help improve guest response rates.

In highly sophisticated systems, geographical information systems can be used to produce maps showing the property's catchments and capacity to draw different market segments. For example, by getting a guest's zip code or even telephone prefix, a restaurant can produce a map of the city showing which suburbs produce the most customers, or which produce the highest average check and so on. These data can even be integrated with census-level population statistics to show how well a restaurant penetrates particular sociodemographic segments in the community.

Forecasting the business

Several new ICT methods and systems can help sigificantly improve forecasting activities in hospitality operations, be they in full service residential hotels, resorts, casinos or food and beverage operations.

First, data warehousing is the technique of storing all operating transactions (including food ordered, mini bar, pay TV and so on) permanently on a computer. This storage, or data warehouse, can contain vast amounts of information about all aspects of the business; in fact, anything that is captured on a cash register or computer can be stored in the data warehouse. The ready availability of all of these data in the warehouse then facilitates the 'data mining' activities wherein extensive and recursive statistical analysis is undertaken of the data to identify patterns and relationships. These data patterns can point to the existence of key trading patterns such as higher average room rates on particular days of the week, higher average food and beverage checks when particular meals are ordered and so on. They can even point to operational standards such as the individual or overall level of compliance with the time allowed in the kitchen to prepare a particular order, as noted previously when discussing PDAs in dining rooms. Data mining can also be used to identify market segments that are more sophisticated and potentially more profitable than traditional segments such as 'groups' and 'corporates'. It can also facilitate customer lifetime value analysis.

The statistical analysis can also more accurately assess the cost structure of the hospitality operation, especially in terms of identifying cost drivers and the nature of the fixed and variable components of stepped costs which can further enhance the quality of budgeting models and forecasts. Highly sophisticated statistical forecasting techniques can also be used to estimate likely volumes of room sales. The most common instance where this large-scale analysis takes place is in yield management. Armed with this information, the hotel can then more accurately forecast and change upcoming room rates to maximize profit. Simlarly, the long-term data from the warehouse can assist in trend analysis of market segments, operating statistics, staff efficiency, financial performance and so on.

Planning for the business

Rather than struggle to produce standard pro forma reports in the hussle and bustle of daily operations, all of this aforementioned information can be extracted out of the system and fullsomely and thoughtfully, yet quickly and cheaply, analysed and synthesized into a strategic and coherent plan for the future of the business, be it hotel, bar or restaurant. Modern 'productivity' software such as PowerPoint, Excel and Word can be used to seamlessly integrate and present a raft of information in a simple, digestible manner. This is vital in long-term strategic planning and thus reinforces the value of ICT to the hospitality industry.

ICT and the Internet are also making a significant impact on labour management and productivity, as reported in *Hospitality Technology* (January 2005), particularly through Internet-based labour scheduling. It reports on two US-based systems – *eRestaurant Services* in use in the 140 company resturants of California Pizza Kitchen, and *TMx 5.0 Labour Management System* adopted by Bertuccis in their 91 locations. In the United Kingdom, *eProductive Systems* has been adopted in a number of hotel chains. In such hotel chains, it is often department heads or supervisors who devise staff rosters, sometimes still using simple pen and paper 'systems'. One hotel that *eProductive* worked with had 55 different people scheduling staff. In this environment, labour management is post-operational, that is, the cost of labour is established after it has been used, when hours worked are calculated and staff are paid. But the Internet can provide an interface that enables all managers with scheduling responsibility to do so in a standard way and incorporate forecasts of how busy the hotel will be, along with 'rules' preventing those doing the schedule to over-staff. Hence Internet-based scheduling can provide immediate feedback to these managers as to the likely outcome of their decision by forecasting labour cost against forecast revenue. Moreover, more senior managers can examine aggregate data or the schedules themselves to see that the plan will not lead to excessive cost. One trial in an international chain found that this system lead to a 25% reduction in labour cost in the housekeeping department.

ICT also has the potential to contribute to the management of the supply chain through e-procurement. Hotel chains have used e-purchasing for many years (Lawlor and Jayawardena 2003), that is, they have used the Internet as a transmission vehicle to send information. In e-procurement, everything is web based, greatly facilitating the coordination of material, information and financial flows between suppliers and customers. One outcome of this is Avendra, a procurement consortium of some of the world's largest hotel chains (Hyatt, Marriott and IHG, among others). Although not just an e-marketplace, it does make use of sophisticated web-based technology. In a detailed study of 14 hotels in Philadelphia, Kothari et al. (2005) found 'lukewarm enthusiasm for e-procurement' due to concerns about their level of control, security and privacy. This was despite the fact that experience in other industries had demonstrated that e-procurement had reduced labour costs in the purchasing process through less paperwork and fewer mistakes; increased access to world markets and hence lower prices; and improved relationships with suppliers.

Impact of ICT on performance

The examples above of how ICT can transform hospitality operations would suggest that the performance of the industry has been significantly improved by the adoption of these systems. However, Weicher et al. (2005) identify that although 85% of IT spending in the 1980s was in the service sector, productivity in this sector increased only 1.9%, while productivity in the manufacturing sector rose 44%. This is because there is a danger that ICT can be a disabler. This is especially the case if it is never used to challenge why things are done in a company, but instead justify and reinforce the way they are done. IT systems in the service sector have been used to generate more unneeded reports, speed up superfluous work steps, generate unnecessary information, encourage shoddy thinking and misdirect attention to spurious details.

An early, largely qualitative study by David et al. (1996) of chief financial officers in the top 100 hotel chains in the United States reported that 'managers often implemented the technology knowing that they would probably not see measurable productivity improvements ... Nevertheless, (they) went ahead ahead with implementation ...'. This was because they saw ICT at this time as boosting customer service levels and augmenting the number of services offered. From their study of 411 hotel managers in the United States, Canada and the United

Kingdom, Van Hoof et al. (1996) also reported that 'much new technology is designed for guest use'.

Paradoxically, a slightly later quantitative study of 5287 individual hotels by Siguaw et al. (2000) reported that 'the U.S. lodging industry has focused on employing technologies that improve productivity and enhance revenue but has not given strategic priority to technologies designed to improve guest services'. They identified that 84% of hotels had adopted technologies that they argued would help with productivity (management e-mail system, voice mail and interactive television guide), 80% had adopted revenue-enhancing technologies (Internet reservations, teleconferencing, automatic teller machines and mobile phone rentals) and 60% had new technology that enhanced guest services (in-room Internet access, in-room fax machines, and in-room modems). There were significant differences between lodging segments. This was largely in terms of the number of these new technologies that had been adopted – budget hotels had fewer upscale properties, with the latter adopting guest service–focused ICT. The study also found differences in the adoption of ICT between nine types of hotel property (all suite, extended stay, convention, casino, conference, condo, standard, motel and bed-and-breakfast). Chain hotels had also adopted more technologies than independents.

Sigala et al. (2004) proposed a new way of assessing ICT productivity, using a non-parametric technique called data envelopment analysis (DEA).[2] Their study of 93 three-star hotels in the United Kingdom identified the nature and type of ICT in use in each property and measured the level of performance of each department within each hotel. Their empirical findings revealed that the hotels had fairly similar ICT infrastructures, but there were significant differences in performance between the hotels, which they categorized into four groups: 58 inefficient hotels, 19 market efficient, 2 operational efficient and only 14 both market and operational efficient. They concluded that 'productivity gains accrue not from investments per se, but from the full exploitation of the ICT networking and informationalization capabilities'. In other words, ICT alone does not lead to improved performance; it is how it is implemented and exploited that makes the difference.

Ham et al. (2005) also researched the effect of information technology on performance. In their sample of 21 upscale hotels in South Korea, they surveyed 638 employees, asking

---

[2] See Chapter 12.

for their assessment of how IT applications had affected performance in their department within the hotel. Front office applications emerged as having the highest perceived impact on performance, followed by restaurant and banquet management systems.

Finally, in one of the few studies of IT implementation in the foodservice sector, Huo (1998) investigated its impact in 57 US-based restaurant chains. This study in particular investigated the factors that were needed to be in place in order for investment in a new IT system to be sustainable. The two most significant factors were identified as investment intensity and asset turnover in capital intensity.

ICT best practice

ICT clearly cannot be dismissed as irrelevant to hospitality operations. The advent of this technology is being driven by powerful market forces and is readily explained by well-established theory.

In the first instance, the seminal work of Peter Keen at Harvard in the late 1980s and the early 1990s set the framework for the way management should deal with the technology. He argued that the pervasive power of the technology means that it should underpin all strategic decisions of the organization (Keen 1993). He went on to identify a model wherein the failure of management to deal with the challenge of this technology, including opportunity and threat, will result in a sub-optimal outcome for the organization. In contrast, he argued that enlightened management will see a 'compelling business vision' for the integration of ICT capacity into their long-term strategic planning.

In the 1970s, John Rockart established the parameters of the information needs of executives. In essence, Rockart (1979) argued that executives and managers should identify those key critical things that drive the success of their business (he called them critical success factors) and that the information system should report only this information. According to him, if something is not vital to your success, then you do not really need to know about it and certainly do not need to waste time and money reporting it. Rockart's work emphasized two key phrases in informations systems management: 'You cannot manage what you do not measure' and 'what gets measured gets managed'. Therefore, the critical thing is to measure and report only those things that are worthy of valuable executive time. Exception reporting, wherein only deviations outside pre-defined acceptable performance boundaries are reported, is the logical conclusion of this thinking. Therefore, it is possible to imagine a hospitality manager who looks at only a single page report to identify those aspects of the business 'not performing to plan', the rest, given that it is performing to plan does not require the manager's intervention.

These two very technological perspectives argue that hospitality managers need to take an assertive and considered approach to how they employ technology to achieve operative efficiency and access to better information for higher quality decision making. There is a danger that managers will only see ICT in terms of tactical improvements. Armijos et al. (2002) in their study of 90 subscribers to *Hospitality Technology* magazine found that this might have been the case, but that a "clear trend is that industry is moving from a state of merely automating manual processes to one of enhancing business performance and sales through enabling technologies". As Siguaw et al. (2000) point out – "the importance of aligning IT choices with the strategic objectives of a hotel will increase in importance as hospitality executives search for additional mechanisms to obtain competitive advantage".

This is not to suggest that traditional hospitality management needs to be taken over by technology. But to apply ICT effectively in this way, managers themselves must be proficient at understanding information technology and its capabilities and limitations. Connolly and Olsen (2001) argue that as technology becomes more pervasive, requires more investment capital and creates greater impact on the organization, it becomes difficult, if not impossible, to separate technology decisions from business decisions. It is one of the largest corporate investments in organizations today, a trend that is likely to continue for several more years, and as such, it has come into the purview of the organization's top executives. Marketing, finance, human resources and operations executives will be required to take information technology into account when making important company decisions. If they are not proficient in information technology or its abilities and limitations, they could be running an ineffective organization. Hence ICT has a boundary-spanning role, as illustrated in Figure 8.1.

In view of this, ICT as a management activity must have a status in the organization similar to other functions within the firm. Within the corporate hierarchy, it should be managed at executive level and integrated into the key initiatives of the business. Cline and Warner (1999) reported that the chief financial officer had the greatest involvement in IT. But forward-thinking and techno-savvy organizations are expanding

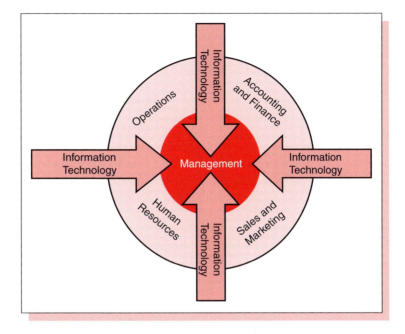

Figure 8.1
IT as the boundary spanner (*Source*: Connolly and Olsen 2001).

and elevating a number of technology positions in the executive ranks to demonstrate a company's commitment toward creating a high-technology infrastructure and to aid in pursuing high-technology strategic initiatives so that along with the chief information officer, there are also the chief technology officer, chief knowledge officer and chief web officer (Connolly and Olsen 2001).

Summary and conclusions

Frew (2000) argued that 1994 was a 'milestone year' in the ICT research literature. In the mid-1990s, there was a major upswing in the studies being undertaken and reported in journals. Shortly afterwards, Frew (2000) identified three major industry-led think-tanks concerned with the impact that ICT was having on tourism and hospitality. The first of these was in Europe under the 5th Framework Programme looking at Informations Society Applications for Transport and Associated Services. In 1997, the Strategic Advisory Group published a report, which led directly to the proposal of specific research fields in this area. Second, between 1997 and 1999, a series of think-tanks were organized by the International Hotel and Restaurant Association leading to major report on ICT in the hospitality industry (Connolly and Olsen 1999). And finally, in 1999 the Hospitality Industry Technology Association wrote a major report (Hamilton 1999) from a more technology-centric perspective, which was published in the first edition of a new journal devoted to ICT in hospitality.

It might be thought that as a result of these initiatives, ICT research in hospitality operations would grow significantly in the early 2000s. In fact this has not been the case. There has been sustained research into ICT, but this has tended to be in tourism rather than hospitality, with focus on marketing rather than operations. And of the research that has been done, especially into the impact that ICT has had on operational performance, the majority has tended to research managerial perceptions of this impact rather than empirically test the actual impact. More research is required in the area of ICT's measurable impact on productivity, employee satisfaction, service quality and innovation.

In conclusion, the advent of the technology presents many opportunities and threats to the hospitality industry. Those that seek to understand the technology and harness it will still be able to offer traditional hospitality, albeit with modern efficiency and effectiveness. Cline and Warner (1999) found that firms were investing 3.1% of their revenue in ICT and were planning to invest more in the future. In contrast, those that fail to invest run the risk of being strategically exposed and ill-equipped to compete with their more technologically literate competitors. It can be said that ICT changes nothing, in the sense that hospitality still requires guest staff interaction to drive guest satisfaction, yet it changes everything, in the sense that it creates a new competitive dynamic.

Acknowledgement

The author would like to acknowledge the contribution of the Editor in drafting this chapter.

References

Armijos, A., DeFranco, A., Hamilton, M. and Skorupa, J. (2002) Technology trends in the lodging industry: a survey of multi-unit lodging operators, *International Journal of Hospitality Information Technology*, 2, 2, 1–18

Cline, R. S. and Warner, M. M. (1999) *Hospitality 2000: the technology*, Arthur Andersen Hospitality and Leisure Executive Report: New York

Connolly, D. J. and Olsen, M. D. (1999) *Hospitality Technology in the New Millennium*, Findings of the Think Tanks on Technology at the International Hotel and Restaurant Association (IHRA): Paris

Connolly, D. J. and Olsen, M. D. (2001) An environmental assessment of how technology is reshaping the hospitality industry, *Tourism and Hospitality Research: The Surrey Quarterly Review*, 3, 1, 73–93

David, J. S., Grabski, S. and Kasavana, M. (1996) The productivity paradox of hotel-industry technology, *Cornell Hotel and Restaurant Administration Quarterly*, 37, 2, 64–70

Davis, S. and Meyer C. (1998) *Blur: The Speed of Change in the Connected Economy*, Capstone: Oxford

Frew, A. J. (2000) Information and communications technology research in the travel and tourism domain: perspective and direction, *Journal of Travel Research*, 39, 2, 136–145

Gates, W. H. (1999) *Business @ the Speed of Thought: Using a Digintal Nervous System*, Time Warner Books: New York

Ham, S., Kim, W. G. and Jeong, S. (2005) Effect of information technology on performance in upscale hotels, *International Journal of Hospitality Management*, 24, 2, 281–294

Hamilton, M. (1999) Vision IT: A report on a hospitality technology think tank, *International Journal of Hospitality Information Technology*, 1, 1, 113–119

Huo, Y. H. (1998) Information technology and the performance of the restaurant firms, *Journal of Hospitality & Tourism Research*, 22, 3, 239–251

Keen, P. W. K. (1993) *Shaping the Future: Business Design Through Information Technology*, Harvard Business School Press: Cambridge

Kothari, T., Hu, C. and Roehl, W. S. (2005) e-Procurement: an emerging tool for the hotel supply chain management, *International Journal of Hospitality Management*, 24, 3, 369–389

Lawlor, F. and Jayawardena, C. (2003) Purchasing for 4,000 hotels: the case of Avendra, *International Journal of Contemporary Hospitality Management*, 15, 6, 346–348

O'Connor, P. and Murphy, J. (2004) Research on information technology in the hospitality industry, *International Journal of Hospitality Management*, 23, 5, 473–484

Porter, M. (1985) *Competitive Advantage: creating and sustaining superior performance*, New York: Free Press

Rockart, J. (1979) Chief executives define their own data needs, *Harvard Business Review,* March–April, 81–93

Sigala, M., Airey, D., Jones, P. and Lockwood, A. (2004) ICT paradox lost? A stepwise DEA methodology to evaluate technology investments in tourism settings, *Journal of Travel Research*, 43, 2, 180–192

Siguaw, J. A., Enz, C. A. and Namasivayam, K. (2000) Adoption of information technology in U.S. hotels: strategically driven objectives, *Journal of Travel Research*, 39, 2, 192–201

Van Hoof, H. B., Collins, G. R., Combrink, T. E. and Verbeeten, M. J. (1996) An assessment of the U.S. lodging industry, *Cornell Hotel and Restaurant Administration Quarterly*, 36, 5, 64–69

Weicher, M., Chu, W. W., Lin W. C., Le, V. and Yu, D. (2005) Business process reengineering: analysis and recommendations, *Communications Horizons*, http://www.netlib.com/bpr1.htm accessed 10 Oct 2007

CHAPTER 9

Outsourcing

Pornpissanu Promsivapallop

Faculty of Hospitality and Tourism
Prince of Songkla University
Kathu, Phuket, Thailand

Introduction

In most industries, the concept of outsourcing is considered from the perspective of firms considering the outsource decision. But in the hospitality industry, there are whole sectors of the industry that exist to supply outsourced products and services, namely hotel management companies, contract foodservice providers and inflight caterers. Many of these firms are large, global companies, such as Four Seasons, Sodexho, Compass and Aramark. Whilst in flight catering, two companies – LSG Sky Chefs and Gate Gourmet – have a combined global market share of 55% (Jones 2004). Hence in this chapter, outsourcing is considered from both the client firm and the supplier perspective. However, the discussion of the supplier perspective will be limited, as almost no operations research into this has been conducted.

The chapter begins with a review of alternative definitions of outsourcing and then explores different types of outsourcing. This is followed by a discussion of the benefits, cost and risks of outsourcing. Two alternative theories of outsourcing – transaction cost economics (TCE) and resource-based view (RBV) – are then compared, before evaluating the research that has been conducted into outsourcing in the hospitality industry. The chapter concludes by considering the provision of outsourced service, through management contracts and franchising, by hospitality companies.

Definition of outsourcing

There is much debate in the management literature concerning the definition of outsourcing. Many agree that the core idea surrounding the outsourcing concept involves moving some of the firm's activities to outside providers. Lankford and Parsa (1999), for example, put forward a simple definition referring to it as the procurement of products or services from sources that are external to the organization. In addition, many authors go on to emphasize that outsourcing should involve only activities that have been performed in-house. Semlinger (1991), quoted in Jenster and Pedersen (2000: 148), defines outsourcing as the market procurement of formerly in-house-produced goods and services from legally independent supplier firms. According to Domberger (1998), Lonsdale (1999) and Bailey et al. (2002) outsourcing is concerned with the transfer of production of goods and services that have been carried out internally to an external provider.

Espino-Rodriguez and Padron-Robaina (2004) explain that the word outsourcing has widely been used, but often as a synonym for the traditional concept of subcontracting, externalization, make-or-buy decision, and disintegration of activities. However, Fan (2000: 213) stresses the fundamental difference between outsourcing and these other concepts, arguing that outsourcing involves only an existing internal activity. Embleton and Wright (1998) and Oates (1998) argue that the creation of a long-term relationship is key to the outsourcing philosophy. Building on the same principle, Greer et al. (1999) maintain that this long-term perspective differentiates outsourcing from subcontracting. They explain that outsourcing possesses a temporal dimension involving long-term and even permanent arrangements, whereas subcontracting and contracting out are rather short-term or temporary contractual interactions between two parties.

Furthermore, some emphasize management strategy as being a significant aspect of outsourcing. In their study of outsourcing strategy in hotels in Shanghai, Lam and Han (2005: 42–43) refer to outsourcing as a management strategy in which a hotel utilizes and forms strategic alliances with specialized outsourcing supplier to operate certain hotel functions, in an attempt to reduce costs and risks and to improve efficiency. The strategic nature of outsourcing is supported by experience in the flight catering industry. In the early 1990s two airlines, Lufthansa and Swissair, decided that the provision of meals onboard was core to their business, and they set up their own flight catering companies, LSG Sky Chefs and Gate Gourmet. At the same time, other airlines were deciding to outsource catering and disposed of their own flight kitchens – usually by selling them and then contracting out to these two firms. For instance, British Airways transferred its two kitchens at London Heathrow to Gate Gourmet. It seems in this sector at least, the strategy was either to get into outsourced services in a big way or to get out completely.

Another essential element put forward by scholars is the tendency of asset transfer from the firm to the outside partners. Quelin and Duhamel (2003: 648) define outsourcing as the operation of shifting a transaction previously governed internally to an external supplier through a long-term contract, and emphasize the transfer of ownership of a business function, often including a transfer of personnel and physical assets, to the vendor. Likewise, McMarthy and Anagnostou (2004) underline that outsourcing not only purchases products or services from sources that are external to the organization, but also transfers the responsibility of the physical business function and often the associated knowledge to the external organization. Chase et al. (2004: 372) explain outsourcing as the act of not only moving some of a firm's internal activities but also including decision responsibility to outside providers. The terms of agreement are established in a contract. It goes beyond the more common purchasing and consulting contracts because not only are the activities transferred, but also resources that make the activities occur, including people, facilities, equipment, technology, and other assets, are transferred as well. This is usually the case when a firm outsources its employee feeding to a contract foodservice company or when a hotel outsources its restaurant to a well-known restaurant brand.

To sum up, although the definition of outsourcing is still debatable, the generally agreed principal philosophy of outsourcing can be drawn from the existing literature. The key elements presented in the outsourcing conception are outlined below:

- externalization of internal activities previously carried out in-house to outside independent suppliers
- the decision is strategic in nature
- it may involve the transfer of assets
- the production responsibility of the activity given to the outside expert can be partial or whole

Types of outsourcing

The outsourcing definition provided by Gilley and Rasheed (2000) includes two types of outsourcing: substitution-based outsourcing and abstention-based outsourcing. This classification is based on the characteristics of activity to be outsourced whether it is the one previously produced in-house or a new activity. Substitution-based outsourcing involves the external purchases for internal activities, the one previously produced in the company. This type of outsourcing may be viewed as vertical disintegration. Another type, abstention-based outsourcing, relates to the purchase of new activities which never occur in-house.

On the other hand, Bounfour (1999: 133) categorizes outsourcing into three types for the purpose of his study about outsourcing of intangibles. These three groups of outsourcing, according to him, are as follows:

- resorting to external sources for carrying out (intangible) activities (mostly professional services)

- putting an activity, until now internalized, on the marketplace
- organizing an internal market within the organization for the supply of (intangible) activities (for instance, via setting up an ad hoc structure dedicated to general accounting for different members of a group)

The third group may apply to a large corporation that consists of a number of groups or companies within it. However, some may question whether the third type of outsourcing fits the concept, since the activity is still produced internally.

Fill and Visser (2000: 43–44) quote Hiemstra and van Tilburg's (1993) classification of outsourcing that includes capacity outsourcing and non-capacity outsourcing. The first refers to activities which are also performed by the company. The reason for capacity outsourcing is that internal production capacity becomes temporarily insufficient perhaps due to seasonal demand fluctuation. Non-capacity outsourcing, on the other hand, concerns the outsourcing of activities which are no longer pursued by the organization itself.

Furthermore, they cite Mylott's (1995) views of different types of outsourcing. According to him, outsourcing takes place in three different forms, namely full outsourcing, selective outsourcing and everything-in-between outsourcing. In full outsourcing, the external supplier is responsible for the whole operation of the activity. Selective outsourcing involves the supplier to provide selected services within the whole activity. Everything-in-between outsourcing falls between the first two types.

Mylott (1995) in Fill and Visser (2000: 44) therefore propose a continuum of outsourcing. At one extreme, outsourcing can be seen in the form of hiring temporary labour or machines to relieve capacity overload for short-term purposes. At the other extreme, complete responsibility is given to the supplier who becomes strategic partner. Various forms of consultancy and skills provision fit in the middle of the continuum. Time is reflected across the continuum with short-term market exchanges at one end and long-term, relational exchanges at the other.

Webster et al. (1997: 829) propose three types of outsourcing as follows:

- Capacity – short-lived and unstable; is set up to meet unexpected or exceptional increases in demand.
- Specialized – long-term and enduring; established by the principal to access specialized expertise or technology which is not available in-house.

- Economic – cost benefits can be obtained by subcontracting work out.

In addition, a more comprehensive classification is provided by Espino-Rodriguez and Padron-Robaina (2004). They distinguish various types of outsourcing according to a range of criteria. Different types of outsourcing can be classified depending on the degree of decision analysis, the range, the degree of integration, the property relationship, the level of administrative control and the ownership, as outlined in Table 9.1.

Espino-Rodriguez and Padron-Robaina (2004) provide a clear explanation to the classification based on the level of decision analysis. According to them, analysis made in the case of tactical outsourcing is very simple. The decision is usually taken intuitively and is based on costs, with no consideration of the other benefits and risks involved in the decision. However, the analysis made in strategic outsourcing is more detailed, and it involves all levels of management and follows a sound process of decision. This creates a long-term co-operation with the supplier. It takes other aspects apart from costs into consideration, including factors such as achieving improved

Table 9.1 Types of outsourcing

Classification criteria	Types of outsourcing
Depending on the level of decision analysis	● Strategic outsourcing
	● Tactical or traditional outsourcing
Depending on its range	● Total outsourcing
	● Selective or partial outsourcing
Depending on the level of integration	● Outsourcing
	● Quasi-outsourcing
Depending on the property relationship	● Group or internal outsourcing
	● Non-group or external outsourcing
Depending on administrative control	● Outsourcing of performance
	● Outsourcing of resources
Depending on ownership	● Private outsourcing
	● Public outsourcing

Source: Espino-Rodriguez and Padron-Robaina (2004).

quality operations and accessing capabilities and knowledge of outside experts. Therefore, strategic outsourcing is a broader, more complete concept of the process. It is regarded as a strategy that becomes part of the company's strategic management.

Benefits of outsourcing

Outsourcing has been reported to provide numerous benefits to the organizations. Clearly, cost savings is the prime reason for outsourcing. Outsourcing firms often achieve cost advantages relative to vertically integrated firms. This view has been supported by an extensive body of literature both conceptually (such as Kakabadse and Kakabadse 2000; Domberger 1998; Blumberg 1998; Jennings 2002) and empirically reported as the top benefit (Outsourcing Institute 1998; Bailey et al. 2002; Kakabadse and Kakabadse 2003; Quelin and Duhamel 2003). It is important to clarify the meaning of costs. The type of costs that tends to fall as a result of efficiency inherent in outsourcing is the operation cost (see the section 'Mechanisms for achieving outsource benefits'). Another type of costs, transaction costs, or the costs of using the market to purchase goods and services, usually increase as firms decide to outsource (Williamson 1979, 1981).

However, outsourcing primarily for cost savings is of concern to a number of scholars. Lonsdale and Cox (1998) and McIvor (2000) view cost saving purpose of outsourcing as a short-term perspective, taking place in an ad hoc fashion. The authors link the increasing failures as a result of outsourcing with this motivating factor. Nevertheless, it is argued here that outsourcing on the basis of cost savings is not necessarily tactical. Increasingly, outsourcing has been employed as the top-corporate-level strategy in many large companies in order to maximize their operation efficiency, and hence minimize costs (Quelin and Duhamel 2003). Furthermore, outsourcing for short-term purposes might not be considered outsourcing in the first place but merely the practice of subcontracting.

The second most often mentioned benefit is the ability of companies to focus on their core business (such as Quinn and Hilmer 1994; Dess et al. 1995; Oates 1998). This is indeed an important benefit since the resources each firm possesses are limited. When freed from devoting resources to areas that are not in its expertise, the company can focus its entire energy and resources on the activities that truly reflect their core competencies.

Another reason for outsourcing is access to external competencies (Quinn and Hilmer 1994; Quinn 1999; Jennings 2002;

Quelin and Duhamel 2003). This argument has been strongly emphasized by Quinn and Hilmer (1994) and Quinn (1999) as the most strategically important benefit the company can gain from outsourcing. Outsourcing presents opportunities for companies to fully leverage the expertise, innovation and investments of the suppliers in the market. These capabilities may be prohibitively expensive or even impossible to duplicate internally.

Being flexible is also frequently claimed as a reason that drives outsourcing decision (Domberger 1998; Jennings 2002; Quelin and Duhamel 2003). Outsourcing allows organizations to quickly response to customer's needs and changes in the dynamic environment. This is particularly true in the case where the company experiences great demand fluctuations (Jennings 2002). In the efforts to optimally manage business upturns and downturns, outsourcing is used as a means to gain flexibility. Furthermore, as explained by Domberger (1998), the company's external suppliers in the form of networks of small organizations can adjust quickly and at lower cost to changing demand conditions compared to integrated organizations.

In addition, outsourcing includes other possible benefits, though less frequently mentioned. For example, it tends to promote competition among outside suppliers. Competition may also result in the availability of higher-quality goods, and services in the future can be reassured (Kotabe and Murray 1990). Cash infusion is another advantage the firms stand to gain from outsourcing (Embleton and Wright 1998; Outsourcing Institute 1998). This is because outsourcing often involves the transfer of assets from the firm to the supplier (Quelin and Duhamel 2003). This asset transfer may result in significant income for the firm, and thus it can use the cash to fund the investment to enhance its core activities. Finally, outsourcing reduces risks (Quinn and Hilmer 1994; Outsourcing Institute 1998). As the business environment is changing extremely quickly, significant investments exhibit tremendous risks. Firms must therefore think carefully not to get into big investments in the areas they lack expertise in order to reduce risks. Indeed, the risks that the firm does not wish to take can be shifted to the outside suppliers who are specialized in the area, willing to invest and more capable of managing the risks inherent in the particular areas. Jones (2002) found that following 9/11, the impact of the decline in demand for air travel affected flight caterers more than airlines. There was 25% fall in passenger numbers, but a 30% fall in demand for airline meals. This was because the fall in demand was significant on long-haul flights, which serve more than one meal, but minimal on short-haul, low-cost airlines that do not provide a complimentary meal service.

Mechanisms for achieving outsource benefits

To begin with, outsourcing contributes to increasing the firm's cost efficiency due to two key factors: market competition (Domberger 1998; Vining and Globerman 1999) and specialization (Domberger 1998; Jacobides 2005). As stated earlier, outsourcing allows firms to focus on its core activities and shift non-core activities to outside suppliers in the market. At the macro-level, this leads to numerous business opportunities to various businesses. For example, many businesses, today, have started to adopt outsourcing strategies by deciding to focus on only their main activities, and thus outsource less important activities such as cleaning and security. This creates significant opportunities to catering, cleaning and security service providers to enter into the market to provide services to all other companies in the area. The higher is the business opportunities for these contract service providers, the more firms will enter this market. Subsequently, this leads to higher competition. Competition forces firms to constantly innovate in order to dominate its competitors and exceed customer's expectations by simultaneously raising productivity and improving quality. Furthermore, in a competitive market, companies are normally forced to price at the lowest possible marginal cost (Vining and Globerman 1999). These pressures leave the firms no options but to keep innovating and investing to maximize efficiency and thus offer the lowest price possible. This was the case in the flight catering industry. The growth of LSG Sky Chefs and Gate Gourmet led to competition for contracts between them, which over a course of five years contributed to a reduction of 15–20% in prices (Jones 2004).

In contrast, producing multiple activities in-house may cause operational inefficiencies in a number of ways. First, the level of competitive pressures faced by the suppliers in the market is not present within the company (Domberger 1998) since the internal production units may act as monopolists who provide services to captive internal customers (Porter 1990). Therefore, internal production units have fewer incentives to be efficient. Secondly, if too many activities are organized within the company, it will experience diseconomies of scope in management (Coase 1996).

Cost efficiency is also created by specialization (Domberger 1998). Apart from increasing business opportunities, outsourcing changes the way firms compete by transforming the entire industry from comprising generalists to specialists (Jacobides 2005). In the past, companies used to vertically integrate to carry out most activities in-house. This self-sufficient practice encouraged organizations to be able to produce everything – but nothing well. However, once outsourcing has become more popular, companies – both the outsourcing firms and suppliers – are presented with opportunities to focus and be best at producing their selected main activities. All firms in the economy, therefore, have evolved to focus and increase specialization in their areas of business.

The link between specialization and cost efficiency is clearly explained by Domberger (1998). He argues that outsourcing enhances specialization in two ways. First, the outsourcing organization can focus on a narrowed range of internal production. Secondly, on the supply side of the market, the suppliers can increase its focused production to serve the entire market once more companies outsource the activity supplied by the supplier. The second point addressed by Domberger is particularly significant because it allows suppliers to undertake an activity in a much greater scale. This directly leads to economies of scale where costs per unit of production declines as a result of an increase in production volume. As mentioned earlier, suppliers, under competitive pressures, are willing to invest in the development of their core capabilities in terms of both technology and human resources development. They, however, need not reinvest in these set-up costs in each transaction they serve the customer. Being a customer, outsourcing firm, therefore, stand to gain from the cost savings offered by the outside specialists who operate at scale economies.

The second group of benefits companies gain from outsourcing is product quality. On the one hand, quality provided by the external specialists is realized by the ongoing innovation forced by market competition as previously explained. Hence, the first source of quality improvements comes from market. It is the organization's leverage of the best supplier's innovations and competencies (Quinn 1999). On the other hand, quality is attained from the specialization within the organization itself. An increased focus on an organization's core competencies and outsourcing non-core activities allows the firm to increase managerial attention and resource allocation to the core activities (Quinn and Hilmer 1994). The firm is permitted to become truly specialized and produce its core activities at a level superior to its competitors. The combined sources of quality attained from the market and that generated within the company lead to an achievement of best performance in both core and non-core activities.

In the UK in the 1980s, the government began requiring all public sector organizations – schools, hospitals, military establishments and others – to put their catering services out to competitive tender. This policy was based on the view that outsourcing this to contract foodservice companies would lead to significant cost savings and improved quality. A number of studies seem to support this view.

Costs and risks of outsourcing

The benefits discussed in the previous section make outsourcing a promising strategy for companies seeking competitive edge. Nonetheless, outsourcing comes with costs. As mentioned in the previous section, there are two main types of costs associated with outsourcing. The first category, production cost, has been proved in favour of outsourcing since outsourcing drives operational cost efficiency. The second category, transaction costs, however increase. As explained by Coase (1996), there are costs of using the price mechanism in the market. These costs include the cost of searching for prices, negotiating and concluding a separate contract for each transaction. Based on this principle, Williamson (1979, 1981) developed the theory of transaction cost economics (TCE) in deciding whether to produce each activity within the company or purchase it from the market based on the costs of each transaction. TCE is frequently used to explain outsourcing and thus requires clarification.

TCE holds that, in certain situations, the costs of market exchange may increase substantially and surpass the production efficiency provided by the market. This is due to two behaviour assumptions: bounded rationality and opportunism of the individuals in the marketplace who are involved with the transactions. Bounded rationality is the assumption where individuals intend to be rational but are limited in solving complex problems and in processing information. Opportunism, on the other hand, assumes that individuals seek to make allowance for self-interest, with guile.

Building on Willamson's assumptions, outsourcing costs have been put forward by several scholars. Vining and Globerman (1999) propose two main costs of a transaction, including bargaining costs and opportunism costs. Both cost circumstances occur when at least one party acts self-interestedly but in good faith in bargaining situations and in bad faith in opportunisms. Bargaining costs include costs of negotiating at pre-contract and post-contract stages to make changes to the contract when unforeseen circumstances arise, costs of monitoring of the performance and costs of disputes. Opportunism costs, on the other hand, are the costs of the outsourcing partner's behaviour to change the agreed terms of a transaction to be more in their favour. Domberger (1998) adds to this the explicit costs of transaction which are the costs of searching for and selecting suppliers, writing specifications, drafting contracts and bidding before the bargaining costs, explained by Vining and Globerman, would occur. Furthermore, because of the risks of the supplier's opportunistic behaviour leading to the dangers of being exploited by the suppliers, the outsourcing company may experience a hold-up risk when they get locked into the disadvantaged contract. This leads to a greater cost of monitoring the supplier's performance to guard against the opportunistic behaviours.

However, these opportunistic behaviours are believed to be present within the organization as well as in the market. The levels of opportunisms by the company's own employees are believed, nonetheless, to be lower than the market since distribution of profits is more relevant in dealings between organizations (Vining and Globerman 1999). Yet this point is not completely convincing (Domberger 1998). He postulates a lack of theory to explain why it is easier to monitor and control internal staff than external suppliers.

Then again, the supplier's opportunistic behaviour assumption seems to dispute the view of several academics who advocate for trust as a key success factor in collaborative relationship (Rugman and D'Cruz 1997; Blomqvist et al. 2005). Furthermore, it can be argued that the opportunism assumption becomes less relevant when outsourcing increases. As explained in the previous section, outsourcing drives market competition and thus suppliers must raise quality to survive. In the competitive market, suppliers need to find their way to delight the customer at a higher level than its competitors. Clearly, outsourcing companies are dissatisfied by being exploited and want to avoid suppliers who exhibit high level of opportunisms. Thus, suppliers are forced to minimize the opportunistic behaviours in order to sustain its business.

Furthermore, the cost of transaction is determined by a number of factors. As explained above, the level of competition in the market is one of the factors that determine the level of opportunisms. Other factors include the level of asset specificity (Williamson 1979, 1981), which refers to the degree of specialization of the asset required for a particular transaction or user. High specificity creates sunk costs and thus raises potential for opportunisms. Another factor is the production/activity complexity level (Vining and Globerman 1999). This refers to the degree of difficulty in specifying and monitoring the terms and conditions of a transaction as a result of uncertainty and information asymmetry. The transaction that exhibits a high degree of complexity leads to high transaction costs.

The majority of outsourcing disadvantages fall into the categories described under the umbrella of transaction costs. The first six types of disadvantages – being exploited, loss of control, dependence on suppliers, confidentiality and security issues, and transfer of know-how that encourages new competitors – are directly related to the fears of supplier's opportunism. Another group of outsourcing pitfalls including loss of critical skills, risk of service provider's deficient capabilities, and being difficult and costly to bring back in-house all happen due to the organization's own false decision made when outsourcing. This is attributed to a number of factors such as inability to identify the correct types of activities to outsourcing. This is a significant problem faced by managers since distinguishing core activities from non-core ones is highly problematic (Kakabadse and Kakabadse 2000; Alexander and Young 1996; McIvor 2000). Failure in market search for true experts could be another factor that leads to receiving inadequate services. Outsourcing in the market that lacks quality suppliers is dangerous (Lonsdale 1999; Gronhaug and Haugland 2005), and thus organizations should not outsource if they cannot identify suppliers that can provide quality service up to the agreed standards.

In addition, other key negative aspects of outsourcing relate to the human resources issues. Since outsourcing normally involves a transfer of assets and possible staff from the outsourcing organization to the external suppliers (Quelin and Duhamel 2003), this can considerably affect the morale of existing staff and may even in some cases generate internal fears and employee resistance (Embleton and Wright 1998; Venkatesan 1992; Blumberg 1998; Oates 1998; Lonsdale and Cox 2000). This can subsequently lead to a negative public image due to large employee layoffs (Embleton and Wright 1998).

However, as argued by Kakabadse and Kakabadse (2000), this problem depends crucially on how well the outsourcing is planned, implemented and communicated to the employees within the organization. Furthermore, outsourcing can provide, in certain cases, good career development opportunities for the employees who get transferred to the suppliers. This is particularly true because their knowledge and skills should match the external expert better than being in less important business functions of the outsourcing firm. In other words, they move from working in non-core activity of one company to working in core activity of another company. Therefore, the external supplier should be able to provide them much more promising career development opportunities.

The final risk of outsourcing is raised by Blumberg (1998). He cautions that outsourcing the direct customer contact activities may put the organization at risks of alienating the customers. However, it is argued here that this risk can be managed if outsourcing is well-planned and the supplier has been carefully selected. More importantly, the risk is over-shadowed by the benefits the outside experts stand to offer in terms of the best quality of the particular activity available in the market. This way, the renewed supplier may even enhance the company's reputation and can indeed add more value to its customers.

In fact, one critical reason explaining why managers are dis-satisfied with the outcome of their outsourcing decisions is due to a deficiency in outsourcing decision-making (Lonsdale 1999; McIvor 2000). Outsourcing is a strategic tool with great potentials to change the way organizations are managed for value maximization. It is argued here that most of the risks presented above, if managed properly, can be limited. This view is supported by Blumberg (1998). He suggests outsourc-ing organizations need to change the management mindset in order to minimize the outsourcing downsides and make the most of the benefits. This argument is well supported by the empirical study of outsourcing best practice in organizations by Kakabadse and Kakabadse (2003). The findings reveal that high-performance companies report greater benefits than do average-performing companies. One factor distinguishing best practice outsourcing organizations from the rest is the degree of top-management commitment to the outsourcing strat-egy and because the organizations are well prepared prior to implementing the outsourcing plan.

In conclusion, it is clear from the above discussion that out-sourcing can generate tremendous benefits needed by organi-zations. These benefits are grouped into two categories: operational cost efficiency and product quality. The benefits primarily stem from market competition and specialization spurred by outsourcing and will subsequently drive more out-sourcing, the never-ending process. Moreover, all activities even at the non-core level within the organization can be of the best quality level since they are provided by the best external spe-cialists in their areas. Once successfully combined, the company starts offering the best-of-everything product to the market.

Alternative theoretical perspectives

Outsourcing is the question of externalization of activities. It directly involves the decision whether to source activities internally or externally. This relates to the problem of the firm's boundaries. It is claimed that outsourcing behaviour of the companies can be explained by two main approaches including economic perspective of transaction cost economics (TCE) and strategic approach based on resource-based view (RBV).

Transaction cost economics

Most outsourcing research has been explained by the TCE perspective; however, the focus is on the context of non-service industries. Outsourcing in the TCE context is organized for efficiency maximization. TCE theorists view firms as governance structures as opposed to production functions explained by neoclassical economists. It is the efficiency gained from administrative instrument that facilitates exchange between economic actors. Markets and hierarchies (the firm) are proposed as alternative instruments for completing the firm's transactions. It is assumed that the governance exchange between economic actors is costly due to transaction governing and monitoring. Transactions are organized to achieve economic optimum of both production expenses and transaction costs.

TCE posits that firms are faced with different sourcing modes of all activities in their operations either to obtain from the suppliers in the market or to produce in-house. It is imperative for any organization to manage each transaction in the most efficient manner by correctly matching a variety of transactions to different sourcing alternatives. By analysing the costs of transactions of each different activity, TCE suggests managers to carry out all activities that possess high transaction costs and outsource all others whose transaction costs are low. The costs of transactions are determined by three key dimensions including asset specificity, uncertainty and frequency.

Resource-based view

More recently, the strategic resource-based approach has emerged as an alternative to explain outsourcing decisions. From this perspective, outsourcing is treated as a strategy that helps raise the firm's competitive advantage. The RBV sees the firm as an entity with a collection of resources. It considers that firms own different types of resources which enable them to develop different strategies. The firm's ability to sustain competitive advantage depends on its ability to effectively exploit its resources and to protect its competitors to imitate its strategy. The RVB theorists reject traditional economic assumptions that resources are homogeneous and perfectly mobile. Instead, they argue that resources are heterogeneously distributed across firms and are imperfectly transferred among them (Barney 1991; Wernerfelt 1984). This suggests firms deliberately position themselves to create differentiation in the market based on their unique resources.

According to Barney (1991), firm's resources include all assets, capabilities and organization processes that enable it to conceive of and implement strategies that improve its efficiency and effectiveness. However, not all resources within the firm have the potential to be a source of sustainable advantage. Barney (1991) contends that the resources that enable firms to sustain competitive advantage are only those that are valuable, rare, imperfectly imitable and non-substitutable. The author explains that a competitive advantage is achieved when a value-creating strategy implemented by the firm is unique in the market. The competitive advantage is sustained if the firm's competitors continue to find it impossible to duplicate it. Furthermore, the strategic resources contributing to the sources of competitive advantage are ascribed by Prahalad and Hamel (1990) as the distinctive core competencies of the organization.

The RBV authors put forward that, in order to gain competitive advantage, organizations need to focus on their unique sets of core resources and competencies. In other words, activities that are based on the company's core resources and capabilities should be produced in-house and all activities that do not truly reflect the company's unique resources and ability should be outsourced.

However, the core conception of RBV, sources of competitive advantage stemming from the resources and capabilities owned and controlled by a single firm, is challenged by Dyer and Singh (1998). They point out that a firm's critical resources may in fact extend beyond its boundaries. Organizations that combine resources in unique ways may realize an advantage over competing firms who are unable or unwilling to do so.

In addition, RBV invites further criticisms. Gronhaug and Haugland (2005) claim that RBV has a less clear-cut conception of sourcing decisions and firm boundaries than TCE. Although it argues that the direction of firm growth is determined by the firm's existing stock of resources and competencies, the viewpoint does not clearly explain which activities should be performed within the boundaries of the firm and which should be performed in the market. Defining core competency for any one organization is real problematic (Kakabadse and Kakabadse 2000) and applying the theory is difficult in practice (Domberger 1998).

Hotel outsourcing research

The outsourcing research in the hotel sector has been dominated by the strategic approach. The findings of the studies generally support the core argument of the theory. Through a series of articles, Espino-Rodriguez and Padron-Robaina provide empirical analysis, employing mainly the RBV theory, in various aspects of outsourcing issues. Using 50 hotels in the Canary Islands in Spain in their study, Espino-Rodriguez and Padron-Robaina (2005a) examine outsourcing of the hotel activities in general. The authors emphasize the need to focus outsourcing study in a single location as outsourcing of activities depends greatly on the offer of services existing in the area. The authors argue that any analysis of several locations could bias the results.

The results report activity performance, substitutability and transferability of the activities as the key determinants of the hotel outsourcing decisions. Non-core activities that yield low degree of competitive advantage to the hotels, described as those which offer low performance or generate less value and comprise resources that are easily substitutable and transferable in the market, are more likely to be outsourced. The authors also confirm that an outsourcing of less strategic activities is positively related to the hotel performance both in terms of financial and non-financial perspectives. Even though the level of outsourcing in the studied hotels is currently low, the managers are reported to perceive outsourcing as having a great potential for operations strategy particularly for improving quality, increasing flexibility and providing better service (Espino-Rodriguez and Padron-Robaina 2004, 2005b). Furthermore, loss of control and autonomy together with distrust of suppliers currently limit the use of outsourcing in the hotels.

In addition, Lam and Han (2005) also take the strategic approach by examining the outsourcing strategy as perceived by hotel managers in Shanghai. Similar to the works of Espino-Rodriguez and Padron-Robaina, a single location is adopted in this study. The findings indicate that the outsourcing market in the city is immature as it is hindered by two key factors including the incompleteness of local laws to protect hotel investors when the outsourcing business conflicts arise and the business cultural incompatibility between hotels dominated by Chinese managers and outsourcing suppliers.

A few studies consider outsourcing of a specific activity or a group of activities in the hotels with a RBV analysis. Within the information systems function, the study by Espino-Rodriguez and Gil-Padilla (2005a) find that hotels tend to retain in-house the critical and differentiating part of IT activity that add more value and improve the hotel's competitiveness. Likewise, the leisure activities that are highly specific to the hotels are found to perform better when they are carried out in-house (Espino-Rodriguez and Gil-Padilla 2005b). Food and beverage operations, normally considered as a key function in hotels, are reported to be increasingly outsourced in both North America and the United Kingdom to well-known branded restaurant chains as this strategy helps the hotel to gain financial stability, know-how and competitiveness (Hallam and Baum 1996). Hemmington and King (2000) found that hotel food and beverage service outsourcing go beyond financial benefits. The results reveal five key dimensions that managers need to take into consideration in relation to the hotel–restaurant outsourcing relationship. These issues include core competencies, brand compatibility, organization culture, operational tension, and systems of review, evaluation and control.

Relatively few outsourcing studies in the hotel industry have adopted TCE in which asset specificity principally explains hotel outsourcing. From the study of Lamminmaki (2005), insourcing is generally preferred in the activities that require high specific asset investments. Likewise, the leisure activities that are highly specific to the hotels are found to perform better when they are carried out in-house (Espino-Rodriguez and Gil-Padilla 2005b). In addition, the findings in Lamminmaki (2007) provide some support for TCE. Other factors found to influence hotel outsourcing decision in this study include managerial risk adversity, availability of specialist suppliers and hotel quality.

Promsivapallop et al. (2007) report on a study of outsourcing in hotels located in Phuket, Thailand. In this study, 22 managers were interviewed using Critical Incident Technique to elicit their opinions about the outsourcing decisions they had made – without any preconceptions derived from TCE or RBV. Analysis of the 64 separate incidents suggests two major influences on outsourcing – asset specificity and capital requirements. Other factors identified include environmental uncertainty, behavioural uncertainty, frequency, prior experience, guest contact and profitability. Profitability has not been identified as an outsourcing factor in the previous literature. This is not surprising given that outsourcing of revenue-generating transactions has rarely been investigated.

Management contracts and franchising

As was explained in the "Introduction" section, hotel and foodservice companies may also be suppliers of outsourced services. A hotel owner who signs a management contract with a hotel company is outsourcing the operation of that property to the hotel chain. Likewise, the clients of a foodservice management contractor are outsourcing their catering provision. Owners and clients decide to outsource in this way, for the same reasons hospitality companies choose to outsource some of the things they could do, as discussed above. So the question is, does it affect how the operations are managed if the business is operated in assets owned by someone else?

The simple answer is almost certainly. Even though the operator does not own the assets, they will still, under the terms of their contract, have responsibility for maintaining and caring for the physical infrastructure. They may indeed be required to make some investment in this infrastructure in order to secure the contract.

A second kind of business format found in the industry is franchising. In this instance, the hospitality operator neither owns the assets nor runs the operation. The franchisor owns the so-called franchise system and brand, and licences franchisees to manage the operations for their mutual benefit.

Again it is unlikely that there will be any major differences from an operations perspective, in terms of how self-operated and franchisee-operated units are managed. The systems, policies and procedures will be almost identical. Bradach (1997) argues that the four main challenges faced by restaurant chains are growth, uniformity, local responsiveness and adaptation. In each of these areas, company ownership and franchising each has its advantages. For instance, with regard to adaptation, franchisees are fast in identifying opportunities but are slow in implementing these throughout the chain, whereas company-owned chains are slow in identifying opportunities but can implement them quickly.

This same research study goes on to suggest that chains that have both these types of operation may have some advantages over those that only operate their own outlets, or exclusively franchise. Bradach (1997) calls this the 'plural form'. Within such companies, he proposes five unique aspects of how operations are managed, which maximize the benefits of both company-owned and franchised outlets. These are:

- Additive processes – growth is achieved by the chain seeding new geographic areas with company units, followed by franchisees; hence the chain focuses on selecting locations, whereas franchisees – with their local knowledge – focus on selecting specific sites.
- Socialization – managers who worked for the company are encouraged to become franchisees. They overcome any shortage of suitable franchisees and ensure greater uniformity between operations.
- Modelling – franchisees are encouraged to take on more units, thereby creating mini-chains.
- Ratcheting – system-wide performance benchmarks are established, and healthy competition between company and franchise units is encouraged.
- Learning – managers and franchisees are routinely brought together in order to learn from each other.

Summary and conclusions

It is clear from the above literature review that hotel outsourcing research is scarce. Most of the few existing studies focus on the strategic management perspective. The majority of the studies cover various activities in many hotels and undertake a single area which avoids result bias from an analysis of multiple areas that have different levels of supplier availability.

However, it is apparent that obtaining small sample sizes is one crucial limitation of these studies (such as studies conducted by Espino-Rodriguez and Padron-Robaina 2004, 2005a, 2005b; Lamminmaki 2005; Promsivapallop et al. 2007). Thus, the results from these studies may not permit generalizable assertions of the observed outcomes. Researchers have discussed numerous advantages and applications of outsourcing. Despite this, hotel outsourcing research is limited. This lack of research interest is surprising as outsourcing has become a crucial component of contemporary hotel management (Ruggless 2004; Holm 2003). This scarcity, however, presents research opportunities for a better insight into this emerging phenomenon.

References

Alexander, M. and Young, D. (1996) Strategic outsourcing, *Long Range Planning*, 29, 1, 116–119

Bailey, W., Masson, R. and Raeside, R. (2002) Outsourcing in Edinburgh and the Lothians, *European Journal of Purchasing and Supply Management*, 8, 2, 83–95

Barney, J. B. (1991) Firm resources and sustained competitive advantage, *Journal of Management*, 17, 1, 99–120

Blomqvist, K., Hurmelinna, P. and Seppanen, R. (2005) Playing the collaboration game right—balancing trust and contracting, *Technovation*, 25, 5, 497–504

Blumberg, D. F. (1998) Strategic assessment of outsourcing and downsizing in the service market, *Managing Service Quality*, 8, 1, 5–18

Bounfour, A. (1999) Is outsourcing of intangibles a real source of competitive advantage? *Journal of Applied Quality Management*, 2, 2, 127–151

Bradach, J. L. (1997) Using the plural form in the management of restaurant chains, *Administration Science Quarterly*, 42, 2, 276–303

Chase, R. B., Jacobs, F. R. and Aquilano, N. J. (2004) *Operations Management for Competitive Advantage,* 10th edition, McGraw-Hill/Irwin: New York, NY

Coase, R. H. (1996) The nature of the firm, In Buckley, P. J. and Michie, J. (Eds.), *Firms, Organizations and Contracts: A Reader in Industrial Organization*, Oxford University Press: Oxford, UK

Dess, G. G., Rasheed, A., McLaughlin, K. and Priem, R. (1995) The new corporate architecture, *Academy of Management Executive*, 9, 3, 7–20

Domberger, S. (1998) *The Contracting Organization: A strategic Guide to Outsourcing*, Oxford University Press: Oxford, UK

Dyer, J. H. and Singh, H. (1998) The relational view: cooperative strategy and sources of interorganizational competitive advantage, *Academy of Management Review*, 23, 4, 660–679

Embleton, P. R. and Wright, P. C. (1998) A practical guide to successful outsourcing, *Empowerment in Organizations*, 6, 3, 94–106

Espino-Rodriguez, T. F. and Gil-Padilla, A. M. (2005a) Determinants of information systems outsourcing in hotels from the resource-based view: an empirical study, *International Journal of Tourism Research*, 7, 11, 35–47

Espino-Rodriguez, T. F. and Gil-Padilla, A. M. (2005b) The relationship between leisure outsourcing and specificity: performance and management perception in hotels in the

Canary Islands, *Journal of Hospitality and Tourism Research*, 29, 3, 396–418

Espino-Rodriguez, T. F. and Padron-Robaina, V. (2004) Outsourcing and its impact on operational objectives and performance: a study of hotels in the Canary Islands, *International Journal of Hospitality Management*, 23, 33, 287–306

Espino-Rodriguez, T. F. and Padron-Robaina, V. (2005a) A resource-based view of outsourcing and its implications for organizational performance in the hotel sector, *Tourism Management*, 26, 5, 707–721

Espino-Rodriguez, T. F. and Padron-Robaina, V. (2005b) The management perception of the strategic outsourcing of services: an empirical examination in the hotel sector, *The Service Industries Journal*, 25, 5, 689–708

Fan, Y. (2000) Strategic outsourcing: evidence from British companies, *Marketing Intelligence and Planning*, 18, 4, 213–219

Fill, C. and Visser, E. (2000) The outsourcing dilemma: a composite approach to make or buy decision, *Management Decision*, 38, 1, 43–50

Gilley, K. M. and Rasheed, A. (2000) Making more by doing less: an analysis of outsourcing and its effect on firm performance, *Journal of Management*, 26, 4, 763–790

Greer, C. R., Youngblood, S. A. and Gray, D. A. (1999) Human resource management outsourcing: the make or buy decision, *Academy of Management Executive*, 13, 3, 85–96

Gronhaug, K. and Haugland, S. A. (2005) A transaction cost approach to a paradox in international marketing, *Scandinavian Journal of Management*, 21, 1, 61–76

Hallam, G. and Baum, T. (1996) Contracting out food and beverage operations in hotels: a comparative study of practice in North America and the United Kingdom, *International Journal of Hospitality Management*, 15, 1, 41–50

Hemmington, N. and King, C. (2000) Key dimensions of outsourcing hotel food and beverage services, *International Journal of Contemporary Hospitality Management*, 12, 4, 256–261

Holm, N. (2003, August 15) Outsourcing – a smart way to do business. Retrieved 20 February 2006, from www.hospitalitynet.org/news/4016775.htm

Jacobides, M. G. (2005) Industry change through vertical disintegration: how and why markets emerged in mortgage banking, *Academy of Management Journal*, 48, 3, 465–498

Jennings, D. (2002) Strategic sourcing: benefits, problems and a contextual model, *Management Decision*, 40, 1, 26–34

Jenster, P. V. and Pedersen, H. S. (2000) Outsourcing – facts and fiction, *Strategic Change*, 9, 147–154

Jones, P. (Ed.) (2002) *Introduction to Hospitality Operations: An Indispensable Guide to the Industry*, 2nd edition, Thomson: UK

Jones, P. (Ed.) (2004) *Flight Catering*, Elsevier: Oxford, UK

Kakabadse, A. and Kakabadse, N. (2003) Outsourcing best practice: transformation and transactional considerations, *Knowledge and Process Management*, 10, 1, 60–71

Kakabadse, N. and Kakabadse A. (2000) Critical review – outsourcing: a paradigm shift, *Journal of Management Development*, 19, 8, 670–728

Kotabe, M. and Murray, J. Y. (1990) Linking product and process innovations and modes of international sourcing in global competition: a case of foreign multinational firms, *Journal of International Business Studies*, 21, 3, 383–408

Lam, T. and Han, M. X. J. (2005) A study of outsourcing strategy: a case involving the hotel industry in Shanghai, China, *International Journal of Hospitality Management*, 24, 1, 41–56

Lamminmaki, D. (2005) Why do hotels outsource? An investigation using asset specificity, *International Journal of Contemporary Hospitality Management*, 17, 6, 516–528

Lamminmaki, D. (2007) Outsourcing in Australian hotels: a transaction cost economics perspective, *Journal of Hospitality and Tourism Research*, 31, 1, 73–110

Lankford, W. M. and Parsa, F. (1999) Outsourcing: a primer, *Management Decision*, 37, 4, 310–316

Lonsdale, C. (1999) Effectively managing vertical supply relationships: a risk management model for outsourcing, *Supply Chain Management: An International Journal*, 4, 4, 176–183

Lonsdale, C. and Cox, A. (1998) Falling in with the out crowd, *People Management*, 4, 20, 52–55

Lonsdale, C. and Cox, A. (2000) The historical development of outsourcing: the latest fad? *Industrial Management and Data Systems*, 100, 9, 444–450

McIvor, R. (2000) A practical framework for understanding the outsourcing process, *Supply Chain Management: An International Journal*, 5, 1, 22–36

McMarthy, I. and Anagnostou, A. (2004) The impact of outsourcing on the transaction costs and boundaries of manufacturing, *International Journal of Production Economics*, 88, 61–71

Oates, D. (1998) *Outsourcing and the Virtual Organization: the Incredible Shrinking Company*, Century Business: London, UK

Outsourcing Institute (1998) Executive survey: the outsourcing institute's annual survey of outsourcing end users. Retrieved 25 November 2005, from http://www.outsourcing.com/content.asp?page=01i/articles/intelligence/oi_top_ten_survey.html&nonav=true

Porter, M. E. (1990) *The Competitive Advantage of Nations*, Macmillan: London, UK

Prahalad, C. K. and Hamel, G. (1990) The core competence of the corporation, *Harvard Business Review*, 68, 3, 79–91

Promsivapallop, P., Jones, P. and Roper, A. (2007, October 25–27) *Factors Influencing Outsourcing: A Study of Hotels in Thailand*, EuroCHRIE conference, Leeds

Quelin, B. and Duhamel, F. (2003) Bringing together strategic outsourcing and corporate strategy: outsourcing motives and risks, *European Management Journal*, 21, 5, 647–661

Quinn, J. B. (1999) Strategic outsourcing: leveraging knowledge capabilities, *Sloan Management Review*, 40, 4, 9–21

Quinn, J. B. and Hilmer, F. G. (1994) Strategic outsourcing, *Sloan Management Review*, 35, 4, 43–55

Ruggless, R. (2004) Hotels keep outsourcing as industry recovers from 3-year slump, *Nation's Restaurant News*, 38, 30, 110

Rugman, A. and D'Cruz, J. (1997) The theory of the flagship firm, *European Management Journal*, 15, 4, 403–412

Venkatesan, R. (1992) Strategic outsourcing: to make or not to make, *Harvard Business Review*, 70, 6, 98–107

Vining, A. and Globerman, S. (1999) A conceptual framework for understanding the outsourcing decision, *European Management Journal*, 17, 6, 645–654

Webster, M., Alder, D. and Muhlemann, A. P. (1997) Subcontracting within the supply chain for electronics assembly manufacture, *International Journal of Operations and Production Management*, 17, 9, 827–841

Wernerfelt, B. (1984) A resource-based view of the firm, *Strategic Management Journal*, 5, 2, 171–180

Williamson, O. E. (1979) Transaction-cost economics: the governance of contractual relations, *Journal of Law and Economics*, 22, 2, 233–261

Williamson, O. E. (1981) The modern corporation: origins, evolution, attributes, *Journal of Economic Literature*, 19, 1537–1568

CHAPTER **10**

Operational
performance

Andrew Lockwood

*Associate Dean Learning and Teaching
Faculty of Management and Law and
Head of the Division of Hospitality and Tourism
School of Management
University of Surrey
Guildford
Surrey*

Introduction

There is a popular management mantra that 'if you can't measure it, you can't manage it', sometimes expressed as 'you won't manage, what you don't measure'. Like many of these management myths, this expression has been credited to a number of management authors, including Kaplan and Norton (1996), Garvin (1983), and Peter Drucker (Singleton et al. 1988), among many others. Indeed it could be claimed to have become a standard of management practice.

The claim for the importance of measurement as part of management practice is based around three key issues:

- *Focus*. Defining the metrics most important to the business allows it to focus on the key issues and so to tune out those areas that are not related to those key measurements. Critics would argue that if the key measurements are not chosen wisely, that focus may be on issues which might lead the business off course – cost control over quality, for example.
- *Vision*. It is claimed that companies that monitor metrics can spot threats and opportunities faster than companies that do not. Metrics provide key insights into what is happening inside the business, and if benchmarked appropriately will also reflect overall trends in the industry, allowing potentially pre-emptive action to be taken.
- *Decision making*. Metrics provide a framework for making appropriate business decisions. With the numbers in black and white, the business is better positioned to make well-reasoned decisions on how to proceed. Again critics might argue that not all the key influences can be presented as black and white and relying completely on metrics might prevent more adventurous and rewarding decisions from being taken.

Two reviews of the hospitality research literature conducted in 1996 and 1997 (Teare 1996; Ingram 1997) identified the areas of business performance and business performance measurement as areas of growing importance and where more research and publications were necessary. It is perhaps strange that given these claims for the centrality of operational performance and its measurement, the number of research publications in the ensuing 10 years has been rather limited.

Measuring operational performance

Harris and Mongiello (2001) in their study of the key performance indicators used by general managers in the European hotel industry identify a number of factors which influence the choice of appropriate measures for the hospitality industry. Their first characteristic is the market orientation of businesses, such as those in the hospitality industry, that have a high percentage of fixed costs to total costs. These businesses need to have a customer and revenue focus and so need to choose performance measures that take this into account. However, they also recognize that hotels and the hospitality industry in general involve the provision of three different elements – accommodation, beverage and food – which require a different focus. While the accommodation side has a service bias, the provision of beverages is largely a retail operation, while the provision of food also involves a production function. Each activity will have a slightly different cost structure and so a different orientation which needs to be reflected in the choice of performance measures or key performance indicators. Part of the results of their extensive study indicates that hotels tend to place considerable emphasis on financially based measures followed by customer-based measures.

Financial measures

Financial performance traditionally has been measured by using ratio analysis calculated directly from a company's financial statements. These ratios can be categorized into five main groups:

- Profitability ratios, which indicate the ability of a company to generate profits from its capital employed or assets (Mclanely 2000).
- Investment ratios, which evaluate business performance from the viewpoint of shareholders and investors (Adams 1997).
- Activity ratios, which show how efficient a company is in using and managing its assets to make sales and profits (Brigham and Houston 2004).
- Liquidity ratios, which indicate a firm's ability to pay off its short-term obligations (Brealey et al. 2001).
- Leverage ratios, which determine the proportionate contributions of owners and creditors to a business structure, for example the extent to which debt is used in a company's capital structure (Brigham and Houston 2004).

While not all the measures above are directly related to operational performance, many of the key measures used in hospitality (indeed any business) are financial. The overall measure is typically profit, derived from sales revenue minus costs. This is then usually broken down in two main ways. First, overall performance may be sub-divided into different parts of the business (such as bar, restaurant, accommodation etc.) in order to understand the contribution each part makes to the overall performance. Second, it may be broken down by the 'elements of cost', usually called materials, labour and overheads. In the hospitality industry, this breakdown has been standardized by the adoption of a uniform system of accounts (Uniform System of Accounts for the Lodging Industry 1996).

Financial performance is monitored closely because ultimately the business only survives if revenues are greater than costs. But financial measures have only a limited value to the operations manager, since if performance is poor they do not provide enough detail to explain why this is so. This is because most financial measures are aggregate data, that is a combination of measures, and because there can be time lags introduced by the recording systems. For instance, labour cost percentages actually derive from four separate elements:

$$\text{Labour cost \%} = \frac{\text{Labour cost}}{\text{Total revenue}} = \frac{\text{Number of employees} \times \text{Average wage}}{\text{Number of customers } \times \text{Average spend}}$$

Hence, this single figure can hide a number of potential reasons for poor performance, such as:

- Too many staff on duty
- Average wages too high, perhaps due to overtime payments
- Fewer customers than expected
- Lower average spend than normal
- Any combination of the above

There are two other problems with financial measures. First, the value of money within a country is not constant. Due to inflation, $1 may buy less next year than it bought last year. If prices go up faster than wages in response to inflation, performance will improve but not through any real improvement in managing the workforce. Second, many hospitality firms are now international. When they compare the performance of all their units, they do so by converting all the financial measures into a common currency, using the current exchange rate. However, exchange rates vary over time and do not necessarily relate directly to local economic conditions and so can give a misleading picture of performance. For all the above reasons, besides using financial measures, most firms will also look at non-financial measures.

Physical measures

The great advantage of non-financial measures is that it is possible to identify if performance has improved over time, irrespective of how much things cost, or how much things are sold for. Occupancy rate is a good example of a non-financial measure. Non-financial measures are particularly useful in measuring productivity,[1] for instance:

$$\text{Productivity of housekeeping} = \frac{\text{Number of rooms serviced}}{\text{Number of staff hours}}$$

Hence, if it takes 400 h to service 300 rooms, the operations manager would know that it takes on average 0.75 h (45 min) to service a room. On this basis, the manager could compare the performance of individual workers, or of teams, to see if some were more productive than others in order to identify what action to take.

Combined measures

As well as having financial and non-financial measures, it is useful to have measures that combine the two. Average spend is a good example here.

$$\text{Average spend} = \frac{\text{Total revenue}}{\text{Number of customers}}$$

Commonly used measures

In the hospitality industry, there are certain performance measures that are regarded as the most important ones. In the hotel industry, it used to be occupancy rate:

$$\text{Occupancy rate} = \frac{\text{Number of rooms occupied}}{\text{Total number of rooms}}$$

However, this measure has been replaced to a large extent, since the introduction of yield or revenue management,[2] by REVPAR

---

[1] See also Chapter 12.
[2] See also Chapter 11.

(revenue per available room). In the foodservice industry, the key measure has always been gross profit, measured as

$$\text{Gross profit} = \frac{\text{Sales} - \text{Food cost}}{\text{Sales}}$$

In fact, due to the complexity of each operation, there are many more measures apart from these that are important. Some can apply to all operations in the industry, while other input or output measures are specific to certain sectors of the industry. This is illustrated in Tables 10.1 and 10.2 that follow – derived from the UK's Department of Trade and Industry (DTI) sponsored initiative designed to improve the performance of small hospitality businesses in the UK.

The generic performance measures shown in Table 10.1 are taken from the DTI's Benchmark Index which is arguably the world's most extensive benchmarking resource for small businesses. Its aim is to help improve the competitiveness and profitability of business in the UK. Run by the DTI and delivered via trained advisors from Business Links, trade associations and private business support organizations, the Benchmark Index

Table 10.1 Generic performance measures

Key performance indicator	Data description
Profitability	Pre-tax profit/total sales revenue
Investment	Pre-tax profit/total assets
Labour productivity – measure a	Total sales revenue: total wage cost
Labour productivity – measure b	Total wage cost/total sales revenue
Innovation	Capital spend/total assets
Revenue development	Revenue from new markets/total sales revenue
Value added	Pre-tax profit/total wage cost
Supplier performance	Value of reject deliveries from suppliers/purchases
Staff turnover	Total leavers during the year/number of employees
Complaints	Value of refunds/total sales revenue
Energy consumption	Energy costs/total sales revenue

Source: www.bestpracticeforum.org

holds the financial data of over 156,000 companies and has a database of benchmarked performance data for a further 18,000.

The benchmark process, which is facilitated throughout by a trained advisor, is simple and practical and centres on the completion and analysis of an in-depth questionnaire aimed at gathering performance information about the company across all key business areas. This data, which is treated with the

Table 10.2 Sectoral performance measures

Key performance indicator	Data description
Hotels, guest houses and other accommodation providers	
Revenue per available room	Total rooms sales revenue/total number of rooms available
Room occupancy	Total number of rooms sold/total number of rooms available
Average achieved room rate	Total rooms sales/total number of rooms sold
Pubs and other licensed retailers	
Income per server	Total sales revenue/number of service staff
Revenue per square metre	Total sales revenue/square metre of retail space
Beverage gross profit %	Beverage gross profit/beverage sales revenue
Restaurants and catering companies	
Average spend per head	Total food and beverage sales revenue/ number of customers served
Food gross profit %	Food gross profit/food sales
Beverage gross profit %	Beverage gross profit/beverage sales revenue
Conference venues and events companies	
Conference occupancy	Total number of actual delegates/total number of delegate spaces
Revenue per square metre of space	Total conference or event sales revenue/ square metre of conference or events space
Average spend per head	Total conference or event sales revenue/ total number of delegates

Source: www.bestpracticeforum.org

strictest confidence, is then fed into a secure database where it is used to provide performance comparisons against other companies of a similar nature. By analysing these comparisons, it is possible to highlight strengths and weaknesses. The generic performance measures have then been customized by the Best Practice Forum for different sectors of the industry by choosing widely used sector-specific measures, as shown in Table 10.2. These measures are then incorporated into the forum's business health check.

Measuring customer satisfaction

It can be seen from Table 10.2 that most of the measures used are related to the revenue, cost or profit performance of the business, but there are other measures of performance that may be critical in service businesses, notably customer satisfaction. The traditional way of eliciting customer feedback is through guest comment cards. Jones and Iannou (1993) identify a number of shortcomings of this method, the most significant of which is the unrepresentative nature of the sample (too small, self-selecting, skewed towards those with complaints) – so that results are biased. Such cards also have to be brief (in order to encourage completion), and hence the question design may not lead to valid results. Comment cards can be used, but their main role is to identify specific problem areas that may need attention.

Another obvious form of feedback is unsolicited compliments and complaints, often in the form of letters from guests or customers. As dealing with service failure is important, such letters can play an important role in retaining loyal customers. But for reasons similar to comments cards, they do not provide a representative sample of all customers on which to base judgements of overall satisfaction. Hence, the best way to elicit such feedback is through a well-designed and executed customer survey.[3] Many hotel companies employ market research firms to routinely telephone a random sample of guests 24 h after departure to ask them about their stay. Likewise, restaurant chains may survey customers at the end of the meal.

Ratios and percentages

Again as can be seen from Tables 10.1 and 10.2, many of the key performance indicators identified are either ratios or

---

[3] See also Chapter 13.

percentages, usually taking the performance of one part of the business and comparing it with the overall performance. Thus, net profit and labour cost are often expressed as a percentage of total sales. The main reason for using percentages is that they enable easy comparison between time periods and between units. For instance, it is difficult to know if £10,500 profit on weekly sales of £115,900 is better or worse than £9,950 profit on £108,300 sales. But when expressed as a profit percentage of 9.06% and 9.19%, it is clear that performance in the second week was better than the first.

Although using percentages makes comparisons easier, they may also be misleading. In the example above, net profit percentage was lower (9.06%) in the first week than in the second. But in terms of actual cash, more profit was made (£10,500) in the first week than in the second (£9,950). Since commercial businesses exist in order to make money (not 'make percentages'), the first week's performance is better than the second. It is surprising how many people forget this. For instance, restaurateurs may choose dishes to promote because they have a high gross profit, rather than those that have the highest cash return. For instance, you make more money from a prawn cocktail selling at £4.50, with a gross profit percentage of 50%, than you do from selling a soup at £2.00, with a GP% of 80% (£2.25 as opposed to £1.60).

Research in hospitality

A number of studies have tried to identify the performance measures used in specific types of operations. As early as the 1980s, research by Umbreit (1986) and Eder and Umbreit (1989) demonstrated that managers were judged on the basis of a balanced hierarchy of performance measures. Hotel companies judged the performance of their general manager on three levels:

- First level: short-term profit indicators
  - Gross operating profit, rooms division profit, food and beverage department profit
- Second level: 'tangibles'
  - Budget compliance, sales, occupancy percent, average room rate
- Third level: 'intangibles'
  - Employee attitude surveys, employee turnover, market share, advanced bookings, customer complaints and employee productivity

Haktanir and Harris (2005) considered the measures used in a 392 room five star, independent resort hotel employing a range of data collection methods in a case study approach. They found that

Clearly, understanding performance measurement practice of an independent hotel requires an understanding of the context of the business, its constituents in terms of the decision-making process and the information flow. Additionally, it became apparent that the kind of measures used and the way the measures are perceived is different at various levels of the business. As a result of the simultaneity element of the service, which requires real-time measures during operations, more guest-related qualitative measures in the form of observation and verbal communication are utilized in operational departments. However, more quantitative measures are reported and used by the senior management in order to assess the outcome of the operational efforts through financial indicators. Thus, interestingly, performance measurement practice in the case hotel identifies guest satisfaction measures as the key indicators at the operational levels and financial measures at the senior management levels.

Haktanir and Harris (2005: 49)

Bergin-Seers and Jago (2007) set their study in small motels in Australia that face particular performance management challenges due to resource shortages, lack of functional expertise and environmental instability. Using a case research approach, they identified the specific monitoring and measurement activities of small motel owner operators, which indicated that the successful managers employ a balanced approach by using a small number of key financial and non-financial measures which are monitored on a regular basis so as to identify problems before they get out of control.

The above discussions highlight the importance of identifying the best measures to use for your business and of building these different measures into a system that will help to maintain operational control and build towards strategic objectives at the same time.

Systems for performance measurement

If business performance measurement is to act as an essential tool to enable managers to achieve and to control their desired objectives as well as their strategies, then they must be co-ordinated into a coherent system that can be used to quantify both the efficiency and the effectiveness of the firm's performance. Jones and Lockwood (1995) suggest that this system should have a number of hierarchical levels, with different measures corresponding to the distinct nature of the inputs and outputs of importance at the strategic, operations management or operating management levels. Southern (1999) also adopts a systems approach to performance measurement in hospitality. He offers a number of insights deriving from systems thinking, principally that in order to ensure good performance, operations should begin with defining the appropriate measures and standards in their operational systems, in order to provide a more systematic approach to the design, operation and control of key processes.

In the generic management literature, there are a number of recognized systems of performance measures that include:

- The Performance Pyramid System developed by Lynch and Cross (1991) to measure business performance through linking the overall company strategy with its operations after developing suitable measures for all levels in the company, following a similar approach to that suggested by Jones and Lockwood (1995).
- The Performance Measurement System for Service Industries (PMSSI) was developed by Fitzgerald et al. (1991) in order to measure the business performance in service companies based on the unique characteristics and features of such businesses. As a result, the PMSSI includes dimensions such as competitiveness, financial performance, quality of service, flexibility, resource utilization and innovation.
- The Integrated Performance Measurement System measures business performance through using seven financial and non-financial factors grouped into internal and external factors. This allows the causal relationships between factors to follow the use of resources from the point of allocation to the point of receiving revenues (Laitinen 2002).
- The Balanced Scorecard was developed by Kaplan and Norton (1992) to measure business performance by using a set of four different perspectives: the financial perspective, the customer perspective, the innovation and learning perspective and the internal business perspective. This approach uses both financial and non-financial measures of business performance.

Research in hospitality

It is this latter approach that has received the most attention from researchers looking at its applications to and implications for the hospitality industry. Probably the first article addressing the balanced scorecard in the hospitality industry in the UK was written by Brander-Brown and McDonnell (1995). This article introduced the concept related to the then existing literature on hotel managers' activities and objectives. They then used a single case study hotel (131 rooms, five star, part of a hotel group) as a pilot study to develop a set of measures to use to form the balanced scorecard for this hotel. Having elicited the hotel's vision and objectives, they continued to build a series of critical success factors that would support these objectives and finally a set of measures to monitor the critical success factors. Their findings saw the balanced scorecard as a dynamic approach that would change from unit to unit and would change over time to maintain its usefulness and relevance.

Writing in the late 1990s, Hepworth (1998) conducted a review of the literature on the balanced scorecard. His review, following from his dissertation work, finds limited evidence of the application of the concept in the hospitality industry, other than the work of Brander-Brown and McDonnell (1995), and reports on his own work in the Food Services branch of the Royal Logistics Corps within the British army. He highlights some concerns about the problems of implementing the 'softer' dimensions of the approach and whether this U.S. management approach would sit well with the British culture.

Harris and Mongiello (2001) acknowledge the changes in the field of performance measurement based on criticisms of narrowness and profit-centric approaches towards more balanced and success-oriented views. Drawing on the views of hotel general managers working in chain-based European properties, their study considers three key dimensions of balance, orientation and coherence as evident in a manager's decision-making process through the selection, interpretation and application of their performance measures. Their research first established what performance indicators managers used regularly to determine their business progress and then tried to establish what these measures actually meant to the managers concerned, before progressing to the decisions these measures allowed managers to take. They found that the most important perspectives concerned human resources, operations and the customer, while in use it is the financial and customer-related indicators that are used as the basis for management decisions and consequent action. It would appear that human resource, operations and customer measures are used to inform the decisions taken that are then checked against their impact on financial performance.

Drawing on work conducted as part of a major study of small- and medium-sized enterprises across the hospitality, tourism and leisure sectors by the University of Surrey on behalf of an Industry Forum Adaptation Programme sponsored by the DTI, Phillips and Louvieris (2005) investigated 10 best practice organizations and the performance measures they used using a theoretical framework derived from the balanced scorecard approach. Results revealed that four key concepts drove measurement systems across these businesses. These were concerned with budgetary control particularly to ensure the achievement and improvement of revenue targets; customer relationship management as a way of improving quality of service and customer retention; strategic management in managing internal business processes; and collaboration both inside and outside the business to drive innovation and learning. Based on this work, they also proposed a balanced scorecard approach identifying critical success factors and key performance indicators that would be suitable for hotel businesses as an exemplar for further development.

Evans (2005) places the balanced scorecard as a tool for strategic implementation and not simply as a tool for operational control and uses a questionnaire to determine the detailed performance measures being used in a sample of hotels and to compare these responses with the balanced scorecard approach. His results suggest that in his sample, hotels are using a wide variety of measures from all of the four categories of the approach and not just relying on short-term financial measures. He does, however, question the nature of the link between the measures being used and the strategy and vision of the company that they are posited to support. He is concerned that managers do not understand the causal links inherent in the framework. He also stresses that there is also a need for a relevant benchmarking system and an understanding of integrating concepts or models such as the service profit chain.

Phillips (2007) has also pursued the strategic importance of the balanced scorecard by conducting a longitudinal study of a hotel company over a three-year period. He found that the implementation within the company had been successful at a number of levels. First, the technique had allowed a clear focus on operational/diagnostic control largely based on adherence to plan and engagement of all levels of the organization in responding to dynamic markets particularly in the areas of quality and customer satisfaction. However, he also found that the technique had been useful in maintaining strategic control to the extent that it helped to inform a key strategic decision to divest a section of the company's up-market hotel portfolio. He again stresses the importance of benchmarking.

Benchmarking

A quick browse through the literature on benchmarking will reveal a number of different definitions of the technique stressing particular aspects or issues. In essence though, benchmarking is simply a systematic way of judging the way your business performs against a reference point, exploring where and why your operation does not work as well as it could and implementing ways of closing the gap. There are, however, many different ways in which this simple idea can be put into operational practice. Figure 10.1 shows the potential range of approaches by combining the key focus of the benchmarking exercise with the potential set of reference points.

The key focal points can be distinguished as

- *Performance.* This approach to benchmarking relies on the identification of key indicators of performance, which are likely to include both physical and monetary measures, and comparing them against an appropriate reference point. This approach is sometimes called statistical or metric benchmarking.
- *Process.* This approach looks at the process and subprocesses that make up the operational capability of the organization – the way in which the key operations are carried out in the conversion of inputs into outputs. The focus here is

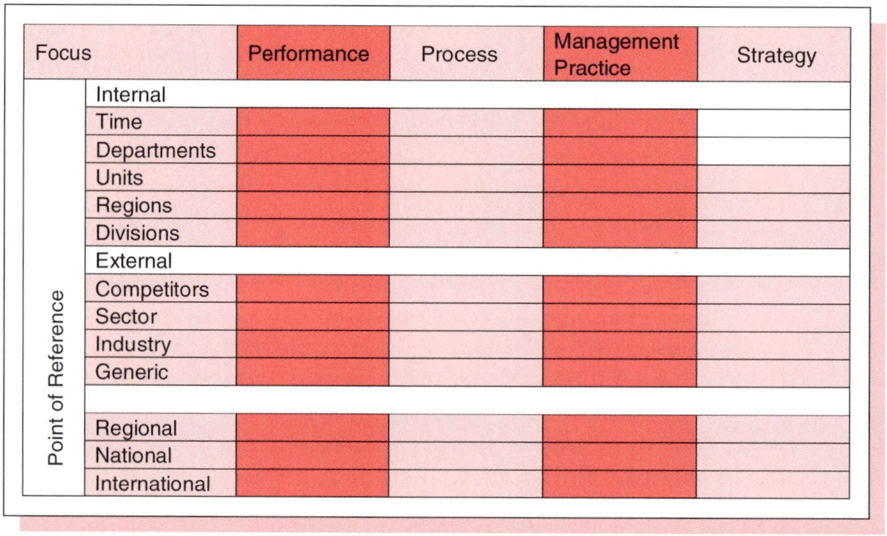

Focus		Performance	Process	Management Practice	Strategy
	Internal				
	Time				
	Departments				
	Units				
	Regions				
	Divisions				
	External				
	Competitors				
	Sector				
	Industry				
	Generic				
	Regional				
	National				
	International				

(Point of Reference)

Figure 10.1
Finding a focus for benchmarking (*Source*: author).

on how things are done, not on the output level achieved. This approach is also sometimes referred to as best practice benchmarking.

In practice, these two approaches are really inseparable. It is difficult to identify the processes within the business that need to be looked at and will result in leveraging improved performance, if you have not collected the data upon which to identify the gaps. Likewise, on its own, knowing that your performance is 5% or 10% poorer than it could be is not much help if you cannot identify ways of changing processes to achieve the gains in performance you could achieve.

- *Management practice.* The focus here moves from the way in which the technology of operations works to the way in which the functions and operations of the business are managed.
- *Strategy.* The focus here moves further up the management hierarchy and is concerned with re-aligning strategies that have become inappropriate. While obtaining data and identifying best practice is relatively straightforward at the well-bounded level of management practices, it becomes much more difficult and therefore potentially more subjective at the level of strategy.

As well as identifying the focus of the benchmarking study, another key decision is choosing the point of reference against which your performance is to be judged. The majority of texts on benchmarking stress the importance of being judged against an external organization, but this should not preclude the potential of the relatively overlooked internal benchmarking. For a single-unit enterprise, unless it is very large and multi-faceted, there is little scope other than to go for external benchmarking but for a multi-unit organization, internal benchmarking can be conducted at a number of levels.

- *Time.* One common response to suggesting that a unit should benchmark itself against others in the chain is that this unit is very different from the others, so you wouldn't expect the same results, would you? However, comparing the same unit over time can be equally revealing. If performance in one week or month is significantly better or worse than another, there is value in exploring systematically what the circumstances were or what was done differently. For example, the nature of labour cost in the hospitality industry is such that it does not vary as directly with the volume of business as most operators would like – it is a semi-variable or stepped cost. There is also likely to be a point at which increased volume will actually incur a reduction in overall performance, for example as overtime or agency staff have to be used, but very little analysis is done (or perhaps with lack of detailed data is possible) to explain and then control this variance.

- *Departments.* Within a large unit such as a hotel, there may be substantial improvements to be made from learning between departments. The banqueting department, for example, is well versed in the logistics of serving people at a distance and moving furniture and food from the point of storage or production to the point of service. There may be important lessons here for the room service team or vice versa.

- *Units.* The most obvious form of internal benchmarking is that between units of the same type within the same chain. The collection of data at this level should be consistent and straightforward as it will probably be part of normal reporting procedures to head office. One obstacle is ensuring that like is compared with like, as even within chains, some groups of units can operate in a very different environment to others. At this point, some form of cluster analysis – a technique that groups together units with statistically similar profiles – may be useful. Another technique used successfully at the University of Surrey in research studies exploring the relative efficiency of pubs, three star hotels and flight catering kitchens is data envelopment analysis. This technique based on linear programming will identify, based on a series of inputs and outputs, the most efficient use of resources and those units that act as a reference for others.

- *Regions.* Another way of maintaining at least some similarity in market conditions between units is to look at geographical groups. This could be grouped by county or regional boundaries, or could be based on city versus rural or airport as the particular circumstances of the chain dictate.

- *Divisions.* Within a large organization with a number of different divisions or brands, the potential for comparison and internal learning is much greater as the potential diversity of operations and approaches widens. There may be many things for hotel operators to learn from restaurant operations within the same group or between brands addressing different markets such as pizzas and fine dining.

The important message here is that before committing the organization to external benchmarking, it is important to consider the potential of internal benchmarking, which may be achieved more easily. Aficionados of the latest management thinking will recognize the close resemblance between internal benchmarking and knowledge management – 'a process of identifying, capturing and leveraging knowledge to help the company compete' (O'Dell and Jackson-Grayson 2000). Internal benchmarking can in fact be a key driver for this process to surface both the explicit and the tacit knowledge within the organization that when shared can result in improved performance.

There is little doubt that for many people the key emphasis of benchmarking is on external comparison, either within the same industry or indeed outside the industry wherever best practice can be found. For Xerox, for example, benchmarking is 'the continuous process of measuring products, services and practices against the toughest competitors or those companies recognized as industry leaders and best in class'. Comparisons with best-in-class operators, wherever they are in the world, can reveal the gaps in performance, processes or practices that could bring about step change. Comparisons with different external points of reference can bring about insights of different types.

- *Competitors.* The emphasis here is on direct comparison with your closest competitors in order to reveal changes that could allow you to catch up with and preferably overtake them. Although we have moved on from the idea of reverse engineering where competitors products were taken apart so that they could be reproduced with modifications and improvements, there is still a feeling here of a combative relationship, and this could make it very difficult to establish useful dialogue. There may be operators who would be reticent about giving information to their 'competitors' even though by doing so they could improve the competitiveness of the sector as a whole.
- *Sector.* As well as comparison between firms in the same sector, comparison between sectors can also be very revealing. A 'league table' of operations within the sector will allow operators to position themselves in the sector, but comparison with other sectors may reveal that they are more effective at controlling certain costs or carrying out certain tasks.
- *Industry.* Similarly, comparisons of all firms in the industry can reveal the relative position of particular firms or sections of the industry, but even more benefit may be gained by cross-industry comparisons. Hotel operators looking at the way airlines handled their reservations and pricing policies has led to the introduction of yield management and the reported substantial gains in income and profitability that this has brought about.

- *Generic.* This leads then to the view that benchmarking particularly of processes should be done with any operation in any industry in any part of the world that can demonstrate world-class performance. If a fast food operation is interested in improving customers' perceptions of queuing, then they could do worse than look at the way Disney handle queues for their theme park rides. By going outside the immediate industry, the problem of competition is removed and the relationship can assume a more collaborative style.
- *Regional.* Carrying out benchmarking of all similar businesses in a local or regional area could also be very revealing.
- *National.* Comparisons at the national level can also be useful. Recently, Pannel Kerr Foster celebrated the 25th anniversary of the PKF UK hotels database of performance with a total sample of 351 hotels covering nearly 57,000 rooms throughout the UK with separate analyses possible for London, England (excluding London), Scotland and Wales. These reports and those from other similar consultancies provide a wealth of comparative data for those firms taking part in the survey but perhaps lack statistical validity as a national standard.
- *International.* International comparisons can highlight many issues that comparisons within a country would not. For example, calculations of the number of full-time equivalent employees per hotel room in Africa might result in a figure over 2, but for a hotel of a similar standard in Scandinavia, it might be around 0.6.

Research in hospitality

There has been a significant interest in studies considering benchmarking in the hospitality industry. These studies can be organized against the four focal points identified above.

Not surprisingly, many of the studies have centred around benchmarking performance, and many have used a multivariate technique called data envelopment analysis (DEA). An early use of the technique is to be found in Morey and Dittman (1995) who compared 54 hotels within a U.S. national chain, combining the physical characteristics of the property, local market or environmental factors and factors controllable by the GM such as expenditures on salaries, materials and energy with outputs such as rooms revenue and customer satisfaction with the physical facilities and the service provided. Johns et al. (1997) also used data from with a single hotel chain, following an internal benchmarking approach, but with only 15 hotels in the chain, their data was limited and so was their range of the input and output variables needed to support the DEA. Their inputs included number of room nights available, total labour hours, total food and beverage costs and total utilities cost, while their outputs were room nights sold, total covers served and total beverage revenue. While their results showed only limited discrimination between the performance of the 15 hotels, it was able to identify that three hotels in particular were not performing at the same level as the rest and needed further investigation. Wöber (2000) reports on the development of a web-based system which allows hoteliers in Austria to input their hotel data and receive an assessment of their overall efficiency compared to other hotels in the database. The system offers the calculation of key financial ratios for each hotel plus a longitudinal analysis for several consecutive periods to allow the identification of trends.

Of particular importance is the possibility of building a peer group of hotels with similar operational characteristics to act as 'best practice' partners. Hu and Cai (2004) focussed specifically on labour productivity, but in this case drew a sample from a specific region, the state of California, and followed an external benchmarking logic. Their eventual sample size was 242 hotels, split into three segments – B&B, limited service and full service hotels to account for disparity in hotel revenues and operational characteristics. They then used the productivity score derived from their DEA analysis to explore whether factors such as service quality, the physical make up of the properties and employees' expertise level could explain the variation in performance and allow for a clearer benchmarking comparator. Barros and Mascharenas (2004) and Barros (2005) report on an exploration of efficiency within a Portuguese state-owned chain consisting of 43 hotels based on cross-sectional data from 2001 again using DEA as the key tool. This article again suggests that the strength of DEA is in providing a benchmark against which poorly performing operations can be judged and remedial action taken. Finally, Sigala et al. (2005) report on a study of productivity in three star hotels in the UK focussing on the rooms division and using a stepwise DEA approach on data received from 93 hotels. An extensive set of input and output data revealed that the factors affecting room division productivity were as follows: achieved room rate, room nights sold, non-room revenue, number of rooms, front-office payroll, administration and general expenses, other payroll, other expenses and demand variability.

Parkan (2005) uses an approach that he has developed called Operational Competitiveness Rating Analysis (OCRA) to compare the results of two hotels of different character owned by the same family-owned company. He uses a common set of cost and revenue data collected over a 13-month period based on existing profit and loss statements to compare the performance of the hotels, first to each other and then benchmarked against industry standard data. This allowed him to draw conclusions about performance in the five most important cost and revenue areas – room costs, food and beverage costs, salaries and wages, revenue from room sales and food and beverage sales.

Yasin and Zimmerer (1995) move away from the purely performance-related issues in benchmarking to incorporate aspects of process and suggest that establishing operational metrics for both the operations and the service subsystems could result in a level of in-depth analysis of processes which would result in significant and continuous quality improvement. This is picked up in a major study reported by Min and Min (1996), Min and Min (1997) and a follow-up study by Min et al. (2002). They identified 14 salient service attributes relevant to Korean luxury hotels based around the two major criteria of rooms and front-office service derived from previous research studies and other sources. They then conducted a survey of 113 guests staying at six different luxury hotels in Seoul asking them to rate the relative importance of these attributes on a five-point Likert scale. In order to provide a benchmark, at the same time, the subjects were asked to rate their perceptions of the service performance of the six hotels on each of the 14 attributes. The data were then analysed using an analytic hierarchy process (AHP) through a series of pairwise comparisons. They then used the results of this analysis to verify statistically the competitive gaps between one hotel's performance and that of its competitors and so identify possible actions to be taken to improve performance in critical areas.

The third area for benchmarking activity is the area of management practice, and some research has been conducted here. Ogden (1998) starts the debate in this area by suggesting that there is a need to view benchmarking as a means to disseminate best practice especially in small hospitality organizations, and he views external agencies such as grading or award schemes as a good means of achieving this. This approach is picked up by Kozak and Rimmington (1998) who again view classification and grading schemes, alongside Investors in People and Excellence Through People, as ways of encouraging small businesses to make improvements. Phillips and Moutinho (1999) concentrate on 15 top hotel groups in the UK for their study of management practice in strategic planning, and they develop a model for measuring the effectiveness of a company's strategic planning process – the Strategic Planning Index (SPI). They then use this index to compare this process for a single hotel with its peer group and so identify gaps. This approach was also used (Phillips and Appiah-Adu 1998) in a slightly earlier comparison of strategic planning in a series of hotel groups in the UK, which showed some significant gaps between the quality of the planning processes and theoretical best practice. Warnken et al. (2004) tackle the increasingly important area of environmental practice and performance in their study of hotels, eco-resorts, condominiums and caravan parks in Queensland, Australia. While their sample size was too small to enable a statistically robust quantitative analysis, they do raise some concerns about the implementation of environmental management in general and the role of environmental accreditation schemes in promoting best practice in particular.

There is limited evidence of research at the level of benchmarking of strategy itself. Drawing on a sample of 189 hospitality firms in Spain, Garrigós-Simón et al. (2005) link the Miles and Snow strategy typologies to business performance. Their analysis revealed four dimensions of performance: profitability, growth, stakeholder satisfaction and competitive position, which they subsequently merged into a single overall performance measure. Their findings reinforced the existing literature in that the prospector, defenders and analyser types had significantly better performance across all variables than the reactors. Within the successful types, prospectors were almost always associated with superior performance, although analysers scored better in the area of profitability.

Phillips et al. (1999) used neural network analysis to consider the effect of strategic planning on business performance in hotels. They distinguished between aspects of the thoroughness and sophistication of the strategic planning process and its market-led formality. While the degree of thoroughness and sophistication of the strategic planning process had a direct positive effect on overall performance, the degree of formality and rigidity of the process could be seen to hamper overall performance.

Once a rigorous benchmarking process has been used to identify gaps in performance at whatever level and against whatever comparator, there is then a need to consider how performance improvements can be made.

Performance improvement: the input–output ratio

For the purposes of this analysis, input refers to the resources used in making a product or providing a service, whilst output is the product or service itself. Inputs may be transformed, that is raw materials, or they may be transforming, that is infrastructure and labour. Early approaches to performance improvement identified two broad strategies. Firms, particularly those with high fixed costs, could concentrate on increasing output whilst holding inputs steady – the so-called market-oriented approach. Alternatively, for those firms with a high proportion of variable costs, the strategy of 'cost reduction' was supported, that is hold output steady but reduce costs. But this model of market orientation or cost reduction seems rather too simplistic. There are in fact five ways in which the ratio of inputs to outputs can be improved, as illustrated in Figure 10.2.

Let us consider each of the five possibilities shown in Figure 10.2 in turn.

- *Decrease inputs (I) and constant output (O).* This option identifies circumstances where existing provision is inefficient – that is to say corrective action should be taken by changing the inputs to achieve the same level of output but at lower cost.
- *Decrease inputs, relatively smaller decrease in output.* This option assumes that a cost reduction exercise will have some impact on output, but that the fall in output will be more than offset by the saving made.

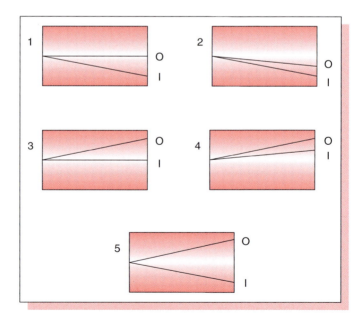

Figure 10.2
Models of improving performance.

- *Constant inputs and increased output.* This option also implies inefficiency, in that the same inputs could produce more output. Unlike option 2 which looks at the operation's costs, this option suggests a marketing approach.
- *Increase inputs, relatively greater increase in output.* This too is a market-orientated approach, but one that recognizes that the change in output can only be achieved at some extra cost.
- *Decrease inputs and increase output.* This option is theoretically possible, but is unlikely to occur very frequently. This is the most challenging alternative and can only be achieved by innovation, that is doing things differently.

For a hospitality manager wishing to improve performance, the value of these five options is that they provide a clear framework for considering the effect of any particular action. However, options 1 and 3, where either input or output is held constant, are extremely difficult to achieve in practice. It is much more likely that a proportional improvement in performance will take place, as explained by options 2 and 4. These options help to forecast or predict the likely effect of a change and set the criteria for measuring the impact of that change.

Research in hospitality

Gray et al. (2000) working in New Zealand isolated the results of 21 hospitality companies from a larger multi-industry sample of over 1000 firms. Comparing the results of the hospitality firms and the top performing service firms, they found some interesting differences. They found the top performing firms were certainly more market oriented and that these firms also encountered greater technological turbulence and had to deal with more powerful suppliers. While there were few performance differences between the two groups, they suggest that hospitality firms should improve their market orientation to be able to cope with future market turbulence where forming closer relationships with customers will be more important. They also suggest developing a corporate culture which emphasizes innovation and the development of efficient new service development processes.

Sigala and Chalkiti (2007) report on their study of the externalization and utilization of tacit knowledge in the Greek hotel industry. Following a disappointing response to their questionnaire survey, they conducted follow-up qualitative interviews which showed a general lack of awareness of tacit knowledge and how it might be used to improve performance.

Summary and conclusions

This chapter has concentrated on four main areas of operational performance – identifying methods and metrics of measurement, combining those measures into a performance measurement system, using benchmarking to identify possible gaps in performance and methods of improving performance to close those gaps.

In all of these areas, considerable research work has been identified that specifically considers the nature of the hospitality industry and the ways in which these generic tools can be applied. Teare's (1996) and Ingram's (1997) calls for more research and publications in this important area would seem to have been answered. However, a consideration of the scale of research and publications in the generic management literature in this area shows that the hospitality industry and hospitality research is still somewhat off the pace.

References

Adams, D. (1997) *Management Accounting for the Hospitality Industry: A Strategic Approach*, 1st edition, Cassell: London, UK

Barros, C. P. (2005) Measuring efficiency in the hotel sector, *Annals of Tourism Research*, 32, 2, 456–477

Barros, C. P. and Mascharenas, M. J. (2004) Technical and allocative efficiency in a chain of small hotels, *International Journal of Hospitality Management*, 24, 415–436

Bergin-Seers, S. and Jago, L. (2007) Performance measurement in small motels in Australia, *Tourism and Hospitality Research*, 7, 2, 144–155

Brander-Brown, J. and McDonnell, B. (1995) The balanced scorecard: short term guest or long term resident? *International Journal of Contemporary Hospitality Management*, 7, 2/3, 7–11

Brealey, R. A., Myers, S. C. and Marcus, A. J. (2001) *Fundamentals of Corporate Finance*, 3rd edition, McGraw-Hill Irwin: Boston, MA

Brigham, E. F. and Houston, J. F. (2004) *Fundamentals of Financial Management*, 10th edition, Thomson South-Western: USA

Eder, R. W. and Umbreit, W. T. (1989) Measures of managerial effectiveness in the hotel industry, *Hospitality Education & Research Journal*, 13, 3, 333–342

Evans, N. (2005) Assessing the balanced scorecard as a management tool for hotels, *International Journal of Contemporary Hospitality Management*, 17, 5, 376–390

Fitzgerald, L., Johnston, R., Brignall, S., Silvestro, R. and Voss, C. (1991) *Performance Measurement in Service Industries*, 1st edition, CIMA: UK

Garrigós-Simón, F. J., Marqués, D. P. and Narangajavana, Y. (2005) Competitive strategies and performance in Spanish hospitality firms, *International Journal of Contemporary Hospitality Management*, 17, 1, 22–38

Garvin, D. (1993, July–August) Building a learning organization, *Harvard Business Review*, 71, 4, 78–91

Gray, B. J., Matear, S. M. and Matheson, P. K. (2000) Improving the performance of hospitality firms, *International Journal of Contemporary Hospitality Management*, 12, 3, 149–155

Haktanir, M. and Harris, P. (2005) Performance measurement practice in an independent hotel context, *International Journal of Contemporary Hospitality Management*, 17, 1, 39–50

Harris, P. J. and Mongiello, M. (2001) Key performance indicators in European hotel properties: general managers' choices and company profiles, *International Journal of Contemporary Hospitality Management*, 13, 3, 120–128

Hepworth, P. (1998) Weighing it up – a literature review for the balanced scorecard, *Journal of Management Development*, 17, 8, 559–563

Hu, B. A. and Cai, L. A. (2004) Hotel labour productivity assessment: a data envelopment approach, *Journal of Travel and Tourism Marketing*, 16, 2/3, 27–38

Ingram, H. (1997) Performance management: processes, quality and teamworking, *International Journal of Contemporary Hospitality Management*, 9, 7, 295–303

Johns, N., Howcroft, B. and Drake, L. (1997) The use of data envelopment analysis to monitor hotel productivity, *Progress in Tourism and Hospitality Research*, 3, 119–127

Jones, P. and Iannou, A. (1993) Measuring guest satisfaction in UK-based international hotel chains, *International Journal of Contemporary Hospitality Management*, 5, 5, 27–31

Jones, P. and Lockwood, A. (1995) Hospitality operating systems, *International Journal of Contemporary Hospitality Management*, 7, 5, 17–21

Kaplan, R. S. and Norton, D. P. (1992) The balanced scorecard-measures that drive performance, *Harvard Business Review*, 70, 1, 71–79

Kaplan, R. S. and Norton, D. P. (1996) Using the balanced scorecard as a strategic management system, *Harvard Business Review*, 74, 1, 75–85

Kozak, M. and Rimmington, M. (1998) Benchmarking: destination attractiveness and small hospitality business performance, *International Journal of Contemporary Hospitality Management*, 10, 5, 184–188

Laitinen, E. K. (2002) A dynamic performance measurement system: evidence from small Finish technology companies, *Scandinavian Journal of Management*, 18, 1, 65–99

Lynch, R. L. and Cross, K. F. (1991) *Measure Up: The Essential Guide to Measuring Business Performance*, Mandarin: London, UK

Mclanely, E. J. (2000) *Business Finance: Theory and Practice,* 5th edition, Financial Times Prentice Hall: Britain

Min, H. and Min, H. (1996) Competitive benchmarking of Korean luxury hotels using the analytic hierarchy process and competitive gap analysis, *The Journal of Services Marketing*, 10, 3, 58–72

Min, H. and Min, H. (1997) Benchmarking the quality of hotel services: managerial perspectives, *International Journal of Quality and Reliability Management*, 14, 6, 582–597

Min, H., Min, H. and Chung, K. (2002) Dynamic benchmarking of hotel service quality, *Journal of Services Marketing*, 16, 4, 302–321

Morey, R. C. and Dittman, D. A. (1995) Evaluating a hotel GM's performance, *Cornell Hotel and Restaurant Administration Quarterly*, 36, 5, 30–35

O'Dell, C. and Jackson-Grayson, C. (2000) *Identifying and Transferring Internal Best Practices*, APQC, www.apqc.org/free/whitepapers/dispWhitePaper.cfm?ProductID-665

Ogden, S. (1998) Comment: benchmarking and best practice in the small hotel sector, *International Journal of Contemporary Hospitality Management*, 10, 5, 189–190

Parkan, C. (2005) Benchmarking operational performance: the case of two hotels, *International Journal of Productivity and Performance Management*, 54, 8, 679–696

Phillips, P. A. (2007) The balanced scorecard and strategic control: a hotel case study analysis, *Service Industries Journal*, 27, 6, 731–746

Phillips, P. and Appiah-Adu, K. (1998) Benchmarking to improve the strategic planning process in the hotel sector, *Service Industries Journal*, 18, 1, 1–17

Phillips, P. and Louvieris, P. (2005) Performance measurement systems in tourism, hospitality, and leisure small medium-sized enterprises: a balanced scorecard perspective, *Journal of Travel Research*, 44, 2, 201–211

Phillips, P. and Moutinho, L. (1999) Measuring strategic planning effectiveness in hotels, *International Journal of Contemporary Hospitality Management*, 11, 7, 349–358

Phillips, P., Davies, F. and Moutinho, L. (1999) The interactive effects of strategic planning on hotel performance: a neural network analysis, *Management Decision*, 37, 3, 279–288

Sigala, M. and Chalkiti, K. (2007) Improving performance through tacit knowledge externalisation and utilisation, *International Journal of Productivity and Performance Management*, 56, 5/6, 456–483

Sigala, M., Jones, P., Lockwood, A. and Airey, D. (2005) Productivity in hotels: a stepwise data envelopment analysis of hotels' rooms division processes, *Service Industries Journal*, 25, 1, 63–86

Singleton, J. P., Mclean, E. R. and Altman, E. N. (1988) Measuring information systems performance: experience with the management by results system at Security Pacific Bank, *MIS Quarterly*, 12, 2, 324–338

Southern, G. (1999) A systems approach to performance measurement in hospitality, *International Journal of Contemporary Hospitality Management*, 11, 7, 366–376

Teare, R. (1996) Hospitality operations: patterns in management, service improvement and business performance, *International Journal of Contemporary Hospitality Management*, 8, 7, 63–74

Uniform System of Accounts for the Lodging Industry (1996) *Uniform System of Accounts for the Lodging Industry*, 9th edition, Educational Institute of the American Hotel and Motel Association: East Lansing

Umbreit, W. T. (1986) Developing behaviorally-anchored scales for evaluating job performance of hotel managers, *International Journal of Hospitality Management*, 5, 2, 55–61

Warnken, J., Bradley, M. and Guilding, C. (2004) Eco-resorts vs. mainstream accommodation providers: an investigation of the viability of benchmarking environmental performance, *Tourism Management*, 26, 367–379

Wöber, K. W. (2000) Benchmarking hotel operations on the internet: a data envelopment analysis approach, *Information Technology and Tourism*, 3, 3/4, 195–212

Yasin, M. M. and Zimmerer, T. W. (1995) The role of benchmarking in achieving continuous service quality, *International Journal of Contemporary Hospitality Management*, 7, 4, 27–32

CHAPTER 11

Revenue management

Stowe Shoemaker

University of Houston

Thomas Gorin

Continental Airlines

Introduction

Revenue management (RM) is frequently defined as selling the right room at the right price to the right customer at the right time (see for instance, Kimes 1997). However, Jones (1999) argues that this is what hoteliers have always tried to do, and hence this simply defines the advanced reservations process in general. In this chapter, the definition of RM will be explored and its practice explained.

Revenue management is often confused with yield management (YM).[1] But YM is just one component of RM. Yield is the ratio between actual and potential room revenue.[2] Actual room revenue is that revenue received from room sales. Potential revenue is what a hotel would have received if their rooms were sold at full price or rack rates. Keep in mind, of course, that for this to be realistic, the full price rates must be realistic. Rack rates that are rarely achieved have little meaning for true yield ratios. Also realize that a hotel will have any number of different rates, including suite rates. All these must be calculated to determine a true yield ratio. Incremental revenue of food and beverages also cannot be ignored. Thus, a hotel can reach the same, better or poorer yield through different combinations of average rates and occupancy.

Revenue management is one the most researched areas in the field of hospitality (Jones and Lockwood 1998). Research interest is mainly focused on particular issues such as the analysis of the RM concept and its development into implementation models (such as Orkin 1988; Rowe 1989; Jones and Hamilton 1992; Brotherton and Mooney 1992; Donaghy et al. 1995, 1997; Jones 1988), the development of an RM culture (Jones and Hamilton 1992) and adoption, understanding and implementation of RM in the hotel industry (Bradley and Ingold 1993; Bitran and Mondschein 1995; Peters and Riley 1997; Jarvis et al. 1997; Badinelli 2000; Upchurch et al. 2002). Savkina and Yakovlev (1997) research the application of YM in Russia.

Griffin (1995, 1996, 1997) has focused on the critical success factors of an RM system. The contribution and value of information technology (IT) use for RM implementation is also heavily mentioned in the literature. These highlight the need for systems integration (Kimes 1989) and for addressing the

---

[1] Also, the usage of these terms has been different in the United States and the United Kingdom. Revenue management replaced yield management as the common terminology in the late 1990s in the United States, but yield management continued to be used in the United Kingdom until four or five years later (Editor).

[2] In the airline industry – yield is revenue per passenger and per mile traveled.

development of different modules and information system architecture of computerized YM systems (Gamble 1990; Jauncey et al. 1995). Sigala et al. (2001) identify the strategic role that IT plays in successful YM practices. Schwartz and Cohen (2003) found from a study of 57 experienced revenue managers that the interaction between a human revenue manager and a computer screen offering revenue management data is influenced by certain attributes of the computer interface.

More recently, researchers have turned their attention to two issues. The first is the extension of RM principles and techniques by either using more sophisticated analysis of customer spend (Dunn and Brooks 1990; Noone and Griffin 1997; Choi and Cho 2000) or applying it not only to rooms but also to banqueting and conference centres (Van Westering 1994; Kimes and McGuire 2001). The second area of research is into the issues of concern about the long-term effect of RM on customer satisfaction and loyalty, as considered by Kandampully and Suhartanto (2000) and Kimes (2003). Huyton et al. (1997) were concerned about the ethical and legal issues of applying RM.

Revenue management overview

Revenue management is best suited to environments where the firm's product is perishable and either is sold to the customer within a specific time frame or remains unused and disappears from the firm's inventory without generating revenue. It was originally developed by airlines in the early 1960s and quickly spread to other industries, such as hotels, rental car companies and cruise lines because airplane seats (hotel rooms, rental cars and cruise ship cabins) are perishable products that must be sold for the flight (night, day or cruise) of interest; otherwise they go unused. Before RM, this was largely limited to balancing group with individual demand on the basis of complementary booking times. Today, through computer technology, the attempt is to juggle all bookings and rate quotations so that on any given night the maximum revenue potential is realized.

Revenue management plans the ideal business mix for each day of the upcoming year and prices the rooms accordingly. It then adjusts the mix and prices on an ongoing basis as reservations do or do not develop.

There are several factors that make the use of RM suitable to the hotel industry. First, a hotel room is a perishable product, so it is sometimes better to sell it at a lower price than not to sell it at all because of low marginal production costs and high marginal capacity costs (i.e. contribution margin pricing).

239

Second, capacity is fixed and cannot be increased to meet more demand. Third, hotel demand is widely fluctuating and uncertain, depending on the days of the week and seasons of the year. Fourth, different market segments have different lead times for purchase. A convention group might reserve hotel rooms three years in advance, a pleasure traveller two months and a businessman a week ahead. Fifth, hotels have great flexibility in varying their prices at any given time.

These factors are very similar to the airline industry and represent the requisite conditions for a successful RM program. Although an operational tool, RM requires hotels to be market oriented. Knowledge of market segments, their buying behaviour and the prices they are willing to pay is essential for maximum success.

The essential rules for successful RM for hotels have been said (Lieberman 1993) to be as follows:

- Set the most effective pricing structure.
- Limit the number of reservations accepted for any given night or room type on the basis of profit potential.
- Negotiate volume discounts with groups.
- Match market segments with room type and price needs.
- Enable reservations agents to be effective sales agents rather than merely order takers.

To these, the following could be added:

- Provide reasons for lower rates, such as advance purchase time, payment in advance, non-refundability and length of stay for a variety of market segments. Marriott has done this deliberately to put the trade-off decision in the hands of the customer. In industry jargon, this is called 'fences'.
- Be consistent across the central reservation system, property reservationists, travel agents and other intermediaries so that quoted rates are the same. This refers to rate parity, discussed earlier in the chapter.

Defining revenue management

There are many definitions of RM. Jauncey et al. (1995: 1111) conducted a literature review of nine RM studies dating back to 1988 and concluded that 'YM (sic) is concerned with the maximization of room revenue through the manipulation of room rates in a structured fashion so as to take into account the forecasted patterns of demand'. Donaghy et al. (1995: 188) suggest that 'RM is a revenue maximization technique which aims to increase net yield through the predicted allocation of available bedroom capacity to predetermined market segments at optimal price'.

Jones (1999) argues that these definitions describe the *purpose* of RM but fail to differentiate it from reservation practices that existed prior to RM implementation. Hence RM is not *meaningfully* defined by its purpose, since hotels have always tried to make as much money as they could out of their fixed capacity. Jones proposes that RM needs to be defined by its 'systems structure', that is, how it enables revenue maximization. Few existing definitions identify this. However, the American Hotel and Motel Association (1994) described RM as 'a set of demand-forecasting techniques used to determine whether prices should be raised or lowered and a reservation request should be accepted or rejected to maximize revenue'. Jones (1999) goes on to develop a more detailed definition based on soft systems analysis – a research methodology designed to distinguish structure and function. The definition that is proposed from this analysis is as follows: 'Yield management is a system for hotel owners to maximize profitability through their senior management in hotels identifying the profitability of market segments, establishing value, setting prices, creating discount and displacement rules for application to the advanced reservations process and monitoring the effectiveness of these rules and their implementation'.

This definition emphasizes the strategic role of RM in managing *profitability*. Increasingly, the hotel industry, and the relevant academic literature, is placing greater emphasis on the profitability of each market segment, not just on the sales value of their custom.

Models of revenue management

One of the earliest models of RM was developed by Orkin (1988) on the basis of four main elements: forecasting; systems and procedures; strategic and tactical plans; and feedback system. Another early model was proposed by Jones and Hamilton (1992) as shown in Figure 11.1. The first stage in their model is to develop a yield (sic) culture, followed by a systematic analysis of market demand. However, the technological input and information systems needed to support RM are not addressed.

In contrast, a later work by Jauncey et al. (1995) gives a more specific view of the elements that are essential for the 'ideal YM applications', as they call it. They identify eight elements

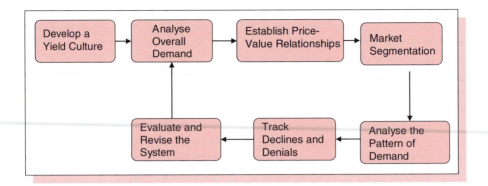

Figure 11.1
The yield management process (*Source*: Jones and Hamilton 1992).

for RM applications and focus on the technological side of the system, as follows:

- Historical demand analysis
- Future demand predictions
- Reservations inventory
- Actual versus forecast sales
- Market composition
- Non-arrival and cancellation analysis
- Analysis and reports
- Advice on rates and restrictions

The model proposed by Donaghy et al. (1995) develops a wide-ranging framework of 10 'key areas' for the effective operation of an RM system in the hotel industry. This framework focuses on identifying both decision-making and information systems (Table 11.1).

Finally, Jones (1999) proposes a systems model[3] of RM. It is divided into two main systems: the decision-making system and the decision support system. The decision-making system is again sub-divided into strategic and operational decision making. As Jones (1999: 1115) states, 'one is concerned with making decisions of a long-term nature and drawing up plans in relation to market segmentation, pricing and operational target setting. The other one is concerned with accepting or rejecting advance reservations in response to customer requests, consistent with pricing, discounting and displacement

---

[3] See chapter 2 for a discussion of systems theory.

Table 11.1 Key stages in a formal YM system

Stage 1	Personnel	Develop employee understanding/ highlight customer or hotel interface/ appoint forecasting committee/sort available customer and market data
Stage 2	Analyse demand	Identify competitors and source of demand/define hotel's strengths and weakness/predict demand levels and booking patterns/constantly monitor external factors
Stage 3	Market segmentation	Identify market (existing and potential)
		Segment market (demographic, psychographic and geographic)
Stage 4	Determine optimal guest mix	Based on propensity to spend
		Based on volume usage
Stage 5	Analyse trade-offs	Extensive calculations of monetary leakages
		Avoid displacing high-spending guests
Stage 6	Establish capacity levels	Set capacity to meet demand of market segments
Stage 7	Introduce YM system	Groups and consortiums need tailor-made system
		Small or independent hotels adopt revised version of above to achieve maximum benefits
Stage 8	Customer reorientation	Train comes into practice by (a) realizing hotel YM objectives and (b) meeting customer needs
Stage 9	Operational evaluations	Revise room allocation
		Evaluate low-demand changes
		Identify additional factors which determine demand
Stage 10	Actions	Implement any changes required immediately

Source: Donaghy et al. 1995.

rules'. The decision support system includes all the functions that aim to assist and support the core of decision-making system, which are an information system, human resource system and technological support system. An information system is concerned on one hand with the actual reservations made, declines, cancellations and no-shows and on the other hand with the analysis of demand used in the strategic and operational decision making. The other two are in effect the outline structure model that supports the RM process. The model also indicates how the external environment continually affects the daily routine of the RM system.

Revenue management in practice

Revenue management is often described as consisting of two distinct components: differential pricing and inventory control (Belobaba 1987).

Differential pricing is the practice of differentiating products by offering different amenities and restrictions and hence setting different prices for each combination of product, amenities and restrictions. Different purchasing patterns of business and leisure customers and the offer of differentiated products add to the complexity of the RM problem and have created the need for inventory control and the development of computerized RM systems.

Inventory control determines how many products of each type to make available throughout the selling period. In particular, it sets the amount of low-price products to make available to ensure that later-purchasing, higher-price customers are able to purchase the remaining products at a higher price without turning away needed low-price demand. An alternative way of thinking about this is termed 'duration control' (Weatherford et al. 2001).

Overview of the history of pricing in the hotel business

It is proposed that pricing in the hotel industry will have five phases of development. In the first phase, hospitality firms had basically the same price for their products. Rates only changed by season, not day by day. Any demand forecasting that was undertaken was used by management not to set rates, but to determine the scheduling of employees.

The second phase of pricing occurred with the advent of YM systems to the airline industry. The YM systems designed for the airlines were then adapted to the hotel industry. Hoteliers used the information provided by the YM systems to forecast demand and change prices accordingly. The standard statistic used to measure results was REVPAR, or revenue per available room.

In the third phase, RM and customer relationship management come together. While setting prices and availability, pricing managers consider not only demand but also the lifetime value of the customer buying the service. Harrah's Entertainment recently implemented a customized RM system which merges their traditional YM system with their total rewards program. Other firms have started doing the same. In this phase of pricing, the standard statistic used to measure results is REVPAC, or revenue per available customer.

In these authors' view, the fourth and next phase of pricing focuses on the value delivered to the customer, not necessarily the availability of the inventory. Essentially, pricing managers will move from being controlled by their RM systems to having their systems as just one part of the overall marketing mix. In setting rates, pricing mangers will examine the different components of value being delivered and price accordingly. This way of thinking about pricing becomes critical in a down economy where there is a tendency in many firms to lower prices to fill capacity. The problem with lowering prices, of course, is that one destroys the brand image, and it also becomes hard to raise prices when demand improves. The statistic used to measure this will be VALUEPAC, or value generated by and for per available customer. The value *by* the customer is the price paid and the value *for* the customer refers to the costs incurred by the firm supplying the value. The key, of course, is for the firm to supply features that the customer really values but have little cost to the service firm. An upgrade on an airplane is but just one example – last room availability is another.

Pricing will reach the final phase when the consumer is completely incorporated in the pricing decision. In other words, pricing managers will use knowledge of consumer behaviour to determine not only how to price but also how the pricing information is presented to the consumer. The measurement here will also be VALUEPAC. The VALUEPAC statistic will be higher in this phase than in the previous phases.

Alternative pricing strategies

Value-based pricing • • •

This strategy involves choosing a price after developing estimates of market demand on the basis of how potential customers perceive the value of the product or service. It has nothing to do with the cost to produce the item. Perceived value is often defined as what one receives divided by the price one paid. Value-based pricing has the advantage that it forces managers to review the objectives they have when marketing their product or service and keep in touch with the needs and preferences of customers.

In establishing prices, there are some elements that are particularly pertinent with regard to the customer. The first of these elements is the perceived price value relationship, as it is commonly called. The importance of price value is illustrated by a study of business travellers (Bowen and Shoemaker 1998) who spend more than $120 per night for a hotel room and make six or more business trips per year. The study revealed that 28% of the 344 who spend more than 75 nights per year in hotels (38% of the total sample) claimed that the feature 'is a good value for the price paid' is important in the decision to stay in the same hotel chain when travelling on business.

The role of the management is to increase the perceptions of price value so that consumers will be willing to spend more money. One way to accomplish this goal is to focus on one or more of the eight components of value, as follows:

- *financial* (e.g. saving money on future transactions, complete reimbursement if service failure, 10% discount at gift shop)
- *temporal* (e.g. saving time by priority check-in)
- *functional* (e.g. availability of check cashing)
- *experiential* (e.g. active participation in the service)
- *emotional* (e.g. more recognition)
- *social* (e.g. interpersonal link with a service provider)
- *trust* (e.g. the organization does what it says)
- *identification with the organization* (e.g. affinity with a sports team)

Prospect pricing

Prospect theory argues that when people make decisions, they do so by examining changes relative to a reference point. That reference point can be established by quoting a high price initially for a premium product, so that subsequent prices for less premium products appear to be good value. Prospect theory is applied in restaurants. In a study on menu pricing (Shoemaker et al. 2006), it was found that menu items with detailed descriptions and high prices were perceived to have the same price value as menu items with modest description and low prices.

Reference pricing

Customers have in mind a price they expect to pay for a given solution. This is called their reference price. Reactions to prices will vary around this reference or expected price, on the basis of some kind of prior experience or knowledge. In understanding reference pricing, it is important to understand some critical pricing definitions. *Reference price* is the first pricing term firms need to understand. This is the price for which consumers believe the product should sell. The reference price is formed when consumers consider such things as:

- the price last paid
- the price of similar items
- the price considering the brand name
- the real or imagined cost to produce the item
- the perceived cost of product failure

The last item is of considerable importance because if reflects consumers' imaginations. For example, the reference price for a meal where one is celebrating a special occasion is higher than the reference price for a meal with some old college friends, even though the restaurant may be the same. The risk of failure is critical in the first case and less critical in the second.

The second definition one needs to understand is *reservation price*. Reservation price is defined as the maximum price the customer will pay for a product. If the selling price is less than the reservation price, the customer will buy the product. Firms that price exactly to the reservation price are said to extract the entire *consumer surplus*. Firms that price less than the reservation price are said to be 'leaving money on the table'. Obviously, firms do not want to leave money on the table. In 1988, Taco Bell used a research methodology based on research originally conducted by Dutch economist Peter H. Van Westendorp to determine customers' reference or expected price. This methodology was developed by Gabor and Clive (1966) and others. However, until Taco Bell picked up on it, this methodology had been largely ignored in the hospitality industry. This process puts a price value on a product as determined by the perception of the target market which, in the final analysis, is the only way to set prices. Basically, this methodology helps determine the reserve price and the reservation price. Through this pricing methodology, Taco Bell learnt to bundle its products – for example, adding sour cream, including a soft drink – in a way and at a price where the customer perceived 'value'. For the fast food industry giants, value pricing and bundling have reduced the former standard practices of discounts, coupons and direct mail as key weapons in the fast food wars.

Lewis and Shoemaker (1997) explain how research can demonstrate the way customers, in some arbitrary fashion, establish an upper price level at which they deem the product to be too expensive and a lower price level below which the quality of the product would be suspect. This is based on expectations. In between is the 'indifference' price – the price perceived as normal for that product in a given market, given one's expectations. There are certain hotels and restaurants where we would expect to pay different prices. When we are 'surprised' by an unexpected price, we may tend to become somewhat irate. Thus, it is the responsibility of the price setter to educate the customer about prices.

Expectations should be built into the pricing decision. Research can determine what the market thinks the product should cost. This can be especially useful in the pricing of services where a cost basis is lacking for developing an expectation. Findings may indicate that the service can be priced higher; contrarily, a lower-than-expected price may offer competitive advantage. Knowledge of price expectation can help firms avoid both overpricing and underpricing.

Psychological pricing • • •

Prices cause psychological reactions on the part of customers just as atmospherics do. As noted, high prices may imply quality and low prices may imply inferiority. This is especially true for services because of their intangibility. Thus, higher priced services may sell better, whereas lower priced services may sell poorly. This is contrary to the standard economic model. Psychological reactions, however, do not necessarily correspond to reality, and it is not unusual for customers to feel that they have made a mistake.

This is also true in the hospitality industry because of the 'visibility' factor. Being 'seen' at an upscale restaurant or hotel is very important to some customers. For example, a businessman might buy inexpensive furniture for his apartment and drink ordinary wine at home. This same businessman, trying to make an impression on peers and customers, will rave about the antique furniture in the lounge and the expensive wine ordered with dinner. In other words, he wants to be seen with the product that offers the highest affordable visibility factor.

Buyers and non-buyers of products also have different perceptions of price. This contrast can be demonstrated best with the case of upscale restaurants. Many such restaurants are perceived by those who have never been there to be far more expensive than is actually the case. Commander's Palace, one of New Orleans' finest restaurants, used large advertisements in the local paper detailing their attractively priced lunch specials to counteract this. In pricing, it is important to understand the price perceptions of non-users as well as of the users.

Another psychological pricing technique is called price-lining.

This technique clumps prices together so that a perception of substantially increased quality is created. For example, a wine list might have a group of wines in the $30–40 range and have the next grouping in the $50–75 range. The perception is a definitive increase in quality, which may or may not be the case.

Still another version of psychological pricing is called odd-numbered pricing. This is a familiar tactic to all. Items sell at $6.99 rather than $7.00 to create the perception of a lower price. Sometimes this is carried to extreme such as a computer that sells for $1,999.99 or a car advertised at $32,999. This tactic is often used in menu and hotel room pricing.

Value-added service pricing ● ● ●

Value-added services are those that are added to the basic product/service that the customer buys to enhance the perception of value. These are worth evaluating because in some cases, they may not add true value, may simply increase the cost base or may eventually be passed on – in the form of higher prices – to a customer who does not really want them or perceive a higher value.

Developing a product/service for customers' specific needs that augments the standard product is a part of loyalty marketing. Business services in a guest room for which an additional charge is sometimes made with turndown service at no charge are perfect examples. Many hotels, however, instead of tailoring added services to individual needs sometimes provide customers with more services than they want or need at prices that do not reflect the value or their cost. Unfortunately, the management sometimes does not even know which services customers with similar needs really want, which should be offered as a part of the standard product or which should be offered as value options that some would pay extra for. Furthermore, because of the intangibility of many services, the management often does not know the cost of providing them; no matter how homogeneous a target market, one size does not fit all.

Because hotel managements rely almost solely on measures of customer satisfaction, they are often misled. Customers are always happy to get something for nothing and they express satisfaction on the overall offering. The property, however, has to absorb the costs, of which they may be unaware, that may or may not have created real value in the first place. The solution to this is called flexible service offerings – particular services valued by individual customers (Anderson and Narus 1995). A hotel should first make an 'inventory' of these services: what is being provided to whom and on what basis. These acts apply especially to group bookings where services are often added just to get the booking. The same thing should be done for any new services that are being considered.

Customers then need to be asked the value of the service to them. This leads to activity-based pricing. The following options are now available:

1. Do not offer the service.
2. Give the service away at no additional charge.
3. Raise the price equal to the cost of providing the service.
4. Raise the price less than the cost of providing it.
5. Raise the price slightly higher to camouflage a price increase on the standard product.

This approach allows hotels to fit the service to customer needs, as well as notify customers that they do not have to pay for something they do not want. Some hotels today have turndown service on request only – but only after realizing how much it was costing them and how many customers did not want it.

Differential pricing through 'fences' • • •

The RM system of a hotel should be set up to offer different categories of rooms for different prices. A hotel has an opportunity to create many different types of guest rooms, some more desirable than others. An effective hotel RM system will open and close categories of rooms, giving the customer greater value for higher pricing.

The key to multiple prices and RM is that each price must represent a different product and that those who have a high reservation price will not be able to buy a lower priced product. Multi-products were discussed above. The chapter now examines how to keep those with high reservation prices from buying less expensive products. This occurs through what is known as fences. Table 11.2 shows some typical fences in the hospitality industry.

In choosing fences, it is important that the 'fence' makes sense to the consumer. That is, the customer must believe that the rate they are paying is based on their choices, not on the firm's greed. For instance, the consumer needs to think 'I need to pay more

Table 11.2 Potential fences

Rule type	Advanced requirement	Refundability	Changeability	Must stay
Advance purchase	3-day	Non-refundable	No Changes	Weekend
Advance reservation	7-day	Partially refundable (% refund of fixed amount)	Change to dates of stay, but not number of rooms	Weekday
	14-day	Fully refundable	Changes, but pay fee; must still meet rules	
	21-day		Full changes, non-refundable	
	30-day		Full changes allowed	

because having flexibility is more important than price' or 'I am paying more because I cannot decide exactly what I want to do'.

One fence that is not listed in Table 11.2 is the 'loyalty fence'. This is a fence for frequent and loyal customers. The firm that offers multiple prices must be careful that the pricing decision does not destroy loyal customers' trust in the organization and hence, their loyalty. In research undertaken in part by one of the authors, loyal hotel customers were presented with a hypothetical situation where the hotel to which they were loyal increased its rate because of anticipated demand. Consumers were then asked how this would change their attitudes and behaviours towards the hotel to which they claimed to be loyal. Findings indicated that 60% of the customers would ask the rate the next time they called for a reservation (normally, loyal customers do not ask about rates). In addition, 35.7% would call other hotels in the area to get their prices. Clearly, the loyal guest needs to be treated differently than the guest who comes for a one-night stay.

History of inventory control

Most of the history of RM and inventory control relates to the airline industry where RM was born. Airlines have been over-booking (accepting more bookings than capacity) their aircraft for close to three decades in an attempt to reduce the revenue loss associated with passenger no-shows. The objective of overbooking algorithms is to determine the total number of seats to sell on a flight while balancing the loss of revenue associated with an empty seat and the cost of 'bumping' a passenger. Overbooking is not illegal, and most airlines overbook their scheduled flights to a certain extent to compensate for no-shows. Passengers are sometimes left behind or 'bumped' as a result. When an oversale occurs, the Department of Transportation, or its equivalent, in most countries requires airlines to ask people who are not in a hurry to give up their seats voluntarily, in exchange for compensation. Those passengers bumped against their will are, with a few exceptions, entitled to compensation.

Airline overbooking research dates back to the 1950s with Beckman's static optimization model (Beckman 1958). Later statistical models include the work of Taylor (1962), Simon (1968), Rothstein (1968, 1985) and Vickrey (1972). While the practice of overbooking is slightly less evident in the hospitality industry, it is nevertheless used to also maximize the occupancy rate. However, the nature of a hotel room makes overbooking a more delicate matter relative to an airline seat, where a delay caused by overbooking may be acceptable to the passenger. Typically hotel guests do not like being 'bumped' to another property, however near it may be.

Overbooking models can be as simple as applying historical averages of show-up rates to the company's inventory to determine the number units of product to make available beyond capacity to maximize utilization. More advanced overbooking methods use statistical models and allow analysts to choose the amount of acceptable risk involved in overbooking, account for revenues and costs associated with overbooking or use customer information to identify unique attributes that might affect the likelihood of each individual customer to no-show.

The first and the most basic inventory control systems consisted of simple databases recording booking behaviour of airline passengers or hotel guests, which allowed the analysts to perform 'post-departure' analyses of the booking behaviour of no-show travellers. The major shortcoming of these systems lay in their inability to automatically identify critical patterns in the booking cycle.

These systems were thus later improved to identify unusual booking behaviour and direct the attention of analysts on departures from the norm. These computerized systems consisted of large databases that allowed analysts to define 'usual' booking patterns and set thresholds beyond which unusual activity was flagged for analyst review. These monitoring systems were not advanced enough to provide automated responses to changes in booking patterns or demand. However, some systems could provide recommendations to the analysts as to the appropriate course of action. The final decision remained in the analyst's hands.

The latest step in RM systems involved the addition of mathematical models to forecast demand and optimize inventory allocation based on historical data collected in booking databases as well as recent behaviour as monitored by these same databases. These mathematical models involve deterministic or statistical optimizers that communicate directly with the firm's reservation system and automatically set the availability of each individual product without user intervention.

These third-generation systems marked a crossroad in RM by moving from user-dependent systems to user-independent systems. In these third-generation optimizers, the analyst monitors the performance of the system and makes corrections for unusual events and departures from 'standard' behaviour that could not be forecasted by the system. The role is therefore reversed from first- and second-generation systems, where the analyst decided on the course of action on the basis of booking behaviour.

We next focus on the individual components of third-generation inventory management systems: overbooking, forecasting and optimization. Overbooking recognizes that travellers may fail to show up for their reserved hotel room (restaurant seat or other product) and artificially inflates the available inventory in an attempt to minimize the number of empty rooms on any given night. Forecasting can be viewed as the critical component of inventory control, as it generates the forecasts of demand for each type of room, which will be used by the optimizer to determine the availability of each product type. Forecasting and optimization involve various levels of refinement from basic day-to-day methods to more advanced length of stay systems (in the case of hotel rooms).

Overview of inventory control techniques

Overbooking • • •

As previously mentioned, overbooking is the practice of accounting for traveller no-show when determining the optimal number of inventory units to make available for sale, with the goal of filling all units. Numerous methods can be used to overbook – from simple deterministic overbooking to more advanced stochastic methods. Deterministic overbooking uses

253

a fixed estimate of the no-show value to set the overbooking level, while stochastic methods estimate the probability distribution of the no-show rate and use this information to make predictions of future no-show. The stochastic approaches to overbooking have the advantage of capturing changes in traveller behaviour that may not be captured in deterministic methods and further account for the stochastic nature of demand and customer behaviour.

The simplest deterministic method uses a pre-determined fixed value of overbooking, based on analyst knowledge of demand. For example, a hotel might choose to overbook by five rooms. More advanced methods might use forecasts of demand – costs of empty rooms and revenue gain of additional room – as deterministic inputs to a linear program that would solve for the optimal overbooking level based on these assumptions.

Traditionally, however, overbooking relies on stochastic models where no-show rates are estimated on the basis of historical data and the optimal overbooking level is then derived from these historical data on the basis of a pre-determined stochastic model (Belobaba 1999). Examples of such models include calculation of simple straight averages of historical no-show rates subsequently applied to future periods. More advanced stochastic models apply confidence intervals techniques to historical data and thus incorporate the history's variability in the calculation of no-shows. These systems thus adjust the forecasted no-show rates (from the simple average) based on an input confidence interval. For example, if the analysts chooses to set the no-show to ensure that the probability of a denied boarding (in the case of airlines) be less than 5%, the recommended no-show rate will be significantly lower than the average, based on the variability of historical no-show rates. Finally, state-of-the-art overbooking techniques include estimates of revenues gained from overbooking, costs incurred from overbooking and customer-specific attributes in the calculation of overbooking levels.

Forecasting • • •

More often art than science, forecasting is the process of predicting future demand on the basis of historical data. Smith (1984) provided a basis for initial research in forecasting of airline demand and led to numerous models of demand forecasting.

Typical demand forecasts are based on historical booking periods, which are further divided into rolling historical periods and holiday or special events periods. Rolling history uses the most recent historical data to forecast demand for future booking periods. Holiday and special events history recognizes that special events or holidays differ from non-holiday periods and use year-over-year data as a historical period. Once the appropriate historical data have been identified, forecasting is typically done using stochastic approaches. For example, future demand can be estimated as the average demand for the historical data or as the sum of historical 'pick-up' between today and date of check-in (in the case of hotels). Pick-up refers to the number of guests who book between the current period and date of arrival. For example, pick-up between 90 days before arrival date and actual arrival is different from demand at the date of arrival and allows demand to be adjusted as this date gets closer. Other methods also rely on historical data but determine the forecasted demand as a weighted average of the history or use exponential smoothing techniques to put more emphasis on recent data.

While actual calculations of a forecast for demand are relatively simple, three major challenges remain. The first challenge pertains to the capacity constraints imposed on demand. Typically, the availability of hotel rooms, airline seats, rental cars or even boat cabins is limited and can be less than demand. As a consequence, historical observations are constrained observations of demand and therefore do not reflect the actual demand, but underestimate it. As a result, it becomes necessary to unconstrain (or detruncate) demand to estimate what historical demand would have been without capacity restrictions. Unconstraining (detruncation) techniques also involve stochastic approaches and can be based on booking behaviours for low-demand periods (when demand did not exceed capacity) relative to high-demand periods.

The second challenge in forecasting, once unconstrained demand has been estimated, involves estimating the impact of seasonal traffic on demand. As observed by many travel industry specialists, demand is cyclical and depends on the season. Airlines typically expect lower demand in the fall and winter, while they forecast much higher demand in the spring and summer. It therefore becomes imperative to account for these seasonal patterns when forecasting future demand so as to avoid forecasting fall demand using unadjusted summer history. Such an approach (in the case of airlines) would invariably overestimate demand for fall travel and underestimate spring demand, ultimately causing the airlines to forego substantial revenues by rejecting low-fare demand in the low-demand months and accepting too much low-fare demand in high-demand months.

Finally, the level of detail involved in a forecast also poses a significant challenge to forecasters. Indeed, the level of aggregation of historical data and future demand is critical in creating a reliable and accurate forecast. Too much aggregation yields too little information on future demand, while too much detail leads to highly variable estimates of demand that are useless. Demand can be broken into finer and finer portions, which better reflect the attributes of individual passengers and thus become more coherent groupings of demand. However, as groupings increase, so too does variability of this demand. For example, when considering the hotel inventory control problem, should the forecaster focus on individual night stays and forecast demand for future nights individually, or should the forecaster attempt to account for length of stay data? Individual night forecasts yield less variable forecasts but lose the information of length of stay, which would allow the optimizer to decide between a single-night-stay customer and a multi-night-customer. Similarly, the length of the booking periods studied to calculate pick-up information affects the reliability of a demand estimate.

All of these challenges have been addressed in some form by RM tools, but no optimal solution has yet been devised.

Inventory control optimization • • •

Given overbooking levels and forecasts of demand for future flights, hotel night stays, rental cars or cruise line cabins, the inventory optimizer sets the availability within each product category to maximize revenues. Three major approaches exist in this final step in inventory control:

1. deterministic control
2. stochastic optimization
3. advanced dynamic programming methods

Deterministic linear programs use forecasted demand as a deterministic input to a linear program, which then sets the amount of seats (hotel rooms, etc.) available at any given price. These linear programs allocate inventory and meet the capacity constraints imposed by hotel or aircraft size and can be re-optimized once a preset threshold of bookings/cancellations is reached. A general formulation of the inventory control linear program can be viewed as follows:

$$\max(\text{Revenues}) = \max\left(\sum_{i,j} X_{i,j} \times R_j\right)$$

subject to

$$\sum_{i,j} X_{i,j} \leq \mathrm{cap}$$
$$\sum_{j} X_{i,j} \leq D_i$$

where D_i represents demands of type I, $X_{i,j}$ the allocation of demand type i to product type j, R_j represents the price of product j.

Stochastic approaches take into consideration the variable nature of demand for travel services or other products and compute the expected marginal revenue to be achieved from selling one additional unit of a specific product category. On the basis of the expected additional revenue from each product compared to the other products available, booking (availability) limits are set within each category. The expected revenue from each incremental unit of product type depends on the distribution of demand for each product.

These stochastic methods are the most commonly used in the travel industry as they have the advantage over deterministic methods of accounting for variability in demand. However, some limitations of these methods are that they often assume independence of product type demand: If a particular product type is unavailable, the customer will not be willing to buy any other product type. In addition, these stochastic methods also make assumptions on the distribution of demand. For simplicity purposes, it is often assumed that demand follows a normal distribution.

Advanced dynamic programming methods involve the relatively new field of dynamic programming and involve far greater computing power than deterministic or stochastic approaches. Without going into the details of dynamic programming, these methods divide the remaining booking periods into sufficiently small time increments so as to ensure that, at most, one booking will occur within each time frame. From any point in the booking period, every possible alternative will be considered and the alternative leading to the highest revenue will be chosen. This process is repeated at each time increment to ensure that the best option is always chosen from that point onwards and, ultimately, that revenues are maximized. These methods show promising results in simulation settings but have been difficult to implement because of the required computing power. In addition, optimization times are generally too long to allow for the frequent re-optimization needed by these methods.

Revenue management 'culture'

It has been argued that hotel companies tend to place too much emphasis on the technical and system-building aspects of RM and too little on the human aspects (Brotherton and Turner 2001). Although computer-based tools are a key component of an RM program, both the technology and the systems are only good as long as there are people handling the data and making decisions on the basis of the analysis. Huge investments in technology also tend to overshadow important organizational issues (Talluri and Van Ryzin 2004).

Cross (1997) argues that top management leadership and support are essential of YM. Kimes (1997: 9) agrees: 'Without a commitment [from top management], RM systems may be doomed to failure'. Top managers set the tone for the organization, and senior managers can also help provide adequate resource to the RM program if the company is to reap the highest potential revenue from the program. Furthermore, they must ensure that the best and brightest people are in the RM team. The top management will be responsible for organizing and putting together the teams and ensure that the system is continuously provided with the necessary for its operation information.

Another factor that easily is lost sight of by hoteliers is employee commitment and their involvement in problem solving. Employee commitment may be seen as a function of the staff's decision-making latitude and involvement (Hansen and Eringa 1997). As Jones and Hamilton (1992: 3) state, 'no computerized system will ever be successful without a range of skilled personnel who are involved in the process'. Revenue management has to become an integral part of everyone's work routine. 'Everyone' means all those managers and employees who have a role to play in the system (Jones and Hamilton 1992: 3), not just the managers. Their involvement in RM can share and provide some important guest information and their 'marketing intelligence'. They often include many more people than usually considered, including reservationists, front office clerks, cashiers and concierges (Jones and Hamilton 1992).

The introduction of computerized RM has also had an impact on the structure of an organization (Jauncey et al. 1995). Successful RM implementation depends on a highly trained and motivated team, often from across different departments of the property, who regularly meet to forecast the forthcoming business of the hotel (Huyton and Peters 1997). Jauncey et al. (1995) state RM team should include all heads of department and other managers concerned with reservations, accommodation and hotel business. They emphasize that the function of the RM team is not simply to overview the process but to become directly involved in all aspects and stages of RM, including the prediction of future levels and patterns of business. Huyton and Peters (1997) stress that RM teams typically consist of the rooms division manager, the sales manager and the reservations manager. They do not mean that anyone else is excluded, but for a speedier and more effective decision-making process they think it is wise not to make the RM team too big and the original three would tend to make the best team. Donaghy et al (1997), through research on the application of RM within the British corporate hotel sector, propose that an RM team is considered essential involving, ideally, the revenue specialists, the functional specialists and a coordinator. They state that the team co-ordinator should be the general manager, who assumes overall responsibility for the implementation of RM and ensures that functional specialists work and learn from each other.

Donaghy et al. (1995) also propose that the effectiveness of an RM system is significantly influenced by the extent to which a training program is developed and provided to RM staff. To enhance awareness of YM within hotels, skills must be developed to practice such techniques proficiently (Brotherton and Turner 2001). All staff, whether managers or employees, must be involved in training sessions, not only on technology but also on company RM philosophy (Lieberman 1993), especially those dealing with sales and inquiries, to develop an understanding of its effects on their job roles and the establishment (Donaghy et al. 1995; Donaghy et al. 1998; Farrell and Whelan-Ryan 1998; Hansen and Eringa 1998). There exist many processes in RM that cannot be completed by the computer. They include isolation of the relevant numbers, discrimination between all the possible combinations of data and focus on only that which is relevant to the forecasting process and the decision at hand (Jones and Hamilton 1992).

Training classes, both before and after implementation, should be conducted at various levels of management (Talluri and Van Ryzin 2005). Talluri and VR suggest that different management level should have different training emphases. For mid-level managers, the main emphasis should be on the principles of RM. For supervisors, more training is needed on the details of the technology (at least at a conceptual level) and how the system 'thinks' in terms of coming up with its recommendations. Revenue analysts need this same training, but they also need specific training in how to use the software effectively and when and when not to override the system recommendations (Talluri and Van Ryzin 2005).

In addition, as Jones and Hamilton (1992) state, training and education should also be considered at some specific job positions which are not direct users of the RM system but their involvement can help make RM more successful. For example, concierge, sales staff, front office staff, customer service agents, and so on. They may pick up information from overhearing guests, talking to guests or through their relationships with other people. In fact, it is easy to lose sight of these staff, but they could help the revenue manager in setting rates and forecasting demand.

To implement RM successfully, it is not only important to get commitment from each department, but there must be effective communication between each department. In the past hotel departments ignored between department communication; as such, they found that because no one really understood what RM was, any problems with rates, guest complaints, or poor pricing decisions were blamed on the RM system (Cross 1997). Cross (1997) suggested organizing road shows to educate the company about RM and how it will help the hotels. Communication can also be undertaken by conducting 'focus group' discussions, by means of attitude surveys and by informally listening to what employees say (Armstrong 2003).

Finally another managerial issue related to RM culture is the development of rational incentives and reward systems. Due to the adoption of a new RM system, hotel managers may have to reconsider the business performance criteria on which they base their incentive schemes for staff in departments such as sales, marketing and reservations (Donaghy et al. 1997). Although incentive schemes ensure that reservations and sales agents are concerned with trying to increase both the occupancy and the average room rate, an incentive system that motivates employees to make decisions which do not increase hotel revenue can counteract the most sophisticated RM system (Kimes 1997). According to Donaghy et al. (1995), a productive incentive scheme within the context of YM must incorporate incentive points that are directly related to the sales generated on high-, medium- and low-demand days. If incentive schemes are based on sales volume and occupancy, or average room rate, there will be a potential conflict between individual and corporate objectives, so reservations agents and sales managers should be rewarded on revenue production rather than on talk time or number of rooms booked. Therefore, the incentive schemes will require revision to ensure that behaviour required by the YM system accords with that encouraged by the personal incentive schemes (Brotherton and Mooney 1992).

Jones and Hamilton (1992) propose formal and informal approaches that can be adopted to develop a revenue culture. The formal approaches are the following:

- Carefully select personnel who have the necessary skills in the use of IT and who can perform analyses.
- Use RM performance criteria to evaluate the business performance of properties.
- Include forecasting and RM in the job descriptions of key personnel.
- Set up a forecasting committee that includes managers from the rooms division, reservations, sales, marketing, food and beverage, banqueting and the front office.
- Modify employee remuneration to reflect improved operating performance resulting from RM.

However, they also emphasize the informal aspects of organizational life which they think as important as the formal ones, and such aspects can be useful in developing a revenue culture. The informal approaches that will support YM are (Jones and Hamilton 1992) as follows:

- Demonstrate a high-level commitment to the YM concept within the organization.
- Accept that mistakes will be made, especially in the early days.
- Involve not only managers but also all employees who have a role to play, including reservationists, front office clerks, cashiers, and concierges.
- Demystify the YM concept by keeping things simple and easy to understand and by rejecting jargon (especially that from suppliers of hardware and software).
- Reward people for implementing new techniques and for suggesting new ideas (such rewards need not be financial – use praise and increased responsibility, too, as a way to acknowledge performance and motivate workers).

Impact on performance

The extent to which YM improves hotel revenue performance has been little researched. Suppliers claim it will give an increase in average achieved room rates of between 3.5 and 5% within the first 12 months (Goymour and Donaghy 1995). One marketer claims that an RM system can earn properties $5–10 more per room night, depending on how well the property was managed before YM was introduced (Rowe 1989). In the late 1980s, Hilton hotels introduced an RM system, and it was reported that one hotel experienced a $7.50 increase in transient average rate with no reduction in occupancy in the first month (Orkin 1988). Bob Regan, President of Revenue Dynamics, reported that three hotels using his company's system experienced a 5–8% improvement in room revenue (Boyce 1991). In 1999, a supplier's website cited increased revenues of 3–7% and profit increases of 50–100% (TIMS Revenue Optimisation Systems 1999).

Despite these claims, objective long-term measurement of such performance improvements has rarely been carried out and was not published in the research literature. This is partly because a number of methodological problems have to be overcome. First, the properties selected as case studies must have adopted and *fully implemented* a YM system. As the Jarvis et al. (1997) study demonstrated, some hotels believe that they have adopted YM, when in fact they have not fully done so. Second, there need to be accurate measurement of the dependent variable (room revenue) and the independent variables (occupancy and achieved room rate) both before and after the implementation and after it. Given that these variables are all key performance measures of hotel operation, such data would be readily available. Greater control over the research would be achieved if it were designed as a longitudinal study, that is, a hotel that was yet to implement YM was studied for some time prior to implementation and studied for some time afterwards. This, however, is very time consuming and costly, so historic data sets were used. The lowest level of aggregation in data would be the most desirable, which could be in weekly or monthly sales performance, but the time frame over which data need to be compared pre- and post-implementation is long. It is suggested by those implementing YM that it takes at least six months for the system to 'bed down'. Furthermore, there may be seasonal fluctuations. This suggests that a minimum of three years' data need to be considered: A full 12-month pre-implementation, 12 months during which the system is installed, tested and established and 12 months post-implementation.

The third methodological problem is the effect of extraneous variables. During the three years of sales activity to be included in the study, a number of factors may have influenced the revenue performance of the hotels, other than YM implementation. These could be either external or internal influences. External influences could be national trends, economic circumstances, national advertising campaigns by the firm or competitors and local developments relating to business demand and competitor behaviour. Internal factors affecting performance could be a change in the management personnel within the property, in-house sales initiatives or refurbishment.

Jones (2000) attempted to tackle these issues in a study of three hotels in the United Kingdom. Despite this, it remained difficult to be sure that any change in performance derived from the implementation of a YM system. However, from discussions with senior managers in each of the properties, it is clear that their *perception* is that YM is extremely effective. What is clear is that post-YM implementation, all hotels appear to be achieving better ARR, although even this depends on the years compared. Managers also agreed that performance improved largely due to YM's impact on rate setting and rate control. Some managers identified that the reduction in discounting that accompanied the 'fair rate' pricing may have deterred some business, but this was more than offset by the improved ARR. Jones (2000) concludes that

- There is growing evidence from a number of sources that YM may improve yield performance by around 4% in the United Kingdom.
- Such improvement largely derives from better management of the average rate achieved (rather than better management of occupancy).
- Yield improvement varies over time, probably in relation to the strength of demand. Most improvement is seen with respect to those periods when demand is strong.
- It takes some time for a YM system to be fully operational so that performance improvement may lag 6–18 months behind implementation.
- Hotels have invested heavily, in terms of both financial investment and human resources, without having any clear system in place to monitor the impact that the YM system will have on operational performance.

A study by Sanchez and Satir (2005) suggested that performance can also be affected by the 'reservation mode, that is, whether it is off-line or online. They looked at the performance of a major hotel chain's system over two years and compared off-line and online modes with respect to average price, occupancy rate and REVPAR. They found that online mode yielded significantly better average prices and REVPAR than the off-line mode. They also investigated a sub-group of hotels and found that those that switched to online mode experienced a substantial revenue increase. The issue of a distribution channel's effect on RM has also been investigated using computer simulation (Choi and Kimes 2002).

Summary and conclusions

Revenue management techniques have been used for close to three decades and have produced significant revenue gains for the companies using them effectively. In the process of improving the efficiency of RM, numerous avenues are currently being explored. Forecasting remains a very difficult discipline in constant need of improvement. Current forecasting methods, while suited to differentiated pricing environments, are rather inadequate at forecasting demand in undifferentiated environments, as currently faced by airlines. Optimization relies on very restrictive assumptions, such as the independence of fare product demand and the normal distribution of that demand. Lastly, alternative approaches to RM currently investigate the possibility of moving away from traditional methods and forecasting altogether to use choice model approaches. Choice models determine the probability that a customer, guest, etc. will choose any of the available alternatives and thus differ from traditional forecasting methods. However, the calibration of such choice models remains a challenge in the transportation industry.

Acknowledgement

The authors would like to acknowledge the contribution of the Editor in drafting this chapter.

References

Anderson, J. C. and Narus, J. A. (1995) Capturing the value of supplementary services. *Harvard Business Review*, 73, 1, 175–183

Badinelli, R. D. (2000) An optimal, dynamic policy for hotel yield management, *European Journal of Operational Research*, 121, 3, 476–503

Beckman, J. M. (1958) Decision and team problems in airline reservations, *Econometrica*, 26, 134–145

Belobaba, P. P. (1987) *Air Travel Demand and Airline Seat Inventory Management*, MIT Flight Transportation Laboratory Report R87-7: Cambridge, MA

Belobaba, P. P. (1999) Flight overbooking models and practice. *Airline Management*. Unpublished, Massachusetts Institute of Technology, Boston

Bitran, G. R. and Mondschein, S. V. (1995) An application of yield management to the hotel industry considering multiple day stays, *Operations Research*, 43, 3, 427–443

Bowen, J. and Shoemaker, S. (1998) The antecedents and consequences of customer loyalty, *Cornell Hotel and Restaurant Administration Quarterly*, 39, 1, 12–25

Boyce, A. (1991) Maximise yields, *Caterer and Hotelkeeper*, 24 January, 27

Bradley, A. and Ingold, A. (1993) An investigation of yield management in Birmingham Hotels, *International Journal of Contemporary Hospitality Management*, 5, 2, 13–16

Brotherton, B. and Mooney, S. (1992) Yield management – progress and prospects, *International Journal of Hospitality Management*, 11, 1, 23–32

Brotherton, B. and Turner, R. (2001) Introducing yield management systems in hotels: getting the technical/human balance right, *Journal of Services Research*, 1, 2, 25–47

Choi, S. and Kimes, S. E. (2002) Electronic distribution channels' effect on hotel revenue management, *Cornell Hotel and Restaurant Administration Quarterly*, 43, 3, 23–31

Choi, T. Y. and Cho, V. (2000) Towards a knowledge discovery framework for yield management in the Hong Kong hotel industry, *Hospitality Management*, 19, 1, 17–31

Cross, R. G. (1997) Launching the revenue rocket: how revenue management can work for your business, *Cornell Hotel and Restaurant Administration Quarterly*, 38, 2, 32–43

Donaghy, K., McMahon-Beattie, U. and McDowell, D. (1995) Yield management: an overview, *International Journal of Hospitality Management*, 14, 2, 139–150

Donaghy, K., McMahon-Beattie, U. and McDowell, D. (1997) Yield management practices, In Yeoman, I. and Ingold, A. (Eds.), *Yield Management: Strategies for the Service Industries*, Cassell: London, 183–201

Donaghy, K., McMahon-Beattie, U., Yeoman, I. and Ingold, A. (1998) The realism of yield. Management, *Progress in Tourism and Hospitality Research*, 4, 3, 187–195

Dunn, K. D. and Brooks, D. E. (1990) Profit analysis: beyond yield management, *Cornell Hotel and Restaurant Administration Quarterly*, 31, 3, 80–90

Educational Institute of the American Hotel and Motel Association (1994) *Yield Management: Concepts and Application*, AHMA: Washington, p. 4

Farrell, K. and Whelan-Ryan, F. (1998) Yield management – a model for implementation, *Progress in Tourism and Hospitality Research*, 4, 3, 266–277

Gabor, A. and Granger, C. W. J. (1966) Prices as an indicator of quality: report on an enquiry, *Economica*, 33, 43–70

Gamble, P. R. (1990) Building a yield management system – the flip side, *Hospitality Research Journal*, 14, 2, 11–22

Goymour, D. and Donaghy, K. (1995) Reserving judgement, *Caterer and Hotelkeeper*, 26 January, 64–65

Griffin, R. K. (1995) A categorization scheme for critical success factors of lodging yield management systems, *International Journal of Hospitality Management*, 14, 3/4, 325–328

Griffin, R. K. (1996) Factors of successful lodging yield management systems, *Hospitality Research Journal*, 19, 4, 17–30

Griffin, R. K. (1997) Evaluating the success of lodging yield management systems, *FIU Hospitality Review*, 15, 1, 57–71

Hansen, C. N. and Eringa, K. (1997) *Critical success factors in YM: a development and analysis.* Paper presented at 2nd International Yield Management Conference, University of Bath, England, 9–11th September

Hansen, C. N. and Eringa, K. (1998) Critical success factors in yield management: a development and analysis, *Progress in Tourism and Hospitality Research*, 4, 3, 229–244

Huyton, J., Evans, P. and Ingold, A. (1997) The legal and moral issues surrounding the practice of yield management, *International Journal of Contemporary Hospitality Management*, 9, 2, 84–87

Huyton, J. and Peters, S. (1997) Application of yield management to the hotel industry, In Yeoman, I. and Ingold, A. (Eds.), *Yield Management: Strategies for the Service industries*, Cassell: London

Jarvis, N., Lindh, A. and Jones, P. (1997) An investigation of the key criteria affecting the adoption of yield management in U.K. Hotels, *Progress in Hospitality and Tourism Research*, 4, 3, 207–216

Jauncey, S., Mitchell, I. and Slamet, P. (1995) The meaning and management of yield in hotels, *International Journal of Contemporary Hospitality Management*, 7, 4, 23–26

Jones, P. (1988) The impact of trends in service operations on food service delivery systems, *International Journal of Operations and Production Management*, 8, 7, 23–30

Jones, P. (1999) Yield management in UK hotels: a systems analysis, *Journal of the Operations Research Society*, 50, 1111–1119

Jones, P. (2000) Defining yield management and measuring its impact on hotel performance. In Ingold, A., McMahon-Beattie, U. and Yeoman, I. (Eds.), *Yield Management: Strategies for the Service Industries*, Continuum: London

Jones, P. and Hamilton, D. (1992) Yield Management: putting people in the big picture, *Cornell Hotel and Restaurant Administration Quarterly*, 33, 1, 89–96

Jones, P. and Lockwood, A. (1998) Operations management research in the hospitality industry, *International Journal of Hospitality Management*, 17, 2, 183–202

Kandampully, J. and Suhartanto, D. (2000) Customer loyalty in the hotel industry: the role of customer satisfaction and image, *International Journal of Contemporary Hospitality Management*, 12, 6, 346–351

Kimes, S. E. (1989) The basics of yield management, *Cornell Hotel and Restaurant Administration Quarterly*, 30, 3, 14–19

Kimes, S. E. (1997) Yield management: an overview, In Yeoman, I. and Ingold, A. (Eds.), *Yield Management: Strategies for the Service Industries*, Cassell: London, 3–11

Kimes, S. E. (2003) Revenue management: a retrospective, *Cornell Hotel and Restaurant Administration Quarterly*, 44, 5/6, 131–138

Kimes, S. E. and McGuire, K. A. (2001) Function space revenue management: a case study from Singapore, *Cornell Hotel and Restaurant Administration Quarterly*, 42, 6, 33–46

Lewis, R. C. and Shoemaker S. (1997) Value pricing: another view and a research example, *Cornell Hotel and Restaurant Administration Quarterly*, 38, 2, 44–54

Lieberman, W. H. (1993) Debunking the myths of yield management, *Cornell Hotel and Restaurant Administration Quarterly*, 34, 1, 34–44

Noone, B. and Griffin, P. (1997) Enhancing yield management with customer profitability analysis, *International Journal of Contemporary Hospitality Management*, 9, 2, 75–79

Orkin, E. B. (1988) Boosting your bottom line with yield management, *Cornell Hotel and Restaurant Administration Quarterly*, 28, 4, 52–56

Peters, S. and Riley, J. (1997) Yield management transition: a case example, *International Journal of Contemporary Hospitality Management*, 9, 2/3, 89–91

Rothstein, M. (1968) *Stochastic Models for Airline Booking Policies*, Ph.D. Thesis, Graduate School of Engineering and Science. New York University: New York

Rothstein, M. (1985) O.R. and the airline overbooking problem, *Operations Research*, 33, 2, 237–248

Rowe, M. (1989) Yield management, *Lodging Hospitality*, 45, 2, 65–66

Sanchez, J. F. and Satir, A. (2005) Hotel yield management using different reservation modes, *International Journal of Contemporary Hospitality Management*, 17, 2, 136–146

Savkina R. and Yakovlev V. (1997) Yield management in Russia: characteristics and evaluation, *International Journal of Contemporary Hospitality Management*, 9, 2/3, 91

Schwartz, Z. and Cohen, E. (2003) Hotel revenue-management forecasting: evidence of expert-judgment bias, *Cornell Hotel and Restaurant Administration Quarterly*, 45, 1, 85–98

Shoemaker, S., Dawson, M. and Johnson, W. (2006) How to increase menu prices without alienating your customers, *International Journal of Contemporary Hospitality Management*, 17, 7, 553–568

Sigala, M., Lockwood, A. and Jones, P. (2001) Strategic Implementation and IT: gaining competitive advantage from the hotel reservations process, *International Journal of Contemporary Hospitality Management*, 13, 7, 364–371

Simon, J. (1968) An almost practical solution to airline over-booking, *Journal of Transport Economics and Policy*, 2, 201–202

Smith, B. (1984) *Overbooking in a Deregulated Airline Market*, Conference Proceedings of ORSA/TIMS Conference, Boston, Massachusetts, March 1984

Talluri, K. T. and van Ryzin, G. J. (2005) *The Theory and Practice of Revenue Management*, Springer-Verlag: Berlin

Taylor, C. J. (1962). The determination of passenger booking levels. *AGIFORS Symposium Proceedings 2*. Fregene, Italy

TIMS Revenue Optimisation Systems (1999) – Retrieved from http://www.tims.fr/increase.html on 16 October 2007

Upchurch, R. S., Ellis, T. and Seo, J. (2002) Revenue management underpinnings: an exploratory review, *International Journal of Hospitality Management*, 21, 67–83

Van Westering, J. (1994) Yield management: the case for food and beverage operations, In Cooper, C. P. and Lockwood, A. (2004), *Progress in Tourism Recreation and Hospitality Management*, John Wiley: Chichester, 139–148

Vickrey, W. (1972) Airline overbooking: some further solutions, *Journal of Transport Economics and Policy*, 6, 3, 257–270

Weatherford, L. R., Kimes, S. E. and Scott, D. A. (2001) Forecasting for hotel revenue management: testing aggregation against disaggregation, *Cornell Hotel and Restaurant Administration Quarterly*, 42, 4, 53–64

CHAPTER 12

Managing labour productivity

Robert Christie Mill

Professor
School of Hotel, Restaurant and
Tourism Management
Daniels College of Business
University of Denver

Introduction

Productivity is one of the most challenging topics of interest in the hospitality industry. It has been written about in depth in the USA (Mill 1989) and the UK (Johns 1996; Jones 1990). There have also been an increasing number of empirical research studies on the topic. Many have commented on the importance of managing labour productivity (Mill 1989; Johns 1996; Riley and Jones 2000), largely because labour represents such a large percentage of the cost of running a hospitality operation. The average full-service hotel spends between 32% and 36% of revenue on direct labour, so improving labour efficiency can have a significant impact on profit improvement and is a key performance area in hotels (Johnson and Ball 2006; Pickens 2006). Despite this, there is still much that is not known about the extent to which any operation's performance can be judged efficient or its labour force productive.

Just what is 'productivity'? Productivity is concerned with the efficient use of resources. It can be defined as outputs divided by inputs (Jones and Lockwood 1989). Going further, it is the total amount of output, goods and services, per unit input used. This can be broken down in several ways (Pickens 2006). Inputs are the resources used in producing a product or service. These can be such things as the labour, customers, capital and natural resources used in creating outputs (Johnson and Ball 2006). Outputs are the products or services that are produced (e.g. meals served, guests housed, rooms cleaned).

In this chapter the challenge of selecting the 'right' input/output measures is identified. The performance of the industry is then evaluated, before discussing specific studies of operational performance. Finally, alternative approaches to labour productivity improvement are reviewed.

The productivity challenge

Productivity is easy to state but difficult to measure (Ball et al. 1986). In its simplest form, it is the ratio of an input (or inputs) to an output (or outputs). The challenge comes from selecting the 'right' input and output variables and developing a ratio which genuinely measure productivity (Johnson and Ball 1989). Three articles in the late 1990s illustrate this in three different sectors – hotels, restaurants and on-site foodservice.

Brown and Dev (1999) proposed six single-factor productivity measures. Three were used to measure 'capital productivity' – SalesPAR (total annual sales per number of available rooms), GOPPAR (gross operating profit per number of available rooms), and ProfitPAR (income before fixed charges per number of available rooms). The other three measured labour productivity – SalesEmp (total annual sales per number of full-time equivalent employees [FTEs]), GOEmp (gross operating profit per FTE) and ProfitEmp (income before fixed charges per FTE).

Muller (1999) approaches this problem for a restaurant setting by suggesting that the unit of production is one complete turn of the service cycle, from the time the guest is seated to the time the table is reset for the next guest. The time period for measurement can range from a meal period to the entire time the restaurant is operating each day. The restaurant's maximum capacity is a function of the number of seats in the restaurant, the service-cycle time and the hours of operation. The ratio of capacity use is found by comparing the number of service cycles in a given period to the maximum number of cycles. This number is then used as a gauge for analysing the effects of changes in the restaurant's operation. What happens, for example, when demand is shifted to off-peak hours or the service-cycle time is shortened?

Reynolds (1998) considers productivity measurement in the context of the on-site foodservice sector. For the business and industry (B & I) segment, he proposes a multiple partial-factor measure with inputs of productive labour cost, cost of goods and amortized leasehold improvements and an output of revenue. For the education segment, he proposes a simpler productivity measure to that for B & I, without including amortized leasehold improvements. Whereas for the healthcare segment, he proposes inputs of food cost, labour cost, direct operating costs and amortized leasehold improvements, with the output of revenue from all activities.

The relationship between productivity and profitability can be viewed as the interaction of two primary factors: profit margin and asset utilization (Douglas 2000). When room revenue and occupancy are combined, the result is a measure of yield – revenue per available room (RevPAR).[1] It is argued that the operational focus of the traditional measures of productivity and performance limit their usefulness (Douglas 2000). They fail to provide a fair picture of the business side of the operation while, as a managerial tool, do not encourage responses that are strategic in nature.

---

[1] See also Chapter 11.

Industry productivity performance

Productivity growth in service industries has generally tended to be lower than in manufacturing industries. This is also certainly true of the hospitality sector. There are a number of reasons for this. Many of the operations management techniques that have proven successful in the manufacturing sector have not been adopted by hotels (Witt and Witt 1989). There are some who claim that many of these techniques are not suitable for adoption in the hospitality industry. Others indicate that some of the practices can work successfully in any type of operation – manufacturing or service. This has led to a conclusion that techniques are not being adopted, in part, because of a lack of management skills on the part of managers in the hospitality industry (Witt and Witt 1989).

A related problem is the labour-intensive nature of the hotel industry. In delivering a service – in being hospitable – there is only so much substitution of machines for people that can be made. In the hotel business, service is tied to people. This puts great pressure on managers to increase the most efficient use of employees rather than rely totally on technological innovations to produce a more productive operation. Although employees are critical to improved productivity, Mill (1989) argues that the industry has traditionally placed little emphasis on employee development and training. He suggests that managers can understand the investment necessary in a machine and the value of a preventative maintenance programme for that machine. However, they do not regard money spent on an employee as an investment; rather it is seen purely as a cost. He proposes that ROI means Return on Individual as well as Return on Investment.

Given the service nature of hospitality, to what extent can technology be used to improve productivity? One study that examines the utilization of information technology (IT) in all hotel sectors in the United States, from deluxe to budget, reveals strategic differences and similarities. Overall, the findings suggest that the U.S. lodging industry has focused on employing technologies that improve employee productivity and enhance revenue but has not given strategic priority to technologies designed to improve guest services (Siguaw et al. 2000). Various studies in the UK indicate that productivity gains come not from the total amount of investments in Information and Communication Technologies (ICT), but rather from the extent to which the entire range of ICT tools and applications are fully exploited. One example is the use of ICT informational and networking capabilities for redesigning and streamlining operations (Sigala 2004).

The study of hotel productivity is made even more complex by the number of variables that might affect performance. Sigala (2004) reviews previous studies of hotel productivity and identifies the following as potentially having some influence:

- Location – rural, city centre or suburban
- Property size
- Hotel design – old/new, purpose built/converted
- Ownership – independent or chain
- Business format – owned, franchise, consortium
- Demand variability
- Level of repeat custom
- Average length of stay
- Market segments served
- Distribution channels
- Proportion of part-time staff

Many of these were then tested in Sigala's (2004) study of 93 three star hotels in the UK. Demand variability, hotel design and ownership were found to affect productivity, but location, level of repeat customer, market segments served and distribution channels did not.

So concerned were the UK government about low productivity in the hospitality industry, especially in small- and medium-size enterprises (SMEs), that they funded a nationwide initiative – 'Profit through Productivity' – in order to improve the situation (Jones 2002). Begun in 2001, the programme's fund of £2.5 million over five years is based on £1.2 million from the Department of Trade and Industry (DTI) to pump prime the project and a similar sum from industry through sponsorship and revenues generated by the sale of deliverables. Profit through Productivity had an annual impact assessment made against seven agreed performance targets. By the end of five years, it was expected that the impact on industry performance would be:

- Sales per employee up by 15%
- Value added per employee (profits) up by 10%
- Levels of customer complaint down by 25%
- Average length of stay per employee up by 20%
- Reject deliveries down by 7.5%
- Capital employed up by 2.5%
- New business from new markets up by 12.5%

One study of North American hotels (Brown and Dev 1999) found that productivity is affected by the hotel's size, its service orientation, its strategic orientation and its ownership arrangement. Large hotels, the study finds, use their labour more productively, and generate the most income from their capital investments. Upscale hotels are more productive overall than mid-market hotels, while hotels operated by branded management companies use their labour resources more efficiently than do hotels operated independently or by independent management companies. Finally, company-owned properties generally employ their labour more productively than do franchised hotels.

Measures of productivity

Before management can improve labour productivity, agreement must be reached on how to measure labour productivity. Measures of productivity have tended to focus on the effectiveness of the labour force based on ratios of input to output. Typically they have been such things as (Mill 1989):

- Payroll ratio: payroll costs divided by sales
- Sales per employee: sales divided by the number of employees
- Sales per hour: sales divided by the number of hours of operation
- Sales per employee-hour: sales divided by departmental employee-hours

If sales were defined as sales per employee, then it could be increased by increasing room rates. A hotel may be housing fewer guests, but the increase in prices could camouflage that – and inefficiencies in management as well.

The best measures of productivity are those that are inflation proof and that measure the performance of output. Productivity could be measured as the number of guests, rooms occupied or meals served divided by the number of employee-hours required. The U.S. Bureau of Labor Statistics defines productivity as output per employee-hour (Mill 1989). It defines output as sales receipts adjusted for inflation and indexed to a base year to facilitate comparisons. Input is the number of hours worked by all employees, both supervisory and non-supervisory. The resulting ratios are productivity indices that are not affected by increases in prices or wages.

A focus on a one-dimensional measure of productivity fails to take into account relationships among resources. Using aggregate or multiple-factor measures allows managers to compare units that are directly managed with those that are, in the case of foodservice, contracted out (Reynolds 1998).

Data envelopment analysis

One particular approach that has been adopted to examine productivity in hospitality is data envelopment analysis (DEA), as advocated by Andersson (1996). First developed by Charnes et al. (1978), DEA is a powerful non-parametric, multivariate, multiple linear programming technique that benchmarks units by comparing combinations of inputs and outputs at the same time. Since DEA uses the production units that are 'best in its class' as reference material, the method is very much in line with the basic ideas underlying the concept of benchmarking. The best performing units are assigned 100% efficiency, and all other units a level of productivity proportional to these best ones. Hence, there is no absolute measure of productivity, as with a ratio. There is also no way of knowing if those units that achieve 100% efficiency are the 'best'. There may be other units, not included in the sample, which are performing even better.

This approach to measuring productivity also has to be applied with care. In particular the right inputs and outputs need to be included. One way to approach this is by the step-wise approach to DEA, based on stepwise regression. This is an iterative procedure in which productivity is measured according to one combination of inputs and outputs and then evaluated by their correlation with the measure of efficiency and applying judgements in terms of cause and effect. Subsequently, inputs and outputs can be added or excluded to see if the correlation increases or decreases, until no further important factors emerge. At that stage, a metric accounting for all the identifiable factors that influence productivity is constructed. The stepwise approach also helps to interpret why particular units are efficient, since the efficiency scores of the units at each step can be produced, thereby identifying how respective inputs/outputs affected their efficiency.

Sigala et al. (2005) summarizes DEA's advantages as follows:

- It provides a comprehensive productivity evaluation as it generates a single aggregate score by comparing simultaneously multiple inputs and outputs of comparable units and using a benchmark of 100% efficiency;
- It is independent of the units of measurement allowing flexibility in specifying inputs/outputs to be studied;
- It objectively assesses the 'importance' of the various performance attributes;

- It evaluates each entity in the best possible light – all alternative priorities will reduce performance;
- It calculates efficiency based on observed best practice – not against an 'average' or 'ideal' model;
- Best practices are identified;
- No functional relationship between inputs and outputs needs to be prespecified;
- Inefficient DMUs are identified as well as the sources and amounts of their inefficiency. Thus, DEA answers both questions: *'how well a unit is doing'*; and *'which dimension and how much could the unit improve'*;
- DEA can identify economies of scale and take them into account.

DEA has been extensively used for productivity benchmarking in the hotel industry (Morey and Dittman 1995; Avkiran 1999; Anderson et al. 1999, 2000; Wöber 2000; Brown and Ragsdale 2002; Hwang and Chang 2003; Sigala 2004; Sigala et al. 2005), as well as in the restaurant industry (Andersson 1996; Reynolds and Thompson 2007).

Hotel productivity

Hwang and Chang (2003) used DEA to measure 'managerial efficiency' of 45 hotels in Taiwan, and how this had changed between 1994 and 1998. They concluded that urban properties, serving international visitors and operated as part of an international chain, were the most efficient type of hotel. Their input/output measures were number of FTEs, number of guest rooms, total floor area for food and beverage (F & B), operating expenses, rooms revenue, F & B revenue and other revenues.

Sigala (2004) explored productivity in both rooms division and F & B. She found that productivity in rooms division was determined by the inputs of number of rooms, front-office payroll, administration and general expenses and demand variability, along with the outputs of average room rate, number of room nights and non-rooms revenue. Whereas F & B productivity was derived from F & B capacity, F & B payroll, F & B materials expenses, demand variability, F & B revenue, percent of banqueting covers to restaurant covers and F & B capacity.

Restaurant productivity • • •

Andersson (1996) explored the use of DEA through applying it to a sample of 46 restaurants in Sweden. He demonstrated that the selection of different combinations of inputs and outputs could have a significant impact on the relative productivity levels of restaurants in the sample. Reynolds and Thompson (2007) investigated 62 full-service restaurants and were concerned with identifying the uncontrollable variables that affected restaurant productivity. They found the inputs to be hourly server wage, number of restaurant seats and whether the unit was standalone or not, and the outputs to be daily sales and tip percentage. They argue that it is only once the effect of these uncontrollable variables is understood, that it becomes possible to understand the effect that management is having on productivity performance.

Improving productivity

In reality, there are five ways in which the input–output ratio can be changed[2] (Jones and Lockwood 1989):

- Decrease inputs and increase output: theoretically possible but unlikely to occur, unless through major innovation.
- Decrease inputs and maintain output: appropriate where there are inefficiencies that can be corrected by reducing costs.
- Constant inputs and increase output: this is a marketing approach to correcting inefficiencies.
- Increase inputs, relatively greater output: this market-oriented approach concedes that an increase in outputs can only be achieved at additional costs.
- Decrease inputs, relatively smaller decrease in output: a reduction in costs will have some impact on output that is offset by savings in cost.

Early attempts to improve productivity focused on two strategies (Jones and Lockwood 1989). Companies with high fixed costs, such as hotel companies, were encouraged to adopt a market-oriented approach that concentrated on increasing output while holding inputs steady. Those companies that had a high proportion of variable costs were encouraged to adopt a cost reduction approach that suggested holding output steady while reducing costs.

Traditionally the focus on how to improve productivity has been to maximize the efficiency with which inputs are

---

[2] See also Chapter 10.

converted to outputs. There are those, however, who argue that the emphasis on efficiency and the quantitative side of productivity has led to researchers and managers ignoring such things as effectiveness and quality. It may be that the application of a holistic productivity metric that combines both traditional operational variables, such as revenue, profit, food cost, and labour cost, and such things as guest and employee satisfaction is what is needed.

One study of restaurants in metropolitan areas in the United States finds that employee satisfaction as an input variable is the most important variable in determining unit-level profit and guest satisfaction (Reynolds and Biel 2007). A study in Cyprus finds that staff recruitment, staff training, meeting guest expectations, and service quality are the main productivity factors in hotels, while research of Wimpy International in England finds that customers consider customer satisfaction and effectiveness as important dimensions of productivity Ball (1993). Lockwood and Bowen (2004) finds that there are significant gains in revenue production (an output) and cost reduction (an input) when such best practices as achieving standards; partnerships and networks; communication; measurement and performance evaluation; transformational leadership; adding value to operators; operational planning and control; and staff development and retention are implemented.

Thus, it is argued that the qualitative dimension of outputs cannot be ignored in any consideration of productivity in hotels. Productivity is not improved if the quantity of output is increased at the expense of lower quality. It is too narrow to view productivity increases only in terms of producing more with the same number of employee-hours (Douglas 2000). Are employees more productive if they register more guests per hour – but in a slipshod, surly manner? Is a hotel restaurant more productive if convenience foods are used to reduce employee preparation time, but food costs are thereby increased to the point that contribution margin is less? Productivity is not improved when more rooms are cleaned, but they are not up to the quality standard of the hotel. When something must be re-done (e.g. the carpet must be vacuumed again), the amount of time to clean the room increases. This increase in input will reduce productivity. Management must set performance standards of both quantity and quality and then manage employees in such a way that these standards are met.[3]

---

[3] See also Chapter 13.

There are three major approaches to improving labour productivity (Mill 1989), to which a fourth can be added. Productivity can be enhanced through better workplace design; through the development of improved work processes; through more efficient employee scheduling; and through workforce flexibility.

Workplace design

The interaction of employees and the environment in which they work affects productivity; designers must develop facilities with productivity in mind. There are several sequential steps in the development of a hospitality operation that will determine how productive the end product is. A market analysis is conducted to determine the potential market. From this information, a mix of products and services are developed that will appeal to the market segments being sought. The operating characteristics are set, the equipment characteristics determined and the resulting space requirements and arrangements finalized.

Little has been researched on the relationship between hotel design and hotel operation. One article describes the Marriott Courtyard concept, in which the construction, services and operational style of the hotels have been expressly designed to maximize productivity (Johns 1996). Rooms were specifically constructed taking employee productivity into account. The amount, type and placement of services and amenities in guest rooms and their impact on productivity is also noted.

Objectives • • •

There are several objectives involved in planning a new facility or revamping an existing one (Mill 1989). First, the planner aims to ease the production process. Spaces are arranged and laid out to ensure a smooth flow of people and things. Employee costs can be reduced through the efficient layout of individual work stations, designed in accordance with the tasks to be performed there (Lawson 1994: 187).

A second objective is to minimize the cost and time required to handle goods within the operation. This means moving many items mechanically rather than by hand; routing things over straight paths while minimizing backtracking; and carrying a minimum amount of inventory while ensuring proper storage to protect materials from damage.

The planner must also try to minimize the investment in equipment. Case-by-case cost-benefit analysis will determine to what extent machines should replace people. Because of the increasing costs of building, the planner must make full use of both horizontal and vertical space for workplaces, aisles and storage so that work can be completed in a minimum of wasted space without the feeling of being cramped.

A final objective should be to facilitate cleaning and maintenance. The wise planner will select surfaces that can be easily cleaned. Maintenance comes into play in the design of equipment. Placing equipment on wheels, for example, allows for ease of movement during cleaning. This is another objective when planning facilities. Portion control, for example, can be made easier by selecting serving utensils of an appropriate size.

The productive use of space and of the people who operate in that space is achieved by applying certain principles of flow to the functions inherent in the operation. The first step is to identify all of the functions that take place in an operation. In F & B, for example, goods are received and sent to either dry or refrigerated storage. From there they might go to preparation, then to the chef, dining room and dishwasher.

Designing flow • • •

Productive use of space occurs when two functional areas – receiving and storage, for example – are placed near each other. Evaluation of flow can be undertaken for materials, employees, guests or paperwork in order to minimize the flow of what is considered important. The same type of analysis can be conducted for a guest entering the hotel in order to ensure a minimum of inconvenience in getting the guest to his or her room. Whichever criteria are considered important, the principles to minimize movement are the same. Wherever possible, flow should be along straight paths. In addition, the amount of cross traffic, backtracking and bypassing should be kept to a minimum.

Keeping flow in a straight line – over the shortest distance – is crucial. Cross traffic causes bottlenecks and congestion; consequently, it should be avoided. Backtracking occurs when a person moves from one place or piece of equipment to another, and then returns along the same path. This probably cannot be eliminated but should be cut down as much as possible, perhaps with wide aisles or circular routes of flow. Bypassing occurs when someone has to move past one or more pieces of equipment to perform the next stage in a process. Different arrangements of equipment, fixtures and areas may be necessary to find the best arrangement.

Flow diagrams or string charts – in which pieces of string are used to simulate movement – can be useful in finding the best arrangement. Five layouts are common in the design of equipment and workplaces. A single straight-line arrangement – in which pieces are placed along a wall or in an island – is simple but limited in the number of pieces that can be accommodated. An L-shaped arrangement can accommodate more pieces of equipment and can be used where space is limited to keep pieces of equipment or workplaces separated better. A U-shaped arrangement is also suitable where space is limited, but the lack of space limits it to where only one or two employees are working. An additional restriction is that pass-through movement through the area is not possible. A parallel, back-to-back arrangement allows for centralizing any utilities required for two banks of equipment, which are set up parallel to each other, their backs adjacent to each other. A parallel, face-to-face arrangement consists of two rows of equipment facing each other, with a work aisle in between. In this arrangement, two utility lines are required.

Work processes

Work processes can be improved through task planning. Task planning involves the analysis of specific actions involved in carrying out a job, in order to establish a more productive procedure for completing that job. The first step in this process is to select the task to be analysed. For the novice task planner, it is wise to select a simple task such as buttering bread or assembling salads. A complex task such as cleaning a room might be broken down initially into components such as making the bed and dusting the room. As the task planner develops more skill and confidence, more complex and time-consuming tasks can be identified and analysed. It is preferable to select tasks that can cause bottlenecks in production or are frustrating for employees. Holiday Inns found that wheeling a small cart into the guest room saved money when cleaning the room. The materials needed were easily accessible, limiting much walking. In addition, the room attendants felt more comfortable cleaning the room with the door closed. Energy costs were reduced because heat or air conditioning did not escape from the room as before, when carts were left outside the open door.

Reynolds (1998) suggests that eliminating unnecessary tasks and doing the same tasks more efficiently are the keys to productivity improvement. All factors must be identified and made part of the analysis. Tasks are affected by the accessibility and storage of raw materials used in performing the job. In one hotel studied by the author, it was found that 20% of a housekeeper's time was spent in getting linen from the linen room. One reason was that a linen shortage made adequate stocking impossible. The answer was to establish a system of stocking linen and other supplies in a closet on each floor. Because housekeepers had adequate, accessible supplies, they were able to clean 16 rooms instead of 13 on a regular day. This resulted in a savings of 10% on the housekeeping payroll. A key principle is that the handling of materials does not add to their value. Such handling, therefore, should be kept to a minimum.

The standard of performance desired affects which tasks must be performed. A hotel restaurant emphasizing its use of fresh ingredients will require different preparation methods for its menu items than a hotel lobby coffee shop that relies heavily on convenience products. Each aims at a quality product – within the boundaries of the price–value relationship. That is, there must be a guest perception that the value received is more than, or at least equal to, the price paid.

The method of preparation and even the process used can be affected by the quantity to be produced. For large-quantity jobs, the capital investment for a piece of equipment may be less in the long run than the labour cost of several employees. Work stations should be sufficiently large to allow for the tools and utensils necessary to complete the required task. Tasks that require the use of the same tools or utensils should be performed at the same place, whenever possible.

The number and type of employees used greatly affects the cost of performing a task. Maximum efficiency results from having the least number of employees necessary. Another factor that must be considered is the quality of the service provided. Sufficient employees must be scheduled to ensure guest satisfaction. The saving of an employee's hourly wage must be weighed against any loss of business through guest dissatisfaction. The skill level of the employee must also be considered. The key is to delegate tasks as far down the line as possible commensurate with the employee's ability to perform the delegated task. In other words, have a seven-dollar-an-hour task performed by a seven-dollar-an-hour employee.

Timing refers to both how long it takes to perform a task and when it has to be done relative to the completion of other tasks. With certain menu items, for example, several tasks may have to be completed at the same time. This probably means that more than one employee would have to be involved. Alternatively, some tasks might be completed ahead of service and the products combined by one employee at the last minute. After a lunch banquet, a decision might be made to leave the washing of the dishware and utensils until later at night. At that time, utility costs are less and the task could be carried out by a skeleton crew who would otherwise be under-utilized.

Employee schedules

The third strategy to improve labour productivity involves creating efficient employee schedules. As noted earlier, payroll costs in the hospitality are typically more than 30% of sales revenue (Kavanaugh and Ninemeier 1999). The importance of controlling labour costs in the labour-intensive hospitality business cannot be over-stressed. Indeed, labour has been identified as the last cost area to be effectively controlled in the hospitality industry. The development of reliable technology sufficient to allow for a cost-effective and systematic approach to the 'purchasing' and scheduling of labour is a relatively recent phenomenon. Labour scheduling means having the right staff with the right skills in the right place at the right time (Mogendorff and Simonds 2003). The process of doing this has typically been carried out in some simple form through the production of manual or spreadsheet rotas for the coming week(s) often by retrospectively using the previous month's financial reports. The type of reactive approach to employee scheduling is no longer sufficient. Recent advances in technology include the development of systems capable of supporting enhanced reservations, table assignment, pre-checking and production and guest service. This technology can assist management in balancing seating and table service patterns. Work loads can be balanced among service staff. Output can be defined in terms of such things as table turns, average chair occupancy and service productivity.

The development of a labour schedule involves four steps (Thompson 1998). The first step is forecasting customer demand, the second involves translating customer demand into employee requirements, while the third requires the development of a labour force schedule. The fourth step involves assessment and real-time control of the outputs of the first three steps to ensure that customers are properly served.

Forecasting demand • • •

There are certain truths about forecasting that must be appreciated (Kavanaugh and Ninemeier 1999). First, forecasts are more difficult to make and are subject to greater error if the forecast is made far in advance of the actual event. It is easier to forecast tomorrow's room occupancy than that of next month's. As a result, forecasts are being reviewed and updated as the hotel moves closer to the actual date.

Second, forecasting involves uncertainty. As a result, judgements have to be made. For example, when making a forecast of room sales one year in advance, it is important to have information on the competition, demand for room nights, room rates, and so on. When definitive information is not available, judgements have to be made.

Third, the starting point for forecasting the future is to look at historical data. This is not always a true reflection of the future if there are significant changes in past environments compared to future scenarios. It may be that several hotels in the vicinity have closed down. If it is not anticipated that new hotels will be built in the short-term and if demand is expected to hold steady, then our hotel should expect a share of the demand that is available because of the closure of the competing hotels.

Finally, it should be noted that forecasts are not as accurate as we would hope. The key is to continuously apply better, more sophisticated methods of forecasting while revising prior forecasts immediately after there is a change in the circumstances that existed when the forecast was made.

A major reason for forecasting is to assist with accurate employee scheduling (Schmidgall 1995). Most hotel revenue-management systems require inputs of the forecasted demand by rate category and length of stay. At least one study demonstrates that a purely disaggregated forecast (even though it meant forecasting smaller numbers) strongly outperforms even the best aggregated forecast (Withiam and Thompson 2004). Most hotels prepare monthly, ten-day and three-day forecasts of business volume (Kavanaugh and Ninemeier 1999). Monthly forecasts are used to prepare an employee schedule which is then refined based on the ten- and three-day updates of upcoming business. The most popular method of forecasting room demand, especially for properties with a reservation system, is to use room reservations at the time of the forecast with an estimate for walk-ins (Schmidgall 1995).

Forecasts of food sales are also used for staffing purposes. However, in a majority of situations, they are also used to determine how much food to order (Schmidgall 1995). The most common forecasting method used (though by less than half of respondents to a major study) is to use the previous period's sales figures and adjust for expected differences. Two other methods are used by approximately the same percentage of hotels. Forecasts are based either on the number of meal reservations plus estimated walk-ins or on a capture rate – the percentage of hotel guests who are expected to eat in the hotel restaurants. This ratio is applied to the number of expected guests and the result, as such, depends on the accuracy of the rooms forecast (Schmidgall 1995).

Employee requirements

There are three basic methods to transition from a forecast of demand to a determination of the number of employees needed – using productivity standards, using service standards and using economic standards (Thompson 1998).

The American Hotel and Lodging Association believes that managers should be able to (Kappa et al. 1997):

- Determine productivity standards taking into account fixed and variable employee positions;
- Develop and utilize a staffing guide as a labour scheduling and control tool;
- Use weekly labour hour reports to evaluate scheduling practices;
- Revise performance standards to increase productivity.

The planning process involves a number of steps (Kavanaugh and Ninemeier 1999). The development of a schedule for housekeepers is used as an exemplar. Area inventory lists and frequency schedules form the starting points for planning the work of employees. Productivity standards are then developed based on performance standards. The standards are then the basis for developing a staffing guide. The staffing guide is combined with a business forecast to create employee work schedules. Productivity is then continuously enhanced by revising the performance standards.

The first step in this process is to develop inventory lists of everything in each area that needs attention. Separate inventories are needed for each type of guest room as well as all of the other areas in the hotel that require cleaning. In preparing a list for a guest room, it is a good idea to follow the sequence in which the room will be cleaned and inspected. In this way, the list can form the basis for developing cleaning procedures, training plans and inspection checklists (Kappa et al. 1997). A list for a guest room might show items listed from right to left and from top to bottom. This replicates the way a room would be cleaned. The idea is to identify all of the items within specific areas that have to be cleaned or maintained.

The next step involves developing a frequency schedule – a chart indicating how often the items in an area should be cleaned or maintained. Items that are to be cleaned on a daily or weekly basis are part of a routine cleaning schedule that is later incorporated into standard operating procedures. This would include making the beds, dusting the room, cleaning the bathrooms, and so on. Some items will be cleaned or maintained on a biweekly, monthly, bimonthly or other schedule. They become part of a deep-cleaning programme that schedules special projects. It may be, for example, that guest elevators, meeting rooms and registration area are shampooed once a month.

Guest rooms that are scheduled for deep cleaning should coincide with periods of low occupancy. The work should also be coordinated with that of other departments. If maintenance is scheduling repair work on several guest rooms, it would make sense for housekeeping to deep clean those rooms at the same time.

The development of performance standards answers the question: 'What must be done in order to clean or maintain the major items within this area?' (Kappa et al. 1997). Standards represent the level of performance required for that task for that particular operation. Performance standards indicate what must be done and how the job should be done. Developing performance standards is the first step to ensuring that all employees carry out the work in a consistent manner. Having the employees who will perform the jobs involved in setting the standards will help ensure that the standards that are developed are accepted by all employees. The developed standards are then communicated through ongoing training programmes.

Productivity standards 'define the acceptable quantity of work to be done by trained employees who perform their work according to established performance standards' (Kavanaugh and Ninemeier 1999: 145). The productivity standard for a housekeeper is the time allocated to clean a room according to the performance standards set by that hotel. Positions within the hotel are either fixed or variable (Kavanaugh and Ninemeier 1999). Fixed staff positions are filled irrespective of business volume. This would encompass positions that are salaried as well as those that are supervisory and managerial. There will typically be a small number of hourly positions that are fixed. Since business demand is variable and management's task is to keep labour costs under control, there is an incentive to minimize the number of fixed staff positions. During slow times, certain positions may be eliminated, salaried employees may perform duties ordinarily done by hourly employees or cross-trained employees may be assigned to another job.

The number of variable staff positions will depend on business volume on any given day. Front-desk employees will be assigned based on the number of expected check-ins and the pattern of their arrival. The number of housekeepers or room attendants will depend on the number of occupied rooms that need to be cleaned. Kitchen and dining rooms staff numbers depend on a forecast of breakfast, lunch and dinner guests.

According to one author, the use of economic standards is better than the use of productivity standards to deliver service most economically (Thompson 1999a). The use of economic standards involves forecasting demand, translating the demand forecast into employee requirements, scheduling the employees and controlling the schedule during the day (Thompson 1999a; Withiam and Thompson 2004).

Workforce scheduling • • •

Labour costs can be controlled through sound scheduling (Pavesic 2004; Thompson 1999a). The task is both essential and complex. The objective is to match the number of workers available to the customer demand that exists in any given time period (Thompson 1999a). Traditional methods of creating the actual schedule tend to match employee supply and customer demand in isolation for each planning period. It is better to take employee-related factors into account when developing the schedule rather than setting a schedule and then assigning employees to fill it (Thompson 1999a). By taking employee work constraints into account in advance, the result is a schedule that reflects a better match between employees and their shifts.

The following tips have been found useful in developing employee work schedules (Kavanaugh and Ninemeier 1999):

- Schedule should cover a full week.
- Schedule should be approved by management before it is posted or distributed.
- Schedule should be posted at least three days before the work week.
- Schedules should be posted in the same place and at the same time.
- Days off and vacation time must be planned as far in advance as possible.
- The daily work schedule should be compared with forecasted demand and revised if necessary.

- Scheduling changes should be made directly on the posted work schedule.
- A copy of the schedule can be used to monitor employee attendance and retained as a permanent record.
- Schedules should be developed to meet the day-to-day and, in some cases, hour-to-hour volumes of business.

Real-time control • • •

To close the scheduling loop, it is necessary to compare employee-hours scheduled with the actual number of hours worked. This is typically done on a weekly basis. Significant variances are noted and investigated. The reasons for the discrepancy are determined and corrective action taken.

The three causes of labour expense variance are volume, rate and efficiency (Mill 2005). Volume variances occur when more work is done than was forecast. If we estimated that 300 rooms would be sold, each requiring 30 min to clean, we would forecast 150 h of work. If, however, 360 rooms were sold, the actual hours worked would be 180. Rate variances look at the average wage rate that was forecast compared to that actually paid. Perhaps, housekeepers are paid $8.50 an hour but, because of increased volume, they were paid overtime and the actual wage was $9.25 an hour. In certain situations, overtime may be warranted. In other cases, it may be the result of poor planning. Efficiency variances refer to the amount of work performed on an hourly basis. It may be that the standard time for cleaning a room is set at 30 min. Perhaps, some unruly convention goers left especially dirty rooms that meant that it took 40 minutes on average to clean a room. The result is an efficiency variance. As before, there is a small effect caused by the interrelationship of these factors.

Increasingly, this is being enabled by web-based rostering systems that enable real-time monitoring of performance (Thompson 1999b; Mogendorf and Simonds 2003). The advantage of scheduling on the web is that it is a common platform that can be shared by everyone within an operation with rostering responsibility. The software can also incorporate forecasts of likely demand, along with rules as to staffing levels relative to demand, so that department heads or line managers cannot over-staff. Moreover, more senior members of the management team can have oversight of the labour scheduling decisions made by their subordinate managers and can forecast the impact these will have on operational performance. Finally, the system can easily facilitate adjustment to the rosters if demand changes in the short term.

Workforce flexibility

Several principles can be identified that, when put into practice, will result in more productive employee scheduling (Mill 1989), notably temporal flexibility and functional flexibility.

Temporal flexibility • • •

Temporal flexibility is concerned with the pattern of hours worked by individual workers and the use of different types of worker – full time, part time, casual and seasonal. Individual workers in the hospitality industry, especially in foodservice, have typically worked split shifts. A split shift means scheduling employees for two time periods during the day with time off in between. This concept is feasible when employees live close to the operation. It does, however, make for a very long day for the employee. It would also encounter strong opposition if the employees were unionized.

The idea of irregular scheduling is that an employee should be called into work at the time that business warrants, rather than starting at the same time each day. For example, businesspeople will tend to check out early during the week to get on the road or to make appointments. On the weekend, the hotel may cater to families seeking a getaway experience. It makes sense to bring in housekeepers later on the weekends compared to during the week. Many hotels employ staff on annualized hours contracts, so that they may work more hours during the peak season and less hours during the off-season.

It is unproductive to staff for peak periods using full-time employees. Full-time personnel can provide a steady, well-trained core of employees to meet average business conditions, while part-time workers can be used to supplement that core during peak periods. As noted above, a staffing guide links forecasted business and productivity standards to determine the number of employees needed at each hour of the day. Its use is critical to establishing control of labour cost.

Functional flexibility • • •

Functional flexibility is the selection and training of staff so that they are able to work in more than one job position within the operation. It is often referred to as 'multi-skilling'. Hospitality operators adopt this for a number of reasons (Jones 2004):

● More efficiently schedule staff, especially during relatively quiet periods of operation.

- Increase staff retention, especially amongst part-time employees.
- Improve team working.

But organizations that have adopted multi-skilling have reported additional benefits to those that they expected:

- Improved work processes, as multi-skill employees approach their second role with experience of the organization but objective insights towards their new department;
- Lower induction training costs, as multi-skilled staff need only be inducted into the organization once;
- Better coordination and collaboration between heads of department

Management have a number of choices to make if they are interested in multi-skilling their organizations. First, there are choices about the breadth of the scheme: the extent to which it will operate across the business unit and the degree of inclusion of the workforce. How are staff to be selected and what skills need they acquire? Secondly, there is the question of depth – will staff be expected to perform all or a selected number of the tasks in their second (or subsequent) role.

At the operational level, there are choices about whether staff will be moved between departments within a shift, or only on separate shifts. In practice, although some of the cases had policies about not moving staff within a shift, this did occur in all cases to cope with unanticipated short-term changes. Seasonal hotels have found that multi-skilling its staff has been particularly useful in keeping labour costs down in periods of low demand. It has significantly reduced the number of staff it employs on a full-time basis during the winter months because of this flexibility. Not only do they report cost savings, but they also report high job satisfaction amongst staff and improved quality of service that derived from the staff working together more closely and understanding each others' roles.

Summary and conclusion

Because hotels are labour intensive, improving the productivity of employees can add significantly to the bottom line. But it remains a challenging area. As Iunius et al. (2006) conclude: 'the concept of labour productivity is still very vague ... the more effort put into understanding [it], the more nebulous the concept becomes'. In the research field, DEA appears to be one approach that addresses many of the complexities of measuring productivity. However, due to its complexity as a technique, it seems unlikely that this will be used in industry itself.

From a practical, applied perspective, productivity can be improved through better workplace design; through improved work processes; through better employee scheduling; and through temporal and/or functional flexibility. A coordinated approach in these areas will result in reduced inputs and increased outputs resulting in improved productivity and greater income.

References

Anderson, R. I., Fish, M., Xia, Y. and Michello, F. (1999) Measuring efficiency in the hotel industry: a stochastic frontier approach, *International Journal of Hospitality Management*, 18, 1, 45–57

Anderson, R. I., Fok, R. and Scott, J. (2000) Hotel industry efficiency: an advanced linear programming examination, *American Business Review*, 18, 1, 40–48

Andersson, T. D. (1996) Traditional key ratio analysis versus data envelopment analysis: a comparison of various measurements of productivity and efficiency in restaurant, In John, N. (Ed.), *Productivity Management in Hospitality and Tourism*, Cassell: London, UK, 209–226

Avkiran, N. K. (1999) *Productivity Analysis in the Services Sector with Data Envelopment Analysis*, Camira: Queensland

Ball, S. D. (1993) *Productivity and Productivity Management within Fast Food Chains – A Case Study of Wimpy International*, M. Phil Thesis, University of Huddersfield, Huddersfield, UK

Ball, S. D., Johnson, K. and Slattery, P. (1986) Labor productivity in hotels: an empirical analysis, *International Journal of Hospitality Management*, 5, 3, 141–147

Brown, J. R. and Dev, C. S. (1999) Looking beyond RevPAR: productivity consequences of hotel strategies, *Cornell Hotel and Restaurant Administration Quarterly*, 40, 2, 23–33

Brown, J. R. and Ragsdale, C. T. (2002) The competitive market efficiency of hotel brands – an application of data envelopment analysis, *Journal of Hospitality and Tourism Research*, 26, 4, 332–360

Charnes, A., Cooper, W. W. and Rhodes, E. (1978) Measuring the efficiency of decision-making units, *European Journal of Operational Research*, 2, 6, 429–444

Douglas, P. C. (2000) Measuring productivity and performance in the hospitality industry, *National Public Accountant*, 45, 5, 15–16

Hwang, S. N. and Chang, T. Y. (2003) Using data envelopment analysis to measure hotel managerial efficiency change in Taiwan, *Tourism Management*, 24, 4, 357–369

Iunius, R. F., Fraenkel, S. and Lacour-Gayet, J. (2006) Productivity perception in the Swiss hospitality industry: preliminary findings, *Information Technology in Hospitality*, 4, 2–3, 83–92

Johns, N. (1996) *Productivity Management in Hospitality and Tourism*, Cassell: London, UK

Johnson, K. and Ball, S. (1989) Productivity measurement in hotels, *Leisure, Recreation and Tourism Abstracts*

Johnson, K. and Ball, S. Productivity measurement in hotels, *Leisure, Recreation & Tourism Abstracts*. http://217.154.120.6/LeisureTourism/show-article.nsp?lastquery=%28Productivity+in+Hotels%29+AND+%28Productivity%29&sortfield=NONE&docindex=2&ranked=3&var_itemsfound=4&var_itemsallowed=4&var_backindex=1 (accessed 7 May 2006)

Jones, P. (1990) Managing food service productivity in the long term: strategy, structure and performance, *International Journal of Hospitality Management*, 9, 2, 143–154

Jones, P. (2002) Researching profit through productivity, *Hospitality Review*, 4, 1, 37–41

Jones, P. (2004) How do small, old, independent hotels get out of the productivity trap and improve quality? *EHLITE*, 7, 39–41

Jones, P. and Lockwood, A. (1989) *The Management of Hotel Operations*, Cassell: London, UK

Kappa, M. M., Nitschke, A. and Schappert, P. B. (1997) *Managing Housekeeping Operations*, 2nd edition, The Educational Institute of the American Hotel and Motel Association: East Lansing, MI

Kavanaugh, R. R. and Ninemeier, J. D. (1999) Managing productivity and controlling labor costs, *CHA Certification Study Guide*, Educational Institute of the American Hotel and Lodging Association: East Lansing, MI, 1, 145

Lawson, F. (1994) *Restaurants, Clubs and Bars: Planning, Design and Investment for Food Service Facilities*, 2nd edition, Butterworth Architecture: Oxford, UK

Lockwood, A. and Bowen, A. (2004) Small business success, *Hospitality Review*, 6, 2, 42–48

Mill, R. C. (1989) *Managing for Productivity in the Hospitality Industry*, Van Nostrand Rheinhold: New York, NY

Mill, R. C. (2005) *Managing the Lodging Operation*, Prentice Hall: Upper Saddle River, NJ

Mogendorff, D. and Simonds, R. (2003, May 27) *Labour Scheduling in Hospitality Where Productivity Blends Brand Standards and Cost Management,* Retrieved on 3 October 2007, from www.wiredhotelier.com/news//4016009.html

Morey, R. C. and Dittman, D. A. (1995) Evaluating a hotel GM's performance, *Cornell Hotel and Restaurant Administration Quarterly,* 36, 5, 30–32

Muller, C. C. (1999) A simple measure of restaurant efficiency, *Cornell Hotel and Restaurant Administration Quarterly,* 40, 3, 31–37

Pavesic, D. V. (2004) Boost productivity to control labor costs, *Restaurant Start-Up and Growth,* 1, 34–39

Pickens, D. (2006) Productivity – the wider context, *Chartered Accountants Journal,* 85, 3, 18–20

Reynolds, D. (1998) Productivity analysis in the on-site food-service segment, *Cornell Hotel and Restaurant Administration Quarterly,* 39, 3, 22–31

Reynolds, D. and Biel, D. (2007) Incorporating satisfaction measures into a restaurant productivity index, *Hospitality Management,* 26, 352–361

Reynolds, D. and Thompson, G. M. (2007) Multiunit restaurant productivity assessment using three-phase data envelopment analysis, *Hospitality Management,* 26, 20–32

Riley, M. K. and Jones, P. (2000) *Multiskilling,* Hospitality Training Foundation, unpublished report

Schmidgall, R. S. (1995) *Hospitality Industry Managerial Accounting,* 3rd edition, Educational Institute of the American Hotel and Motel Association: East Lansing, MI

Sigala, M. (2004) Integrating and exploiting information and communication technologies (ICT) in restaurant operations: implications for restaurant productivity, *Journal of Foodservice Business Research,* 6, 3, 55–76

Sigala, M., Jones, P., Lockwood, A. and Airey, D. (2005) Productivity in hotels: a stepwise data envelopment analysis of hotels' rooms division processes, *Service Industries Journal,* 25, 1, 61–81

Siguaw, J. A., Cathy, A. E. and Namasivayam, K. (2000) Adoption of information technology in U.S. hotels: strategically driven objectives, *Journal of Travel Research,* 39, 2, 192–201

Thompson, G. M. (1998) Labor scheduling, part 2: knowing how many on duty employees to schedule, *Cornell Hotel and Restaurant Administration Quarterly,* 39, 6, 26–37

Thompson, G. M. (1999a) Labor Scheduling, part 3: developing a workforce schedule, *Cornell Hotel and Restaurant Administration Quarterly,* 40, 1, 86–96

Thompson, G. M. (1999b) Labour scheduling, part 4: control-ling workforce schedules in real time, *Cornell Hotel and Restaurant Administration Quarterly*, 40, 3, 85–96

Withiam, G. and Thompson, G. (2004) View labor as a value-maximizing asset when scheduling, *Hotel and Motel Management*, 219, 19, 14

Witt, C. A. and Witt, S. F. (1989) Why productivity in the hotel sector is low, *International Journal of Contemporary Hospitality Management*, 1, 2, 28–34

Wöber, K. W. (2000) Benchmarking hotel operations on the internet: a data envelopment analysis approach, *Information Technology and Tourism*, 3, 3/4, 195–212

CHAPTER 13

Quality management

Mohamed Fawzy Afify

Assistant Lecturer
Faculty of Tourism and Hotels
Menoufia University
Egypt

Introduction

Quality management is the most researched operations management topic in hospitality (Jones 2007). This chapter begins by examining different definitions of quality and goes on to look how quality can be designed into hospitality operations and organizations. Five basic approaches are reviewed: quality inspection (QI), quality control (QC), quality assurance (QA), total quality management (TQM) and continuous improvement (CI). Operators may also seek external recognition or accreditation of their quality standards. A number of schemes exist and have been adopted in the industry – these are explained and reviewed. Within strategies, specific approaches to measuring quality are adopted – mystery guest, customer surveys and audits – so research in these areas is reviewed.

The whole approach to quality in industry in general and in hospitality in particular has gradually become more sophisticated over the years. The most unsophisticated strategy – QI – was largely the way quality was managed up to and including the 1950s. During the 1960s, a number of sectors introduced new technologies and created new systems, along with which QC systems were established. For instance, the adoption of cook-chill led to the development of HACCP (hazard analysis and critical control point). However, as with many service operations, the service worker can directly impact a customer satisfaction so that the control approach in some cases was further modified in order to achieve QA. Finally, the 1990s saw the development of the concept of TQM, and more recently CI.

What do we mean by quality?

Quality in the dictionary is defined as 'the degree or standard of excellence of something'. This suggests that there is an absolute standard against which all things can be measured. So, for instance, it is sometimes assumed that five star hotels are of a higher 'quality' than three star hotels, or fine dining restaurants are of a higher 'quality' than quick service outlets. This is wrong. Quality is not absolute, it is relative – like has to be compared with like. So it is possible to have high-quality five star hotels and poor-quality ones, and high-quality quick service restaurants and low-quality examples.

The so-called Quality Gurus – Japanese experts like Shingo, Ishikawa and Taguchi, and Americans like Deming, Crosby and Juran – spent several decades developing concepts and practice in this area and have always thought of quality as relative. Juran, for instance, has defined quality as fitness for purpose. The British Standards Institution likewise defines it as 'the totality of features and characteristics of a product or service that bear on its ability to meet a specific need'. For Crosby (1979: 15), quality means 'conformance to requirements'. Those requirements must be clearly established, as not conforming to the requirements means that quality is absent. Nevertheless, being free from defects does not guarantee quality (Anand 1997). Crosby coined the phrase 'quality is free' as he saw that non-quality items were adding costs, which would only be avoided by *doing things right first time* (Crosby 1979). This echoes the Zero defect programme nurtured in the Martin Company (Garvin 1987).

Taguchi and Clausing (1990) suggest that quality begins in the design stage, as such the Zero defect programme may not help to deliver quality. Instead of chasing defects, the design in the first place must not allow defects to occur, shifting most of the burden to the design team. This programme is seen by Anand (1997) as a means to reach quality. However, Anand (1997: 196) attacks seeing quality as 'conformance to standard' accusing it of being 'the biggest enemy of quality' and holding it 'largely responsible for poor quality products being produced at high cost'. Juran (2000) also criticizes it as it ignores the customers' interests, and Smith (1993: 237) believes it does not differentiate between 'a concept's meaning with its operationalization or method of measurement'.

Feigenbaum defines quality as 'the total composite product and service characteristics of marketing, engineering, manufacture, and maintenance through which the product and service in use will meet the expectations of the customer' (Feigenbaum in Kolarik 1995: 5). Feigenbaum's first definition of quality had the products as its object, but later service found its way into his definition, reflecting realization of the growth and importance of the service sector (Reeves and Bednar 1994). Feigenbaum's call for 'Total Quality Control' brought a more integrated look to quality, reflecting a sense of responsibility sharing among the 'inter-functional teams'. However, Feigenbaum did not think of quality as a strategy, according to Garvin (1987). Garvin stresses that quality should be thought of as a strategy. He subdivides product quality into eight dimensions or categories, namely *performance, features, reliability, conformance, durability, serviceability* and the most subjective *aesthetics* and *perceived quality. Conformance* and *reliability* are 'the most traditional notions'.

It can be concluded that there is no universal definition that can be applied to all businesses and cases. The different definitions have evolved over time; each one represents a certain focus that reflects the prevailing thinking in its time. For that reason, new dimensions or even definitions may be added as the need arises. However, every business should define quality according to its environment and situation, and as Garvin stresses, it is better to consider many definitions of quality and not to rely on just one.

Why is quality difficult to achieve?

A number of models have been developed to describe service quality, many of which are just as relevant to products. Brogowicz et al. (1990) usefully integrate these into a single model, which identifies five main areas where service quality problems are likely to arise.

Gap 1 is called the *positioning* gap. It develops if the product or service concept diverges from customer requirements, as may happen if fashions or demographic changes affect the market place or new products and services come into the market place. Long-term control of the positioning gap can be achieved by regular top-level reviews of the established concept. This is usually done through both qualitative and quantitative market research, aimed at identifying customers' current wants and needs.

Gap 2 is the *specification* gap. This occurs when management set standards of performance that are different to what they perceive to be customer requirements. This may occur because these requirements are contradictory, difficult to execute or too costly to achieve. It may also occur when firms move into new markets, perhaps overseas, where they apply existing brand standards to new customers.

Gap 3 is the *delivery* gap and occurs when employees do not, or cannot, deliver the product or service to the standard required. It is this gap that is most frequently managed in operations through management audits and mystery shopper programmes (see below).

Gap 4 relates to promotional *communication*. This has an important influence upon customer perceptions of service quality, because for many operations, it is the basis upon which customers build their expectations. It should therefore reflect products and service accurately and faithfully.

Gap 5 is the *perception* gap, that is the difference between what customers expect and what they perceive they have received. The perception gap may be monitored by SERVQUAL (see below), customer satisfaction questionnaires or market research surveys.

From an operations perspective, these gaps are very different in nature, and hence how they should be managed differs greatly. The positioning gap is highly strategic and relies heavily on expertise in the marketing field. The specification gap is the point at which operations managers seek to develop policies, systems and technologies that can deliver customer requirements. The expertise needed here has very much to do with socio-technical systems and how this relates to process design and job design.[1] A failure to design quality in will lead to systemic failures in products and service delivery. The delivery gap is clearly the responsibility of the operations management team at all levels within the organization, from first-line supervisors up to the operations director. The communications gap relies heavily on the marketing and operations functions working closely together to ensure the operation's capabilities are not exaggerated, whilst the final challenge, the perception gap, is entirely inside the customer's head. It is this gap that the SERVQUAL instrument seeks to measure. Managers dealing with dissatisfied customers have to realize that it is customers' perceptions they have to deal with, even if these are at variance with 'reality'. For instance, customers who complain about waiting too long typically exaggerate the time they have waited for.[2] Finally, gap theory also has implications for the design of quality measurement tools, which are discussed later in this chapter.

SERVQUAL

One of the most influential research instruments in researching service quality has been SERVQUAL. Parasuraman et al. (1988) developed SERVQUAL as a scale to measure the quality of service, where perceived service quality is the outcome of a comparison between a customer's expectations of the ser-vice and the perceived service. The original 10 service quality determinants were reduced to five dimensions, namely tangibles, reliability, responsiveness, assurance and empathy. It is worth noting that not all the dimensions are equal in their importance. Some have higher importance than the others, as identified by Parasuraman (1988) where reliability was more important and empathy the least important. The relative importance of dimensions depends on the nature of the service (Ghobadian et al. 1994).

Tsang and Qu (2000) used SERVQUAL to examine the gaps between the expectations and perceptions of international tourists and hotel managers in nine hotels in three Chinese cities. In addition to the traditional five gaps, two more gaps were examined: 'the difference between consumer perceptions of service delivery and what management believes they deliver' and 'the difference between management's perception of consumer expectations and management's perception of its

---

[1] See Chapter 2.
[2] See Chapter 5.

service delivery' (Tsang and Qu 2000: 318). The study by Ekinci et al. (2003) explored British tourists' evaluation of the accommodation in Crete. Intangibles, more than tangibles, were appreciated by the tourists, especially female respondents.

Parasuraman et al. (1988: 30–31) do not claim that SERVQUAL is applicable to all kinds of operations – 'The instrument has been designed to be applicable across a broad spectrum of services it provides a basic skeleton through its expectations/ perceptions format, encompassing statements for each of the five service-quality dimensions'. They understand also that it may need modification – '[It], when necessary, can be adapted or supplemented to fit the characteristics or specific research needs of a particular organization'. Hence it has been adapted to specific contexts in hospitality. Knutson et al. (1991) proposed LODGSERVE to evaluate quality in hotels, and Raajpoot (2002) developed TANGSERV for the foodservice sector. Stevens et al. (1995) and Knutson et al. (1995) reported on DINESERVE which was a modified version of the SERVQUAL to fit the restaurant business. DINESERVE has 29 items, distributed on five dimensions – tangibles, reliability, responsiveness, assurance and empathy. Heung et al. (2000) studied service quality using DINESERVE in their study of four restaurants in Hong Kong – Chinese, casual dining, full service and quick service. Akbaba (2006) used an 'adapted/modified' SERVQUAL of 29 attributes, subsequently reduced to 25, in studying business hotels in Turkey. He found that tangibles was the most critical service quality dimension to most hotel guests, and identified a new dimension – convenience. He also found that for the business travellers, convenience received the highest expectation scores, while understanding and caring came the last. Juwaheer (2004) applied SERVQUAL on hotel international guests in Mauritius, identifying nine factors – reliability, assurance, extra room benefits, staff communication skills and additional benefits, room attractiveness and décor, empathy, staff outlook and accuracy, food and service, hotel surrounding and environmental factors.

However, SERVQUAL has been heavily criticized (Ekinci 2002). Davies et al. (1999) argue that SERVQUAL has been promoted because of its alleged universal applicability, but even this, according to Davies et al. can be rejected as many studies have modified the model to adapt it to their contexts. SERVQUAL was criticized by Cronin and Taylor (1992) on the grounds that perceptions alone can be used to predict service quality; the dimensions of SERVQUAL are not believed to be applicable to all service encounters and they may need to be altered (Carman, 1990). Buttle (1996) noted that SERVQUAL is decried on both theoretical and operational grounds. Table 13.1 summarizes this critique.

Table 13.1 Critical issues with SERVQUAL

Theoretical	Operational
Paradigmatic objections SERVQUAL is based on a disconfirmation paradigm rather than an attitudinal paradigm (Cronin and Taylor 1992; 1994); and SERVQUAL fails to draw on established economic, statistical and psychological theory (Buttle 1996).	*Expectations* The term expectations is polysemic; consumers use standards other than expectations to evaluate SQ; and SERVQUAL fails to measure absolute SQ expectations (Buttle 1996).
Gap model There is little evidence that customers assess service quality in terms of P-E gaps (Buttle 1996).	*Item composition* Four or five items cannot capture the variability within each SQ dimension (Buttle 1996).
Process orientation SERVQUAL focuses on the process of service delivery, not the outcomes of the service encounter (Buttle 1996; Ekinci 2002).	*Moments of truth (MOT)* Customer's assessments of SQ may vary from MOT to MOT (Buttle 1996).
Dimensionality SERVQUAL's five dimensions are not universals; the number of dimensions comprising SQ is contextualized (Carman 1990); items do not always load on to the factors which one would a priori expect (Carman 1990); and there is a high degree of intercorrelation between the five RATER dimensions (Buttle 1996; Ekinci 2002).	*Polarity* The reversed polarity of items in the scale causes respondent error (Buttle 1996).
	Scale points The seven-point Likert scale is flawed (Buttle 1996).
	Two administrations Two administrations of the instrument causes boredom and confusion (Buttle 1996; Carman 1990).
	Variance extracted The overall SERVQUAL score accounts for a disappointing proportion of item variances (Buttle 1996).

Source: Adapted from Buttle (1996).

Strategies for managing quality

Another potential measure of overall quality is the *cost* of quality. According to Wyckoff (1984) and Crosby (1979), quality costs fall into four main categories:

- *Prevention*. Costs of setting up standards and a system to maintain them, for example training staff, preparing purchase specifications, developing processes, monitoring and documenting procedures (setting up costs).
- *Assurance*. Cost of actually maintaining standards, for example resources required for inspection, measurement and documentation (staff time and administrative costs).
- *Internal failure*. Costs due to waste or losses before the product or service reaches the customer, for example rejection of raw materials, losses due to faulty storage, products rejected as a result of inspection (cost of waste and inefficiency).
- *External failure*. Costs due to defective items reaching the customer, for example a free meal or room offered to placate offended individuals (ultimately marketing costs and loss of repeat business).

Crosby (1984) does not count the costs of setting up and maintaining a quality system as part of the cost of quality. These are costs which diligent management would have to bear anyway to set up an effective system. He argues for what he calls the price of non-conformance (PONC), namely the cost to management of not getting it right first time and every time. In other words, this is the cost of internal and external failure. However, calculating PONC is not easy, because it is not easy to assess the value of lost repeat business customer dissatisfaction and negative word of mouth. However, companies do assign such costs to their operations. PONC calculations are usually carried out department by department, and individual mangers are consulted as to what constitutes a 'non-conformance'. The normal procedure is to decide standard costs for specific failure events and to multiply them by the number of such failure events.

There are five main approaches to managing quality that focus on managing processes – QI, QC, QA, TQM and CI. These are not mutually exclusive. Hence, there may be QI as part of the TQM approach, and QA is typically found in CI programmes. Each of these will now be discussed.

Quality inspection

The simplest way to manage quality is to inspect the product before it is sold to the customer. Therefore, the goals of a QI system are very simple: set up a specification of the product, cost it, and detect any defects before delivering it or selling it to the end user. It is very much a 'shop-floor' activity, involving only those employees directly concerned with the making of the product or delivery of the service, and their superiors. While it is easy to install, the point at which quality is checked is at the output point. This means QI takes place *after* the product has been produced. This approach has been used extensively in the hospitality industry for many years. For example, hotel rooms are routinely checked by floor housekeepers before being made available for the next customer and food items are routinely checked at the hot plate by the chef before being taken into the restaurant.

Whilst QI may prevent external failure, this system may lead to high internal failure costs. There is little spent on prevention and assurance, so failure may be high and systemic. The system can only be improved by increased inspection, thus increasing cost, so there is often a trade-off between quality and cost. It is a simple system often found in small hospitality businesses, but does not achieve a great deal in quality terms. Finally, QI cannot easily be applied to intangible aspects of the product/service package, and it therefore provides the operator with only a partial quality management system.

Quality control

A range of models have been proposed with regard to QC in the hospitality industry, for instance Wyckoff (1984), Jones (1983) and King (1984). King's approach, based on the manufacturing model of QC, is fairly typical of the QC strategy, as illustrated in Table 13.2.

The decision to segment the market has major implications for quality management. Each market sector has discrete quality standards which must be communicated both to the customer and to the staff. Once the operator has determined its market requirements, it can then translate these into definite product specifications in terms of the layout, décor and design of room facilities, equipment and materials to be used, ancillary items, and in a broader context, the scale and nature of other facilities and services within the operation. Furthermore, the operating procedures for the implementation of service provision must also be specified in this approach by detailed standards of performance manuals, detailed training of staff and specific organizational systems.

In this control model of quality management, after designing the quality level and setting product standards, the principal

Table 13.2 Model of quality control

1. Design quality level
   Define customer requirements
   - Identify desired quality characteristics.

2. Set product standards
   Design product to meet standards:
   - Drawings
   - Equipment and materials specification
   - Document procedures
   - Plan organization and training.

3. Check conformance
   Output
   - Inspecting
   - Quality audit
   - Guest complaint.

   Process
   - Check employee performance
   - Equipment monitoring.

4. Correct non-standard output
   - Redo or defer sale of rejects
   - Analyse rejects for cause of failure
   - Adjust production process.

Source: King (1984).

role of the manager is checking on conformance. Two features can be monitored, the actual outcomes and the process of working practices employed. Both can be evaluated internally or by an external auditor. Typically, a number of approaches are adopted – internal inspection, quality audits, mystery shopper or mystery guest programmes and so on. These are discussed in more detail later in this chapter.

The final stage of the control system is to 'correct non-standard output'. For instance, in housekeeping this would mean that if a room is not up to the expected standard, the maid or supervisor will put it right. If for some reason the room cannot be brought up to the standard, perhaps due to inundation by water, vandalism or some other serious defect, then the room will be put 'off' until the necessary work has been carried out to restore it to the level of quality expected. Management should ensure that the reasons for failing to meet the required standards are investigated so that action can be taken to ensure that it does not happen again. Two approaches to QC; statistical process control (SPC) and HACCP, will now be discussed.

Statistical process control

SPC is a quality technique based on statistics. It was developed by Shewhart, Dodge, and Roming in the Bell Telephone Laboratories in the 1930s. The British Standard Institute describes SPC as: 'The in-process application of statistical data analysis methods to identify out of tolerance conditions for a specific production process and to notify the operator of the current or impending problem' (BSI 1994 in Herbert et al. 2003: 64). The technique aims to eradicate the special causes of variation; it is used to observe, control, canvas and improve the process performance. Although it is the tool most associated with SPC, the control chart is not all SPC (Barker 1990). The other tools constituting SPC include check sheets, histograms, scatter diagrams, Pareto analysis, cause and effect diagrams, and graphs. Two studies have looked at the application of SPC in the hospitality industry. Jones and Dent (1994) reported on a study in a cafeteria, and Jones and Cheek (1997) compared SPC with mystery shopper programmes to assess the efficacy of these two alternatives.

HACCP

Hazard analysis and critical control point (HACCP) is a specific approach to QC designed for large-scale catering and food manufacturing largely to assure the safety of food products. Food poisoning is a major problem. In Hong Kong, poor food-handling procedures caused 60% of the food-borne illnesses between 1997 and 1999 (Kivela et al. 2002). In the United States, it accounted for 9,000 deaths and 33 million illnesses, resulting in costs of $9.3 to $12.9 billion annually (Riswadkar 2000). In Australia, more than 700 people suffered from food poisoning in three individual cases in Queensland which took place in November 1996, and one month later, a salmonella-contaminated sandwich was the reason for an old patient's death in a hospital in Queensland (Morrison et al. 1998). The two incidents were preceded by the disclosure of a microbial inspection results of salad bars in retail and foodservice outlets revealing the presence of *Listeria monocytogenes*, *Staphylococcus* and *Bacillus cereus* in eight out of twenty-four tested operations (Morrison et al. 1998).

The adoption of HACCP in the UK was suggested as a result of the excessive incidents of food poisoning all over the kingdom in the 1980s (Barnes and Mitchell 2000). According to Wilson et al. (1997), the worries regarding food-related problems, food poisoning incidents and the BSE crisis resulted in increased concerns for better food hygiene and handling procedures. They argue that with the change in the life style of consumers, and the observed growth of eating out, the need for a system that guarantees the correct food handling is proving to be a necessity. Morrison et al. (1998) elaborate the same view, suggesting that demographic changes produced more vulnerable people who can contract diseases easily, new pathogens are discovered, and species are becoming more resistant to the traditional safety practices, and the food supply chain has more intensive farming.

The foodservice industry is accused of being a major source of ill health as 70% of the food poisoning incidents caused by bacteria are accounted for by caterers (Wilson et al. 1997). But the situation is more significant than such numbers suggest, since the reporting of food poisoning incidents is less than 10% (Morrison et al. 1998). A high percentage of foodservice operations are managed by their owners, and many do not have adequate food safety background. In addition, the special nature of the foodservice business, where large batches of food are prepared beforehand, and busy periods where the hygiene rules may be forgotten or ignored, make increases in risk more likely (Eves and Dervisi 2005).

Food safety programmes that concentrated on final product inspection proved to be a failure – unable to protect the consumers, the producers and the service providers (Ehiri et al. 1995; Riswadkar 2000). The need for a system that expects the problems and takes the necessary precautions to prevent them was required. Initially HACCP was developed to provide space programmes in the United States with food (Sperber 2005a; Riswadkar 2000). HACCP can be defined as a 'risk-based food safety assurance system that concentrates prevention strategies on known hazards' (Morrison et al. 1998: 101). The system tries to pinpoint the possible hazards by identifying the stages in an operation where they are likely to happen (Wilson et al. 1997). A hazard may be a microbiological, chemical or physical substance (Riswadkar 2000; Wilson et al. 1997), or a 'condition of food with the potential to cause an adverse health effect' (Mortimore 2001: 212). HACCP identifies and eliminates hazards that could result in a food-borne illness instead of depending on examining samples of final products randomly, as it incorporates quality in every stage of food processing and handling (Riswadkar 2000).

Hazard identification is the first step of the process and this step is followed by an evaluation of the identified hazards. The typical way to identify hazards is by reviewing the sensitivity of the ingredients being used or through the brain-storming process performed by the HACCP team. Where hazards are greatest in the process, theses points are termed critical control points (CCPs). These are 'subsystems within the food production/service process for which loss of control would result in an unacceptable risk of food-borne illnesses' (Wilson et al. 1997: 151). HACCP works by practicing control over those points. Initially HACCP was based on three principles which over time expanded to be seven, as illustrated in Table 13.3.

Sun and Ockerman (2005) provide a comprehensive look over the situation of HACCP implementation in the foodservice area. Microbial examination of food items is an indication of the success of an HACCP programme. Soriano et al. (2002) report the observed decline in the microbial count in Spanish omelette and pork loins after the implementation of HACCP in 19 university restaurants. HACCP proved another success in the fight against Salmonella which was reduced by 50% on chicken carcasses (Billy 2002). Kokkinakis and Fragkiadakis (2007) examined tomato salads (a raw prepared food with high risk) in six mass-catering businesses in Greece – operations that adopted HACCP had less microbial count than those that did not.

However, HACCP has not been adopted industry wide due to some concerns with the system. Panisello and Quantick (2001: 168) identify the 'technical barriers' which are 'all those practices, attitudes, and perceptions that negatively affect the understanding of the HAACP concept and hence the proper

---

Table 13.3   HACCP principles (1972 and 1997)

HACCP principles, 1972
1. Conduct hazard analysis
2. Determine critical control points
3. Establish monitoring procedures

HACCP principles, 1997
1. Conduct hazard analysis
2. Determine critical control points
3. Establish critical limits
4. Establish monitoring procedures
5. Establish corrective actions
6. Establish verification procedures
7. Establish record keeping procedures

Source: Sperber (2005b).

and effective implementation of the HACCP principles'. Such obstacles may happen before, during or after the adoption of HACCP. Documentation is crucial under HACCP, as a means to affirm the adherence to the right procedures and to prove 'due diligence' (Azanza 2006; Eves and Dervisi 2005). Nevertheless, it is seen as a 'restraining factor' (Eves and Dervisi 2005). IT solutions, such as Hygiene Management System software, are helping to overcome this. It is user friendly, with an ability to generate many reports and using the multimedia to help guide the step-by-step implementation of HACCP. Maher (2001) argues that it makes it much easier for those involved in the production and processing of food to adopt HACCP. The effective use of technology is also reported by Eves and Dervisi (2005), where HACCP computer-based training (CBT) was provided for the food handlers.

HACCP audits can be conducted through two approaches, internally or independently (Motarjemi 2000). Internally the food business carries out self-audit, and independently it can be done by regulatory bodies (representing the government) or a third party (an external firm) (Souness 2000). Governmental institutions have a crucial responsibility for HACCP implementation and assessment and this is explained in the joint consultation of the Food and Agriculture Organization of the United Nations (FAO) and the World Health Organization (WHO). Motarjemi (2000) highlights this consultation. While some operations appreciated the role of the enforcement officers and recognize their assistance, others felt that the officers made it more complicated and added to their confusion, as the officers lack catering work experience that qualifies them to understand the nature of the tasks carried out (Eves and Dervisi 2005). The same negative regard is shared by another operator in the study by Taylor and Taylor (2004), who described them as 'bureaucratic', 'suits' and having 'no intimate knowledge'.

Operations that implement HACCP benefit from the advantages it offers. The system is proactive, not reactive; it does not wait for problems; instead it prevents them (Morrison et al. 1998; Wilson et al. 1997). Those who support the system argue that it concentrates on the critical phases of food handling, from the raw material till it is ready for consumption, in a 'cost effective manner' (Morrison et al. 1998). Control is relatively easy, focusing on time, temperature and appearance. Execution of the system is the responsibility of the staff as part of their daily duties, and it should raise staff morale and increase their sense of ownership (Wilson et al. 1997). In food manufacturing, Ehiri et al. (1995) report that HACCP increases the potentials of exporting for the food industry, as many countries would prefer HACCP-certified traders to non-certified ones. This is also confirmed by Gagnon et al. (2000) who see HACCP as 'food passport' to international trade. Ehiri et al. (1995) argue that the benefits gained from HACCP implementation exceed any related costs, even if spending on staff training, which is just one of the different associated expenses, was estimated to be £35–42 million in the UK food industry. A cost-benefit analysis should convince operators to adopt HACCP (Ehiri et al. 1995).

Wilson et al. (1997) reports some disadvantages associated with HACCP. HAACP adoption represents a considerable financial burden especially for small businesses. Taylor (2001) argues that small companies are considered an essential part of the economic development in most countries. In the UK, small companies represent 99% of all food operations, offering jobs to 50% of the work force and a 38% contribution to turnover. A glance over these percentages warrants the concerns over the food safety practices, and systems applied in that sector. Taylor (2001) also noted that HACCP implementation in small operations proved to be mediocre. Small companies are lacking motivation to adopt HACCP. If they apply, it is due to compliance with legislation not persuasion (Morrison et al. 1998; Taylor 2001).

Likewise keeping documents and records is basic to HACCP, but this practice is not sufficient, as they can be faked. Moreover, watching all the practices of staff at one time is impossible, especially in the catering industry which has multiple functions. For small business, HACCP is considered a complicated system (Hilton 2002), described as 'bureaucratic nightmare' (Taylor and Taylor 2004). Taylor (2001) explains the impediments that confront small businesses in their implementation of HACCP, and she also reports on the 'theoretical benefits' they can gain. Taylor and Kane (2005) investigated how HACCP could be simplified for SMEs. They developed a tool kit for HACCP implementation, finding that problems 'can be partially helped by providing simplified documents or streamlined verification methods, but only in an overall context of training and support that addresses the primary problem – that of the SME's basic lack of understanding of the HACCP approach' (Taylor and Kane 2005: 837). Worsfold (2006) reports on the experience of assisting small fast food businesses through workshops to understand and adopt the Food Standard Agency (FSA/UK) guidance manual on HACCP. Finally, Adams (2002: 357) argues that 'HACCP is not a magic wand nor magic bullet. Even the best and the most elegant HACCP plan is still prone to human error, and failed execution'. Sperber (2005a: 514) observes that 'food safety is not synonyms with HACCP', as 'Food safety is HACCP plus prerequisite programs' and 'Farm to Table Food Safety' should be stressed rather than 'Farm to Table HACCP'.

A number of studies have been conducted with respect to the application of HACCP to the foodservice industry. Jones (1983) and Farkas and Snyder (1991) both identified how this might be applied to catering, and O'Donnell (1991) describes its application in a specific firm. Eves and Dervisi (2005) undertook a detailed study of HACCP in seven different types of foodservice outlet, identifying that compliance with regulations was the main motivation for adopting it.

Quality assurance

Quality assurance (QA) is built on the principle 'get it right first time every time'. More is invested in assurance costs, which should ensure a significantly greater decline in internal and external failure costs.

With regard to the business environment, most employees can easily identify what the business is but may have a very wide range of views about the most important aspect of that business. Quality can be brought to the forefront of their thinking by an overt use of the word from the moment of recruitment, right throughout the induction period and during any on-the-job training. Since this concept may also be consistent with the image the operation wishes to create in the consumer's mind, it can become part of an advertising slogan. This emphasis on one feature of the operation can then become central to the shared value system of the organization, whereby management praise high-quality performance; promotion or bonuses are seen to be relative to the quality of work done; the physical resources, such as equipment and work environment, provide the necessary tools to achieve quality and are of high quality themselves; and so on. It will be difficult for management to convince their work force of the need for quality front-of-house if their changing rooms are poor, their work clothes ill-fitting, and management do not appear to care about time-keeping, personal appearance and standards. Both management and staff can therefore help to set standards by behaving as role models, thereby contributing to the cultural climate.

In the hotel sector, a number of studies have considered how the industry has gone about adopting a quality management programme. Walker and Salameh (1990) assessed the impact of the American Hotel and Motel Association sponsored QA programme, finding that hotels with QA had higher employee satisfaction and lower labour costs than hotels without QA. Breiter et al. (1995) investigated how Bergstrom Hotels had implemented their quality programme. Lockwood et al. (1996) report on quality management in six hotels, and Harrington and Akehurst (1996) survey hotel managers to investigate their quality management practices. Baldacchino (1995) reported on an in-depth study of total quality management (TQM) being applied in a single property. Hsieh and Hsieh (2001) research the role that job standardization has in delivering service quality.

Quality circles

As well as these general principles aimed at creating the appropriate climate in which quality can thrive, there is a particular technique that is meant to result in total commitment to the idea – namely the quality circle. A quality circle has been described as 'a group of four to ten volunteers working for the same supervisor who meet once a week, for an hour, under the leadership of the supervisor, to identify, analyse and solve their own work-related problems' (Robson 1983: 8). The typical features of such circles are that they are entirely voluntary, intensely practical and unbureaucratic. But there is widespread confusion about both the objectives and the appropriate format of quality circles in the USA and the UK. Originally modelled on circles developed in Japan, certain features of Japanese work ethics and culture do not exist in the West. For instance, Japanese workers are very loyal, expect to work for the same employer for their lifetime, exhibit a group-based work ethic and are prepared to join in many company-organized activities, including quality circles, outside their normal working hours.

On the basis of the Japanese model, it has been proposed that the growth and development of the circles depends entirely on the employees and is not dictated by the organization. The way in which each circle works should be as follows:

- Originate list of problems by brainstorming;
- Reject those problems outside own work area;
- Select those problems that are possible to solve;
- Rank problems in priority order;
- Analyse the problem;
- Collect relevant data;
- Solve problem;
- Sell this solution to management.

This approach, however, often has had only mixed results (Jones and Merricks 1994). The UK has a very different labour relations and industrial climate to Japan. In particular, by involving employees in a more open and participative style of management, employee expectations may be raised, but frustration may set in when these expectations are not met. Because of this, it may not be practical to think of quality circles as a long-term approach, but one with relatively short-term and specific quality objectives.

The reported benefits of quality circles are numerous. Most importantly, they change attitudes within the organization: staff are better motivated, supervisor gain confidence, problem solving is more competent, communication at all levels is improved and there is the creation of a problem-solving ethic rather than blame-shifting ethic. As well as these unquantifiable results, organizations have found that the solutions that circles generate can in some cases save them thousands of pounds per year. And a better motivated work force has resulted in less absenteeism and lower rates of staff turnover.

These reported benefits have also caused some confusion as to the role that circles play. In Japan and as described above, quality circles are all about solving problems and issues broadly related to quality. The 'side effects' of improved work relations are largely taken for granted. In the West, however, quality circles have sometimes been formed with the intention and objectives of improving work relationships. Such objectives should be viewed as possible, but quite separate and distinct from the quality issue. The use of circles to effect such changes at work are in effect using them as a devise to modify organizational culture and as such they require even more support, commitment and depth than the QC model described above. In this context, circles should always be viewed as a long-term device since cultural shifts cannot take place in the short term unless very great external forces for change exist.

Total quality management

A significant development of the 1980s was the emergence of the concept of TQM. The strategy is entirely customer driven and its holistic approach is adopted with an almost missionary zeal. TQM is a way of organizing and involving the whole organization, every department, every activity, every single person at every level. Soriano (1999) researched the application of TQM to hotels in Spain, whilst Breiter and Bloomquist (1998) reviewed TQM in American hotels.

Jones and Riggott (1992) proposed that a TQM strategy in the hospitality industry involves a number of key steps. Whilst this includes some of the features of the QC and QA strategies, TQM differs from these in a number of ways. First, it is holistic and involves the whole organization. Secondly, senior executives play a key role in leading the quality drive and communicating the quality message. A further key aspect is employee empowerment which involves staff more actively in the decision-making process. While it can be thought of as allowing employees to do something about quality defects as they notice them so that organizations can continuously correct their performance, it encompasses more than that. Employees at all organization levels should be allowed to make decisions (which should be monitored) within clearly defined parameters in order to free up their superiors for their tasks. Developing the appropriate organizational culture and a concomitant leadership style are fundamental to the development of TQM in line with the requirements of the effective introduction and reinforcement of any major organizational change. Because of this it can take up to five years to get the system up and running, and many organizations give up before they have achieved their goal.

Continuous improvement

In services especially, TQM has tended to become enshrined as *the* 'best practice' in quality management, partly through the accreditation such as European Foundation for Quality Management (EFQM) and recognition schemes such as Malcolm Baldrige. However many firms, notably in manufacturing, are highly effective in managing their quality, without adopting TQM, through CI. CI has many similarities to TQM, but is more flexible in its philosophy and approach. Originating in Japan as *kaizen*, CI is 'a strategy to continually, and incrementally change and improve all operational components: equipment, procedures, skills, throughput time, quality, supplier relations, product and service designs, and so on' (Lowson 2002: 84).

Lowson (2002: 85) identifies 'ten guiding principles' of CI. These are:

1. Process driven across all organizational functions
2. Total employee involvement
3. Good labour-management relations
4. Effective leadership and cross communication
5. Adaptability to changing environment

6. Visibility and control of all processes
7. Reducing waste
8. Customer orientation
9. Standardization
10. Quality awareness and QC

External accreditation of quality

Whichever of the quality strategies a firm adopts, it may also seek to gain recognition or accreditation of quality through any one of a number of schemes. In many cases, firms use these schemes as one of the ways to upgrade and improve their approach to quality, since they provide a specific objective for management and employees to work towards. The cost of introducing such quality schemes is hard to quantify. Quality systems generally result in considerable savings in staff time and wastage. There is usually an ongoing requirement of at least one high-level full-time quality manager with administrative support, and time will have to be allocated by many other staff to operate this system. In general, in the long term the benefits would outweigh the costs. The implementation of a quality scheme is best carried out by initially briefing senior managers on what is involved in introducing quality systems and then launching the scheme as a pilot scheme focusing on a particular area of operations. The pilot scheme should have clearly definable goals and should maintain a high profile with regular reports being issued so that all members of the institution are aware of what progress is being made. Regular briefing sessions will be required in order to maintain a high profile of the project, so that staff realize the importance of the introduction of quality. When the initial project has been completed, other areas can be targeted and the programme rolled out.

Some of the major schemes being currently used in the hospitality industry are BS 5750 (ISO 9000), the EFQM Scheme, the Malcolm Baldrige Award, and six sigma. These are briefly described below.

BS 5750 (ISO 9000)

The British Standard BS 5750 was initially published in 1979 to define to suppliers and manufacturers what is required for a quality-orientated system and later developed into the international standard ISO 9000. Although originally devised for manufacturing industry, it was quickly adopted by service organizations, including financial services, foodservice, health care and educational establishments. The standard is very process orientated, relying heavily on fully documenting and controlling all aspects of 'production processes.' The standard covers the definition and description of a wide range of operational activity, as illustrated in Table 13.4. Contract foodservice firms particularly are adopting these standards, largely because their clients specify that suppliers should be so accredited. ISO 9000 was researched by Ingram and Daskalakis (1999) in their study of hotels in Crete. Nield and Kozak (1999) investigated the gained benefits of ISO 9000 in 34 hospitality operations in UK.

Table 13.4 BS 5750 specifications

1 Management responsibility.
2 Quality system principles.
3 Internal quality auditing.
4 Quality-related cost considerations.
5 Quality in marketing including contract review.
6 Quality in specification and design (design control)
7 Quality in procurement (purchasing control).
8 Quality in production (production process control).
9 Control of production.
10 Material control and traceability (product identification and traceability).
11 Control of verification status (inspection and testing).
12 Product verification (inspection and testing).
13 Control of measuring and testing
14 Control on non-conformity of product.
15 Corrective action.
16 Handling of post-production functions (handling, storage, packaging and delivery).
17 After-sales servicing.
18 Quality documentation and records (document control).
19 Quality records.
20 Personnel (training).
21 Product safety and liability.
22 Use of statistical methods.
23 Purchaser supplied products.

European foundation for quality management scheme

The EFQM was formed in 1988. A TQM model for self-appraisal was issued in 1992. The scheme allows institutions to introduce a TQM scheme which is self-assessed for the purposes of obtaining a quality award. However, a representative of the foundation may request a site visit to validate the information given in the self-assessment. The scheme is not focused on products, customers or services but is a total quality scheme which attempts to address all aspects of quality within an organization including:

- Leadership
- Policy and strategy
- People management
- Resources
- Processes
- Customer satisfaction
- People satisfaction
- Impact on society
- Business results

Each of the categories can be further split down, describing the major issues to be addressed. Camison (1996) researched the application of the EFQM to hotels

Malcolm Baldrige National Quality Award

The Malcolm Baldrige National Quality Award (MBNQA) originated in the United States in 1987 as a government-backed accreditation programme (Ghobadian and Woo 1996). Ghobadian and Woo (1996: 23) describe it as 'an audit framework which enables organizations to perform internal self-assessment and identify the areas that need improvements and the values they need to enact in order to attain a culture and operating system capable of attaining CI and customer satisfaction'. The award is regarded as 'standard for performance excellence' (Lau et al. 2004: 705).

The MBNQA criteria are based on seven dimensions that are used to assess the performance of the organization. The total score is 1000 points distributed as:

1. Leadership (95 points);
2. Information and analysis (75 points);
3. Strategic quality planning (60 points);

4. Human resources development and management (150 points);
5. Management of process quality (140 points);
6. Quality and operational results (180 points); and
7. Customer focus and satisfaction (300 points).

Annually, there are two champions in each of three classes – manufacturing, service and small business. Evaluation of the candidates includes examining their documents, besides on-site visits to their operations. Garvin (1991: 80) proposes that the award 'has become *the* most important catalyst for transforming American business', just a few years after its introduction. However, Leonard and McAdam (2002) observe that some of the Quality Gurus – Deming and Crosby – are less convinced about its impact.

The Ritz-Carlton hotel company won the MBNQA in 1992 and 1999 (Bacon and Pugh 2003). Ritz-Carlton remains the pioneer and single hospitality establishment to achieve this. It is also the first and only service organization to win the award twice (Cai and Hobson 2004). In 2000, the Canadian company Delta Hotels acquired the National Quality Institute's (NQI's) 'Canada Awards for Excellence' (Pallet et al. 2003).

Six sigma

Six sigma is not new – it originated in the1980s (Klefsjö et al. 2001). It was developed by Motorola (Antony 2006; Behara et al. 1995). It can be defined as a 'business improvement strategy used to improve profitability, to drive out waste, to reduce quality costs and improve the effectiveness and efficiency of all operations or processes that meet or even exceed customers' needs and expectations' (Antony and Coronado 2001: 119). Specifically it is a '[statistical] term that refers to 3.4 defects per million opportunities (DPMO), where sigma is a term used to represent the variation about the average of any process'.

Behara et al. (1995: 9) observe that six sigma is an echo of Crosby's zero defects programme; however, six sigma is more of 'possible near-perfection'. Six sigma works not by chasing defects but by preventing their possible occurrences (Antony 2006). He identified that business strategy linked to six sigma was the major critical success factor for implementing the programme successfully. Antony (2006: 244) also notes that six sigma is very like TQM but argues it is better at 'achieving measurable and quantifiable financial returns to the bottom-line of an organisation'.

There are many advantages that businesses can gain from six sigma implementation: enhanced inter-departmental cooperation, promotion of proactive culture rather than reactive one, reduction of costs, reduction of variability, and more sound decisions can be rendered by management as it is based on facts (Antony 2004). Nonthaleerak and Hendry (2006) have reviewed literature on six sigma, identifying more than 200 studies. In the hospitality industry, Starwood has a global six sigma strategy – '[it] has helped increase our financial performance by improving the quality and consistency of our guests' experiences as well as those of our internal customers' (www.starwoodhotels. com 2007). The Intercontinental Hotels Group PLC (IHG), with the assistance of Xerox, adopted six sigma to overcome IT problems, thereby achieving cost savings of $1.2 M, and increasing customer satisfaction (www.xerox.com 2007).

Quality measurement techniques

There are three main methods used by the hospitality industry to monitor quality – mystery guest programme, customer satisfaction survey and quality audit. Each of these will now be explained and critiqued.

The mystery shopper or mystery guest

The 'mystery' customer, shopper or guest technique is used by some hospitality companies to monitor service standards. Mystery shoppers are trained personnel who buy a meal as a member of the public (i.e. without announcing themselves) or stay in a hotel and report the standard of service to head office. This procedure aims to evaluate the performance of the retail and service units within the firms (Finn and Kayandé 1999), to ensure consistent process and procedures (Wilson 2001). It was started in the 1940s, but became a sophisticated technique by the 1980s (Calvert 2005). It may be called 'secret, phantom, or anonymous consumer shopper' (Finn and Kayandé 1999). The financial sector was the first client of the mystery shopping service, followed by fast food chains and hotels (Erstad 1998). The volume of the mystery shopping business in the UK was estimated to be £20–30 million in 1996, with many sectors benefiting from it; financial services, governmental departments, leisure and travel and transport (Wilson 1998b).

Although the mystery shopper programme is used on a wide scale, there is little published about its details and stages (Wilson 1998a). Finn and Kayandé (1999) found that mystery shopping is more cost effective than customer surveys, considering the enhanced quality of the information it provides with regard to service quality, yet it is estimated to cost 10 times the costs of customer surveys. A key feature of the mystery shop is that it is carried out deliberately, with the aim to observe, evaluate and report. This is not present in customer surveys, which ask customers about their perceptions of an experience that has ended (Finn and Kayandé 1999).

There is usually a precisely laid out shopping or dining procedure, and observations may be reported on a standard form. Stopwatches may be used to measure the timing of service, and the food temperature may be determined with a probe thermometer. The steps needed to conduct the mystery shopper programme are demonstrated in Figure 13.1. The disguised shopper evaluates the physical facilities and the environment (tangibles) and also, most importantly, the shopping interaction (intangibles). Then s/he completes the evaluation form allowing the identification of the shortfalls and strengths in the performance of the shopped outlet (Baggs and Kleiner 1996; Finn and Kayandé 1999). The number of visits required per business unit is determined according to the objective of the evaluation and what is to be measured. Finn (2001) cites that 40 visits per unit is needed to benchmark service quality, and 10 visits for benchmarking a store environment may be needed. Consequently, that affects the costs associated with the scheme.

The mystery shopper programme may be managed in-house or outsourced to specialist firms. The use of internal shoppers may offer some advantages in terms of money savings and the high degree of the internal shoppers' knowledge of the company's goals and products. This, however, has its shortfalls, namely the possibility of unmasking the identity of the mystery shopper. Other drawbacks are the subjectivity of employees and the resistance of employees of such practice, not liking to be shopped by colleagues (Erstad 1998). The rapid growth in service organizations typically led to the use of external shoppers, as there were not enough internal shoppers to cover the increasing volume of business to be shopped. However, the shortcomings of outsourcing are the efforts and resources needed to gear up the external shoppers to perform the visits and the impact of shoppers' turnover on reliability (Erstad 1998).

To create an evaluation form, it is recommended to use the contributions of the front-line employees, which can be extracted through focus groups or by interviewing them. This helps to involve the staff in the programme and increases their sense of responsibility. Questions should be simple and open ended, focusing on the description of the process. The evaluation form

Step 1

The Objectives
Know what you want to get out of the shopping programme. The objectives should be related to having satisfied customers as well as satisfied employees. Mystery shopping is meant to reinforce positive behaviour and modify improper behaviour but not to punish.

Step 2

The Evaluation Form
Use employees to define and set the measurable standards to be met. Find out what customers value and incorporate these into the evaluation form.

Step 3

The Mystery Shopper
Select, inform, and train the mystery shopper in line with the company's objectives.

Step 4

The Evaluation
Produce an unbiased, mainly objective evaluation (but include a limited amount of subjective information) of the shopped unit.

Step 5

The Analysis
Identify gaps in the service delivery and determine origin.

Step 6

The Action Needed
Develop a reward and incentive scheme related to employee performance in mystery shopping programmes. Provide coaching to further develop employees' technical and behavioural skills. Work on the service delivery system if gaps exist because of poor design. Repeat the shopping experience.

Figure 13.1
The mystery shopping programme steps (*Source*: Erstad 1998).

can be produced in the form of a checklist, a service rating (which places value on overall standard) of service or a performance index, which gives points for certain actions (Erstad 1998).

The results of the visit can be produced in the form of reports with each report having a special focus matching the interests of its audience, such as employees, managers, top management, customers and suppliers (Wilson 1998a). Each may be interested in different ways and act upon the findings differently. All stakeholders need to be informed of the improvements adopted as a response to the findings (Erstad 1998). Two studies in hospitality were conducted in the United States. Beck and Miao (2003) investigated how the mystery shopper is operated and hotel senior management perceptions of the effectiveness of the scheme in assessing the service quality. Beck et al. (2004) aimed at developing and assessing the mystery shopper scheme at a U.S. Air Force base.

The threefold outcomes of the mystery shopping visits are as follows:

Act as a diagnostic tool: It can be used to highlight the main components of the service and the weakness areas that need to be remedied. This is revealed from the perspective of customers not as a result of a managerial assessment (Wilson 1998a).

To encourage, develop and motivate: The results of mystery shopping are used to appraise the service staff, to acknowledge those with high accomplishment, whether individuals or teams, and to reward them. This requires a systematic communication between the management and the staff, as they must be informed on what attributes they would be assessed and consequently rewarded (Wilson 1998a; Erstad 1998). This sends a message to the service staff that the programme is not about fault finding nor simply rewards for managers (Baggs and Kleiner 1996). In some instances, the feedback from the visit can be declared upon completion, before the shopper leaves the unit. Immediate reward can be given to the deserving staff member, serving to ground the seriousness of the programme (Erstad 1998). From the motivation perspective, Wilson (1998a) claimed that mystery shopping has limited impact in the long run. Although the service performance level rises with the initiating of the programme, it gradually becomes steady. To overcome this, some organizations would start a new programme, whilst others would halt it.

Assess competitiveness: Mystery shopping is used to benchmark the competitors and can be used to benchmark other firms in other lines of business. This may inspire new standards or help develop better standards (Finn and Kayandé 1999).

Employees can perform mystery visits to competitors. This approach provides an evaluation of the competitors and alerts the employers to the strengths and weaknesses of the competitors, and develops a sense of criticism in them (Erstad 1998).

However, mystery shopping is not without criticism. Covert observations as applied in the mystery shopper programme may worry some people and raise ethical concerns (Slack and Rowley 2001). Wilson (2001) described the use of mystery shoppers as 'using deception'. He mentions that observing people without notifying them is considered a privacy violation, so the service staff should be informed of the mystery programme. According to Shing and Spence (2002), mystery shopping is a means of competitor intelligence gathering, although it is practiced 'on the edge of the public domain' as information is readily available for whoever seeks it. But they express ethical concerns about dishonesty, misrepresentation and unapproved observation. Wilson (1998a) warns that when shopping at competitors, some ethical matters must be considered. A purchase is to be done not just an enquiry, and enquiries should be simple and not meticulous ones. Other ethical concerns may include assigning shoppers to evaluate interactions they do not approve of, for example, shopping a casino or a bar (Calvert 2005). The world Association of Opinion and Marketing Research (ESOMAR) provides guidelines and instructions on the usage of the mystery shops and introducing them in business (Wilson 2001).

There are a number of advantages of this approach to quality measurement. Finn (2001) argues that the use of customer satisfaction surveys and SERVQUAL in businesses classified as 'hit-and-run', such as fast food and petrol stations, is not practical – the mystery shopper is more suitable as a measurement tool in such operations. Roberts and Campbell (2007: 59) claim that using the mystery shopper 'have been shown to produce accurate and stable results even with a small number of observations'. They argue that this approach compared to other means of customer surveys is heedful, and its deliberate observation is a distinctive feature. Wilson (2001) suggests that 'only' mystery shopper is able to evaluate the service performance against the service standards, especially the factors related to the staff behaviour. Although Finn (2001) admits it is expensive to conduct a mystery shopper programme, he claims it as 'cost-effective tool' to obtain 'reliable' assessment.

The major disadvantage of a mystery shopper programme is the sample size. Judgements cannot be based on one or two visits to an operation as this is not valid statistically (Calvert

2005), and management cannot rely on such information to make decision (Finn 2001). Reliability is very crucial in a mystery shopping programme, as the outcomes of such a programme would provide management with insights of what requires their attention.

To increase its reliability, the shoppers must be selected carefully and be provided with the proper amount and quality of training (Wilson 1998a). Such training may be done through video tapes, photographs and simulations (Wilson 1998a). The shoppers' skills of data gathering can be improved through training in the situations they will experience. Data-gathering training concentrates on the attributes to be observed, and the keeping and recording of data which cannot be done while carrying out the visit itself (Calvert 2005). Training may also include memory training and testing; whilst technology may help with this, as the use of 'aides-memoir' may be allowed to help in recording data (Wilson 1998a). The service situation involves two parts: the service provider and the customer. The quality of that experience depends on the two sides. The personal attributes of the mystery shopper may have an influence over the service interaction. However, this should not represent a problem as the rule is to treat all customers the same regardless of their characteristics (Wilson 1998a).

Customer satisfaction surveys

Customer satisfaction has been heavily studied with more than 15,000 published papers in trade and academic journals since 1960. However, it remains an 'elusive concept' (Ekinci 2004). Baggs and Kleiner (1996) argue that customer satisfaction could determine the success of any company. Thus, measuring customer satisfaction is very crucial as, based on the outcomes of the evaluation, the company can identify which areas should be developed and compare its performance against its competitors. Competition is a major driver behind the interest in customer satisfaction (Fečiková 2004); the growing globalization and relationship marketing are also contributing to such pursuit (Veloutsou et al. 2005). Ensuring customer satisfaction is the means to stand out from competitors and to achieve long-term profitability. However, not having highly competitive market does not dictate that customer satisfaction is not a major concern (Jones and Sasser 1995). Companies are obliged to satisfy their customers, so customer satisfaction can be seen as 'the glue that holds various corporate functions together and directs resource allocation' (Peterson and Wilson 1992: 61).

Pizam and Ellis (1999) suggest there are nine salient customer satisfaction theories:

1. Expectancy disconfirmation;
2. Assimilation or cognitive dissonance;
3. Contrast;
4. Assimilation–contrast;
5. Equity;
6. Attribution;
7. Comparison-level;
8. Generalized negativity; and
9. Value-precept.

However, the expectancy disconfirmation theory of Oliver (1997) is the most adopted one (Pizam and Ellis 1999).

Oliver (1997: 13) defined satisfaction as 'the consumer's fulfilment response. It is a judgement that a product or service feature, or the product or service itself, provided (or is providing) a *pleasurable* level of consumption-related fulfilment, including levels of under- or overfulfilment'. He notes that 'satisfaction is a post usage phenomenon, purely experiential and results from a comparative process'. Understanding the way customers form their satisfaction helps to measure it. Oliver (1997) developed a model based on the expectancy disconfirmation in which a comparison between performance and expectations yields objective disconfirmation, leading to the formation of subjective disconfirmation and that result in satisfaction.

Measuring customer satisfaction can be done through direct methods such as customer satisfaction surveys or indirect methods like customer re-purchase profiling (Adebanjo 2001). Other market research techniques that can be used are:

1. Customer satisfaction surveys methodologies (Fečiková 2004); mail surveys, telephone surveys, call back and survey through personal contact (Babbar 1992);
2. Focus group (Fečiková 2004; Babbar 1992);
3. Standardized packages for monitoring customer satisfaction (Fečiková 2004);
4. Evaluation and suggestion slips (Babbar 1992);
5. Delphi or nominal group method (Babbar 1992);
6. Various computer softwares (Fečiková 2004).

Using different ways to collect the customer satisfaction information – such as telephone, mail or personal contact – may influence the level of reported satisfaction, with personal and telephone surveys raising the satisfaction level by almost

10–12% than self-administered surveys (Peterson and Wilson 1992). Response to mail surveys is dependent on the memory of the respondent and even if the time lapse between the service encounter and the survey is small, this diminishes its accuracy and reliability. Other problems associated with mail surveys are non-response rates as generally mail surveys yield the lowest response rates (Lin and Jones 1997). To overcome this, a reply paid envelope may induce respondents to participate in the survey. Cost and multiple mailings are other problems associated with this type of survey, and this may explain why mail surveys are not as popular as they were (Babbar 1992). There are limitations and problems with every technique; selecting the technique is not the sole problem; of more importance is that they are 'being used infrequently and often at arbitrary points in time by management' (Babbar 1992: 41).

Danaher and Haddrell (1996) identify that there are more than 40 different scales to measure customer satisfaction for products or service. Scales used in customer satisfaction surveys are classified into two main categories: single and multi-item scales; other scales used in consumer research include 'rank order, constant sum, graphical, Likert, semantic differential, paired comparison and staple scales' (Danaher and Haddrell 1996: 6). The scales can be sorted in three classes:

- Performance scales – poor, fair, good and excellent;
- Disconfirmation scales – worse than expected to better than expected;
- Satisfaction scales – very dissatisfied to very satisfied.

Lin and Jones (1997) stated that there are four methodological issues related to the customer surveys.

1. *Sampling structure*: the sample needs to be representative of the population of the customer, so the way the sample is selected is very crucial. The sample size, target population and the segment of the target population are all factors to be considered when sampling.
2. *Enhancing quality of survey data and tool*: timeliness, completeness, usability and accuracy are the crucial characteristics of data quality. Response error and procedures error are two kinds of errors associated with measurement using customer satisfaction surveys. Improving the quality of the surveys instrument can be done through eradicating scales which demonstrate undesirable psychometric qualities.
3. *Non-response*: this is common to all customer surveys. Low response rates diminish the validity and generalizability of a

survey. To improve response rates, incentives can be offered to respondents, and if that does not help, 'post-survey adjustments' can be adopted.
4. *Reporting and interpretation*: customers can be segmented into certain clusters and that should be considered when designing surveys. Multi-item scales help to cover broad concepts and increase the reliability but should be analysed carefully. The time lapse between the customer experience and the survey makes it hard to rectify failures identified by the customers. Applying wrong statistical analysis yields false results that may mislead management.

Peterson and Wilson (1992: 62) note that 'virtually all self-reports of customer satisfaction possess a distribution in which a majority of the responses indicate that customers are satisfied and the distribution itself is negatively skewed'. They identified this as a 'striking characteristic' and pointed out reasons for this. First, it may be truly the perception of the customers. Second, satisfaction may have a distribution different than the normal distribution, due to the antecedents of satisfaction. Third, the customer satisfaction distribution may be influenced by the 'artifacts of the research methodologies', that is the instruments used to conduct the research. Peterson and Wilson (1992) also examined several factors that may cause this, such as response rate bias, data collection mode bias, question form, question context, measurement timing, response styles and mood. They concluded that 'unless viable unobtrusive measuring devices become available, it is probably not possible to measure "true satisfaction". True satisfaction is probably so intertwined with both intrapersonal characteristics and methodological considerations that it may never be possible to disentangle them' (Peterson and Wilson 1992: 69). Lin and Jones (1997) also expressed concerns over the usage of the customer satisfaction surveys such as disposition to express a high degree of satisfaction, deficiency of satisfaction scales, the incremental employment of surveys and customers reporting being over-surveyed.

Customer satisfaction surveys have been compared to the mystery shopper. Wilson (2001) notes that the customer satisfaction surveys are implemented to measure the results of the service encounter, while mystery shopper measures the process. He conducted interviews with four service organizations that reported that they cannot depend solely on customer satisfaction surveys to discover and rectify failures in the service delivery process as customer satisfaction surveys do not yield adequate information. Interviewing service managers revealed that they stressed that customer satisfaction levels remain relatively constant and therefore they are not utile (Wilson 2001).

Rust and Oliver (1994) propose that quality and satisfactions have different meaning. While some researchers consider that satisfaction is antecedent to quality, there is another group who argue that service quality is antecedent to the satisfaction, while others see that 'there is a non-recursive relationship'. Oliver (1997) cites some conceptual differences between quality and satisfaction:

- *Experience*: quality perceptions do not require consumption, while satisfaction is based on experiencing the service.
- *Attributes and standards*: the elements inherent in quality judgements are quite particular, whether they are cues or properties. Satisfaction judgements, however, can be brought about from any factor, quality related or not.
- *Expectations and standards*: expectations for quality are founded on ideals or 'excellence' perceptions; satisfaction judgements are built on many non-quality factors: needs, equity or fairness.
- *Cognition or affect:* while quality judgements are principally cognitive, satisfaction is made up of cognition and affect.
- *Conceptual antecedents*: 'Quality has fewer *conceptual* antecedents, although personal and impersonal communications play a major role'. Satisfaction is affected by a 'number of cognitive and affective processes including equity, attribution and emotion' (Oliver 1997: 179).
- *Short- or long-term temporal focus*: quality endures over longer periods; quality is linked to a certain product or service in a *'global sense'*, while satisfaction is *'experience specific'*.

Both customer satisfaction and service quality are based on the comparison between pre-consumption expectations and post-consumption perceptions (Oh and Parks 1997). Oh (1999) examined the expectancy-disconfirmation principle in SERVQUAL and customer satisfaction surveys. He argues that expectancy and disconfirmation in SERVQUAL aims to 'describe' the perceived service quality, whereas in the customer satisfaction, it tries to 'explain and theorize' a consumption process. Oh and Parks (1997: 44) state that the distinctive difference between the two constructs is that customer satisfaction is seen as 'a result of customers' *subjective* comparison between expectation and performance, while SQ is viewed as the researcher's *objective* comparison between the two components'. However, measuring expectations subject-ively in the expectancy disconfirmation model proved to be more

327

valid than in the objective measurement of SERVQUAL (Oh 1999). Ekinci (2004) investigated the relationship between customer satisfaction and service quality, attitudes, self-concept congruence, desires congruence and behavioural intentions. His findings showed that service quality evaluation results in customer satisfaction, a reverse relationship was not sustained and the overall attitude is affected by customer satisfaction rather than service quality.

Quality audits

Quality audits can be used either to test hypotheses or substantiate hunches about the organization's service effectiveness, or they can be used as part of a total quality improvement programme. An audit has been defined by Juran and Gryna (1980) as 'independent evaluation of service quality to determine its fitness for use and conformance to specifications'. As we shall see, such an audit attempts to overcome the problems we have identified above by ensuring objectivity through independence from the organization and by expert and articulate evaluation of the experience through observation and participation. Prior to any such audit taking place, management and auditor will discuss and agree the objectives, methodology, scheduling and reporting procedures of the study.

A quality audit is a systematic appraisal of a service process. A checklist of items is drawn up and compared by the author with each aspect of the service. It is a quick and effective way (often the only practicable way) to get an impression of service quality, and it is therefore used by many types of service organizations. Audits may be conducted either by in-house personnel or by specialized consultants. There are two main types: auditing by department and customer perception audits.

In the case of hotels, Haywood (1983) suggests that the nature of the service is so complex that an audit cannot be made of the entire service experience. Therefore, it is necessary to establish the objectives of the audit. A commonly used method is Pareto analysis, in which every possible problem is listed and then ranked in their order of importance. A second technique, advocated by Wyckoff (1984) is 'fishbone' analysis which helps to identify cause and effect.

Once the objectives are established, the next step is for the auditor to adopt the consumer's frame of reference. This is done by familiarization with the profile of typical customers in terms of their age, background, occupation, income and so on.

From this, some judgements can be made concerning their life style and likely attitudes towards the service provision. Some attempt will also be made to assess the purpose and importance of the service, that is for instance in a hotel stay for pleasure or business purposes.

As with other forms of measurement, there are advantages and disadvantages with audits. Jones and Merricks (1994) argue that the advantages are:

- They are consumer orientated;
- Auditors take a consumer's perspective but can explain themselves to management in a way that management can understand;
- The audit is independent and therefore objective;
- It provides a wealth of detail;
- The data collected is actionable, that is to say management can act to correct below-standard performance.

The disadvantages are (Jones and Merricks 1994):

- In terms of statistical sampling, an audit does not provide any valid evidence of actual guest's level of satisfaction;
- There may be bias on the part of the auditor;
- The auditor's experience is unique and may provide misleading evidence;
- An audit can only be carried out infrequently due to its complexity and cost;
- The detail of the audit may result in results that do 'not see the wood from the trees'.

Audit by department is mainly concerned with the way in which the service conforms with management's perception of the operation, that is with gaps 1 and 2 of the service provision model of Brogowicz et al. (1990). Audit checklists therefore tend to emphasize the departmental nature of the foodservice outlet. For example, they may involve a detailed study of kitchen hygiene or an evaluation of the behaviour, dress and attitudes of service personnel. If access is regarded as an auditable issue, it will tend to be associated with separate departments, for example the grounds and car park, or disabled facilities at reception.

An organizational quality audit is defined as 'an examination of an organization's arrangements to control and ensure the quality of its products or services' (Øvretveit 1993: 75). Quality audits are conducted to help organization to compete in markets and as evidence that they are pursuing quality (Øvretveit

1993). Evaluating the effectiveness of the QA endeavours and ensuring the compliance with quality standards such as ISO 9000 have given quality audits its salient task (Karapetrovic and Willborn 2000).

According to Fuentes (1999), audits are known as 'performance protocols'. They try to measure numerically the performance of the professional during a specific process. Fuentes (1999: 231) regards this as implementing the 'Acceptable Levels of Quality' and 'the ultimate aim of audits is not to exceed the minimum requirements, that is to say, at no time is it intended is improve the quality of the processes'. This is contradictory to Karapetrovic and Willborn (2000: 679) who suggest that 'many authors argue that one of the primary purposes of audits is continuous improvement'.

Summary and conclusion

This chapter has reviewed five main ways in which quality can be managed in foodservice operations. Moving on from QI, through QC and QA, to TQM and CI, these strategies increase in complexity and sophistication. Organizations that have adopted a strategic approach to quality can also seek external recognition of their quality. The industry has consistently adopted certain ways of measuring quality, through mystery guest, customer surveys and quality audits, albeit these are increasingly being questioned as the most effective approach.

Acknowledegment

The author would like to acknowledge the contribution of the Editor in drafting this chapter.

References

Adams, C. E. (2002) Hazard analysis and critical control point-original "spin", *Food Control*, 13, 6–7, 355–358

Adebanjo, D. (2001) Understanding customer satisfaction – a UK food industry case study, *British Food Journal*, 103, 1, 36–45

Akbaba, A. (2006) Measuring service quality in the hotel industry: a study in a business hotel in Turkey, *International Journal of Hospitality Management*, 25, 2, 170–192

Anand, K. N. (1997) Quality: an evolving concept, *Total Quality Management*, 8, 4, 195–200

Antony, J. (2004) Six Sigma in the UK service organisations: results from a pilot survey, *Managerial Auditing Journal*, 19, 8, 1006–1013

Antony, J. (2006) Six sigma for services processes, *Business Process Management*, 12, 2, 234–248

Antony, J. and Coronado, R. B. (2001) A strategy for survival, *Manufacturing Engineer*, 80, 3, 119–121

Azanza, M. (2006) HACCP certification of food services in Philippine inter-island passenger vessels, *Food Control*, 17, 2, 93–101

Babbar, S. (1992) A dynamic model for continuous improvement in the management of service quality, *International Journal of Operations and Production Management*, 12, 2, 38–48

Bacon, T. R. and Pugh, D. G. (2003) Ritz-Carlton and EMC: The gold standards in operational behavioral differentiation, *Journal of organizational Excellence*, 23, 2, 61–76

Baggs, B. C. and Kleiner, B. H. (1996) How to measure customer service effectively, *Managing Service Quality*, 6, 1, 36–39

Baldacchino, G. (1995) Total quality management in a luxury hotel: a critique of practice, *International Journal of Hospitality Management*, 14, 1, 67–78

Barker, R. L. (1990) SPC and total quality management, *Total Quality Management*, 1, 2, 183–196

Barnes, J. and Mitchell, R. T. (2000) HACCP in the United Kingdom, *Food Control*, 11, 5, 383–386

Beck, J., Lalopa J. and Hall, J. (2004) Insuring quality service: training mystery shoppers, *Journal of Human Resources in Hospitality and Tourism*, 2, 2, 41–56

Beck, J. and Miao, L. (2003) Mystery shopping in lodging properties as a measurement of service quality, *Journal of Quality Assurance in Hospitality and Tourism*, 4, 1/2, 1–21

Behara, R. S., Fontenot, G. F. and Gresham, A. (1995) Customer satisfaction measurement and analysis using six sigma, *International Journal of Quality and Reliability Management*, 12, 3, 9–18

Billy, T. J. (2002) HACCP – a work in progress, *Food Control*, 13, 6–7, 359–362

Breiter, D. and Bloomquist, P. (1998) TQM in American hotels: an analysis of application, *Cornell Hotel and Restaurant Administration Quarterly*, 39, 1, 26–33

Breiter, D., Tyink, S. A. and Corey-Tuckwell, S. (1995) Bergstrom hotels: a case study in quality, *International Journal of Contemporary Hospitality Management*, 7, 6, 14–18

Brogowicz, A. A., Delene, L. M. and Lyth, D. M. (1990) A synthesised service quality model with managerial implications,

International Journal of Service Industries Management, 1, 1, 27–45

Buttle, F. (1996) SERVQUAL: review, critique, research agenda, *European Journal of Marketing*, 30, 1, 8–32

Cai, L. A. and Hobson, J. S. P. (2004) Making hotel brands work in a competitive environment, *Journal of Vacation Marketing*, 10, 3, 197–208

Calvert, P. (2005) It's mystery: mystery shopping in New Zealand's public libraries, *Library Review*, 54, 1, 24–35

Camison, C. (1996) Total quality management in hospitality: an application of the EFQM model, *Tourism Management*, 17, 3, 191–201

Carman, J. M. (1990) Consumer perceptions of service quality: an assessment of the SERVQUAL dimensions, *Journal of Retailing*, 66, 1, 33–55

Cronin, J. J. Jr. and Taylor, S. A. (1992) Measuring service quality: a reexamination and extension, *Journal of Marketing*, 56, 3, 55–68

Cronin, J. J. Jr. and Taylor, S. A. (1994) SERVPERF versus SERVQUAL: reconciling performance-based and perceptions-minus-expectations measurement of service quality, *Journal of Marketing*, 58, 1, 125–131

Crosby, P. (1984) *Quality Without Tears: The Art of Hassle-Free Management*, McGraw-Hill: New York, NY

Crosby, P. B. (1979) *Quality is Free*, McGraw-Hill: New York, NY

Danaher, P. J. and Haddrell, V. (1996) A comparison of question scales used for measuring customer satisfaction, *International Journal of Service Industry Management*, 7, 4, 4–26

Davies, B., Baron, S., Gear, T. and Read, M. (1999) Measuring and managing service quality, *Marketing Intelligence and Planning*, 17, 1, 33–40

Ehiri, J. E., Morris, G. P. and McEwen, J. (1995) Implementation of HACCP in food businesses: the way ahead, *Food Control*, 6, 6, 341–345

Ekinci, Y. (2002) A Review of the theoretical debates on the measurement of service quality: implications for hospitality research, *Journal of Hospitality and Tourism Research*, 26, 3, 199–216

Ekinci, Y. (2004) An investigation of the determinants of customer satisfaction, *Tourism Analysis*, 8, 2–4, 197–203

Ekinci, Y., Prokopaki, P. and Cobanoglu, C. (2003) Service quality in Cretan accommodations: marketing strategies for the UK holiday market, *International Journal of Hospitality Management*, 22, 1, 47–66

Erstad, M. (1998) Mystery shopping programmes and human resources management, *International Journal of Contemporary Hospital Management*, 10, 1, 34–38

Eves, A. and Dervisi, P. (2005) Experiences of the implementation and operation of hazard analysis critical control points in the food service sector, *International Journal of Hospitality Management*, 24, 1, 3–19

Farkas, D. F. and Snyder, O. P. (1991) How to describe a food process for quality control, *Journal of Foodservice Systems*, 6, 147–153

Fečiková, I. (2004) An index method for measurement of customer satisfaction, *The TQM Magazine*, 16, 1, 57–66

Finn, A. (2001) Mystery shopper benchmarking of durable-goods chains and stores, *Journal of Service Research*, 3, 4, 310–320

Finn, A. and Kayandé, U. (1999) Unmasking a phantom: a psychometric assessment of mystery shopping, *Journal of Retailing*, 75, 2, 195–217

Fuentes, C. M. (1999) Measuring hospital service quality: a methodological study, *Managing Service Quality*, 9, 4, 230–239

Gagnon, B., McEachern, V. and Bray, S. (2000) The role of the Canadian government agency in assessing HACCP, *Food Control*, 11, 5, 359–364

Garvin, D. A. (1987) Competing on the eight dimensions of quality, *Harvard Business Review*, 65, 60, 101–109

Garvin, D. A. (1991) How the Baldrige award really works, *Harvard Business Review*, 69, 6, 80–93

Ghobadian, A., Speller, S. and Jones, M. (1994) Service quality: concepts and models, *International Journal of Quality and Reliability Management*, 11, 9, 43–66

Ghobadian, A. and Woo, H. S. (1996) Characteristics, benefits and shortcomings of four major quality awards, *International Journal of Quality and Reliability Management*, 13, 2, 10–44

Harrington, D. and Akehurst, G. (1996) An exploratory investigation into managerial perceptions of service quality in UK hotels, *Progress in Tourism and Hospitality Research*, 2, 2, 135–150

Haywood, K. M. (1983) Assessing the quality of hospitality services, *International Journal of Hospitality Management*, 2, 4, 165–177

Herbert, D., Curry, A. and Angel, L. (2003) Use of quality tools and techniques in services, *The Service Industry Journal*, 23, 4, 61–80

Heung, V. C. S., Wong, M. Y. and Qu, H. (2000) Airport-restaurant service quality in Hong Kong: an application of SERVQUAL, *Cornell Hotel and Restaurant Administration Quarterly*, 41, 3, 86–96

Hilton, J. (2002) Reducing foodborne disease: meeting the food standard agency's targets, *Nutrition & Food Science*, 32, 2, 46–50

Hsieh, Y-M. and Hsieh, A-T. (2001) Enhancement of service quality with job standardisation, *Service Industries Journal*, 21, 3, 147–166

Ingram, H. and Daskalakis, G. (1999) Measuring quality gaps in hotels: the case of Crete, *International Journal of Contemporary Hospitality Management*, 11, 1, 24–30

Jones, P. (2007) From the bottom up: operations management in the hospitality industry, In Brotherton, B. (Ed.), *Handbook of Hospitality Research*, Sage: London, UK

Jones, P. and Cheek, P. (1997) Service quality: an evaluation of approaches to measuring actual performance against standards in the hospitality industry, *6th CHME National Research Conference*, Oxford Brookes University

Jones, P. and Dent, M. (1994) Lessons in consistency: statistical process control in Forte Plc, *The TQM Magazine*, 6, 1, 18–23

Jones, P. and Merricks, P. (1994) *The Management of Foodservice Operations*, Casell: London, UK

Jones, P. and Riggott, G. (1992) TQM in five star hotels – old style hospitality or modern day operations management? *International Operations Management Conference*, Operations Management Association (UK), University of Manchester

Jones, P. A. (1983) The restaurant – a place for quality control and product maintenance, *International Journal of Hospitality Management*, 2, 2, 93–100

Jones, T. O. and Sasser, W. E. (1995) Why satisfied customers defect, *Harvard Business Review*, 73, 6, 88–91

Juran, J. M. (2000) How to think about quality, In Juran, J. M. and Godfrey, A. B. (Eds.), *Juran's Quality Handbook*, 5th edition, McGraw-Hill: New York, NY

Juran, J. M. and Gryna, F. M. (1980) *Quality Planning and Analysis*, McGraw Hill: New York, NY

Juwaheer, T. D. (2004) Exploring international tourists' perceptions of hotel operations by using a modified SERVQUAL approach – a case study of Mauritius, *Managing Service Quality*, 14, 5, 350–364

Karapetrovic, S. and Willborn, W. (2000) Quality assurance and effectiveness of audit systems, *International Journal of Quality and Reliability Management*, 17, 6, 679–703

King, C. A. (1984) Service-oriented quality control, *Cornell Hotel and Restaurant Administration Quarterly*, 25, 3, 92–98

Kivela, J., Lam, M. L. and Inbakaran, R. (2002) Food safety in school catering in the People's Republic of China, *International Journal of Contemporary Hospitality Management*, 14, 6, 301–312

Klefsjö, B., Wikland, H. and Edgeman, R. L. (2001) Six sigma seen as a methodology for total quality management, *Measuring Business Excellence*, 5, 1, 31–35

Knutson, B., Stevens, P. and Patton, M. (1995) Dineserv: measuring service quality in quick service, casual/theme and fine dining restaurants, *Journal of Hospitality and Leisure Marketing*, 3, 2, 35–44

Knutson, B., Stevens, P., Wullaert, C., Patton, M. and Yokoyama, F. (1991) LODGSERVE: a service quality index for the lodging industry, *Hospitality Research Journal*, 14, 3, 277–284

Kokkinakis, E. N. and Fragkiadakis, G. A. (2007) HACCP effect on microbiological quality of minimally processed vegetables: a survey in six mass-catering establishments, *International Journal of Food Science and Technology*, 42, 1, 18–23

Kolarik, W. J. (1995) *Creating Quality: Concepts, Systems, Strategies, and Tools*, McGraw Hill: New York, NY

Lau, R. S. M., Zhao, X. and Xiao, M. (2004) Assessing quality management in China with MBNQA criteria, *International Journal of Quality and Reliability Management*, 21, 7, 699–713

Leonard, D. and McAdam, R. (2002) The role of the business excellence model in operational and strategic decision making, *Management Decision*, 40, 1, 17–25

Lin, B. and Jones, C. A. (1997) Some issues in conducting customer satisfaction surveys, *Journal of Marketing Practice: Applied Marketing Science*, 3, 1, 4–13

Lockwood, A., Baker, M. and Ghillyer, A. (1996) *Quality Management in Hospitality: Best Practice in Action*, Cassell: London, UK

Lowson, R. H. (2002) *Strategic Operations Management: The New Competitive Advantage*, Routledge: London, UK

Maher, D. (2001) Integrated software for hygiene management, *Nutrition & Food Science*, 31, 1, 27–30

Morrison, P., Caffin, N. and Wallace, R. (1998) Small establishments present challenge for Australian food safety code, *International Journal of Contemporary Hospitality Management*, 10, 3, 101–106

Mortimore, S. (2001) How to make HACCP really work in practice, *Food Control*, 12, 4, 209–215

Motarjemi, Y. (2000) Regulatory assessment of HACCP: a FAO/WHO Consultation on the role of government agencies in assessing HACCP, *Food Control*, 11, 5, 341–344

Nield, K. and Kozak, M. (1999) Quality certification in the hospitality industry: analysing the benefit of ISO9000, *Cornell Hotel and Restaurant Administration Quarterly*, 40, 2, 40–45

Nonthaleerak, P. and Hendry, L. C. (2006) Six sigma: literature review and future research areas, *International Journal of Six Sigma and Competitive Advantage*, 2, 2, 105–161

O'Donnell, C. D. (1991) Implementation of HACCP at Orval Kent Food Company Inc., *Foodservice Research International*, 6, 3, 197–207

Oh, H. (1999) Service quality, customer satisfaction, and customer value: a holistic perspective, *International Journal of Hospitality Management*, 18, 1, 67–82

Oh, H. and Parks, S. C. (1997) Customer satisfaction and service quality: a critical review of the literature and research implications for the hospitality industry, *Hospitality Research Journal*, 20, 3, 35–64

Oliver, R. L. (1997) *Satisfaction: A Behavioural Perspective on the Consumer*, McGraw-Hill: New York, NY

Øvretveit, J. A. (1993) Auditing and awards for service quality, *International Journal of Service Industry Management*, 4, 2, 74–84

Pallet, W. J., Taylor, W. W. and Jayawardena, C. (2003) People and quality: the case of Delta Hotels, *International Journal of Contemporary Hospitality Management*, 15, 6, 349–351

Panisello, P. J. and Quantick, P. C. (2001) Technical barriers to Hazard Analysis Critical Control Point (HACCP), *Food Control*, 12, 3, 165–173

Parasuraman, A., Zeithaml, V. A. and Berry, L. L. (1988) SERVQUAL: a multiple-item scale for measuring consumer perceptions of service quality, *Journal of Retailing*, 64, 1, 12–40

Peterson, R. A. and Wilson, W. R. (1992) Measuring customer satisfaction facts and artifacts, *Journal of the Academy of Marketing Science*, 20, 1, 61–71

Pizam, A. and Ellis, T. (1999) Customer satisfaction and its measurement in hospitality enterprises, *International Journal of Contemporary Hospitality Management*, 11, 7, 326–339

Raajpoot, N. A. (2002) TANGSERV: a multiple item scale for measuring tangible quality in the foodservice industry, *Journal of Foodservice Business Research*, 5, 2, 109–127

Reeves, C. A. and Bednar, D. A. (1994), Defining quality: alternatives and implications, *Academy of Management Review*, 19, 3, 419–445

Riswadkar, A. V. (2000) An introduction to HACCP, *Professional Safety*, 45, 6, 33–36

Roberts, B. and Campbell, R. C. (2007) Being new-customer friendly: determinants of service perceptions in retail banking, *International Journal of Bank Marketing*, 25, 1, 56–67

Robson, M. (1983) *Quality Circles: A Practical Guide*, Gower: Aldershot, UK

Rust, R. T. and Oliver, R. L. (1994) Service quality: insights and managerial implications from the frontier, In Rust, R. T. and Oliver, R. L. (Eds.), *Service Quality: New Directions in Theory and Practice*, Sage: London, UK, 1–20

Shing, M. N. K. and Spence, L. (2002) Investigating the limits of competitive intelligence gathering: is mystery shopping ethical? *Business Ethics: A European Review*, 11, 4, 343–353

Slack, F. and Rowley, J. (2001) Observation: perspectives on research methodologies for leisure managers, *Management Research News*, 24, 1/2, 35–42

Smith, G. F. (1993) The meaning of quality, *Total Quality Management*, 4, 3, 235–244

Soriano, D. R. (1999) Total quality management: applying the European model to Spain's urban hotels, *Cornell Hotel and Restaurant Administration Quarterly*, 40, 1, 54–59

Soriano, J. M., Rico, H., Molto, J. C. and Manes, J. (2002) Effect of introduction of HACCP on the microbiological quality of some restaurant meals, *Food Control*, 13, 4–5, 253–261

Souness, R. (2000) HACCP in Australian food control, *Food Control*, 11, 5, 353–357

Sperber, W. H. (2005a) HACCP doesn't work from farm to table, *Food Control*, 16, 6, 511–514

Sperber, W. H. (2005b) HACCP and transparency, *Food Control*, 16, 6, 505–509

Stevens, P., Knutson, B. and Patton, M. (1995) DINESERVE: a tool for measuring service quality in restaurants, *Cornell Hotel and Restaurant Administration Quarterly*, 36, 2, 56–60

Sun, Y. M. and Ockerman, H. W. (2005) A review of the needs and current applications of hazard analysis and critical control point (HACCP) system in foodservice areas, *Food Control*, 16, 4, 325–332

Taguchi, G. and Clausing, D. (1990) Robust quality, *Harvard Business Review*, 68, 1, 65–75

Taylor, E. (2001) HACCP in small companies: benefit or burden? *Food Control*, 12, 4, 217–222

Taylor, E. and Kane, K. (2005) Reducing the burden of HACCP on SMEs, *Food Control*, 16, 10, 833–839

Taylor, E. and Taylor, J. Z. (2004) Perceptions of "the bureaucratic nightmare" of HACCP: a case study, *British Food Journal*, 106, 1, 65–72

Tsang, N. and Qu, H. (2000) Service quality in China's hotel industry: a perspective from tourists and hotel managers, *International Journal of Contemporary Hospitality Management*, 12, 5, 316–326

Veloutsou, C., Gilbert, G. R., Moutinho, L. A. and Goode, M. M. H. (2005) Measuring transaction-specific satisfaction in services: are the measures transferable across cultures? *European Journal of Marketing*, 39, 5/6, 606–628

Walker, J. R. and Salameh, T. T. (1990) The QA payoff, *The Cornell Hotel and Restaurant Administration Quarterly*, 30, 4, 57–59

Wilson, A. M. (1998a) The role of mystery shopping in the measurement of service performance, *Managing Service Quality*, 8, 6, 414–420

Wilson, A. M. (1998b) The use of mystery shopping in the measurement of service delivery, *The Service Industries Journal*, 18, 3, 148–163

Wilson, A. M. (2001) Mystery shopping: using deception to measure service performance, *Psychology & Marketing*, 18, 7, 721–734

Wilson, M., Murray, A. E., Black, M. A. and McDowell, D. A. (1997) The implementation of hazard analysis and critical control points in hospital catering, *Managing Service Quality*, 7, 3, 150–156

Worsfold, D. (2006) HACCP workshops – practical guidance for small fast food businesses, *Nutrition & Food Science*, 36, 1, 32–42

Wyckoff, D. D. (1984) New tools for achieving service quality, *Cornell Hotel and Restaurant Administration Quarterly*, 25, 3, 78–91

CHAPTER 14

Innovation management

Michael Ottenbacher

Associate Professor
School of Hospitality and Tourism Management
San Diego State University

Introduction

No matter which business you are involved in, innovation is important. Innovation is a critical issue for sustaining and growing firms, not only at the corporate level, but also at the small, entrepreneurial level. Much has been written in recent years about innovation and what it represents to countries, businesses and the hospitality industry. Innovation drives a country's economic engine. For example, Britain's weak economic performance in the early 1980s is attributed to its industries' insufficient design and innovation efforts (Ughanwa and Baker 1986). Conversely, Japan's economic strength after World War II was mainly due to the ability of Japanese industries to develop new, high-quality products that satisfied consumer needs (Barclay and Benson 1990). Hence, there is considerable historical evidence for Drucker's (1999) assumption regarding management challenges of the 21st century: that innovation is one core competence that every organization needs.

There are several benefits of innovation, but in the context of business and hospitality, the major benefit of successful innovation is to be, or become, more competitive (Ottenbacher and Gnoth 2005). Every product and service seems to go through a life cycle: it is born, goes through several phases and eventually dies as newer and better products and services come along.[1] Because all products and services eventually decline, organizations must develop new products and services to replace ageing ones. Innovation helps companies keep their product or service portfolio competitive and thereby achieve long-term competitive advantages. Moreover, a significant proportion of revenue and profits is likely to come from innovations introduced in the last few years. Innovations launched during the last five years of a company's existence generated nearly 40% of company sales and could be expected to account for 46% of company profits (Cooper and Kleinschmidt 1995). The less quantifiable benefits of successful innovations include enhancement of a business's reputation and increased loyalty of existing customers.

The innovation challenge

The environment of hospitality organizations is characterized by growing social and governmental constraints, downsizing, restructuring, technological change, competitive pressures,

---

[1] See also Chapter 15.

mature markets and changing customer demands. These challenging conditions mean that hospitality companies cannot afford to rely on past success; instead, they have to work on new services and nurture an innovative climate. Consequently, hospitality organizations must integrate continuously changing market trends into their portfolio. Hospitality organizations often compete in mature markets; therefore, innovation is important because it supports both growth in market share and growth into new markets. Cooper and Edgett (1999) stated the purpose of hospitality innovation even more vehemently. They argued that hospitality organizations have two choices: succeed at innovation or fail as a company.

The dilemma facing hospitality organizations is that although innovations are critical for the long- and short-term success of a firm, the failure rate of new products and services is high. The failure rate of product innovations is between 25% and 45%, depending on the industry (Cooper 2001). The average success rate for new service projects is 58% (Griffin 1997); in other words, four out of ten new services fail in the marketplace. But these failure rates do not include new product or service projects that were eliminated during the development process and before the launch. The high rate of innovation failure results in wasted time, money and human resources.

Aside from having a high failure rate, innovation can be risky and expensive. Not only small companies have problems in innovation management, but large and usually successful organizations have also had several new service failures. For example, Ford lost US$350 million on its Edsel car, and Texas Instruments lost US$660 million before withdrawing its Selectra Vision videodisc player. In the hospitality industry, McDonald's, with several billion in sales annually, had unsuccessful new menu offerings that had to be removed a short time after their introduction. McLean Deluxe, Arch Deluxe, fajitas and pizza have been marketplace flops for McDonald's restaurants in the past. Not only were these fiascos expensive and resources wasted, but the corporate image was damaged as well.

So what is the 'secret' of successful hospitality innovations? Actually, it is no secret at all; it is the combination of applying some creativity and a high degree of professional innovation management. Creativity is the ability to develop new, useful ideas and to discover new ways of looking at problems and opportunities. Innovation management is the ability to implement creative solutions to those problems and opportunities. Thus, having an innovative idea is not sufficient; converting the idea into a product or service is the critical aspect.

341

Although service innovation is an important aspect of hospitality management, there is relatively little published research on the topic. The body of literature focusing on innovation in the hospitality industry could still be regarded as being in its infancy. As a result, managers often rely on gut feeling, speculation and their own limited experience about the keys to innovation success. It is obvious that that there exists a need for further research and understanding in this field. Although many hospitality firms recognize the importance of innovation, it is not always clear how to create and design new hospitality services. The objective of this chapter is to increase hospitality managers' knowledge about hospitality innovation. It is hoped that this knowledge will enable managers to focus on innovation more strategically and professionally in order to reduce the high failure rate of new service projects. The following discussion will focus on five important hospitality innovation subjects. First, the term *innovation* will be defined. The next part will present the different types of service innovation by illustrating several classifications of new services. The third section will explain the service innovation process and the extent to which this is the same across all sectors. The fourth section looks at characteristics of innovation management and the factors that make hospitality innovations successful. The final part will focus on the differences between the innovation activities of small, independent hospitality firms versus those of large, chain-affiliated organizations.

Definition of innovation

There is some confusion about what exactly innovation means and what it characterizes. Often the words *invention* and *innovation* are used interchangeably, but although they are related, they have different meanings. Invention is only the beginning of a process of transforming an idea into effective use. Invention is part of innovation or the innovation process. The term *innovation* comes from the Latin *innovare*, meaning to make or create something new (Tidd et al. 1997).

Schumpeter (1934) was one of the first to develop a theory about innovation. He maintained that innovations – new ways of doing things, or unique or better combinations of production factors – are part of the entrepreneur's work. Schumpeter distinguished five areas in which companies can introduce innovations:

(a) generation of new or improved products
(b) introduction of new production processes

(c) development of new sales markets
(d) development of new supply markets
(e) reorganization or restructuring of the company.

According to Drucker (1985), innovation should be viewed and implemented as an opportunity that results in the creation of a new product or service or a change to a different one. An innovation can be an idea, practice, process or product, perceived as new by an individual who then transforms a new problem-solving idea into an application. Innovations are thus 'the outcome of the innovation process, which can be defined as the combined activities leading to new, marketable products and services and/or new production and delivery systems' (Burgelmann and Maidique 1996: 2).

Innovation comprises the two literature streams of new product development (NPD) and new service development (NSD). The NPD field focuses on the development of tangible goods, while NSD concentrates on the development of new service offerings. NSD involves developing new services such as financial, health care, telecommunications, information and leisure and hospitality services (Johne and Storey 1998). NSD is particularly important as developed countries shift from manufacturing to service economies. Service sectors have the highest growth rates, accounting for the greatest proportion of gross domestic product (Froehle et al. 2000), and have the highest levels of innovation (de Brentani 2001). The terms *service innovation* and *new service development* are often used interchangeably.

Classifications of innovation

Lovelock (1983) identified six classifications of service innovations, ranging from major innovations through to style changes. Gadrey et al. (1995) distinguished four types of new financial service developments: innovations in service products, architectural innovations that bundle or unbundle existing service products, modifications of an existing service product, and innovations in processes and organization for existing service products. Debackere et al. (1998) suggested three types of new services: breakthrough projects, platform projects and derivative projects (see Table 14.1).

The most popular classification of new products and services was developed by the consulting firm Booz-Allen and Hamilton (1982). Although Booz-Allen and Hamilton's categories were developed for manufactured goods, these definitions

Table 14.1 Classifications of new service innovation

Author(s)	Type of service innovation
Booz-Allen and Hamilton (1982)	● New to the world products/services ● New product/service lines ● Additions to existing product/service lines ● Improvements in/revisions to existing products/services ● Repositionings ● Cost reductions
Lovelock (1984)	● Major innovations (new service for markets as yet undefined) ● Start-up business (new services for a market that is already served by existing services that meet the same generic needs) ● New service for the currently served market (new services that are offered to the firm's existing customers) ● Service line extension (represents an augmentation of the existing service line or different way of service) ● Service improvements (changes in certain features for existing services currently on offer to the currently served market) ● Style changes (highly visible changes to existing services)
Gadrey et al. (1995)	● Innovations in service products ● Architectural innovations (bundling–unbundling of existing service products) ● Modifications of service products ● Innovations in processes and organization for existing service products
Debackere et al. (1998)	● Breakthrough projects (fundamental changes to existing products and processes) ● Platform projects (new product lines) ● Derivative projects (incremental changes to products and processes)
Avlonitis et al. (2001)	● New to the market services ● New to the company services ● New delivery processes ● Service modifications ● Service line extensions ● Service repositionings

have been adapted for service innovations. Service innovation can be any of the following:

1. *New-to-the-world services:* new services that are seen to be quite new in the eyes of customers because they are the first of their kind, creating entirely new markets (e.g. the introduction in the UK of the Little Chef Lodge concept, now known as Travelodge);
2. *New service lines:* services that are not new to the marketplace but are new to the firm (e.g. the development of the Courtyard concept by the Marriott hotel group);
3. *Additions to an existing service line:* new services that supplement a company's established service line and are not significantly new to the service producer, but may be new to the customers in the existing market segment (e.g. menu development in restaurant concepts);
4. *Improvements and revisions to an existing service:* new services that provide improved performance or greater perceived value and so replace existing services (e.g. hotel refurbishment, improved food quality);
5. *Repositionings:* existing services that are targeted to new markets or market segments (e.g. repositioning of the Ramada brand in 2004); or
6. *Cost reductions:* new services that provide similar performance at a lower cost of supply (e.g. introduction of buffet breakfast, better productivity).

While hospitality innovations can embrace the whole spectrum of service innovations, from new-to-the-world services to cost reductions, most hospitality-related innovations are modifications of existing services.

The innovation process

Innovation process models are based on NPD models. In the 1960s, the National Aeronautics and Space Administration (NASA) in the United States implemented a product development process for its space programme. These pioneering first-generation processes were largely engineering driven and mostly a measurement and control tool. The processes contained discrete phases, with review points at the end of each phase. However, they were bureaucratic and slow, and dealt mainly with the development phase rather than the entire process from idea to launch (Cooper 2001).

Most of the innovation process models implemented today are second-generation models, which usually involve seven required steps for managing the process effectively and transforming new ideas into new products or services. Third-generation innovation process models have also been developed; these flexible and informal models involve the parallel processing of stages to reduce the development time. However, these are only recommended for very experienced innovation managers or teams, as many hospitality managers have limited knowledge and experience in regard to innovation management. Therefore, second-generation models might be more appropriate for achieving innovation success in the hospitality industry (Cooper 2001).

Differences between NSD and NPD process models

The four characteristics that distinguish services from products – intangibility, heterogeneity, perishability and inseparability – impact on the NSD process (Edgett and Parkinson 1994). Because of the differences between tangible products and services, strategies for NSD can vary considerably from those for developing new tangible products.

Intangibility • • •

The relative intangibility of services influences NSDs in several ways. Because customers have difficulty evaluating the service prior to purchase and comparing competitive service offerings, they have to take a risk by purchasing a promised outcome. To alleviate the evaluation and comparison difficulties of new services, hospitality firms should offer unique characteristics or benefits and build a strong image and unique reputation. One way to make a new service less abstract and the examination easier is to provide some tangible evidence of the service, such as a logo or inclusion in the hotel brochure.

Another implication of intangibility is that new services can be copied quickly. Because new services often require little investment and are not patentable, competitors can copy services easily and without legal barriers, thus destroying the originator's competitive advantage (Atuahene-Gima 1996).

A third operational problem in NSD that evolves from the intangibility of services is the risk of conducting the development too quickly by skipping some stages of the development process. For example, testing new services is difficult, because there are often no physical prototypes to test market, and conducting R&D and quantitative market research is a problem. Therefore, close interaction with customers is necessary in order to get feedback during the development process.

Heterogeneity • • •

Heterogeneity is the inability of service producers to provide consistent performance and quality, because production and delivery of services depend significantly on the staff of the company. Services, especially those with higher labour content, are heterogeneous because the 'performance often varies from producer to producer, from customer to customer and from day to day' (Zeithaml et al. 1990: 16). The extent of heterogeneity depends mainly on the degree to which a service firm controls the system for variation and how the customers and employees impact on the process of the service.

Heterogeneity has several implications for NSDs. Heterogeneity of services contributes to difficulties in concept testing because of the people factor. Each time the service is delivered, different people affect the quality. Furthermore, service companies have to decide what degree of heterogeneity is desirable, because there are positive and negative consequences for both directions. Customized services can respond more effectively to customer needs, but service quality lacks consistency. On the other hand, standardization increases the consistency of processes and output and reduces customer uncertainty, but it can be less effective in satisfying individual customer needs. This means that when developing new services, firms face the dilemma of deciding between efficiency and personalization. The opportunity exists to develop customized services that are tailored to the customer; such services offer potential for unique selling advantages over competing services. On the other hand, a standardized delivery system is of critical importance to service introduction. Through quality control and staff training, it is possible to maintain the consistency of service delivery performance.

Perishability • • •

The third difference between goods and services is that services are produced at the time they are consumed and so cannot be stored, saved, resold or returned (Zeithaml and Bitner 2000). That is, unused capacity cannot be reclaimed, and a revenue opportunity is lost forever. However, some specific services, such as information-based services, can be recorded or stored for later use (Gummesson 2002). Furthermore, because of variations in demand, service companies can incur high costs as a result of under-used capital (e.g. hotel rooms or banquet room) or human resources (employee salaries) during low levels of business, as well as lost revenue when they cannot meet peak demand levels.

Therefore, capacity planning is a significant management task in the service industry. The main implication of this service characteristic for NSD is that the service firm should develop further new services to meet cyclic demand. Hospitality firms can solve the problem of perishability through developing new services that use existing resources in low-demand periods and through diverting demand at peak times. The integration of these new services with existing ones requires more planning and employee training and higher levels of integration among departments, in addition to stronger marketing activities that avoid wasted service capacity. Service firms can also sometimes reduce costs through substituting labour with technology, and the design phase of the development process should therefore include consideration of the appropriate mix of human labour and technology in the delivery of the service.

Inseparability • • •

Authors refer to the fourth characteristic as either simultaneity or inseparability, as services tend to be produced and consumed at the same time in the presence of the user (Zeithaml et al. 1990). Therefore, consumers may take part in the production process, and the outcome may be affected by this interaction. The service providers must ensure that customers understand their role and agree to be involved in this interaction. Meanwhile, not only customers affect the outcome of a service, but the quality of the employees who deliver the service is even more important.

As consumers have direct contact with the service process, they impact the design of new services. Production and delivery become fundamental design elements. Therefore, it is important to have high levels of customer involvement in the different stages of the development process. The simultaneity of production and consumption also means that employees with customer contact are a critical factor in the success of new services, because these employees often represent the delivery system (Shostack 1984). Front-line employees must have technical and interpersonal skills for optimal job performance (Hochschild 1983). Therefore, when developing new services, firms have to put strong emphasis on training, hiring, and performance standards. Furthermore, because employees delivering new services are particularly important to the development process, increased employee involvement in the development process is necessary (Cooper and Edgett 1999).

New service development process models

The NSD process could be defined as a formal blueprint, road-map or thought process for driving a new service project from the idea stage through to market launch and beyond. These process models, if applied in a disciplined way, can help firms to improve the effectiveness and efficiency of innovations so that scarce resources are not wasted during the development. However, not all the steps of the proposed models may be necessary; the decision will depend on time pressures, resources, the nature of the new service and the character-istics of the target market. The use of NSD process models will not necessarily guarantee success, but the use of a model does increase the chances of success. Service innovation pro-cess models are based on NPD models, and these approaches tend to follow the format of Booz-Allen and Hamilton's (1982) model.

As Table 14.2 illustrates, Shostack's (1984) model, the result of an analysis of case studies, outlined 10 stages in design-ing and developing new services. According to Shostack, the design and control of the process are the key to success-ful NSD, because control of the process is the critical aspect of controlling output. Bowers's (1989) model was developed through an investigation of how closely banks and health ser-vices follow the Booz-Allen and Hamilton (1982) model when developing new services. Therefore, Bowers's eight stages of service development (see Table 14.2) are similar to those for NPD. The main difference between Bowers's stages and those of the Booz-Allen and Hamilton model is that Bowers added one strategy stage (development of a new service strategy) and omitted the screening stage.

Cooper and Edgett (1999) proposed a stage-gate model, which includes a cross-functional team approach and up-front homework as two major ingredients. Between each stage is a gate, a 'quality-control checkpoint' at which a new product/service project has to meet a list of criteria in order to move to the next stage. These criteria contain qualitative components such as risk, strategic role, internal strengths and competi-tion, as well as quantitative aspects such as gross margin mini-mum, payback period, return on invested capital and return on assets. The stage-gate system prevents managers from skip-ping certain steps and guides the development in a successive order. Such a system detects early unpromising projects and saves resources that might be necessary for other, more prom-ising projects.

Table 14.2 New service development process models

Shostack (1984)	Bowers (1989)	Cooper and Edgett (1999)
	Business strategy	
	New service strategy	
Service definition	Idea generation	Ideation
Information search and alternatives		Preliminary investigation
Draw boundaries of service	Concept development and evaluation	Detailed investigation
	Business analysis	
Blueprint	Development	Development
Blueprint analysis		
Decision to implement		
Implement service (test)		
Pre-launch marketing activities	Market testing	Testing and validation
Market launch	Commercialization	Full operations and market launch
Post-introduction audit		Post-launch review

Scheuing and Johnson (1989) expanded the development process to 15 stages (see Figure 14.1). Scheuing and Johnson's model – which was based on a review of existing models, conversations with service managers and a survey of 66 financial services – included the complexity of service design and key factors that influence the design process, both internally and externally. This model indicates the unique conditions prevailing in service industries, because it places more emphasis on user and employee involvement and interaction during the development process.

Jones (1996), based on research in the fast food sector (Wan and Jones 1993), flight catering (Jones 1995) and tourism operations (Jones et al. 1997), proposed that the 15-stage process, shown in Figure 14.1, is highly contingent. It should be thought of as a checklist of options rather than as a rigid script

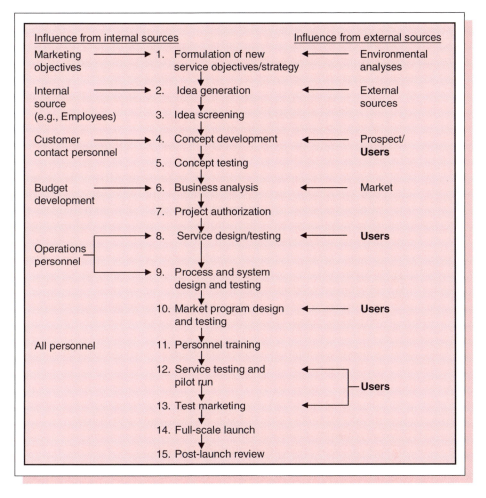

Figure 14.1
NSD process model suggested by Scheuing and Johnson (1989).

to follow. Jones (1996) suggested that a systematic and formal approach to innovation is likely to be adopted when:

- new products, with major process impact, are developed;
- a number of interrelated innovations are being developed simultaneously;
- the new product is protected by a licence or patent;
- product life cycles are long;
- competitors are unlikely to enter the market with a similar product/service;
- the innovation is original or 'new-to-the-world'.

Innovation is likely to follow a shorter, simplified development process when:

- simple modifications are made to existing products or services;
- innovation is not part of a major change programme;
- there is no licence or patent protection;
- competitors are actively innovating;
- the 'new' product is largely a copy of a competitor's product.

Jones (1996) also argues that an organization may create internal conditions that either foster or hinder innovation. Often these are strongly influenced by the external environment. Conditions that may encourage a systematic but rigid approach to innovation are:

- a bureaucratic culture;
- mature marketplace;
- the involvement of external consultants;
- formal research and development departments.

Conditions that encourage a dynamic and flexible approach to innovation are:

- growing supply chain integration;
- an organizational culture founded on innovation;
- industry association sponsorship;
- creative and entrepreneurial leadership;
- deregulated markets.

Whatever the precise nature of the innovation process, NSD can be divided into three major stages: predevelopment, development and launch preparation.

Early stages of the process

The NSD process starts with the clear formulation of objectives and an NSD strategy that leads and directs the entire service development activity. A product innovation chart can be used as a strategy statement, but very few service firms have written NSD strategies. The sources of new service ideas can come from internal or external sources, either formally or informally. External sources of new ideas include customers, competitors, channel members, and trade associations and shows. However, hospitality firms should not rely exclusively on external sources. Front-line staff, because of their under-standing of the service operation and customer needs, can be viewed as a logical source of ideas. Unfortunately, hospitality firms seldom have a formal idea-generation process for solicit-ing ideas (Ottenbacher and Shaw 2002).

Because not all new hospitality ideas can or should be developed, the objective of screening is to eliminate most sug-gestions and concentrate resources on those ideas that have the best potential for success. Hospitality firms use different screen-ing practices with different degrees of formality. However, hos-pitality firms should use rigorous screening concepts, because once a new service is introduced, not only is it difficult to withdraw, but financial and human resources are also wasted. Whether an innovation enhances or supports the organization's image is a significant screening criterion, because the new serv-ice has to uphold the corporate reputation. Further, screening criteria often include potential competitive advantage, market size, development cost, price, ROI, market share and other pre-determined 'must have' or 'would like to have' criteria (Cooper and Edgett 1999).

The business analysis stage includes a detailed investiga-tion that defines the service and what is required to make the project successful. The first part consists of a customer analy-sis, competitive analysis and market research of potential con-sumer needs and wants. The second part includes a financial analysis – including details on costs, revenue and internal rate of return – to justify an investment in new resources.

The development stage • • •

The development stage is the translation of an idea into an actual service for the market. It involves three steps:

(a) service concept development, that is, the description of customer needs and wants;
(b) service system development, that is, the resources required for the service, including employees, service environment and administrative structure;
(c) service process development, that is, the service delivery process.

The second and third steps emphasize the importance of operational staff and their training, and the overall cross-functional coordination. All three steps can be combined by the use of service blueprinting, which is one of the most commonly applied techniques for analysing and managing complex service processes in the pursuit of operational efficiency (Shostack 1984). A service blueprint gives meaning and structure to an otherwise partly intangible abstraction.

A service blueprint is a flow chart that shows in a diagrammatic form all the main functions of the service, all possible fail points and the processes in place to correct these, the relationship between the front and back office, and time. The key aspects of blueprinting are to match service specifications to customer expectations and to accurately portray the service system. A service blueprint visually displays the service by simultaneously depicting the process of service delivery, the point of customer contact, and the evidence of service as the customer experiences it. The service blueprint thus allows management and employees to organize and manipulate the entire service system. The main components of the service blueprint are customer actions, contact employee actions, backstage employee actions and support processes. A significant feature of service blueprints, as opposed to product processes, is the inclusion of customers and their views of the process.

Final stage of the process • • •

The final stage of the innovation process is the most expensive and resource intensive. Launch preparation includes the process activities at the final stage of the development process, such as the internal marketing of the project and training of employees. Before the launch, the commercial feasibility of the new service concept is tested and validated. Market testing is often undertaken in an effort to expose potential customers to the new hospitality innovation and test its marketing strategy under near-realistic purchase conditions, in order to find out whether and to what extent customers will actually purchase. This provides the organization with valuable feedback about the new service and its marketing programme. The reluctance of some service organizations to implement market testing may be explained by the difficulty of patenting a service, with innovators fearing that competitors might hear about the new service being tested and copy it. The final stage of the process includes the implementation of the market launch plan, the operations and delivery plan, and a post-launch evaluation of the new service project. With the help of an effective evaluation system that analyses sales, market reactions and problems, managers can benchmark the performance and undertake necessary changes.

Innovation management

In addition to implementation of a formal and well-planned process, success in hospitality innovation depends on the proficiency and ability of management to coordinate the process and harness the necessary resources. Successful projects appear to be guided by a clear, well-communicated strategy and vision, and by managers who strongly and visibly support the project. Furthermore, innovation success depends on getting the necessary commitment and interaction from management and from the different departments and employees, which is accomplished by creating a supportive and innovative environment. Innovations are also significantly affected by outstanding hospitality individuals, 'best practice champions' who have leadership qualities and problem-solving skills and are responsible for guiding the whole project (Enz and Siguaw 2003). Furthermore, failure to understand customers and competitors has been linked to unsuccessful outcomes. Involving employees throughout the process is therefore doubly important, because of their ability to improve service quality and their knowledge of customer demands.

One of the greatest handicaps to innovation is the lack of input by employees, who have the skills and the experience necessary for the development of new services (Johne and Storey 1998). Employees can help to identify customer requirements and how they might be fulfilled. In addition, employees who have been involved in the development will probably treat customers better, thus increasing the chances of successful implementation (Schneider and Bowen 1995). Furthermore, employee involvement in the process helps the organization to focus more strongly on the customer instead of focusing on process efficiencies. However, employees are often hesitant to get involved in NSD activities, because to do so might enlarge their workload. One way to increase employee buy-in is to adequately reward staff for their NSD involvement (de Brentani 1991).

Successful hospitality innovators are effective communicators who can raise customer awareness and convince customers of the benefits of the new service. It is not sufficient simply to create an innovation and announce its existence. Even the best products and services do not sell themselves. Innovations should be supported by a strong marketing communications strategy. An effective marketing communications strategy must include clear targeting, so that the new service will have a distinct position in the marketplace. Because services are often largely or partly intangible, the marketing communication should explain the potential benefits of the service well, as customers cannot try or test the service before purchase. Creating awareness and communicating the service's benefits can be supported by a strong brand image and a unique positioning in the buyers' minds.

Innovation success factors

In addition to disciplined application of a new service process model and effective management of the process, the following eight aspects are also very critical to the success of hospitality innovations.

Tangible quality • • •

The tangible quality of a new product has perhaps the most influence on success in NPD. Because of the simultaneity of production and consumption and the nature of intangibility, the control of perceived quality is more difficult and challenging for service organizations than it is for manufacturing firms. Groenroos (2000) distinguished between technical and functional quality: Whereas the technical quality involves the tangible output dimension of the service (what is received), the functional quality includes the service experience quality (how it is received). Because of the intangible nature of services, customers sometimes have difficulty understanding and evaluating new services; therefore, customers may use tangible cues such as staff and physical evidence to judge the service (Johne and Storey 1998).

New business service projects that incorporated service quality evidence to help buyers make evaluations had significantly greater success rates (de Brentani 1991). Services in the hotel sector are often intangible, and therefore customers may look for tangible and physical representations of the service in order to judge quality. Tangible features and tangible qualities are not only important for new products but are also a key factor for hospitality innovations (Ottenbacher and Gnoth 2005). Tangibles include the reliability, accuracy and consistency of the service product. Additionally, tangibility relates to the quality of the actual implements that are involved, that is, the facility and equipment used. The quality of these tangibles needs to match the quality of commitment required of staff and management.

Service advantage • • •

Relative advantage has been recognized as an important factor in developing new products and new services, even though the level of influence is lower for new services. Successful new hospitality service developments offer a significantly better value than competitive services and offer the customer unique benefits not available elsewhere. Furthermore, successful hospitality services are difficult to copy, significant improvements over those offered by the competition and considered to be more innovative than those of the competition. New business services that offered a service advantage are more than three times as successful as services lacking such advantages (Cooper and de Brentani 1991). Service advantage is very difficult to achieve and sustain, because services can be easily and quickly copied and lack legal protection (Atuahene-Gima 1996). However, new hospitality services should offer a service advantage if possible, even though to do so is more challenging for services than it is for new products.

Innovative technology • • •

Technological advantages are drastically modifying the ways in which many service firms do business, and they also impact NSDs in several ways. In particular, the integration of computers and telecommunications affects many service industries, including hospitality and tourism. Innovative technology can create new markets for new services and aid NSD by making it more cost effective, improving quality, making the use of the service simpler and faster, or providing a competitive advantage. Innovations in technology should be used in NSD not simply to replace labour input and control costs, but mainly as a tool to develop value for the customer and to provide a unique service benefit. Implementation of new technology in NSD can thus be used as an opportunity for differentiation. The creative application of technology, rather than the technology itself, has had an enormous impact on the hospitality industry.

Market responsiveness • • •

Market responsiveness relates to the fit between the new service and the demands of the market. Successful hospitality innovations have a higher level of market responsiveness (Ottenbacher and Gnoth 2005). In the financial industry, service innovations that satisfied clearly identified customer needs and responded to important changes in customer needs and wants were more than five times as successful as those that lacked market responsiveness (Cooper and de Brentani 1991). Such innovations are based on active market research and respond to actual as well as anticipated customer demand. Successful innovations require close customer contact, detailed consumer research and a comprehensive understanding of consumer needs in order to distinguish between fad, fashion and trend (Ottenbacher et al. 2006a). Effective customer responsiveness relies on the ability to comprehend the market, and on competently trained and flexible staff to respond to the challenges of the market. The ability to respond thus underpins market selection.

Market Selection

Market selection turned out to be one of the most important factors in determining the success of new hospitality service developments (Ottenbacher et al. 2006a; Ottenbacher and Gnoth 2005). Both the potential and the attractiveness of the target market are crucial parameters. The potential relates to both the current and the future size of the market. The current market needs to be large enough to promise a worthwhile return. Yet, this is not the only criterion, as the future potential needs to be carefully assessed as well. Because hospitality firms often have to make significant financial investments, managers perceive as successful only those innovations that release an almost immediate ROI as well as promise a long-term volume potential (e.g. building a scenic spa facility on the rooftop). Consequently, hospitality organizations should have a firm understanding of the potential size of the markets they target with their innovations.

Reputation

The image or reputation of a company represents the value that customers, potential customers, lost customers and other groups of people link to the organization (Groenroos 2000). A positive image can be an asset for a service firm, but image impacts NSD in several other ways. A service firm's image also communicates expectations. Additionally, external marketing communications regarding the firm's image influence the perception of the new service's performance and have an impact on employees' attitudes. Successful new hospitality services are more likely to be developed by organizations that have a high reputation for quality and service and whose customers have high levels of confidence in the company and its services. Furthermore, successful new hospitality services are more likely to fit with the current image of the operation. Image and word of mouth are crucially important for hotel organizations and therefore present significant challenges and opportunities for hotels and their service offerings (Kandampully 2002). The emphasis on image is greater in hospitality firms than in other service segments, and hospitality consumers' perceptions of differences in hotel services are often based only on hotel image (Kotler et al. 2006).

Overall synergy

Synergy refers to the fit, position and level of harmony in the product portfolio. Successful hospitality innovations have higher levels of synergy between the project and management expertise and resources, including existing range of services and products, marketing expertise, financial expertise and human resource capabilities. The fit between the innovation, the marketing mix and the capabilities of the firm are especially critical (Ottenbacher and Gnoth 2005). A successful hospitality innovation fits into the existing skills and the product and service mix offered by the hotel. In other words, it is appropriately priced, advertised and delivered. Although there can be no doubt about the need for perfection, managers perceive the gestalt of the service in its totality rather than merely concentrating on perfecting the technical aspects of the service.

Employee management

Because of the intangible nature of services, the simultaneity of production and consumption, and the importance of human factors in service delivery, employees play a more important role in service innovation than in product innovation. The human element in services means that service quality depends heavily on human resource strategies, which are the tools for effective management of employees (Ottenbacher et al. 2006a). Successful innovations are developed by hospitality organizations that implement strategic human resource management practices – which are linked to the organization's strategic business planning – in order to attract excellent staff. Employees are also viewed as a competitive advantage rather than a cost factor. Successful hospitality innovations evaluate front-line employees' performance in relation to customer-oriented behaviours (such as their ability to provide courteous service), rather than specific work-related outcomes such as quotas. Furthermore, successful new hospitality service developments are characterized by an approach in which the organization considers training a high priority and spends a lot of money on systematically structured interpersonal and general skills training. Such firms also transfer responsibilities, provide opportunities for personal initiative, trust their employees and allow them to use their discretion and judgement in solving problems. Wong and Pang (2003) investigate what motivated managers and supervisors to be creative and through factor analysis found five factors that influenced this: training and development, support and motivation from the top, open policy, recognition, and autonomy and flexibility.

Innovation in small versus large businesses

New chain-affiliated hospitality operations have flourished all around the world, and it seems that new hospitality chain operations have mastered the challenging market conditions. Is it their financial strength or their powerful and sophisticated marketing systems, or do they have a more structured approach to innovation? In general, independent hospitality firms are smaller, family-owned operations, while chain hospitality firms are larger organizations. Although larger organizations have shown strong growth, there are also many success stories among small hospitality businesses. The frontrunners of small hospitality firms are entrepreneurs who understand and apply the principles of successful innovation, because there are plenty of opportunities within the areas of change.

Entrepreneurship is driven by an attitude of opportunity and a management style that is innovative, flexible, responsive and efficient (Guth and Ginsberg 1990). Entrepreneurial management tends to be proactive, innovative, risk taking, future oriented and aggressive in the pursuit of business growth (Miles et al. 2000). In addition, entrepreneurial management considers innovation to be a vital and central aspect of strategy (Miller and Friesen 1982).

For large firms, the innovation advantage tends to be in industries that are capital intensive, advertising intensive and highly unionized (Audretsch 2004). The competitiveness of smaller firms' innovation activities is limited by the lack of financial resources, shortfall in marketing and management expertise, lack of access to external information, and weak networks

(Rothwell 1992). However, smaller firms have several advantages. Because of their smaller size, they are more flexible and have closer contact and relationships with their customers. This means that independent firms can be more adaptable to changing conditions and able to respond more quickly to customer needs and problems (Rueckert et al. 1985). Small firms usually have a dynamic and entrepreneurial management style (Rothwell 1992), so innovations can be less expensive. Therefore, innovation in small firms can be more efficient and effective (Vossen 1998).

A recent study (Ottenbacher et al. 2006b) investigated success factors of innovations in corporate versus independent hotels. The results suggested that corporate growth in the hospitality sector has been accompanied by the successful innovation activities of many independent hotels. Therefore, innovation success in the hospitality industry is not only a matter of money and structure. Only two success factors are common to both chain-affiliated and independent hotels: empowerment and market attractiveness. The secret of successful hospitality innovation appears to be that chain-affiliated and independently operated hospitality firms should have different priorities when developing innovations. Hospitality firms should vary their emphasis between market, process and organizational factors in order to develop successful corporate or independent hospitality innovation and offer the quality products and services that their customers demand. The results of the study suggest that, aside from market attractiveness and empowerment, the predictors of success for chain-affiliated hotels are process management and market responsiveness. In independent hotels, the factors of NSD success (other than empowerment and market attractiveness) are effective marketing communication, employee commitment, behaviour-based evaluation, employee training and marketing synergy.

Summary and conclusions

Innovation management may be even more difficult and challenging in the future. Intense competition has led to increasing market fragmentation, so that companies must aim at smaller market segments rather than at the mass market. This results in smaller sales and profits for each product or service. The rapidly changing business environment will also be a substantial challenge for hospitality businesses. The speed of change over the last decade may have been merely a warm-up for the upheaval to come in future years. Hence, innovation management is one of the most important challenges hospitality managers face in the new millennium.

Many hospitality firms still fail with their innovation activities; however, in the past we also saw some very successful innovative hospitality firms. For example, who would have thought 20 years ago that there would be potential for a coffeehouse concept to become so successful? The successful launch and growth of coffeehouse chains such as Starbucks, Second Cup and Costa have not only challenged the hospitality industry, but they have also created a new hospitality segment that did not exist before. Certainly, the developments of these coffee store concepts have lower levels of innovativeness than, for example, new breakthroughs in medicine or technology. However, these coffee shop chain stores have shown that there are still immense opportunities for innovation in the hospitality industry. The idea to create a coffeehouse chain with a large variety of coffee drinks in a comfortable atmosphere was not an outstanding innovative idea. As stated earlier, having an innovative idea is not the important aspect; rather, converting the idea into a product or service is critical.

New-to-the-world innovations are rare in a service environment such as the hospitality industry. Many would argue that most new hospitality services are versions of existing services or copies of competitors' services. Of course, it is important that hospitality firms consistently improve, revise or reposition their services. Unfortunately, however, too many hospitality firms shy away from more innovative categories and focus on low-risk service modifications that do not produce enough new streams of revenue. Hospitality firms should find a balanced innovation portfolio mix that combines highly innovative and low-risk new service projects.

Each year, more hospitality firms are looking to innovation as a weapon in the increasingly competitive environments in which they operate. Companies such as Marriott and McDonald's have installed internal processes to systematically and effectively develop and launch innovations. Most of the hospitality innovation success factors are directly controllable. For example, adoption of a market-oriented development process with a strong emphasis on market research and market knowledge is an aspect missing in many hospitality companies. There are no easy roads to successful innovations in the hospitality industry. Success in hospitality innovation is not the result of competence in one aspect; it is a combination of having many factors in place and doing many things well.

References

Atuahene-Gima, K. (1996) Differential potency of factors affecting innovation performance in manufacturing and services firms in Australia, *Journal of Product Innovation Management*, 13, 1, 35–52

Audretsch, D. (2004) Sustaining innovation and growth: public policy support for entrepreneurship, *Industry and Innovation*, 11, 3, 167–191

Avlonitis, G. J., Papastathopoulou, P. G. and Gounaris, S. P. (2001) An empirically-based typology of product innovativeness for new financial services: success and failure scenarios, *Journal of Product Innovation Management*, 18, 324–342

Barclay, I. and Benson, M. (1990) Success in new product development: the lessons from the past, *Leadership and Organization Development Journal*, 11, 6, 4–12

Booz-Allen and Hamilton (1982) *New Product Management for the 1980s*, Booz-Allen Hamilton Inc: New York, NY

Bowers, M. R. (1989) Developing new services: improving the process makes it better, *Journal of Services Marketing*, 3, 1, 15–20

Burgelmann, R. A. and Maidique, M. A. (1996) *Strategic Management of Technology and Innovation*, Irwin: Homewood, IL

Cooper, R. G. (2001) *Winning at New Products: Accelerating the Process from Idea to Launch*, 3rd edition, Perseus Books: New York, NY

Cooper, R. G. and de Brentani, U. (1991) New industrial financial services: what distinguishes the winners, *Journal of Product Innovation Management*, 8, 2, 75–90

Cooper, R. G. and Edgett, S. J. (1999) *Product Development for the Service Sector*, Perseus Books: Cambridge, UK

Cooper, R. G. and Kleinschmidt, E. (1995) New product performance: keys to success, profitability and cycle time reduction, *Journal of Marketing Management*, 11, 315–337

Debackere, K., Van Looy, B. and Papastathopoulou, P. (1998) Managing innovation in a service environment, In Van Dierdonck, R., Van Looy, B. and Gemmel, P. (Eds.), *Services Management: An Integrated Approach*, Pitman Publishing: London, UK, 387–405

de Brentani, U. (1991) Success factors in developing new business services, *European Journal of Marketing*, 25, 2, 33–59

de Brentani, U. (2001) Innovative versus incremental new business services: different keys for achieving success, *Journal of Product Innovation Management*, 18, 3, 169–187

Drucker, P. F. (1985) *Innovation and Entrepreneurship: Practice and Principles*, Elsevier Butterworth-Heinemann: Oxford, UK

Drucker, P. F. (1999) *Management Challenges for the 21st Century*, Butterworth-Heinemann: Oxford, UK

Edgett, S. and Parkinson, S. (1994) The development of new financial services: identifying determinants of success and failure, *International Journal of Service Industry Management*, 5, 4, 24–38

Enz, C. and Siguaw, J. (2003) Revisiting the best of the best: innovations in hotel practice, *Cornell Hotel and Restaurant Administration Quarterly*, 44, 5/6, 115–123

Froehle, C. M., Roth, A. V., Chase, R. B. and Voss, C. A. (2000) Antecedents of new service development effectiveness: an exploratory examination of strategic operations choices, *Journal of Service Research*, 3, 1, 3–17

Gadrey, J., Gallouj, F. and Weinstein, O. (1995) New modes of innovation: how services benefit industry, *International Journal of Services Industry Management*, 6, 3, 4–16

Griffin, A. (1997) PDMA research on new product development practices: updating trends and benchmarking best practices, *Journal of Product Innovation Management*, 14, 6, 429–458

Groenroos, C. (2000) *Service Management and Marketing: A Customer Relationship Management Approach*, 2nd edition, Wiley: Chichester, UK

Gummesson, E. (2002, June) *Service research at the crossroad: Useful axioms or just myths?* Paper presented at the 11th AMA Frontiers in Services Conference, Maastricht, Netherlands

Guth, W. and Ginsberg, A. (1990) Guest editor's introduction: corporate entrepreneurship, *Strategic Management Journal*, 11, 5, 5–15

Hochschild, A. R. (1983) *The Managed Heart: Commercialization of Human Feelings*, University of California Press: Berkley, CA

Johne, A. and Storey, C. (1998) New service development: a review of literature and annotated bibliography, *European Journal of Marketing*, 32, 3/4, 184–251

Jones, P. (1995) Developing new products and services in flight catering, *International Journal of Contemporary Hospitality Management*, 7, 3, 28–32

Jones, P. (1996) Managing hospitality innovation, *Cornell Hotel and Restaurant Administration Quarterly*, 37, 5, 86–95

Jones, P., Hudson, S. and Costis, P. (1997) New product development in the UK tour operating industry, *Progress in Hospitality and Tourism Research*, 3, 4, 283–294

Kandampully, J. (2002) *Service Management: The New Paradigm in Hospitality*, Pearson Education: Frenchs Forest, NSW, Australia

Kotler, P., Bowen, J. and Markens, J. (2006) *Marketing for Hospitality and Tourism*, Prentice Hall: Upper Saddle River, NJ

Lovelock, C. H. (1983) Classifying services to gain strategic marketing insights, *Journal of Marketing*, 47, 9–20

Lovelock, C. H. (1984) Developing and implementing new services, In George, W. R. and Marshall, C. E. (Eds.), *Developing New Services*, American Marketing Association: Chicago, 44–64

Miles, M., Covin, J. and Heeley, M. (2000) The relationship between environmental dynamism and small firm structure, strategy, and performance, *Journal of Marketing Theory and Practice*, 8, 2, 63–78

Miller, D. and Friesen, P. (1982) Innovation in conservative and entrepreneurial firms: two models of strategic momentum, *Strategic Management Journal*, 3, 1, 1–25

Ottenbacher, M. and Gnoth, J. (2005) How to develop successful hospitality innovation, *Cornell Hotel and Restaurant Administration Quarterly*, 46, 2, 205–222

Ottenbacher, M., Gnoth, J. and Jones, P. (2006a) Identifying determinants of success in development of new high-contact services: insights from the hospitality industry, *International Journal of Service Industry Management*, 17, 4, 344–363

Ottenbacher, M. and Shaw, V. (2002) The role of employee management in NSD: preliminary results from a study of the hospitality sector, In Kahn, K. B. (Ed.), *Proceedings of the 2002 Product Development and Management Association (PDMA) Research Conference*, Product Development and Management Association: Orlando, FL, 109–133

Ottenbacher, M., Shaw, V. and Lockwood, A. (2006b) An investigation of the factors affecting innovation performance in chain and independent hotels, *Journal of Quality Assurance in Hospitality and Tourism*, 6, 3/4, 113–128

Rothwell, R. (1992) Successful industrial innovation: critical factors for the 1990s, *R&D Management*, 22, 3, 221–239

Rueckert, R. W., Walker, O. C. and Roering, K. J. (1985) The organization of marketing activities: a contingency theory of structure and performance, *Journal of Marketing*, 49, 1, 13–25

Scheuing, E. E. and Johnson, E. M. (1989) A proposed model for new service development, *Journal of Services Marketing*, 3, 2, 25–34

Schneider, B. and Bowen, D. E. (1995) *Winning the Service Game*, Harvard Business School Press: Boston

Schumpeter, J. A. (1934) *The Theory of Economic Development*, Oxford University Press: New York

Shostack, G. L. (1984) Designing services that deliver, *Harvard Business Review*, 62, 1, 133–139

Tidd, J., Bessant, J. and Pavitt, K. (1997) *Managing Innovation: Integrating Technological, Market and Organizational Change*, Wiley: Chichester, UK

Ughanwa, D. O. and Baker, M. J. (1986) *The Role of Design in International Competitiveness*, Routledge: London

Vossen, R. (1998) Relative strengths and weaknesses of small firms in innovation, *International Small Business Journal*, 16, 3, 88–94

Wan, L. and Jones, P. (1993) Innovation in the UK foodservice industry, *International Journal of Contemporary Hospitality Management*, 5, 2, 32–38

Wong, S. and Pang, L. (2003) Motivators to creativity in the hotel industry – perspectives of management and supervisors, *Tourism Management*, 24, 5, 551–559

Zeithaml, V. A. and Bitner, M. J. (2000) *Service Marketing: Integrating Customer Focus Across the Firm*, McGraw-Hill: Boston

Zeithaml, V. A., Parasuraman, A. and Berry L. L. (1990) *Delivering Quality Service: Balancing Customer Perceptions and Expectations*, Free Press: New York

Chain restaurant management

Dennis Reynolds

Associate Director and Ivar Haglund
Distinguished Professor
School of Hospitality Business Management
Washington State University

Robin B. DiPietro

Assistant Professor
Hospitality, Restaurant and Tourism Management
Department of Nutrition and Health Sciences
University of Nebraska-Lincoln
Lincoln, NE

Introduction

Restaurants have been part of the human experience for millennia. The modern restaurant industry's entrepreneurial roots date back to 3500 B.C., when the first restaurant opened as an extension of its proprietor's home (Reynolds 2003). The target market, as it were, consisted of weary travellers who wanted a meal in a family setting while away from home. The modern retail landscape is of course vastly different; restaurants are ubiquitous in everyday life. Throughout the civilized world, humans embrace the convenience, epicurean pleasure and value of eating meals outside of the home. The seeds of the chain restaurant industry were, however, sown long before the advent of contemporary chains. Restaurant patrons have always sought consistency, value and availability, the hallmarks of the chain experience.

In 1955 – when chain restaurants began to establish a foothold in the market – Americans spent approximately 25% of their food dollars outside of the home; the National Restaurant Association (2006) now predicts that, during the current decade, this number will exceed by 50%. Worldwide, annual consumer expenditures on restaurant visits during the same time frame should exceed $1 trillion (Reynolds and Namasivayam 2006). More than 900,000 restaurants blanket the United States today. Of these, some 270,000 are chain restaurants (National Restaurant Association 2005). Sales statistics suggest, however, that chains command an even bigger share of the restaurant business – chain outlets capture half of all restaurant revenues in the United States. As Muller (2005) also noted, more than nine out of every ten hamburgers eaten away from home are purchased from a chain restaurant.

The preponderance of chains appears to be increasing. While foodservice industry revenues in the United States are growing at a rate of approximately 4% annually, total revenues at the top 25 chain restaurants have in recent years grown by approximately 5.1% (National Restaurant Association 2005; Technomic, Inc 2004). Global chain restaurant growth is also increasing faster than growth in the foodservice industry in general, a phenomenon that is projected to continue long into the twenty-first century.

Segmentation and definition

So what is fuelling this growth? To answer this, we must understand all the factors affecting chain restaurant operations. Howard Johnson, an entrepreneur who realized that he could maximize operational efficiencies and sustain excellence in quality across many units through replicating a solid business concept, was the first to describe his restaurants as links in a *chain of restaurants* (Muller 2005). He achieved a competitive advantage by leveraging brand recognition through multiple operations with the same identifiable physical attributes and service offerings. Yet he also appreciated that the failure of one link in the chain could have dramatic consequences throughout the system.

Researchers, in attempting to conceptualize the chain restaurant in a way that would be conducive to quantifying chain restaurant operations, have offered a variety of definitions. The most widely accepted, however, stems from Wyckoff and Sasser (1978) – two or more eating establishments at separate locations under common ownership or related through other legal entities (e.g. franchising), which, as the dominant activity, provide food for consumption on or off premises. Such a definition supports the understanding that a chain restaurant can take on many forms (e.g. kiosks, quick-service counters with limited seating, steakhouses) and can be located in almost any location, even non-traditional sites such as healthcare settings, sports stadiums or within hotels.

Today, the quick-service segment claims the largest number of chains. Chains in the full-service, casual-theme segment, while dramatically fewer than those in the quick-service segment, nevertheless comprise a substantial share of restaurants globally. The smallest number of chain restaurants, in terms of both units and concepts, is in fine dining.

The benefits of chain operations remain the same across all segments. Chain restaurant organizations have the advantage of economies of scale regarding materials and supplies, with vast market reach generated by brand recognition allowing for quick penetration into new markets (Muller and Woods 1994). Siguaw et al. (1999) describe a variation on the advantage for chain operators in the competitive restaurant industry discovered by Howard Johnson: the ability to leverage brand personality. As these researchers noted, 'A well-established brand personality has been shown to result in increased preference and patronage, higher emotional ties to the brand, and trust and loyalty' (Siguaw et al. 1999: 49). In large part because of these advantages, chain restaurant management requires specialized acumen. Furthermore, there are a number of considerations that, if left unattended, can result in business failure. These include:

- Understanding the differences between single- and multi-unit management

- Appreciating the need for ongoing management training and development
- Embracing best practices in chain restaurant management
- Understanding the chain restaurant business lifecycle

Single- versus multi-unit management

Chain restaurant operations are very different from independent operations and therefore require different managerial approaches. Jones (1999) notes the following differences between chain and independent operations: ownership and management are usually separate in large chains; large firms assign management functions such as operations, marketing, human resources and financial accounting to specialists; the role of management changes as a firm grows in size; and large firms are geographically dispersed.

To understand chain restaurant operations, however, it is more important to understand the difference between the single-unit manager and the multi-unit manager. In an independent restaurant, the person at the top of the hierarchy has overarching responsibility for that single operation. Such a manager may report to an owner, partner or investors, but ultimately decision making occurs at this level. For multi-unit managers, who – depending on the industry segment – may face a span of control of anywhere from 5 to 15 restaurants, decision making fits into a more complex decisional structure. Decisions in a chain may stem from corporate policy, from the multi-unit level involving a manager who oversees some subset of all units in the chain, or – for minor issues – from the unit-manager level. Moreover, the multi-unit middle manager typically reports to a vice president or director of operations who has at least another layer of management above him.

Recent research emphasizes that single- and multi-unit managers need different management skills, primarily because of the multi-dimensional structure of the chain operation. Researchers have identified five key dimensions of multi-unit management: financial management, restaurant operations, marketing and promotions management, facilities and safety management, and human resources management. Successful management across these dimensions requires a more complex set of skills than those that are required in single-unit management. Reynolds' (2000) qualitative study involving a survey of leading restaurant executives found that the top five characteristics required of a single-unit manager are organizational skills; interpersonal skills; restaurant experience, knowledge and skills; honesty, integrity and strong ethics; and leadership skills. Similar key characteristics have been reported in several previous studies (e.g. Kakabadse and Margerison 1988; Boulgarides and Rowe 1983; Van der Merwe 1978).

While such skills are arguably necessary in any position, research regarding multi-unit manager success characteristics suggests that they are more specifically reflective of the broader perspective and varied priorities that face multi-unit managers. For example, Umbreit (1989) interviewed executives and practicing multi-unit managers to determine key job requirements for a manager of two or more restaurants. The results suggested that managing restaurant operations was the most important component of the multi-unit manager position, followed closely by human resources management. The respondents in this study indicated that they spent over half of their time on the job performing tasks related to problems in restaurant operations and resolving issues in human resources in the restaurants.

More particularly, Umbreit and Smith (1990) listed some key, self-determined success factors that multi-unit managers said they needed prior to promotion from single-unit management. These included knowing how to manage managers, how to motivate people, how to work with a diverse group of people, how to get things done and solve problems through other people, how to build teams, how to manage time and set priorities, how to deal with unstructured time, how to enforce standards in multiple restaurant units and how to recognize differences in each unit's operational situation.

A follow-up study completed by Muller and Campbell (1995) was conducted to validate the Umbreit findings through a large empirical study with a single quick-service restaurant chain. The researchers analysed differences in perceptions on the part of single-unit (store or restaurant) managers, multi-unit managers (often referred to as 'district managers') and headquarters or corporate staff personnel regarding the tasks or skills needed by the multi-unit manager. The results indicated that, while all respondents believed that they were competent at their own positions, they were not comfortable with being promoted to the next level of supervision. Unit managers felt especially that they needed more training in marketing and interpersonal skills to move up to the district level. This study also emphasized that multi-unit managers need strong human resources skills.

Among the key findings in related studies (e.g. Umbreit and Tomlin 1986; Campbell 1994) was that all levels of management were in consensus regarding the rank order of the three most important job dimensions of a multi-unit manager. Of the five key dimensions noted above, the most important was human resources, followed by restaurant operations and then finance. These findings can serve as the foundation of a programme for the successful promotion of single-unit managers to multi-unit managers (Muller and Campbell 1995).

More recently, Umbreit (2001) published a qualitative Delphi-style study of 10 chain restaurant executives who were asked to review and comment on the changing role of the multi-unit manager. The findings suggested that the trend towards expanding the span of control for multi-unit managers seen in the late 1980s and early 1990s had reverted to the tighter spans of control that characterized previous decades. One additional outcome of this study was the suggestion from surveyed executives that multi-unit management titles and responsibilities have changed. In their view, the district management role in 2001 required more 'soft skills' of the sort that facilitate productive interpersonal relationships as compared with the more traditional 'hard' or technical skills of previous times. This finding re-emphasizes the importance of the human resources skills that previous studies had found to be a critical component of the success of the multi-unit manager.

The Umbreit (2001) study also suggests that organizations are increasingly viewing employees in new ways. Traditionally, most organizations saw labour mainly as an expense. More recently, organizations are realizing the importance of embracing employees at all levels as assets that can be leveraged in many creative ways.

Training and development of multi-unit managers

The continued growth of the chain restaurant industry and the corresponding organizational complexity it brings translates to a distinct need in the market for well-trained and qualified multi-unit managers. These are the professional knowledge workers whom Peter Drucker called the 'manager[s] of managers' (Drucker 1955: 24). Clearly, as the roles and duties of these knowledge workers change over time, continued development is required.

Building on the seminal work cited above regarding the identification of key attributes and role dimensions in multi-unit restaurant management, Muller and DiPietro (2006) developed a model of multi-unit manager development (see Figure 15.1). The highlights of this model include a pathway along which the developing multi-unit manager progresses from 'super operator' with strong technical organizational skills to master of the more complex management issues entailed by human resource development. The model helps us understand how to

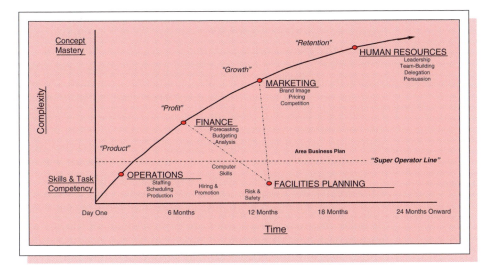

Figure 15.1
Phases in multi-unit (district) manager development (*Source*: Muller and DiPietro 2006).

augment skills mastered at the unit level with those needed to succeed at the multi-unit level across the five key managerial dimensions.

As shown, a developmental training programme for the newly promoted multi-unit manager would be constructed on an assumption of personal growth over a period of time. Upon promotion from a successful single-unit position, the new multi-unit manager would most likely exhibit the attributes and behaviours associated with a 'comfort zone' of existing skills (McKenna 1994). These skills might include those required for the dimensions of restaurant operations and facilities management and would by necessity have a tactical short-term decision window.

As the multi-unit manager gains experience and perspective, the next step in managerial development is the understanding of multi-unit profit, which represents a shift in focus from the actual output of the individual unit. A new focus on finance complements the focus on multi-unit profit. This includes a shift in the multi-unit manager's approach to longer-term thinking, particularly as it applies to budgeting for preventive maintenance or capital investment in physical plant equipment. Associated training, then, should centre on methods for driving district-level profits, which include a better understanding of forecasting, budgeting and cash flows (Littlejohn and Watson 1990). Finally, this phase in management development includes a broader, macro-oriented focus, as the multi-unit manager learns to consider individual units within the district as small parts of the greater organization.

In order to facilitate district-level growth in sales and eventually in number of units, the multi-unit manager's development turns next to marketing. This shift in outlook can be difficult and may take as much as a year to accomplish. As Nakata and Sivakumar (2001: 269) stated, 'Activating the marketing concept is a complex process of interdependent steps facilitated and inhibited along the way by particular cultural values'. Such cultural values include those brought into the situation by the manager and those embodied in the organization's operations and human resources management approach. Because the manager's values are inevitably shaped by unique past experiences, it may take some time to develop the proper philosophical fit of individual and corporate behaviour.

As part of such a programme of marketing training and development, the multi-unit manager begins to appreciate the importance of managing the brand image. As Muller (1998) noted, a brand can build equity when it focuses on product and service quality, the execution of service delivery, and the advantageous leveraging of a symbolic and evocative image. This is particularly challenging given that brand management relies on positioning strategies based on clearly defined product attributes and demographic-cohort identities.

A thorough understanding of pricing and competition naturally becomes more critical during this phase. As Reynolds (2003) noted, pricing must reflect market and demand drivers. Prices are market driven in that they must be responsive to competition, particularly for menu items and service systems that are common across multiple providers. Demand-driven pricing can be adopted more fully only when there are few providers or alternatives in the marketplace.

The final phase in a multi-unit manager's development centres on retention and, correspondingly, human resource issues. This is underscored by assertions made by Baum et al. (1997: 221) wrote, 'Human resource management is a central strategic and operational concern ... with implications for quality and market positioning at [the] local, regional, and national levels'. The notion that such human resources skills as leadership, team building, delegation and persuasion characterize strong managers is not unique to chain restaurant middle management. For example, more than two decades ago the U.S. Office of Personnel Management (1985) developed a competency-based model of managerial performance that identifies success characteristics including leadership and interpersonal sensitivity. Moreover,

McClelland and Burnham (1995) found similar success factors necessary at higher levels of management.

Human resources skills that improve employee and customer retention and increase market share are not developed in the vacuum of a workshop or training session but rather require feedback to develop properly. This is underscored by the role that feedback plays as an antecedent in various forms of social-cognitive theory. As noted in Reynolds' (2006: 65) empirical study of 296 managers at differing organizational levels, 'Positive feedback in the workplace may lead to broader outcomes such as enhanced retention, productivity, and loyalty'.

As this model appears to be useful for researchers and practitioners alike, it can easily be expanded by drawing on future empirical work on key success factors within existing conceptual frameworks. For corporate trainers, the model provides the basis for a programme in which multi-unit managers can develop skills that lead to success in the chain restaurant industry. As Becton and Greatz (2001) noted, a lack of rudimentary skills in key areas of hospitality management can best be addressed through such management-development programmes. Managers, too, understand the importance of such training and development. As Berger and Ferguson (1986) reported, although experience is vital in developing the necessary skills to run multiple operations, in an age of rapidly changing industry trends, managers increasingly turn to training programmes to tailor those developing skills to newly emerging market conditions and competitive situations.

Embracing best practices

The term 'best practice' refers to any process, know-how or experience that has proved valuable or effective in a specific setting and that may apply to other situations. For multi-unit managers, the study of best practices 'allows [the manager] to integrate proven practices with minimal trial and error – it lessens the risk' (Reynolds 2003: ix). Of still greater importance, the study of best practices can spark new ideas and suggest new possibilities for a manager's specific district of operations.

Research on best practices in chain restaurants covers a broad range of functional areas. For example, chain managers learn early on that managing revenue requires managing dining duration. As Taylor (1994) explained, lengthy wait times or perceived delays during any part of the dining experience increase customer dissatisfaction. Unnecessarily long dining durations also result in lower seat turnover, reducing revenue accordingly.

As Noone and Kimes (2006) reported, restaurant customers prefer promptness during the seating and first-course-delivery processes; they also desire promptness once the meal is completed and the check-out process begins. The time between courses, however, must be managed so that guests feel neither rushed nor neglected. This is sometimes difficult to accomplish since customers possess differing interpretations of 'too fast' or 'too slow', often owing to variations in previous dining experiences, differing reasons for the patronage (e.g. a celebration versus a 'quick meal') and differing chain restaurant segments (Hui and Bateson 1991; Woodruff et al. 1983).

A related area is shifting time-variable demand. As Kimes and Chase (1998) noted, shifting time-variable demand – practiced in the airline industry for decades – is a strategic revenue-management lever that is intended to fill restaurant seats during traditionally slower times. For example, a typical mid-scale chain restaurant is busy from 6:00 p.m. until 8:00 p.m. in most suburban settings. Shifting time-variable demand means reducing possible waiting times during such a peak period by shifting customers to non-peak periods.

Research on best practices related to shifting time-variable demand has focused on alternative pricing structures that vary with demand (a technique used by airlines and hotels) and incentives that work without changing pricing structures. Alternative pricing structures can be effective (see Kelly et al. 1994), but operators must use caution to avoid perceptions of unfairness. For example, if prices are varied such that they increase at a specified time, two tables could conceivably order at the same time yet be charged different prices (if, say, guests at one of the tables arrived before the cutoff time but lingered over cocktails).

Incentives have often taken the form of 'early bird' pricing. As Susskind et al. (2004) demonstrated, customers generally are willing to shift their dining time in exchange for discounts on menu items. Such research indicates that an optimal approach is to offer such incentives in tandem with a specialized menu in order to prevent a perception of unfairness similar to that noted in the case of alternative pricing structures.

Research on yet another best practice that is specifically targeted at multi-unit management is menu engineering. Noting that menus in chain operations are the most critical component of revenue management, Miller (1980, 1987) developed a matrix model that focused on food cost and product mix to analyse menu-item profitability in quick-service operations. Kasavana and Smith (1982) used the Boston Consulting Group Portfolio Analysis as the basis for the menu engineering matrix approach to menu analysis for mid-scale and fine-dining restaurants.

Atkinson and Jones (1994) suggested this could use simpler performance criteria (popularity and cash gross margin), whilst Pavesic (1986) modified these matrix models by using food cost and weighted averages of gross profit and popularity.

While others have added unique additions to these existing models (e.g. LeBruto et al. 1995), the most provocative menu-engineering research that has the promise of best-practice applicability posits holistic models. For example, Hayes and Huffman (1985) developed an individual profit and loss statement for all menu components in an attempt to allocate all costs, including labour and fixed costs, to individual menu items. Horton (2001) segmented the menu prior to analysis and evaluation into categories of comparable items for comparison. He modified the Kasavana and Smith model to include pure variable labour costs defined as those labour costs that could be calculated in the direct production of a menu item. Bayou and Bennett (1992) included a profitability-analysis model to evaluate the financial strength of menu items in an attempt to allocate variable costs such as labour. They did not, however, specify how the specific labour costs associated with a specific menu item would be ascertained.

Cohen et al. (1998) introduced a multidimensional approach that takes food cost, price, labour cost, popularity and contribution margin into account to evaluate menu effectiveness. Unfortunately, they did not specify how such variables, including labour, would be calculated and did not include other potential factors related to food production. Most recently, Taylor et al. (2007) developed a robust multi-factor menu analysis model that employs data envelopment analysis,[1] a technique that simultaneously integrates quantitative and qualitative variables to fully assess menu efficiency and profitability.

Such studies suggest that further research on best practices – or approaches that may lead to best practices – will pay off in yielding successful new techniques for chain restaurant management. While the majority of these will likely pertain to revenue management, research in related areas such as human resources, marketing and service management offer the promise of contributing strongly to the industry's evolution.

The chain restaurant business lifecycle

When chains became entrenched in American society in the mid-1900s, the notion that understanding each chain's lifecycle

---

[1] See Chapter 12 for a more detailed explanation of DEA.

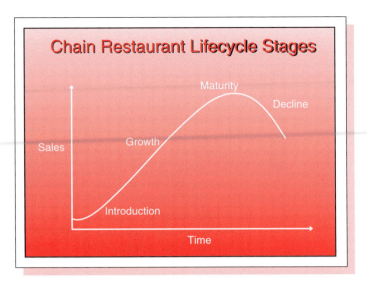

Figure 15.2
Restaurant lifecycle.

would be necessary to success was implausible. However, as Sasser et al. (1978) noted, effective service-sector management must recognize the importance of the unique periods in a concept's evolution. These researchers observed phases they classified as introduction, multi-site rationalization, growth, maturity and decline. Kotler (1988), drawing from related work on competitive strategy (e.g. Porter 1980), pared the model's phases down to introduction, growth, maturity and decline (see Figure 15.2).

Shay (1997) summarized the lifecycle concept within an integrated framework, arguing that each of these stages has unique market characteristics, objectives and strategic levers. For example, in the introduction stage, when a concept is created and launched, sales are typically low and customers can best be described as early adopters. The operator's goal is to create awareness in the marketplace and convey to potential customers the value associated with the core offerings.

In the growth stage, units are added to the chain, resulting in increased market share and sales. As Pearce and Robinson (1997) noted, the goal during this phase is to offer product extensions (as explicated by Muller 1998) and ensure service consistency. Both of these strategies serve to forestall competitors who seek to create similar concepts and therefore impinge on the success and popularity of the concept.

As a chain matures, its sales stabilize, its brand identity achieves widespread recognition and acceptance, and business becomes predictable in the context of an established market. The objective now, as D'Aveni (1994) explains, is to raise barriers to entry for potential competitors while ensuring retention of the concept's heaviest users. Such barriers may include building a more intensive distribution network, thereby lowering costs (and allowing for creating greater value), and diversification of offerings, such as menu items or delivery methods (e.g. adding take-out as an option). To keep the loyal customer loyal, advertising and discounting (if used) are targeted almost exclusively at the core customer.

Often owing to overwhelming competition and newer concepts that are more responsive to current trends, when a chain enters a period of decline, it sees sales and profit margins, and possibly standards, begin to fall, and market share shift away. Chain restaurants in this stage are faced with two choices: invest in a new 'rebirth' strategy, where product offerings are changed and a fresh approach is applied to operations, or launch an exit strategy and harvest available assets before they decrease in value (Muller 1997).

The goal, then, for chain restaurants is to identify these stages for each of their concepts. In doing so, they can employ appropriate competitive strategies and plan for future stages along the curve. Handy (1994) noted that the sigmoid curve shown in Figure 15.2 also offers opportunities in that operators can launch new concepts progressively: When concept one is in a growth phase, concept two can be launched. Later, when concept one is in decline, it can be readily replaced by a later concept. In this way, organizations can protect against losses during the decline of a single concept, whether from evolutionary growth leading to decline in the lifecycle or loss in market share from competitors.

With growth in the number of chain restaurant concepts increasing on a global scale, conducting lifecycle analyses and related research fills a correspondingly critical need. The main objectives of such research should be to identify defensive strategies that lead to desired outcomes at each lifecycle phase and to integrate changes in consumer behaviour that affect chain operators in the various segments as the four phases unfold. Such research will increase the body of knowledge in this area and can result in stronger business models for operators.

Summary and conclusions

In this chapter we have considered every aspect of chain restaurant management, including concept introduction through segmentation and definition, the unique requirements of multi-unit management, personnel development and training, the use of best practices, and the business lifecycle. A thoughtful discussion of chain restaurants must also, however, address the various controversies that accompany this field of study. For example, there is a misconception that a chain's entry into a new market will inevitably result in the demise of 'mom and pop' restaurants. Controversy also arises about a perceived nationwide homogenization of culture, the low wages often paid to chain restaurant employees and the contribution of chain proliferation to suburban sprawl. Such concerns are hardly unique to chain restaurants, applying equally to any large service-sector business. Critics argue that existing operations cannot defend against such new market entries and that any such entry will have negative net consequences (e.g. Quinn 2005).

In truth, chain restaurants have evolved naturally in an industry that must cater to customer demand. As customers become more globally aware, and as they continue to seek new concepts with which they can identify, new concepts will be born. In a global, market-driven, capitalist environment, such concepts must replicate in order to maximize market share, revenue, and ultimately, profit. Furthermore, customers ultimately determine whether a chain restaurant is desirable through their purchasing behaviour. Can we blame a concept for its success with customers?

There is also a counter-argument to those who view chains as destructive. Chains are becoming increasingly important in educating customers regarding nutrition and promoting healthy lifestyles. As Gregory et al. (2006) explain, quick-service chain restaurant leaders such as Wendy's have made adjustments in their children's menus that include healthier options in combo meals. In other segments, too, chain restaurant operators are emphasizing the importance of moderation (Frumkin 2003). And these trends are no less demand driven than the convenience and low cost that built the market in the first place. If customers demand healthier food and lower environmental impacts, chain corporations will deliver.

Chain restaurants are a critical part of the foodservice landscape. This segment of the foodservice industry is continuing to grow and will continue to capture increasing percentages of total foodservice expenditures globally. For researchers, this equates to a rich source of interest and opportunities on the basis of which to conduct rigorous empirical studies.

References

Atkinson, H. and Jones, P. (1994) Menu engineering: managing the foodservice micro-marketing mix, *Journal of Restaurant and Foodservice Marketing*, 1, 1, 37–56

Baum, T., Amoah, V. and Spivack, S. (1997) Policy dimensions of human resource management in the tourism and hospitality industries, *International Journal of Contemporary Hospitality Management*, 9, 5–6, 221–229

Bayou, M. E. and Bennett, L. B. (1992) Profitability analysis for table-service restaurants, *Hotel and Restaurant Administration Quarterly*, 33, 2, 49–55

Becton, S. and Graetz, B. (2001) Small business – small minded? Training attitudes and needs of the tourism and hospitality industry, *International Journal of Tourism Research*, 3, 2, 105–113

Berger, F. and Ferguson, D. H. (1986) Myriad management methods – restaurant managers tell all, *Cornell Hotel and Restaurant Administration Quarterly*, 26, 4, 16–24

Boulgarides, J. D. and Rowe, A. J. (1983) Success patterns for women managers, *Business Forum*, 8, 2, 22–24

Campbell, D. F. (1994) *Critical Skills for Multi-Unit Restaurant Management*, Unpublished Monograph, Master's Thesis

Cohen, E., Mesika, R. and Schwartz, Z. (1998) A multidimensional approach to menu sales mix analysis, *Praxis*, 2, 1, 130–144

D'Aveni, R. (1994) *Hypercompetition*, Free Press: New York

Drucker, P. (1955) *The Practice of Management*, Heinemann: London

Frumkin, P. (2003, September 22) Chains shift from defense to proactive menu stance to deflect finger pointing on the fat flak, *Nation's Restaurant News*, 37, 38, 86–92

Gregory, S., McTyre, C. and DiPeitro, R. B. (2006) Fast food to healthy food: a paradigm shift, *International Journal of Hospitality and Tourism Administration*, 7, 4, 43–64

Handy, C. (1994) *The Age of Paradox*, Harvard Business Scholl Press: Boston, MA

Hayes, D. and Huffman, L. (1985) Menu analysis: a better way, *Cornell Hotel and Restaurant Administration Quarterly*, 25, 4, 64–70

Horton, B. W. (2001) Labor and menu category: effects on analysis, *FIU Hospitality and Tourism Review*, 19, 2, 35–46

Hui, M. K. and Bateson, J. E. (1991) Perceived control and the effects of crowding and consumer choice on the service experience, *Journal of Consumer Research*, 18, 2, 174–184

Jones, P. (1999) Multi-unit management in the hospitality industry: a late twentieth century phenomenon, *International Journal of Contemporary Hospitality Management*, 11, 4, 155–164

381

Kakabadse, A. and Margerison, C. (1988) Top executives: addressing their management development needs, *Leadership and Organization Development Journal*, 9, 4, 17–21

Kasavana, M. L. and Smith, D. I. (1982) *Menu Engineering: A Practical Guide to Menu Analysis*, Hospitality Publishers: Okemos, MI

Kelly, T. J., Kiefer, N. M. and Burdett, K. (1994) A demand-based approach to menu pricing, *Cornell Hotel and Restaurant Administration Quarterly*, 35, 1, 48–52

Kimes, S. E. and Chase, R. B. (1998) The strategic levers of yield management, *Journal of Service Research*, 1, 2, 156–166

Kotler, P. (1988) *Marketing Management: Analysis, Planning, Implementation, and Control*, 6th edition, Prentice Hall: Englewood Cliffs, NJ

LeBruto, S. M., Quain, W. J. and Ashley, R. A. (1995) Menu engineering: a model including labor, *FIU Hospitality Review*, 13, 1, 41–51

Littlejohn, D. and Watson, S. (1990) Management development approaches for the 1990s, *International Journal of Contemporary Hospitality Management*, 2, 2, 36–42

McClelland, D. C. and Burnham, D. H. (1995) Power is the great motivator, *Harvard Business Review*, 73, 1, 126–139

McKenna, D. (1994) Leveraging complexity: the middle manager's dilemma, *The Learning Organization*, 1, 2, 6–14

Miller, J. (1980) *Menu Pricing and Strategy*. CBI: Boston, MA

Miller, J. (1987) *Menu Pricing and Strategy*, Van Nostrand: Reinhold, NY

Muller, C. C. (1997) Redefining value: the hamburger price war, *Cornell Hotel and Restaurant Administration Quarterly*, 38, 3, 62–73

Muller, C. C. (1998) Endorsed branding: the next step in restaurant-brand management, *Cornell Hotel and Restaurant Administration Quarterly*, 39, 3, 90–96

Muller, C. C. (2005) Chain restaurants, In Pizam, A. (Ed.), *International Encyclopedia of Hospitality Management*, Elsevier: Oxford, 61–62

Muller, C. C. and Campbell, D. F. (1995) The attributes and attitudes of multiunit managers in a national quick-service restaurant firm, *Hospitality Research Journal*, 19, 2, 3–18

Muller, C. C. and DiPietro, R. B. (2006) A theoretical framework for multi-unit management development in the 21st century, In Reynolds, D. and Namasivayam, K. (Eds.), *Human Resources in the Foodservice Industry: Organizational Behavior Management Approaches*, Haworth Hospitality Press: New York, 7–26

Muller, C. C. and Woods, R. H. (1994) An expanded restaurant typology, *Cornell Hotel and Restaurant Administration Quarterly*, 35, 3, 27–37

Nakata, C. and Sivakumar, K. (2001) Instituting the marketing concept in a multinational setting: the role of national culture, *Journal of the Academy of Marketing Science*, 29, 3, 255–275

National Restaurant Association (2005) Restaurant industry 2005 fact sheet, Retrieved on 5 May 2005, from http://www.restaurant.org/research/ind_glance.cfm

National Restaurant Association (2006) Restaurant industry 2006 fact sheet, Retrieved on 7 November 2006, from http://www.restaurant.org/research/ind_glance

Noone, B. and Kimes, S. E. (2006) Dining duration and customer satisfaction, *Cornell University Center for Hospitality Research Report*, 5, 9, 1–22

Pavesic, D. (1986) Prime numbers: finding your menu's strengths, *Cornell Hotel and Restaurant Administration Quarterly*, 26, 3, 70–77

Pearce, J. A. and Robinson, R. B. (1997) *Strategic Management: Formulation, Implementation, and Control of Competitive Strategy*, Irwin: Boston, MA

Porter, M. E. (1980) *Competitive Strategy*, Free Press: New York

Quinn, B. (2005) *How Wal-Mart is Destroying America (and the World): And What You Can Do About It*, Ten Speed Press: Berkeley, CA

Reynolds, D. (2000) An exploratory investigation into behaviorally based success characteristics of foodservice managers, *Journal of Hospitality and Tourism Research*, 24, 1, 92–103

Reynolds, D. (2003) *On-Site Foodservice Management: A Best Practices Approach*, Wiley: Hoboken, NJ

Reynolds, D. (2006) To what extent does performance-related feedback affect managers' self-efficacy? *International Journal of Hospitality Management*, 25, 1, 54–68

Reynolds, D. and Namasivayam, K. (2006) *Human Resources in the Foodservice Industry: Organizational Behavior Management Approaches*, Haworth Hospitality Press: New York

Sasser, W. E., Olsen, P. R. and Wyckoff, D. D. (1978) *Management of Service Operations*, Allyn and Bacon: Boston, MA

Shay, J. P. (1997) Food-service strategy: an integrated, business-life-cycle approach, *Cornell Hotel and Restaurant Administration Quarterly*, 38, 3, 36–49

Siguaw, J. A., Mattila, A. and Austin, J. R. (1999) The brand-personality scale, *Cornell Hotel and Restaurant Quarterly*, 40, 3, 48–55

Susskind, A. M., Reynolds, D. and Tsuchiya, E. (2004) An evaluation of guests' preferred incentives to shift time-variable demand in restaurants, *Cornell Hotel and Restaurant Quarterly,* 45, 1, 68–84

Taylor, J. T., Reynolds, D. M. and Brown, M. (2007) Multi-factor menu analysis using data envelopment analysis, Manuscript submitted for publication, 11th Annual Conference on Graduate Education and Graduate Research in Hospitality and Tourism

Taylor, S. (1994) Waiting for service: the relationship between delays and evaluations of service, *Journal of Marketing,* 58, 2, 55–69

Technomic, Inc. (2004) Top 100 chain restaurants, Retrieved on 5 May 2005, from http://www.technomic.com/facts/top_100.html

Umbreit, W. T. (1989) Multiunit management: managing at a distance, *Cornell Hotel and Restaurant Administration Quarterly,* 30, 53–59

Umbreit, W. T. (2001) Study of the changing role of multi-unit managers in quick service restaurant segment, In Parsa, H. G. and Kwansa, F. A. (Eds.), *Quick Service Restaurants, Franchising and Multi-Unit Chain Management,* The Haworth Hospitality Press: Binghamton, NY, 225–238

Umbreit, W. T. and Smith, D. I. (1990) A study of opinions and practices of successful multiunit fast service restaurant managers, *The Hospitality Research Journal,* 14, 2, 451–458

Umbreit, W. T. and Tomlin, J. W. (1986, August) Identifying and validating the job dimensions and task activities of multi-unit foodservice managers, *Proceedings of the 40th Annual Conference on Hotel, Restaurant, and Institutional Education,* 66–72

U.S. Office of Personnel Management. (1985) *The Management Excellence Framework: A Competency-Based Model of Effective Performance for Federal Managers,* Government Printing Office: Washington, D.C.

Van der Merwe, S. (1978) What personal attributes it takes to make it in management, *Ivey Business Quarterly,* 43, 4, 28–32

Woodruff, R. B., Cadotte, E. R. and Jenkins, R. L. (1983) Modeling consumer satisfaction processes using experience-based norms, *Journal of Marketing Research,* 20, 3, 296–304

Wyckoff, D. D. and Sasser, W. E. (1978) *The Chain Restaurant Industry,* Lexington Books: Lexington, MA

CHAPTER 16

Crisis management

Dolf A. Mogendorff

Research Director
Eproductive Ltd
Dorking, England

Introduction

'Events, dear boy, events'. Harold MacMillan, former British prime minister, when asked what worried him most.

While most of the time the management of hospitality operations typically takes place under relatively stable conditions, in a dynamic environment there may be periods of extreme turbulence. This may be due to internal events, such as a fire, a death or crime on the property, or external events, such as a strike by transport workers, terror incidents, extreme weather and natural disasters. This chapter will discuss how operations managers may need to respond to crises, both in the short- and longer term, for the benefit of the organization, its customers and staff and the external environment.

It would be wrong to make the bold statement that all crises can be 'managed'. Especially, external incidents which impinge on the organization can at best be ameliorated by management in its effects on that organization and its stakeholders. Even internal incidents may not be wholly manageable, simply because they might not have been expected. However, what management can do is to plan and put mechanisms in place to ensure prevention of crises where possible, the minimization of the effects of any crisis, and the recovery from those effects as quickly and efficiently as possible.

Crisis management: definition and types

Crisis management is a means of proactively preparing a company for a worst-case scenario. It involves the careful planning of approaches that will minimize the effects on its operation in both short- and longer terms. Selbst (1978), quoted in Faulkner (2001), refers to a crisis as 'any action or failure to act that interferes with an (organization's) on-going functions, the acceptable attainment of objectives, its viability or survival, or that has a detrimental personal effect as perceived by the majority of its employees, clients or constituents'. Faulkner (2001) extrapolates from this that, whilst crises tend to be induced by the actions or inactions of the organization (e.g. a fire started by a cigarette or a kitchen fire created by the non-cleaning of extractor ducting), disasters tend to be induced natural phenomena or external human action (e.g. earthquakes, tsunamis, forest fires, floods; hijackings and terrorism). Jones (2003) disputes this analysis. He agrees that Faulkner's definition of a disaster is correct, but he argues a crisis is defined as 'a crucial or decisive point or situation; a turning point'. Hence it is likely that an event (whether internally or externally caused), which could be a disaster, will lead to a crisis. Hence *by definition* it is possible to have a crisis without a disaster. He goes on to propose that disasters cannot be managed (although they might be predicted and planned for), whereas crises must be managed.

Crisis management became a catchphrase towards the end of the 1980s following incidents such as the Exxon Valdez oil spill in Alaska (seen to this day as *the* example of how not to handle a crisis), the UK's Piper Alpha, oil rig explosion in the North Sea and the Union Carbide chemical release in Bhopal in India. In each case it became clear, albeit after the events, that these crises had been preventable and could be so in the future. For instance, in the case of Piper Alpha the technology was changed to make it safer, but also to reduce sharply the number of personnel exposed to the potential hazard. In the early 1990s, management practitioners developed crisis management as a vital tool of business management to provide an orderly and efficient transition from crisis condition to normal.

Methods to deal with internal events such as breakdown of services, financial difficulties, bad publicity, loss of a key employee or manager, or strikes, fire or flooding have been developed over a number of years. External events can also create a crisis situation, for instance violent crime, drug-related crime, illegal immigration, and strikes by other employees which impact on the business (e.g. transportation or fuel workers' strikes). Even from these few examples given so far it is obvious that the operations manager has often to work not only with the rest of the management team but also with external agencies if he or she wants to be effective in minimizing the effects on operational outcomes in such circumstances.

Santana (2003) has developed an operational model of crisis management (Figure 16.1). This shows that a comprehensive effort is required at all management levels to provide an integrated approach to crisis management in terms of crisis planning, training and stakeholder involvement in designing and implementing preventive mechanisms aimed at business continuity. These matters will be discussed in this chapter.

Crisis management: planning

Crisis management planning means identifying the nature of a crisis, the steps to be taken to minimize damage and recover from the crisis, and communicating effectively throughout the

387

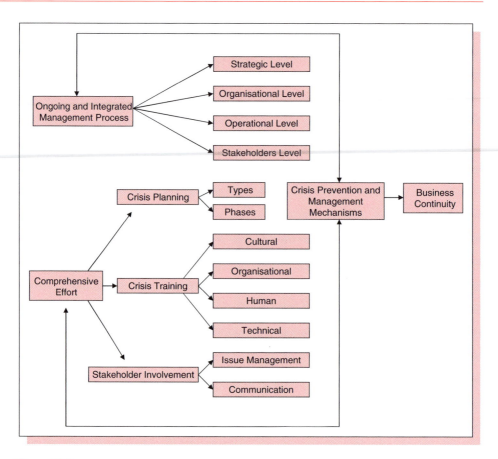

Figure 16.1
Model of crisis management (*Source*: Santana 2003).

process with all stakeholder groups to prevent harm to the company's resources, results and reputation. A relatively simple crisis created by the sudden resignation of a key staff member, such as the executive chef, could ruin a reputation built over a long period, and may require a huge effort to recover and maintain the organization's reputation. In the case that harm cannot be prevented, a plan should be in place to start rebuilding the business and the reputation as soon as possible after the event – known as crisis/disaster recovery planning. This will be discussed later in this chapter. In particular circumstances, the lack of such planning could mean the difference between the business recovering or having to file for bankruptcy.

Like any well-executed planning cycle, the crisis management process carries the added benefit of getting the management team to focus and think through the related issues. This in itself will help the team to recognize a crisis when it occurs. If a risk management process is already in place which assesses day-to-day risks, its team can be extended to deal with crisis management.

According to Campbell (2005), the team needs to comprise a core group of senior people on that site or in that business so that both policies and plans can be developed. The team will be skilled in a number of critical disciplines, assigned specific responsibilities and given the requisite authority. Team members must have an understanding both of the internal interests and of the external perspective. So, as will be seen, it requires both internal and external specialists.

A good core crisis management team needs a team leader, an incident response specialist, that is somebody who can link with the emergency services, a legal representative – and ideally both legal and financial representatives – IT, human resources, operations and recovery specialists. Last but not least is the public affairs or public relations coordinator. In addition, the core team should have access to skills banks and extra specialists who can be called on in the case of specific situations such as kidnap, ransom or special emergencies (see below). Finally the team needs a log keeper. Log keeping is a very important part of the process and in some countries a legal requirement – and such a log needs to be kept from the beginning of the planning process right through an incident and thereafter as evidence of processes planned and implemented.

The process would start by brainstorming possible crises, some of which might be specific to the property; then they should be ranked from most to least damaging in a matrix of incident types which takes account of effects on all stakeholders: customers, management, staff, suppliers, shareholders, lenders, the public at large and the media.

Incident types might include:

- altercations (amongst guests, amongst staff, between these two groups, with stakeholders and the public at large);
- various types of crime, with or without weapons, such as physical assault, sexual assault, drugs, theft, robbery, kidnap, sabotage, bomb threat or prostitution;
- personal injury whether inside the property or while in, or caused by, a company vehicle; suicide within or near the premises;
- water damage whether caused by pipe bursts or by external flooding;
- breakdown of systems with immediate safety implications, such as elevators or escalators, electronic locking systems and so on;

- fires of various types;
- medical incidents including food and other types of poisoning;
- unauthorized entry;
- property damage, internal and/or external;
- supply chain failures, especially of major and/or specialist items such as specialty foods;
- breakdown of essential systems, for example loss of power, air conditioning;
- information damage, for example to computer systems, communications systems;
- in addition, there may be crises that are not immediately obvious, such as creeping competition which, at a 'tipping point', might engender a crisis.

All such issues should be subjected to a crisis vulnerability audit – how likely is it that such a scenario might occur? A separate section might deal with (external) disaster incidents (see later in this chapter).

Then, possible damage to people, property and information for each incident type should be assessed with effects cast as widely as possible, differentiating between short- and long-term damage, identifying relevant timelines for recovery in a matrix of business functions and timescales. Both the severity and its scope should be taken into account for impact assessment. This would also clarify the interrelationships between issues, people and events, as well as the range of possible scenarios that could develop – a solution should be identified for each route. Basic questions will need to be asked, such as the following: how will customers be able to contact the business; how will suppliers supply the business; how will customers pay bills; how will the company pay suppliers? Solutions to these matters might be covered by the organization itself, by willing competitors (on a temporary basis) or by specialist business continuity suppliers who have the facilities and knowledge to provide fast and efficient support. For instance, during the SARS outbreak in Hong Kong in 2005, flight catering companies organized their shifts so that one group of workers had completely vacated the premises before the next group arrived for their shift – to minimize the possible transmission of the disease.

Once all this has been carried out, functions and individuals, both internal and external, should be identified, who could mitigate the crisis and who would be essential at such a time. These would include those who would be in charge of an emergency such as a fire, to those responsible for the safety of

ICT data and the temporary setting up of alternative facilities. With each of these individuals or teams, concrete plans should be developed and written up. Once this is done, they should be approved by authorities and regulatory agencies where relevant (e.g. fire policy).

By taking the time to think through the what-ifs, and by creating possible policies and plans, one can work more quickly should the need ever arise. It is important to be flexible; no plan should be hard and fast since one cannot plan for every scenario (who could have foreseen the exact events of 9/11?). Instead, the plans should be used as a guide to help the operation recover. Such contingency plans can also act as a guide to sanity during difficult times. In many crises, the immediate ability to respond effectively can often save lives, assets and reputations. The Hyatt Hotel in New Orleans had highly developed plans in place that enabled it to respond effectively to the 2005 flooding of that city. What was completely unexpected was that the property became the crisis management centre for the whole city, and was occupied and utilized by the various federal, state and city authorities for several months.

Training and maintenance

The plans that have been developed need to be rehearsed on a regular basis. This allows the management team to ensure that the crisis management plans are functionally up to date. People must talk in a language of response that is quick, clear and efficient and all of that must be organized beforehand. The only way to do this is to practise.

It is essential that a team member is responsible for the maintenance of relevant crisis resources that enable effective crisis management, for example immediately contactable crisis management teams (including the use of 'telephone trees'), crisis control emergency packs and so on. In a 24-h operation such as a hotel, it is vital that there is such an identified individual on duty at all times.

Plans may be rehearsed as paper-based exercises which allow clarification questions and the discussion of 'what if' written scenarios. Alternatively, the so-called telephone cascading can be done by sending out a test message without warning to everyone at the top of the telephone tree. The message then cascades down, and all persons at the bottom of the tree contact the anchor person who in turn logs those calls. In this way, the effectiveness of this communications system can be tested for speed and accuracy. The third method, and the most costly and time consuming, is the full rehearsal which provides an opportunity to test the integrity of all the parts of the plan. In a 24-h hospitality operation, this method is particularly challenging for those planning it.

The final step in the development cycle of any crisis management plan is maintenance, that is reassessing all risks and looking out for new ones, keeping the plans up to date, and keeping the teams involved and interested in this continual improvement process. The manager's aim here is to promote awareness of the need for ongoing crisis preparation and to combat so-called fire drill fatigue. Such plans, therefore, need to be tested with good and exciting simulations that challenge the team's ability to act and interact. As the crisis management process develops, one can start to tackle the more difficult scenarios. By running simulations and drills of potential crises, those who are given tasks during a crisis have the opportunity to play out their roles under stressful conditions while also being challenged intellectually. It is also important that everyone rehearses together to ensure that each individual understands their role as well as the roles of the rest of the team, building a culture of awareness.

After each such simulation, it is essential that lessons are learnt and the plans updated. A great tool is gap analysis which allows the team to model the scenario against the plan, and revise accordingly. This involves looking at the 'gap' between what should have been and what actually occurred at each step of the process and to find solutions that would close those gaps.

External agencies

Business continuity suppliers provide crisis recovery solutions to companies that are unable to continue to operate due to (unforeseen) disruption. Depending on the company, they can offer end-to-end service, from consultancy in the planning stages to the provision of all alternative ICT and other (office) services. Agreements with such organizations are known as either 'hot site' agreements with desks normally available within about 4h of a service request or 'cold site' agreements where a temporary building can be erected on a suitable site where the company in crisis can move in about two working weeks. In each case there are issues of cost as well as the ability to rehearse such scenarios. A further option may be to make a mutual agreement with another company to use their facilities – a relatively cheap option but difficult to rehearse. Again, the function/time matrix will help decide which departments/people require such facilities, and for what time period.

There are a number of external organizations which need to be consulted and/or be kept informed and who often have expertise not available in-house. These include the local authority emergency planning officer who deals with major incidents; the emergency services (police, fire, ambulance); neighbouring businesses (managements might be able to help each other); utility companies; suppliers and (major) customers; and banks/financial services companies. Also, guests and suppliers are increasingly willing to claim their rights in an ever more litigious environment, so being able to call on the services of a good experienced legal practice is essential.

It is vital to ensure that the organization is properly insured to the right values and that, following a crisis, insurance companies can work closely with the property to help recovery as soon as possible. This requires that the insurer has all relevant information to make quick loss-adjusting decisions, such as P&L statements, occupancy and sales data, invoicing and inventory records, and reservation data so that they can project losses during the crisis.

Another key organization would be a good PR agency which has experience in the media side of crisis management. This prevents the organization's reputation being adversely affected by events and allows experts to deal with external relations while the management team is trying to get the business back on its feet. But the responsibility lies with the company to get the message right and to be seen to be involved with the crisis and its aftermath.

The following is based on key issues set out by Loretta Ucelli, a former White House Communications Director (Ucelli 2002). It sets out the key issues that senior management need to keep in mind during and after such a crisis period:

- News is global, not just local: especially where brand values have to be protected across a (geographically spread) estate, a crisis in one property might affect a whole brand;
- News is democratized (live and blogged): it travels fast and bloggers in most countries are not controlled;
- Rumours and falsehoods can spread fast, so clarity, truthfulness and timing are of essence;
- A communications protocol should be devised, so the team is clear about who the spokespersons are and to ensure that only they deal with the media;
- A communications crisis manual should be developed so that all relevant team members have clear and same instructions which they can access wherever they are and can speak with one voice;

- A stakeholder strategy should be devised so that all these parties are kept informed and up to date – the biggest problems doing lasting damage to the organization are often caused by a lack of communication with those who matter;
- Media relationships should be prioritized to those who can do most damage if they mis-report at the time of crisis and those who might be most helpful during the recovery period;
- The most senior manager possible should front the communications during and after an incident to show leadership – this requires training;
- Such a manager might need to be accompanied by an experienced PR person who can 'manage' media presentations, especially question and answer sessions;
- Respond quickly, accurately, fully and frequently.

Data protection

With organizations' ever greater reliance on data, and in particular those generated through ICT systems, crisis management needs to include clear contingency plans in case of a crisis which prevents the use of such systems or the loss of their data. Day-to-day good practice includes regular data and system back-ups, system utilities and diagnostics, secure environments (including various anti-hacking and anti-virus systems), and keeping copy data off-site in a protected environment (e.g. special safes). This may require the involvement of third parties where systems are Internet based and data held on server farms at remote sites.

In addition, there are specific matters to deal with during a crisis situation. These include:

- Keeping original software secure so that it can be uploaded again after the crisis;
- Making sure that clear responsibility has been allocated for system management, with deputizing team members to ensure constant cover;
- Mission-critical systems – those systems without which the operations manager cannot manage the basic functions of the property, for example PMS, EPOS, payroll, address lists of key personnel, customers and suppliers, will require back-up systems at all times, possibly off-site;
- Lack of an accounting system could lead quickly to cash-flow problems and loss of key management information;

- There are legal responsibilities in managing company data under Data Protection legislation, for example protecting personal information of employees; this requires staff training at all levels for normal trading conditions but is of particular importance during a crisis, for example to check on and possibly locate missing personnel;
- If the Internet is used with a reservation system, credit card details may be stored on the system, and again the organization has legal responsibilities for the confidentiality of such data;
- Crises can be created by bad system management – for example loss of data during upgrades. Careful management of such procedures is essential, including frequent back-ups and the use of master and working copies;
- Ensuring file compatibility throughout all systems makes the management of a data-related crisis much easier. Although many are now data based, there are still often compatibility issues between programmes;
- If using Internet-based systems, guarantees should be obtained from vendors on system up-time, back-up and data integrity;
- Up-to-date contact details of hardware and software support companies should be held within the crisis management system.

Information security management is now well recognized on an international basis, and quality standards organizations may offer advice under ISO/IEC 17799:2005 *Code of Practice for Information Security Management* and ISO/IEC 27001:2005 *Specification for Information Security Management.*

Effects on branding

Brands are often built over many years, but as already stated, the reputation attached to a brand can be lost in a matter of moments. Therefore, the kind of policies and procedures mentioned earlier in this chapter need to be in place to ensure the brand is protected as much as possible, and standards regained as soon as possible.

It is often the case that the brand can suffer because it is that which is in public view. A franchisor may suffer much damage to its franchise system from the fallout of a crisis in one unit – for example food poisoning. Two high-profile fires through grease built-up in ventilation systems at a major hospitality chain at a London airport and a London railway station, both of which required evacuation of these major sites, caused major travel delays and huge costs and litigation. It was the brand that suffered in the public's perception, not the unknown operator who actually caused the fires through lack of relevant training.

Another example of how a company may deal with protection of their brand relates to a fire at a large branded forest-based resort when a major fire destroyed all central facilities and services. Crisis policy dictated that staff not be laid off but to:

1. use them to deal with developing site security problems by training staff to act as security patrols;
2. use the time to retrain staff for reopening;
3. redeploy staff at other of the chain's sites.

Creative deployment of staff after this incident was done to strengthen brand standards through retraining and retaining staff loyalty through continued employment. In addition the fire created a major rethink of the design of the central facilities, with a physical division of these services in two halves intersected by a road that acts as a fire break. As will be discussed at the end of the chapter, crises can often be used as an opportunity to review facilities and procedures and create a more effective operation.

Crisis management after disasters

Unlike most crises, disasters cannot be managed as such, but the catastrophic changes they create might be ameliorated through crisis management. Recent events such as 9/11 and other such incidents in Spain and the UK, as well as natural disasters such as earthquakes, floods and tsunamis, have taught that all that has been said in this chapter so far in relation to planning, training, communication, leadership and team building applies, but in even greater measure, to managing the aftermath of such disasters. Management and their teams cannot prevent such occurrences, so they have to ensure that the proper systems are in place to rescue people and assets and to try and rebuild the business.

A lot of organizations, both governmental and NGOs, have published advice on how to deal with terrorism and its consequences. In the USA, the Department of Homeland Security has published advice for business on their Ready Business website (www.ready.gov/business/index.html). In the UK the internal security service, MI5, has published recommendations: *Protecting Against Terrorism* (Security Service MI5 2006) and is linked to the UK Government's initiative Preparing for Emergencies (see www.preparingforemergencies.gov.uk) which also includes advice on other matters such as avian flu and drought. This in turn is also linked to the Government's UK Resilience website which is run as a news and information service for emergency practitioners by the Civil Contingencies Secretariat at the Cabinet Office. There is also a special website for London as a defined terrorist target (www.londonprepared.gov.uk) prepared by The London Development Agency and Visit London, the local tourism department.

Britain is not often subject to natural disasters although flooding emergencies have recently been on the increase. Again, government agencies and NGOs have issued advice – see, for instance, Business Link's Protect Your Business From Flooding (www.businesslink.gov.uk). Companies have to be continually up to date on planning for possible disasters that might affect them in the future.

Business continuity planning

The UK's Confederation for British Industry (CBI) has also published advice for businesses: *Contingency and Security Planning* (CBI 2006), where the issue of business continuity planning is specifically set out as follows:

- *It is critical that continuity plans are regularly reviewed and tested.* This should be done once or twice a year, across the whole company.
- *All staff should be trained to execute the crisis management plans.* Staff need to understand where the evacuation points are, their role in the event of an incident, who is the in charge, and where the operation's back-up locations are. Most importantly, staff must have easy access to the plan and key contact details.
- *Consider the operation's position in the immediate aftermath of an event.* Does the property have the equipment and the facilities available on site to protect and tend to staff and guests? Companies should consider designated shelters where evacuated staff and guests can assemble. One shelter should be at the heart of the business premises, to protect staff and guests against a bomb attack, with another, more distant shelter, in case of fire or evacuations. These will need to be equipped with food, water, communications and sanitation, and should be big enough to accommodate both staff and guests.

• *Is there a separate location to go to, to continue operations?* If so, its location should be considered carefully – much will depend on the nature and location of the business and the potential threat. If chemical or biological weapons were being released in the city centre, it would be vital to find a relocation site upwind from there.

Crisis management: opportunities for change

Faulkner (2001) quotes Berman and Roel's (1993) description of reactions to the 1985 Mexico City Earthquake:

'Crises bring about marked regressions as well as opportunities for creativity and new options. They are turning points in which regressive tendencies uncover discrimination (and) resentment about ethnic and socioeconomic differences … yet they also trigger progressive potentials and solidarity'.

Examples of opportunities to positively affect the variables include:

• Narrow the service concept: an opportunity to reinvent the product for today's/tomorrow's markets/(re)differentiate your product;
• Refocus markets: if a crisis or disaster has reduced access to certain markets, use the opportunity to attract different market segments;
• Resize: reduce your organization to a more manageable size in the circumstances until new opportunities present themselves;
• Relocate: to a safer environment;
• Simplify processes: use the situation to review all processes and simplify/automate them;
• Combine activities and/or departments for more effective management/better customer service/cost control;
• Update assets: in line with market expectations;
• Redefine staff needs and skills: in line with the new priorities;
• Retrain staff: to better cope with the existing situation or the new direction.

The extent to which companies may take up such opportunities depends very much on how dynamic they are. Those that are better at facilitating change as an inherent part of their culture will be better both at managing crises and at exploring new avenues for their businesses.

Summary and conclusions

In January 2008, John Holmes, the United Nations Under-Secretary General for Humanitarian Affairs and Emergency Relief Coordinator wrote: 'In 2006, 426 disasters affected 143 million people and resulted in $35 billion in economic damage. The number of floods and related disasters was 43% greater than the 2002–2004 average…. All but one of these disasters resulted from extreme weather' (Holmes 2008). Crisis management is now an important concern of management, not least in the hospitality industry as it is vulnerable to many crises (e.g. food poisoning) and attacks (due to drugs, alcohol, gathering of groups of people in a limited space, easy access and egress). Best management practice, added to specific planning, training and communication skills and the involvement of expert third parties can prevent the worst effects of such incidents.

References

Berman, R. and Roel, G. (1993) Encounter with death and destruction: the 1985 Mexico City earthquake, *Group Analysis*, 26, 81–89

Campbell, R. (2005) *Emerald Now … Management Learning into Practice. The Role, Scope and Goal of Crisis Management,* Spotlight on Ross Campbell, Retrieved on 12 October 2007, from http://www.emeraldinsight.com/info/about_emerald/emeraldnow/archive/dec2005spotlight.jsp

CBI (The Confederation of British Industry). (2006) *Contingency and Security Planning,* Confederation for British Industry: London

Faulkner, B. (2001) Towards a framework for tourism disaster management, *Tourism Management*, 22, 2, 135–147

Holmes, J. (2008, January 3) Disasters are the 'new normal', *USA Today*, p. 13A

Jones, P. (2003) Review of Hall, M. C., Timothy, D. J. and Duval, D. T. (Eds.), Safety and security in tourism: relationships, management and marketing, *Journal of Hospitality and Tourism Research,* The Haworth Press Inc.: London, 29, 2, 279–281

Santana, G. (2003) Crisis Management and tourism: beyond the rhetoric, In Hall, M. C., Timothy, D. J. and Duval, D. T. (Eds.), *Safety and Security in Tourism: Relationships, Management and Marketing,* The Haworth Press Inc.: London, 299–322

Security Service MI5 (2006) *Protecting Against Terrorism,* MI5 National Security Advice Centre (NCAS): London

Selbst, P. (1978) In Booth, S. A. (1993) *Crisis Management Strategy: Competition and Change in Modern Enterprises,* Routledge: London, quoted in Faulkner, B. (2001), op cit

Ucelli, L. (2002) The CEO's "how-to" guide to crisis communications, *Strategy and Leadership,* 30, 2, 21–24

C H A P T E R **17**

Environmental management

David Kirk

Vice Principal (Learning & Teaching)
Queen Margaret University, Edinburgh

Introduction

The environment has become one of the major issues facing not only the hospitality industry but also humankind, with the increasing acknowledgement that human activity is causing global climate change. In the tourism industry, the importance of the environment has long been recognized. Indeed, the concept of 'sustainability' originated and developed in this sector. This is largely because much of leisure tourism is based on visitation to places with natural or manmade resources that people can enjoy. Paradoxically, the more people seek out natural resources such as Ayers Rock in Australia or beaches in Thailand, and manmade attraction such as Egypt's pyramids or Disneyworld, the less attractive they become. This is because the effect of visitation is to erode or reduce the very resource that is being visited. For example, in the Veneto region of Italy, hotels noticed a sharp downturn in business in the early 1990s. They discovered this was due to northern European visitors being dissatisfied with the region's attitude to the environment. In response, hotels and tourism operators formed a consortium to demonstrate and promote green values. As a result, Hotel Ariston in Milan implemented an environmental policy and increased its occupancy by 15% (Ball et al. 2002: 112).

Given the importance of this subject, there has been relatively little research into environmental management in the hospitality industry. The most prolific and influential source of information has been *Green Hotelier*, a magazine aimed at industry practitioners. Over an extended period, this publication has provided a very large number of articles, often based on case studies of highly applied 'research'. Stipanuk (1996) argued that in the USA, the lodging industry responded to environmental issues long before they became 'politically correct, market-opportunity driven or governmentally mandated'. He argues that this history of concern should mean that the industry will continue to care about the environment irrespective of incentives or legislative pressures. Writing at the same time, however, Brown (1996) expressed some reservations about how proactive the industry was, based on her survey of 106 hotel general managers in the UK. She based this on the failure of hotel companies to incorporate environmental measures into their management reporting and control systems. Kirk (1998) also surveyed hotel managers, in this case in Edinburgh, and found a similar lack of action. Of 85 respondents, only 19 reported an environmental policy in operation.

Environmental action

Sustainable development has been described as a new paradigm for management theory and practice. The World Commission on Environment and Development (i.e. The Brundtland Commission) defined sustainable development as development which meets the needs of the present without compromising the ability of future generations to meet their own needs (WCED 1987). A concrete result of the Rio meeting of the world's leaders was the development of the publication known as *Agenda 21* (UN 1992). Subsequently, this was translated by the WTTC into *Agenda 21 for the Travel and Tourism Industry*. This developed priority areas for both the public and private sectors.

In order to achieve sustainability, a wide number of stakeholders have to be involved – governments, environmental agencies, business and consumers. Governments are increasingly introducing legislation and regulation to manage our impact on the environment. In addition to international and governmental pressures for change, we are also seeing the growth of the green consumer. Hospitality businesses are subject both to the 'push' of governmental pressure, for example through the 'polluter pays' principle, and the 'pull' of the market, as increasing numbers of consumers express a preference for green products and services. They have responded to these pressures in a variety of ways.

Some business managers simply think of the environment as part of a raft of government regulations, that is, as an issue of compliance with laws and codes of practice. Others have seen environmental management as a means of differentiating themselves and have gone in for environmental or 'green' award schemes. A more sophisticated approach is to see environmental responsibility become part of the search for total quality. The parallels between aiming for total quality and cradle-to-grave environmental management can be seen through similar audit systems (ISO 9000 and ISO 14000).

Increasingly, however, companies are accepting the ethical case for developing sustainable strategies. Such businesses feel that they have a corporate responsibility to go beyond what is legally required and to operate on a sustainable basis. Some have incorporated environmental management and waste management procedures into their existing operations; some have developed new procedures, based on an environmental policy; and many companies now have environmental reports in their annual company reports.

The five main drivers for change towards sustainable development in an organization are:

- the need for compliance with legislative and fiscal requirements
- opportunities for financial savings
- consumer attitudes and pressure
- public opinion
- enlightened senior management

Companies often progress through a number of evolutionary changes in their approach to environmental management. The first stage of development is sometimes referred to as an 'end of pipe mentality', where the concern is with dangerous or toxic wastes, disposal of the waste materials and waste of scarce resources. This approach leads to an emphasis on waste minimization and waste recycling.

The second stage of development is based on an evaluation of an existing process holistically, through consideration of the input–transformation–output process.[1] This leads to a consideration of the measurement of the ratio of input to output (system efficiency) and policies designed to maximize the use of resources. These considerations lead to better controls over purchasing, storage, production and service.

The third stage of development reflects the approach of a company which has an environmental vision, reflected in a holistic design of their systems, environmental principles designed into the total organization, and consideration for all the internal and external processes in the organization. By considering all these factors as a system and how all the parts of an operation interact, it should be possible to make sensible decisions which allow it to obtain the optimum benefit to the environment while not threatening the financial viability of the hotel. Treating the operation as a whole, and considering interactions between design, purchasing specification, production planning, stock management, waste management and waste disposal, it is found that it is possible to gain both environmental and financial benefits, the latter savings being able to be used to finance environmental initiatives with no immediate short-term payback.

The extent to which large international hospitality chains have reached the third stage is debatable. A study by PricewaterhouseCoopers (2001) researched the environmental

---

[1] See Chapter 2 for an explanation of this model.

practices of Europe's 10 largest hotel chains. Nine of these had environmental policies, but only one of these was externally accredited and verified. Four had environmental management systems (EMSs) in place and a fifth was planning to do so. Most adopted some form of communication about the environment with various stakeholders – annual reports to shareholders, notices in rooms to guests, bulletins or newsletters to staff, and to the world at large on their website. Such chains also face the challenge that their environmental policy may not fulfil the legislative and regulatory demands of the individual countries in which they operate. Moreover, the environmental issues and challenges can vary widely from one country to another. In some parts of the world, water is a critical resource, notably on islands and in the Asia Pacific region. The Mandarin Oriental in Jakarta, Indonesia, has been able to save 13% of its water consumption, through the use of practical measures, such as reduced flow shower-heads (Clements-Hunt 1995). In other parts of the world, the issue is air quality, as demonstrated by concerns with regards the Olympic Games in Beijing.

However, some companies do adopt a holistic approach. The Scandic Group of hotels opened a 194-room hotel in Oslo, Norway, in 1997. This hotel incorporates features such as natural wood and fibres in the construction (each room is 97% recyclable), individual computerized bedroom heating controls, low-energy light bulbs, sub-metering of energy and water and segregated waste bins in each bedroom (paper, organic waste, metal/plastic) (Green Hotelier 1997a). Iwanowski and Rushmore (1994) strongly argue the case for such eco-friendly hotels.

Environmental accreditation

One of the most significant influences has been the International Hotels Environment Initiative (IHEI). Based on an initiative by the CEO of Intercontinental Hotels in 1991, and subsequently sponsored by the Princes Trust, the IHEI was set up by 11 of the world's largest hotel chains. The hotels which made up IHEI were able to demonstrate considerable progress in the first five years (Green Hotelier 1998). Subsequently in 2004, the IHEI became the International Tourism Partnership (ITP). As well as continuing to publish *Green Hotelier* and the standard work on this issue – *Environmental Management for Hotels* – originally published in 1993, ITP is also publishing in 2007 *Sustainable Hotel Siting and Design Guidelines*. In addition it has developed a website that will easily enable hotels to benchmark their environmental performance against other similar properties (www.benchmarkhotel.com). Finally it publishes a quick and easy checklist – *Going Green* – that enables hoteliers to adopt environmental polices and procedures.

However, the principal accreditation scheme in this field is the internationally recognized ISO 14001 Environmental Management Standard. This has five core elements – policy, planning, implementation, checking and corrective action, and management review. The Hong Kong Shangri-La became the first hotel in the Asia Pacific region to be awarded ISO 14001 (Green Hotelier 1997b). In 2000, 8791 certificates were issued, but only 61 of these were to hotel and restaurant firms (Chan and Wong 2006). In their study of 164 hotels in southern China and Macau, Chan and Wong (2006) investigated the motivation for adopting this standard. They found that the two most important influences were the corporate head office and legislation.

Other accreditation schemes include the Green Globe certification (United States), the Green Gum Tree classification (Australia), the Green Leaf Award (Canada) and the Green Tourism Business Award (Scotland). But one of the challenges is the extent to which these schemes, along with benchmarking, are effective in helping the industry to become more environmentally friendly. Bohdanowicz et al. (2005) compare four schemes and conclude that they differ with regard to geographic and climatic areas covered, types of facilities included, nature of environmental information required, benchmarking methods, user friendliness and implementation cost. They go on to arguing the case for an internationally agreed standard approach to benchmarking.

Chan and Wong's (2006) study also suggested that small hospitality businesses were less engaged with environmental issues than large chains. Brown's (1996) study also found this, as did Stabler and Goodall's (1997) study of the hospitality sector on the island of Guernsey. Stabler and Goodall (1997) also concluded that external influences were most likely to change attitudes and behaviours. They strongly recommended action by central and local government to achieve this, through grading schemes, building regulations, incentives, and leafing by example.

Environmental management

The application of systems theory[2] is particularly relevant to the environment, since the natural world is made up of a

---

[2] See Chapter 2.

number of highly complex and interacting systems that have come to be called the 'ecosystem'. The purpose of an EMS is to manage the exchange of materials between the operation – that is to optimize inputs, processes and outputs. Much of environmental management is concerned with the nature of systems outputs, particularly those we consider as waste. However, it is becomingly increasingly clear that in order to manage the impact on the environment, we need to consider not only the outputs, but also the inputs and processes.

There is always a danger that the focus is on the wrong sub-system or system component. What happened in the case of pollution control was an exclusive concentration on treating *undesirable* outputs through pollution control – an expensive option. However, it was later recognized that looking at inputs and processes, which themselves contain hidden pollution costs, and innovating to eliminate all undesirable pollution (pollution prevention) can be more effective. Pollution is not simply an inevitable outcome, but a symptom. The cause may be close in time and space, for example the production process; or more remote, for instance a design flaw; or both.

Planning and designing 'green' buildings

Some authors have expressed the view that the whole economic and business system has to be redesigned to integrate with the natural environment. They advocate the redesign or start up of a business so that it does maintain a holistic relationship between economy and ecology, and is not therefore limited to 'end-of-pipe' remedies such as reducing existing emissions. Many companies in the hospitality industry have attempted the design or redesign approach.

Apart from hospitals, hotels have the highest environmental impact of commercial buildings due to the amounts of energy, water and other resources they consume every day of the year. Indeed, the construction industry, in general, consumes half of the resources produced on the planet every year, and is directly and indirectly responsible for about 40% of emissions (Rada 1996). One of the most obvious commercial advantages of environmentally designing a new hotel or restaurant is that it will have lower operating costs than a conventionally designed structure. Rada (1996) suggests that the main principles of environmental design are:

- *minimizing the use of resources*, the advantages of which cascade down into reduced maintenance and technical equipment costs;

- *thinking of a building as a complete system* rather than as a collection of engineering disciplines; and
- *multifunctional use of parts, features and systems* which have the twin advantages of reducing costs and increasing functionality.

Stipanuk (1996) reports that even in 1954, Statler Hotels Corporation was building properties designed with a 'conscious consideration of recycling, use of daylight for lighting restaurant space, reuse of guest linens, a minimization of materials in construction, and reductions in energy usage'. Today hotels may be constructed and operated completely with the environment in mind, as with the Orchid Hotel in India (Jones 2002). Whilst renewable sources of energy are desirable, there are some constraints. Solar power is particularly suitable for new hotels in sunny climes, and other renewables are available (derived from the wind, hydroelectric, wave, tidal and geothermal power), but currently they account for only a very small proportion of the world's energy supplies.

Environmental management systems characteristics

The characteristics of an EMS are:

- A written policy statement
- A set of targets against which to measure progress
- Agreed specific actions
- Monitoring results against targets

An EMS requires to be 'fed' from a variety of sources, including internal subsystems and the external environment. Some of these may be considered as 'tools' of environmental management which provide feedback. The EMS then responds to this feedback. There is a need 'to establish structures and norms which will ensure that environmental performance is improved over time'. This may be achieved through the organization first assessing its own performance and then responding to that data by setting benchmarks (Stainer and Stainer 1997). Just as the implementation of a TQM programme requires the full support of top management, so does an EMS. Indeed, those organizations that have already implemented TQM find it easier not only to meet legal requirements but also to integrate 'total quality environmental management' into their TQM system.

An EMS may be seen as hierarchy, starting with, at the highest level of the organization, a policy statement. Below this will be operational systems which impact on the day-to-day management of all of the areas of a hospitality business: purchasing, food production, food service, rooms division, maintenance, transport and so on. Achievements against targets will be measured against a regular audit of environmental performance.

The environmental policy and mission statements • • •

All employees have to play their part in moving the organization towards sustainable development. The production and dissemination of clear environmental policy and mission statements, endorsed by senior management, is essential. These must include specific and attainable goals and targets, including performance targets, and details of the arrangements for monitoring, control and communication. The policy statement should also clarify responsibilities. Whether issued as a new policy statement or incorporated into the company's mission statement, the environmental initiative must be linked to action and targets. Hence, in larger companies, a specific environmental manager or co-ordinator is probably needed to ensure the environmental strategy is implemented.

While no responsible company would aim at minimum targets, it is important to know what these are. Naturally, the organization has to meet local and national legal requirements and may wish to incorporate the requirements of a standard such as ISO 14001. Any existing company standards will have to be incorporated in the new policy, and the standards used by suppliers and recommended by trade bodies may also influence policy. A policy should:

- be brief, maximum two pages
- be such that it is understood by, and communicated to, all levels of the company
- be available to the public
- include a commitment to progressively reducing areas of environmental impact
- include a commitment to meet all current legislation
- aim to go beyond legal compliance
- indicate that individuals will be assigned direct responsibility
- indicate that an auditing programme will be set up to measure the implementation of the policy
- have a commitment to review the policy after a specified period
- be consistent with health and safety policies of the company

A possible model for effective environmental performance appraisal, in the form of a continuous loop, is given in Table 17.1.

The environmental audit ● ● ●

The term 'audit' is usually associated with finance, and a financial audit involves the application of rigid rules. By contrast, environmental auditing is based on balancing of facts and values, rather than just on financial measures. The purpose of an environmental audit (EA) is to assess the performance of an organization against prescribed targets related to inputs, processes and outputs.

- *Input* measures include indicators, targets and measures of plant efficiency, materials quality and recyclability. It may be seen as much broader than simply material input and might include, for example, the effectiveness of training staff.
- *Process* measures aim at percentage improvements in reducing waste in stock holding, processing and packaging.
- *Output* measures record impact on, or damage to, the community, including waste, emissions and pollution.

Clearly, such an audit on the whole organization must be carried out at regular intervals, feeding back internal information for control of the EMS. As we shall see, audits of subsystems of the EMS, such as those of specific resources – water, energy and so on – feed back into policies relating to the specific management of these resources.

Table 17.1 The environmental performance appraisal model

---

1. Define the environmental context and objectives
2. Identify potential measures
3. Select appropriate measures
4. Set targets
5. Implement measures
6. Monitor and communicate results
7. Act on results
8. Review

Source: James and Bennett (1994).

Energy management

Hotels were forced to look for energy economies when the cost of oil soared in 1973–1974. The American Hotel and Motel Association conducted annual surveys of energy usage between 1977 and 1984, which showed reductions of 35% over this period (Stipanuk 1996). Hotels use more energy, in terms of dollars per square metre, than industrial buildings, naturally ventilated offices and schools. The benefits of good energy management to the environment include conservation through a reduction in the use of non-renewable energy resources, and also a diminishing of atmospheric pollution, global warming, ozone depletion and acid rain.

The principle of energy management is to minimize the amount and cost of energy used by the hotel without any perceived loss of comfort to the guests unless this is done with their consent, for instance if they agree that they do not need fresh towels every day. Deng and Burnett (2000) studied the energy performance in 16 quality hotels in Hong Kong. An average Energy Use Index (EUI) based on unit floor area was derived for these properties using energy consumption data for 1995. The breakdown of energy use showed that electricity dominated total energy consumption and that, on average, about one-third of total energy was used for air conditioning. A number of factors that affect the energy use in hotel buildings, such as year of construction, hotel class, among others, were reviewed. The difficulties in assessing hotel-building energy performance were also discussed, and methods for adequately evaluating energy performance for hotel buildings were proposed.

Energy in existing buildings may be saved by implementing the following measures (Kirk 1996; International Tourism Partnership 2007):

- A review of the mix of energy sources used;
- A review of tariffs used or other contractual arrangements with energy supply companies;
- Staff training leading to practical steps that can be taken to reduce energy consumption;
- A programme of capital investment on the building, plant and equipment in order to reduce energy consumption;
- Checking and maintaining all equipment regularly;
- Implementing low-cost measures such as energy-efficient light bulbs and motion detectors;
- Improve insulation;
- Use bicycles or other environmentally friendly vehicles around resort properties.

A study of 158 hotels in Greece (Santamouris et al. 1996) found that the annual average total energy consumption was 273 kWh/m². This was a very high level compared with other types of building. Based on simulations, it was estimated that 20% savings could be made by making changes to the building's outer envelope, heating and cooling systems, and lighting. In comparison, Chan (2005) investigated energy usage in 17 hotels located in the subtropics and found annual energy usage to be 313 kWh/m², nearly 40% more than the Greek properties. However, this was an improvement on an earlier study of 17 hotels in Hong Kong (Chan and Lam 2002) which reported consumption of 342 kWh/m².

The energy management programme • • •

For the programme to be successful, someone within the hospitality business should be given managerial responsibility for energy use. In many cases this will be the individual responsible for both building and maintenance and possibly the total environmental management programme. Staff may also be designated to collect energy data (International Tourism Partnership 2007). Alternatively, some hospitality businesses have outsourced their energy management to a contract company, to exploit their expertise and economies of scale.

The first step in any energy management programme is an energy audit. By analysing and evaluating historic records and hotel statistics, a measure of the energy performance of the entire building can be obtained. Deng and Burnett (2000) studied the energy performance of 16 hotels in Hong Kong. They found that the age of the building, star rating and occupancy had no impact on usage. However, they strongly recommended separating guest floors and non-guest floors for assessing energy performance. The energy performance of individual departments, such as restaurants, bars and kitchens, may require specific investment in sub-metering. Another complication is that comparisons can only be made if the units of energy are standardized to kWh (kilo-Watt hours). In estimating costs, account must be taken of the differing price per kilo-Watt hours of the various sources of energy used and of their relative efficiency.

The energy audit should provide:

- energy consumption and cost data for up to five years;
- frequent meter readings to show day-time, night-time and weekend energy consumption; and

- an inventory of all energy-consuming equipment showing age, power loading and maintenance record, together with data on frequency of use

As with an EA, an energy audit requires the full involvement of employees. It will show where the energy is being spent, and energy-saving opportunities. It should also quantify achievable energy targets. However, it is important to note that energy performance indicators are meaningless without having an external comparator, such as the equivalent for other hospitality businesses and industry average data. Care must be taken in comparing one hotel with another as there are many factors associated with the construction, location and operation of a hotel that can affect energy consumption, for example facilities like leisure centres and swimming pools, and air conditioning.

Materials and waste management

Cummings (1992) clearly articulated the 'urgent' need for solid waste minimization in the hospitality industry. A waste management scheme will reduce the amount of waste produced, partly through recycling, where feasible, and thus also make savings in resources such as time, materials and money. For economic reasons, such a scheme will concentrate first on achieving maximum waste minimization and only then on disposal of the residual waste. As in other environmental management programmes, problems must be viewed holistically, waste management being perceived as a process affecting all stages of an operation from design to production and aimed at maximizing the value of all resources.

Every employee must make their personal contribution to waste management, including product and services designers, those responsible for purchasing, stock control, operations and sales management, with the aim of achieving the best possible financial return.

As with other environmental management programmes, the first stage is the design of a waste audit. It is, however, inevitable that some waste will occur, unless there is appropriate, local, multi-sector co-operation to close the waste loop. Management of this waste must be carried out within the constraints of the hotel's legal duty of care in a prioritized manner as follows:

1. re-use the material if possible;
2. if not, collect and separate waste streams for possible recycling;

413

3. if this is not possible and the material has potential energy value, contribute it to local incineration or power generation schemes;
4. if none of the above options are possible, consign to a landfill site.

A holistic approach to waste management must take account of waste which is not measurable as an 'output', for example the excessive use of detergents and cleaning fluids. This is often called 'invisible waste' and can be detected by means of a more comprehensive input–output analysis, combined with measures of efficiency, including comparisons with other hospitality businesses in a chain or industry standards. Particular attention should be paid to levels of food waste. Around 15.5% of edible food has been found to be wasted in hotels and restaurants (Ball et al. 2002). Paper is another commodity where waste can be minimized by reducing consumption, re-use and recycling where necessary. An analysis of present use, including purchases and waste, should yield some solutions to the problem.

The advantages to the environment of recycling are obvious. However, there are also financial advantages, including a reduction of the cost of waste disposal and the cash value of some of the products of recycling. Table 17.2 identifies some common recyclable materials and the resulting products.

Many hospitality businesses throughout the world are still using refrigeration systems which predate the new generation of CFC- and HCFC-free units, despite international initiatives and legal sanctions. Technological advances have produced alternatives to these hazardous chemicals which are cheaper and more efficient and it is now a relatively easy task for maintenance engineers to carry out the necessary conversion. As already noted, safe collection and disposal of the CFCs and HCFCs is essential so that the gases do not escape into the atmosphere. Clearly, when buying new refrigeration units or air-conditioning plant, managers should buy only CFC- and HCFC-free equipment. Energy savings of 10–50% are possible with modern equipment.

Management of the indoor environment

The indoor environment comprises air quality and levels of lighting and noise. These can impact upon the comfort, health and well-being of customers.[3] Each country will have its own

---

[3] See also Chapter 3.

Table 17.2 Recyclable materials

Aluminium, for example cans and foils with high waste value, made into new aluminium products.

Steel cans: the tin coating is removed and the steel melted down for steel-based products.

Paper: separated into differing qualities; the high-grade paper is treated and made into boxboard, tissue, printing and writing paper, newsprint and liner board.

Glass: usually clear glass is separated from coloured glass. The glass is crushed and treated, then melted, the molten glass being made into new containers, fibre glass or glass beads for reflective paint.

Plastic: plastic goods require careful sorting. The plastic can then be melted and remoulded into drainpipes, insulation, rope, carpet backing and many other goods.

Frying oil: this has a commercial value and may be collected by manufacturers for a variety of uses, including the base for cosmetics.

Source: Kirk (1996: 117–118).

---

regulations covering health and safety. In the UK, the Health and Safety at Work Act 1974 and the Health and Safety at Work Regulations 1992 provide the main legal requirements. These are supplemented by the Control of Substances Hazardous to Health Regulations 1988. The UK regulations cover, in particular, the dangers of occupational lung diseases caused by exposure to dust, smoke and chemicals.

Comfort is a subjective experience even though attempts may be made to measure it objectively in terms of temperature, purity of air, humidity, ventilation and noise levels. When we look at comfort holistically, it will become clear that the above factors affect one another, ventilation and acceptable temperature, for instance. A comfortable temperature will also depend on people's level of activity and what they are wearing. There is no absolute optimal temperature defining comfort, but rather a range of temperatures known as the 'comfort zone', within which most people will feel comfortable under defined conditions. Other factors that interact within the bedroom environment system are bedroom temperature, ventilation and energy loss – arising out of guests opening their windows if too hot. The need for individual control of temperature and ventilation by the guest will be obvious.

Operations managers have a responsibility for reducing to a minimum the risks to guests, other visitors and employees from a variety of hazards. There are five groups of chemical hazards:

- toxic, for example herbicides and pesticides,
- flammable (solvents and fuels),
- explosive,
- corrosive, and
- infectious.

Software may be used to create, update and monitor a database of all potentially harmful materials, chemicals and substances in the hotel. In the UK, under the Chemicals (Hazard, Information and Packaging) Regulation (CHIP) (1993), manufacturers of hazardous chemicals must provide data sheets giving the information necessary to build up such a database. The principle which should be applied to dangerous materials is that of substitution with a safer alternative or, if this is impossible, ensure that safe handling, use, storage and disposal procedures are in place.

Air quality

Poor air quality can affect both the comfort and the health of guests and staff. The parameters by which air quality may be measured are (i) the proportion of normal air gases and (ii) pollutants. Concern has been expressed over the effects of mechanical ventilation and air conditioning on indoor air quality. The competing claims of energy conservation and ventilation have resulted in poor levels of the latter. This can result in headaches, mucosal irritation of the eyes, nose, throat and respiratory problems.

The principal potential sources of air pollutants (Kirk 1996: 89–90) are:

- Combustion products, including gases such as carbon dioxide, nitrogen oxides, sulphur dioxide or hydrocarbons; and suspended particulates from boilers, cooking stoves, vehicle engines, among others.
- Chemical vapours from cleaning solvents, pesticides, paints and varnishes, and photocopier emissions.
- Building materials which may include toxic substances, for example formaldehyde in foam insulation, textile finishes, pressed wood, fibre glass or mineral fibres, plasticizers, among others.
- Tobacco-smoking products. A number of places around the world – New York, Ireland, and most recently England – have now introduced bans on smoking in public places.

- Radon gas and radon products which can be released by the soil beneath the building or by stone (especially granite), cement or brick building materials.
- Methane gas from decomposition of any nearby landfill facility or from leaks in the gas distribution system.
- Water vapour which may result in high humidity and mildew, discoloration, odours and damage to materials.
- Odours, both chemical and naturally arising odours from human activity.
- Asbestos, in older buildings, capable of producing asbestosis and cancers.
- Dust and particulate matter, causing allergic reactions, damaging equipment and decor and increasing cleaning costs.
- Airborne micro-organisms, such as *Legionella pneumophilia*, normally associated with moisture in air-conditioning and ventilation systems.

Air quality can be analysed by diagnostic screening to identify problems which can then be eliminated. Comments from staff and guests and objective measurements should be used over a time frame, as single measures can be misleading. The three ways to improve air quality are to eliminate or reduce the pollutant source, filter or purify the air, and ventilate or dilute pollutants. Thereafter, monitoring and evaluation are essential for maintaining high air quality.

Noise

The most common sources of irritating noise are traffic, including aircraft, construction, industry and production, and other human activities such as entertainment and sport. Noise can have many effects on the health of guests and employees, from migraines to sleeplessness. Noise can also impair employees' creative and productive performance. New hospitality businesses should be designed to physically separate noise-producing activities from noise-sensitive ones. Existing hospitality businesses should carry out a noise audit, based partly on an analysis of complaints, and take steps to change procedures and, where necessary, invest in noise control measures.

Light

The properties and quality of light available within different areas of a hotel or restaurant have important effects on the overall experience of guests/customers and the efficiency of staff. The intensity of light for detailed work should be between 500 and 1000 lux (or lumen per square metre), a measure of 'illuminance'. Only 200–300 lux is necessary for non-detailed work. Corridors and public areas require an illuminance of between 100 and 250 lux. Within bedrooms, the overall illuminance will vary according to the number of lighting units, and the most important factor is the degree of control that the guest has over lighting.

Artificial light can cause distortions, for example in the colour of foods, and therefore lighting effects must be tested. Types of fluorescent lighting, in particular, must be tested with furnishings, crockery and food to check for any undesirable colour distortion.

Non-ionizing radiation

The most common sources of radiation in hotel operations are microwave radiation from microwave ovens, visible radiation associated with lasers in printers and ultraviolet radiation used in sun beds. Radioactivity (ionizing radiation) is rarely found in hospitality businesses, other than emissions of the radioactive element radon from certain types of building materials. Microwave radiation in the form of heat can affect the eyes, giving symptoms similar to a cataract. Regular checks on microwave ovens for leakage should be carried out to ensure that any exposure is below the recommended maximum exposure level of $100\,W/m^2$. Laser printers which use lasers have built-in protection against this form of radiation which can damage the retina of the eye and burn the skin. Staff should be trained to limit their maintenance activities to that recommended in the handbook and leave repairs to the manufacturer.

Water management

Fresh water is becoming increasingly scarce, and conservation must be a high priority for all managers. There are several reasons why hospitality operations managers focus on the management of water consumption and water quality. These include:

- waste water reduces the supply of what is often a scarce resource and adds to the hotel's costs;
- a waste of hot water is also a waste of energy;
- poor quality water supplies may pose a health risk to customers and employees;

- poor quality water often adds to the running and maintenance costs of equipment and reduces its life;
- contaminated waste water is a hazard to the health of other stakeholders in the community and increases the load on effluent plants.

Water quality

Evaporated water is pure, but it then becomes contaminated with impurities as it passes through the 'water cycle', for instance the nitrate-based chemicals from fertilizers which may only emerge from deep underground supplies up to a decade later. Other contaminants include phosphates and the acid rain that results from absorption of the sulphur dioxide in the atmosphere. Rivers are also used for waste disposal which may accidentally rise to danger levels, despite stringent precautions, regulations and 'lateral thinking' solutions such as making companies draw their water from downstream. For all these reasons, water is usually treated before being used for drinking and cooking. In addition to rivers and lakes (natural and artificial), water supplies come from wells which tap natural groundwater that has accumulated through seepage in underground structures called aquifers. In many areas, demand is exceeding natural supply and aquifer water levels are falling.

Utility companies provide most hospitality businesses with their water supply, though wells bored into aquifers may be the source in remote areas. Within the UK, cold water supplies for drinking and cooking are taken direct from the main supply. For all other purposes, the source will be an intermediate storage tank within the property, containing either cold or hot water. Note that the removal of waste water is controlled by local regulations. Roof and site drainage water is usually separated from sanitary waste, and kitchen waste is often passed through grease filters before entering the waste system.

Most water supplies have been treated by the utility company before reaching the hotel, though those using wells will need on-site treatment. Quality levels are related to intended use. Thus lower-quality water may be used in WCs and for gardening purposes, but non-potable and potable supplies must be physically isolated to prevent contamination. There are three classes of pollutants: chemical, such as lead, aluminium, nitrates and pesticide residues and chemicals causing 'hardness'; bacteriological, as indicated by the presence of coliform bacteria and removed by chlorine-based disinfectants; and organoleptic factors (affecting taste, smell or colour).

419

An action plan on water quality should include setting appropriate standards, for both the operation and its location; maintenance and monitoring of the property's water plant; and assessment of the performance of the plant, especially with regard to potential sources of stagnant water. Issues that might need to be addressed could include contamination by airborne particles, infestation by insects and rodents and the selection of additional in-house water treatment measures. Common defects and their treatment include the filtration of suspended solids, desalination, water softening, chlorination to remove bacterial contamination, and filtration through an active carbon filter to remove odours and improve taste. Particular care is needed to ensure *Legionella pneumophilia* cannot survive.

Control of water consumption

Water costs account for typically 15–20% of a property's outgoings of a hotel's overall utilities bill. Hot water wastage is more costly due to associated energy loss. Reducing water loss must not be at the expense of the comfort of guests, unless they specifically agree to certain measures. It has been estimated that the average hotel can reduce its water bill by 40%. The main savings come from managing flushing systems which account for 33% of total water usage, compared to only 3% for drinking or preparing food. The used water may be treated and reused in non-contact areas such as toilet cisterns and gardening (International Tourism Partnership 2007). This is called a grey water recycling system and is quite invisible to the customer. Other savings may be made through rainwater harvesting and self-closing taps, and through adapted shower-heads which reduce water usage while maintaining customer satisfaction.

Control of water consumption is accomplished by assessing current performance through conducting a water use audit which relates the measure of water consumption to the time of year and the hotel's level of business and gives a detailed evaluation of efficiency. The performance is then compared with previous figures for the hotel or those of other hospitality businesses. Comparisons with other hospitality businesses' water consumption, obtained in cubic metres per customer per year by dividing the annual consumption of water by the average number of guests per day for the year, can provide a basis for benchmarking. However, in such comparisons, specific factors affecting consumption, such as indoor laundries and swimming pools must be taken into account. This was found to be the case in a study of water usage in 17 hotels in

Hong Kong (Deng and Burnett 2002). They measured consumption by cubic metres per floor area (m^3/m^2) and found that this varied widely from $2.1\,m^3/m^2$ up to $7.7\,m^3/m^2$. This was largely due to whether or not the hotel had an in-house laundry, the average for the 10 hotels that did so being much higher than those without this facility. They also found that average water usage was highest in five star hotels and lowest in three star properties. Specific action that can be taken includes (International Tourism Partnership 2007):

- Change routines, for example reduce wash/rinse cycle in laundry
- Check regularly for leaks from cisterns, taps, pipes and basins
- Fit water-saving devices or sensors in kitchens, bedrooms and public washrooms

Green marketing

Marketing has been blamed for contributing to environmental damage simply because it produces increased consumption, particularly of raw materials. There has therefore been an increasing emphasis on the social dimension of marketing, often in response to consumer concerns. There is a sense in which customer needs must be viewed holistically over time. Marketing decisions in future will have to take account of ecological factors if sustainable development is to become a reality. Welford (1994: 26) asserts that it is in this functional area (of marketing) that a company's commitment to sustainability will be judged, particularly by the consumer and wider public. Some companies, such as Scandic Hotels, The Body Shop and Tescos, have been proactive, rather than reactive, and this is likely to become a trend.

Gustin and Weaver's (1996) study is one of the few to investigate consumers' perspectives. They found that 73% of respondents considered themselves environmentally minded and 71% were positive about staying in ecofriendly properties. Hence marketing may have to be part of a company's holistic approach to environmental management. Despite consumer pressure relating to the environment, firms will also have to recognize that consumers' wants do not always coincide with the long-term interests of the environment. This challenge can be met, at least in part, by marketing strategies that educate and inform on environmental issues and benefits.

Although some experts stress exclusively the rights and expectations of shareholders (Reinhardt 1999), businesses will increasingly have to meet the demands of other stakeholders, such as customers, employees and the local community. For this reason, it is necessary to make public part at least of the results of the EA. However, consumers may not always be supportive of green initiatives. Manaktola and Jauhari (2007) studied consumers using hotel services in India and how conscious they were of environmentally friendly practices. They found consumers would prefer to use lodging that follows these practices but were not willing to pay extra for these services. Despite this, there is likely to be an upsurge in green branding. This may be by chains, such as the subtle highlighting of 'eco' in the Grecotel chain's logo (Konopka 1998). Alternatively this may be through awards given by professional bodies (such as the Green Globe scheme) or by local tourism organizations (such as the Scottish Tourist Boards Green Tourism Business Award).

Environmental management issues and trends

Such is the complexity and regional diversity of the global hospitality industry that it is very difficult to identify clear trends (Jones 1999). Indeed the very word 'trends' implies a degree of stability which is rapidly being supplanted by 'complexity' or 'chaos'. Nevertheless, the International Tourism Partnership (2007) is clearly shifting 'environmentalism' into sustainability. It therefore proposes that operators should work with their suppliers to green the supply chain. Part of this is to work much more closely with local suppliers to reduce transport emissions (and costs). Linked to this are links with local people and communities, so that they too benefit from the hotel development. Finally, operators should 'maintain a "sense of place" that supports the geographic character of a place – its environment, culture, heritage, aesthetics, and the well-being of its citizens' (International Tourism Partnership 2007).

Although some people in the hospitality industry take their environmental responsibilities very seriously, others are only willing to act if there is some compulsion. Legislation is being, and will continue to be, used to change the behaviour of businesses. For example, in the UK we have seen legislation on waste disposal, on energy use and on reduction in the use of packaging materials. These have all affected the hospitality industry. Wan Yim King Penny's (2007) study of hotels in Macau revealed that low customer demand, poor environmental knowledge and the lack of governmental regulations enforcing environmental practices are the reasons hindering hoteliers in Macau from practicing green polices. But the major barrier was that hotel managers do not recognize the importance of environmental management to hotel effectiveness and competitiveness. Consequently, hotels were only interested in improving areas where there are direct financial gains and where there is a fiscal/legislative requirement. A fragmented approach to managing their environmental performance has resulted.

This approach is reactive rather than proactive and does not address the added value of environmental management. Too often, managers adopt a 'cost effective' consideration of compliance, rather than a 'cost-benefit' or 'value added' approach. There is no encouragement either to go beyond strict compliance, or to attempt to influence future legislation. The guidelines suggested by Piasecki et al. (1999) are therefore neither holistic nor entrepreneurial. The language of compliance used by Piasecki is that of the manager seeking only to minimize the costs of this inconvenience without extinguishing a creative approach to other aspects of the business. These weaknesses arise from an unimaginative response to regulation which is perceived purely in terms of cost. By contrast, the entrepreneur, or enlightened senior manager, actively seeks competitive advantages from the creative use of imposed legislation and regulation, and attempts to influence other stakeholders and competitors and to influence future legislation in alignment with the company's environmental investment programme.

Hospitality businesses can only optimize their contribution to global sustainability through local and regional co-operation. Welford (1994: 28–29) advocates the development of environmental networks, including multi-sector networks, amongst small businesses, voluntary organizations and the public sector. As other companies, through promotion, become aware of best practice in this kind of initiative, expanding numbers of such networks will enable controlled and sustainable growth to occur. Rivera's (2004) study in Costa Rica aimed to identify how institutional forces, such as regulatory and stakeholder pressures, are related to proactive environmental behaviour by hotel facilities participating in the Certification for Sustainable Tourism, a voluntary environmental programme established by the Costa Rican government. This programme was among the first third-party performance-based environmental certification initiatives implemented in the developing world. The study suggested that voluntary environmental programmes that include performance-based standards and third-party monitoring may be effective in promoting beyond-compliance environmental behaviour when they are 'complemented by isomorphic institutional pressures exerted by government environmental monitoring and trade association membership' (Rivera 2004).

The International Tourism Partnership is another example of co-operation within one industry, based on sharing of environmental information and examples of best practice. The World Commission on Environment and Development is an example of an initiative to introduce inter-sectoral and international co-operation. However, to meet the global environmental challenge, there will need to be a meeting of minds, a consensus worldview on the integration of economics and the environment. A fundamentally new paradigm relating to economics and development is difficult for many economists and business experts to accept. However, the 2007 Stern Report clearly demonstrated the economic and business impacts of global warming and the need for positive action, and it may well lead to a fundamental paradigm shift.

Summary and conclusions

Environmental management is concerned with all aspects of the operation, starting with the inputs to the business, the design and management of all processes and the output or waste from the system. Environmental management should start, first with a policy statement and then an audit, to establish current performance. This usually leads to a number of planned and measurable changes, designed to improve performance with regard to energy management, materials and waste, water management and indoor environment.

Although hospitality businesses were fairly slow to get into environmental management, a number of high-profile initiatives have promoted environmental awareness. A number of countries and/or regions have also developed environmental awards or grading schemes as a means of promoting their initiatives. In the future, it is likely that we will see more of these developments, pressured by inter-governmental agreements. However, many companies are at an early stage of development. Initially it is often possible to link environmental management with financial savings. Plans that result in lower consumption of energy or water or reduced costs of waste disposal are relatively easy to sell to the boards of companies. Beyond those changes, others may cost money to implement, with less tangible returns, often based on hard-to-quantify marketing or public relations benefits. This differentiates those companies that only respond to a business case from those that take an ethical stance on environmentalism and sustainability.

References

Ball, S., Jones, P., Kirk, D. and Lockwood, A. (2002) *Hospitality and Operating Systems*, Continuum London

Bohdanowicz, P., Siminic, B. and Martinac, I. (2005) Sustainable hotels – environmental reporting according to Green Globe 21, Green Globes Canada/GEM UK, IHEI Benchmarking and Hilton environmental reporting, *The 2005 World Sustainable Building Conference*, Tokyo, 27–29 September

Brown, M. (1996) Environmental policy in the hotel sector: "green" strategy or stratagem? *International Journal of Contemporary Hospitality Management*, 8, 3, 18–23

Chan, W. W. (2005) Predicting and saving the consumption of electricity in sub-tropical hotels, *International Journal of Contemporary Hospitality Management*, 17, 3, 228–237

Chan, W. W. and Lam, J. C. (2002) Prediction of pollutant emission through electricity consumption by the hotel industry in Hong Kong, *International Journal of Hospitality Management*, 21, 4, 381–391

Chan, E. S. W. and Wong, S. C. K. (2006) Motivations for ISO 14001 in the hotel industry, *Tourism Management*, 27, 481–492

Clements-Hunt, P. (1995) Asia on stream, *Green Hotelier*, 1, 6–7

Cummings, L. E. (1992) Hospitality solid waste minimisation: a global frame, *International Journal of Hospitality Management*, 11, 3, 255–267

Deng, S. M. and Burnett, J. (2000) A study of energy performance of hotel buildings in Hong Kong, *Energy and Buildings*, 31, 1, 7–12

Deng, S.-M. and Burnett, J. (2002) Water use in Hong Kong Hotels, *International Journal of Hospitality Management*, 21, 1, 57–66

Green Hotelier (1997a) Scandic opens 'recyclable' hotel, *Green Hotelier*, 8, 6

Green Hotelier (1997b) Shangri-La's path to ISO 14001, *Green Hotelier*, 8, 30–31

Green Hotelier (1998) Members profile – Hilton International, Accor, Bass hotels, Inter-Continental hotels, Starwood hotels, Manarin Oriental hotels, Marriott international, Forte hotels, Marco Polo hotels, Radisson SAS hotels, Scandic hotels, The Indian Company of hotels, *Green Hotelier*, 12, 12–25

Gustin, M. E. and Weaver, P. A. (1996) Are hotels prepared for the environmental consumer? *Hospitality Research Journal*, 20, 2, 1–14

International Tourism Partnership (2007) Retrieved on 22 October, from *http://www.tourismpartnership.org/pages07/Practical_Solutions.html*

Iwanowski, K. and Rushmore, C. (1994) Introducing the eco-friendly hotel, *Cornell Hotel and Restaurant Administration Quarterly*, 35, 1, 34–38

James, P. and Bennett, M. (1994) *Environmental-Related Performance Measurement in Business: From Emissions to Profit and Sustainability?* Ashridge Management Research Group: Berkhamsted

Jones, P. (1999) Operational issues and trends in the hospitality industry, *International Journal of Hospitality Management*, 18, 4, 427–442

Jones. P. (2002) The Orchid Hotel, *Tourism and Hospitality Research*, 3, 3, 277–280

Kirk, D. (1996) *Environmental Management for Hotels*, Butterworth-Heinemann: Oxford

Kirk, D. (1998) Attitudes to environmental management held by a group of hotel managers in Edinburgh, *International Journal of Hospitality Management*, 17, 1, 33–47

Konopka, C. (1998, October 15) The greening of Grecotel, *Caterer and Hotelkeeper*, 32–33

Manaktola, K. and Jauhari, V. (2007) Exploring consumer attitude and behaviour towards green practices in the lodging industry in India, *International Journal of Contemporary Hospitality Management*, 19, 5, 364–377

Piasecki, B. W., Fletcher, K. A. and Mendelson, F. J. (1999) *Environmental Management and Business Strategy: Leadership Skills for the 21st Century*, Wiley: New York

PricewaterhouseCoopers (2001) *Hospitality Directions – Europe Edition*, PWC: London

Rada, J. (1996) Designing and building eco-efficient hotels, *Green Hotelier*, 4, 10–11

Reinhardt, F. L. (1999) Bringing the environment down to earth, *Harvard Business Review*, 77, 4, 149–157

Rivera, J. (2004) Institutional pressures and voluntary environmental behavior in developing countries: evidence from the Costa Rican hotel industry, *Society and Natural Resources*, 17, 9, 763–857

Santamouris, M., Balaras, C. A., Dascalaki, E., Argiriou, A. and Gaglia, A. (1996) Energy conservation and retrofitting potential in Hellenic hotels, *Energy and Buildings*, 24, 1, 65–75

Stabler, M. J. and Goodall, B. (1997) Environmental awareness, action and performance in the Guernsey hospitality sector, *Tourism Management*, 18, 1, 19–33

Stainer, A. and Stainer, L. (1997) Ethical dimensions of environmental management, *European Business Review*, 97, 5, 224–230

Stipanuk, D. M. (1996) The U.S. lodging industry and the environment, *Cornell Hotel and Restaurant Administration Quarterly*, 37, 5, 39–45

UN (United Nations) (1992) *Report of the UN Conference on Environment and Development*, General Assembly Resolution A/RES/47/190, UN: New York

Wan Yim King Penny (2007) The use of environmental management as a facilities management tool in the Macao hotel sector, *Facilities*, 25, 7/8, 286–295

WCED (The World Commission on Environmental and Development) (1987) *Our Common Future (The Bruntland Report)*, Oxford University Press: Oxford

Welford, R. (1994) *Cases in Environmental Management and Business Strategy*, Pitman Publishing: London

Index